Studies in Spinoza

Studies in Spinoza

Critical and Interpretive Essays

Edited by S. Paul Kashap

UNIVERSITY OF CALIFORNIA PRESS
BERKELEY LOS ANGELES LONDON 1972

University of California Press
Berkeley and Los Angeles, California

University of California Press, Ltd.
London, England

Copyright © 1972 by
The Regents of the University of California

ISBN: 0–520–02142–8
Library of Congress Catalog Card Number: 71–174459

Designed by Wolfgang Lederer
Printed in the United States of America

To the memory of

DR. G. D. KASHAP,

MAYA DEVI KASHAP,

and

JOSEPH SHERRY

Acknowledgments

ACKNOWLEDGMENT is gratefully made to the following publishers, editors, and authors for permission to include previously published material:

To the Editor and Secretary of The Aristotelian Society for the following essay from the *Proceedings of the Aristotelian Society* (Vol. XXVII): "Spinoza's Conception of the Attributes of Substance," by A. Wolf, Copyright 1927 The Aristotelian Society.

To the authors, and to the Editors of *The Philosophical Review* for the following essays: "Spinoza and the Status of Universals" (Vol. LIX, 1950) and "Spinoza's Definition of Attribute" (Vol. LXII, 1953), both by Francis S. Haserot, and "Spinoza and Language" (Vol. LXVII, 1958), by David Savan.

To George Allen & Unwin Ltd., London, for an extract from *Spinoza and Time* by S. Alexander, first published in 1921.

To the authors, the Editor of *Inquiry*, and Universitetsforlaget, Oslo, for the following essays: "Personal Identity in Spinoza" (Vol. XII, no. 1, 1969), by Ruth L. Saw, and "Spinoza's Theory of Knowledge Applied to the *Ethics*" (Vol. XII, no. 1, 1969), by Guttorm Fløistad.

To the Editor of *Mind* for "Some Incoherencies in Spinozism," Parts I and II (Vol. XLVI, 1937), by A. E. Taylor, and "Notes on the Second Part of Spinoza's *Ethics*," Parts I, II, and III (Vol. XLVII, 1938), by H. Barker.

To the Editor of *The Review of Metaphysics* and Mrs. Marian Farrant for "On a Reputed Equivoque in the Philosophy of Spinoza" (Vol. III, 1949–50), by H. F. Hallett.

To the author and the Clarendon Press, Oxford, for "Truth and Falsity," from *Spinoza's Theory of Knowledge* by G. H. R. Parkinson, first published in 1954.

To the author and Oxford University Press for "Spinoza and the Idea of Freedom," by Stuart Hampshire, from *Proceedings of the British Academy 1960*, published by Oxford University Press.

To the author's executors and the Editor of *Philosophy* for "Spinoza's Doctrine of God in Relation to His Conception of Causality" (Vol. XXIII, 1948), by T. M. Forsyth.

To the author's executors and the Editor of *Philosophy* for "Spinoza's Doctrine of Privation" (Vol. VIII, 1933), by Raphael **Demos.**

Contents

Introduction

Spinoza is one of those great men, as Santayana rightly observed, whose eminence grows more obvious with the lapse of years. His thought was centuries ahead for his own time and still is ahead in our own. The more one understands him the more one marvels at his genius in having conceived of a philosophical system capable of giving a surprisingly coherent account of a number of philosophical issues in such fields as philosophy of mind and philosophy of action, which only recently have begun to receive the attention they deserve. For this reason Spinoza's thought today assumes a greater philosophical relevance than perhaps that of any other philosopher in history apart from Aristotle.

E. M. Curley, in his study of *Spinoza's Metaphysics*, observes that: "No philosopher should be easier to understand than Spinoza, for none has taken so much trouble to explain himself, defining his key terms, listing his basic assumptions, and arguing carefully for each conclusion he draws from these assumptions. But few have proved harder." For as Bayle in his *Dictionary* remarked rather gloatingly, few men have made any serious effort to study his theories, and among those who have, "there are few who have understood it and have not been discouraged by the perplexities and the impenetrable abstractions that are found in it. . . ." Insofar as the essays in this volume make an attempt not only at understanding Spinoza but also at explaining his thought in terms of a modern philosophical vocabulary, they make Spinoza more accessible to those who wish to study the philosopher but are deterred by his "impenetrable abstractions."

All the studies in Spinoza that are collected here were written in English. Most of them were written after 1937. The two exceptions are S. Alexander's lecture on "Spinoza and Time," delivered in 1921, and A. Wolf's paper on "Spinoza's Conception of the Attributes of Substance," which was read at the Aristotelian Society meetings in 1926–27. My own article here is the only one that has not been published before.

Compared to the number of articles published in English on other philosophers such as Descartes, Hume, and Kant, there are very few on Spinoza, and of these fewer still are of sustained merit. This does not mean of course that everything worthwhile that has been written in English on Spinoza has been included in this volume. The essays that appear in this collection are self-contained studies of one or the other specific aspect of Spinoza's thought. Some are openly critical of Spinoza's views, others defend Spinoza against misunderstandings, and some attempt to present a more or less neutral interpretation. In general, however, each article does all this in varying degrees.

The discussions included here deal with Spinoza's metaphysics, theory of knowledge, and moral theory. It has not been possible to devote equal space to each of the three areas. The final selection of the essays was made not so much from the point of view of their textual criticism but on the basis of their ability to advance one's philosophical appreciation of Spinoza's thought.

Forsyth's article attempts to explain Spinoza's notion of cause—in particular the notion of self-caused cause—in its application to Substance or God. Forsyth argues that in identifying God with one substance or ultimate reality, Spinoza is neither merely using conventional language nor forcing his own terminology upon a conception to which it is inappropriate. He is expressing his own insight into the real meaning of the concepts concerned through a reinterpretation of extant thought and usage. Spinoza identifies the God of religion with ultimate reality which philosophical thought compels him to affirm, and thereby makes it possible for him to unite the philosophical search for truth with the intellectual love of God. The article also analyzes the difficult notions of immanent and free causality in Spinoza.

Wolf's article is an analysis and interpretation of Spinoza's conception of the attributes of substance which forms the very foundation of Spinoza's philosophy. He argues that for Spinoza the relation of cause-effect is not identical to that of ground and consequent, and explains briefly but brilliantly what it means for Spinoza to speak of substance as "constituting of infinite attributes."

Haserot, in his article on attribute, discusses and analyzes the nature of attributes in Spinoza's philosophy by raising the question of whether they are essentially forms of cognition and hence subjective or whether they refer to the inherent character of substance and are hence objective. Haserot acutely examines the ambiguities and difficulties involved in Spinoza's definition of an attribute and other related notions such as intellect. In doing so he refers to the original Latin version of Spinoza's definition. But the article is written in a way that does not presuppose knowledge of Latin to appreciate and understand the argument and analysis.

In his article on universals Haserot examines the question of whether Spinoza was a nominalist or a realist in his stand regarding the nature of universals. This throws some important light on the nature of attributes. Haserot has very ably argued in his other article in this volume that attributes are not mental entities but have an objective reference. Here he argues that a nominalist view of universals logically leads through positivism to pragmatism, whereas "Spinoza's philosophy represents the antithesis of pragmatism." Through a careful analysis and interpretation of the relevant passages from the text, Haserot clarifies Spinoza's real position in regard to universals and compares it illuminatingly with that of Plato.

Alexander's is an insightful discussion of the concept of time in Spinoza's philosophy. He begins with an examination of the relations between attributes, infinite modes, and finite modes, and argues that if motion-and-rest is the infinite mode of extension (and if motion is not to be understood statically in Cartesian terms as merely change of place), then extension must not be space, but space-time. In that case, time itself becomes an attribute of reality. The implications of this conclusion are further examined in light of the impossibility of regarding time as an attribute in Spinoza's thought.

Ruth L. Saw argues that when Spinoza said "our highest knowledge is of the individual" it is generally believed that Spinoza was promising us an account from which one might arrive at individuals such as Peter and Paul in all their particularity as the object of our highest knowledge. But this belief is mistaken. For Spinoza, what we know when we know Peter fully is not Peter as a person but Peter who is a unique system of interrelated finite modifications of substance under the attributes of extension and thought existing in its own place in the spatiotemporal scheme of *natura naturata*. So that although Spinoza's aim was to increase human happiness and to show man the way to that end, the men who finally emerge as having attained happiness are not individuals in their emotional and passionate uniqueness but human beings as "rational men" with nothing to individuate them.

The three articles by Barker include some of the most provocative and intensive discussions of Spinoza's theory of knowledge written in English. The first article is devoted to a severe and critical examination of whether Spinoza's assertions with regard to questions about knowledge and mind and the relation of knowledge to its object and of mind to body are true of our actual experience. If they are not true, then the formal scheme of *Ethics* I, so far as it cannot be true if they are not, must be rejected with them.

In the second article Barker analyzes the most important and critical proposition in *Ethics*—Proposition 7 of Part II—and discusses the difficulties concerning the nature of attributes and those concerning the relation between the *idea* and the *ideata* which are involved in it.

The third article deals specifically with the relation of mind and body as involved in Spinoza's theories of *idea ideae* and truth and error.

Hallett discusses and clarifies the equivocal use made by Spinoza of the term *idea* as at once the mental correlate of some physiological state of the body of the percipient as well as of an external object. While making a very able defense of Spinoza against misinterpretation of one of the most important notions in his theory of knowledge, Hallett also throws light on the difficulties involved in the causal theory of perception.

In his first of two articles in this volume Taylor discusses the difficulties one has to face in Spinoza with regard to the relation between finite modes and infinite substance, which is an extremely important issue in connection with the existence of individuals in Spinoza's philosophy. The metaphysical framework of *Ethics* I, Taylor argues, requires the admission that finite modes are mere illusions, while the doctrines elaborated in *Ethics* II–V demand that they must not be treated as such. He also deals with problems concerning the nature of mind and its relation to the body, self-consciousness, the process from imagination to knowledge, and freedom in Spinoza.

Parkinson analyzes the relation of Spinoza's theories of substance, attribute, and infinite mode to his theories of truth, falsity, and error, and by way of clarifying the relation between the idea and object in his theory of knowledge, discusses whether or not Spinoza can be said to have held the coherence theory of truth.

Savan examines the extent to which Spinoza's views on language affect his philosophy and its formulation. Savan's argument is that the language Spinoza uses to express his thoughts cannot be identified with or taken as a literal exposition of philosophical truth or true ideas. An idea, in Spinoza's sense, does not consist of words. This leads not only to Spinoza's rejection of the semantic theory of truth but to his acknowledgment that no simple, direct, precise and consistent verbal account of the true philosophy is possible. Spinoza's words do, nevertheless, have a proper role to play in the formulation of "entities of reason" which function as tools or mental aids to a true idea or philosophical truth. But a thing is truly understood, in Spinoza's view, when it is perceived simply by the mind without words and images.

Guttorm Fløistad discusses the relation between knowledge and language, the distinction between two types of imagination in Spinoza, and the relation between reason and intuition. He examines Savan's thesis that Spinoza's writings are not and were not intended to be a direct or literal exposition of philosophical truth, by raising a question regarding the kinds of knowledge implied in the propositions of the *Ethics*. An answer to this question as well as to the question of whether true knowledge can (or may) be adequately expressed in language is provided by the arguments of his essay. His thesis is as follows: (a) there are no instances of imagination (Spinoza's first kind of knowledge) to be found in the *Ethics*; (b) the larger part of the *Ethics* contains propositions that belong to Spinoza's second kind of knowledge, namely reason; and (c) instances of Spinoza's third kind of knowledge, namely intuition, not only occur frequently but play a crucial role in the *Ethics*.

Demos's article contains a critical analysis of Spinoza's views on moral freedom, moral judgment, and the nature of moral consciousness. The fundamental question raised in this article is whether it is possible in Spinoza's philosophy to seek to better one's condition in life. Demos argues that the denial of "genuine possibility" by Spinoza leads to the denial of moral freedom, moral judgment, and purposive behavior.

In his second article on Spinoza, A. E. Taylor argues that if Spinoza's statement "We do not desire a thing because it is good, it is good because we desire it" means that *good* is only a name for whatever is in fact desired by the person using the word, then it would be in principle impossible for a Plato, an Aristotle, or a Kant to agree with him. Spinoza's proposal to treat moral actions exactly as though they were geometrical figures leads to his ignoring their specific character as *moral*. For, Taylor says: "To construct a morality from which the distinctions of the objectively good and evil, right and wrong are absent is like proposing to construct a geometry superior to the 'vulgar prejudice' that there is a distinction between straight and curved." In short, Taylor maintains that the exclusion of the notion of moral value excludes the possibility of a genuinely ethical doctrine in Spinoza. The article also includes a brief discussion of the doctrine of "intellectual love of God."

Hampshire's contribution is not only a penetrating analysis of the notion of freedom but also a brilliant defense of Spinoza. The central question raised concerns the precise connection between a man's knowledge of the distinction between different levels of knowledge and his freedom of action. This connection, it is suggested, is to be found in Spinoza's theory of individuals. Hampshire's argument consists of an illuminating analysis of this theory and its relation to the freedom of man.

I argue in my paper that the commonly accepted view that Spinoza's philosophy makes no allowance for purposive behavior rests upon the misconception that he fails to distinguish "appetite" from "desire." If it can be shown, as I try to do, that Spinoza not only makes a clear and crucial distinction between the above two concepts but also accepts the idea that the direction of one's energies toward a consciously pursued ideal is a necessary condition for self-improvement, then it would follow that his system cannot have rejected the applicability of the concepts of intentional and purposive action to man.

S. PAUL KASHAP

Notes on the Contributors

T. M. FORSYTH taught philosophy in Scotland and South Africa. He was Professor of Philosophy at Rhodes University, Grahamstown, before his death in 1958.

ABRAHAM WOLF, who died in 1948, was Professor of Logic and Scientific Method in the University of London. Among his publications are *Spinoza: His Life and Treatise on God and Man* (1910), *The Oldest Biography of Spinoza* (1927), and *The Correspondence of Spinoza* (1928).

FRANCIS SAMUEL HASEROT is Professor Emeritus of Philosophy at the College of William and Mary.

SAMUEL ALEXANDER, who died in 1938, was Professor of Philosophy (1893–1924) in the University of Manchester. His Gifford Lectures were published as *Space, Time, and Deity* (1920).

RUTH LYDIA SAW is Professor Emeritus in Aesthetics in the University of London, and former head of the Department of Philosophy, Birkbeck College. Among her publications are *The Vindication of Metaphysics* (1951), *Leibniz* (1954), and *Aesthetics* (1970).

HENRY BARKER taught at the University of Edinburgh until his retirement in 1934. He died in 1948.

HAROLD FOSTER HALLETT, who died in 1966, was Professor of Philosophy (1931–1951) in the University of London, Kings College, and British Secretary of Societas Spinozana (1929–1935). Among his publications are *Aeternitas: A Spinozistic Study* (1930), *Benedict de Spinoza: The Elements of His Philosophy* (1957), and *Creation, Emanation and Salvation: A Spinozistic Study* (1962).

ALFRED EDWARD TAYLOR, who died in 1945, was Professor of Moral Philosophy in the University of Edinburgh (1924–1941). Among his publications are *Elements of Metaphysics* (1903), *Plato: The Man and His Work* (1927), and several translations of Plato.

G. H. R. PARKINSON is Professor of Philosophy in the University of Reading. Among his publications are *Spinoza's Theory of Knowledge* (1954) and *Logic and Reality in Leibniz's Metaphysics* (1965).

DAVID SAVAN is Professor of Philosophy in the University of Toronto.

GUTTORM FLØISTAD teaches philosophy at the University of Oslo.

RAPHAEL DEMOS, who died in 1968, was Alford Professor of Philosophy at Harvard (1945–1962). He edited *The Complete Works of Plato* (1936), and was the author of *The Philosophy of Plato* (1939).

STUART HAMPSHIRE is Warden of Wadham College, Oxford. He was Grote Professor of Philosophy of Mind and Logic in the University of London (1960–1963), and Professor of Philosophy at Princeton University (1963–1970). Among his publications are *Spinoza* (1951), *Thought and Action* (1959), and *Freedom of the Individual* (1965).

S. PAUL KASHAP is a Fellow of Merrill College and Lecturer in Philosophy in the University of California, Santa Cruz.

Studies in Spinoza

Spinoza's Doctrine of God in Relation to His Conception of Causality

T. M. Forsyth

"THE TRUEST VISION ever had of God came, perhaps, here."[1]

IN A PREVIOUS ARTICLE I considered Aristotle's view of God as final cause and its relation to the philosophy of Plato;[2] and at the end of the article I remarked on the affinity of both doctrines with that of Spinoza. The present paper is concerned with Spinoza's doctrine of God as it is related to his conception of causality and seeks, *inter alia*, to show that his explicit rejection of final causes does not prevent his philosophy from having in it something like the true principle of final causation. In each section I first quote the chief relevant definitions or propositions in Spinoza's *Ethics*,[3] and then state what seems needful in the way of interpretation or comment.

Causa Sui = Ultimate Reality

"By cause of itself I understand that whose essence involves existence, or that whose nature cannot be conceived unless existing."[4]

---

[1] Santayana's beautiful rendering of the concluding words of Ernest Renan's commemorative address at the unveiling of the statue of Spinoza at The Hague. The whole address is contained in *Spinoza: Four Essays* (edited by Knight).

[2] "Aristotle's Concept of God as Final Cause" (*Philosophy*, Vol. XXII, No. 82, July, 1947).

[3] The passages cited are all from the *Ethics*, and I have followed Hale White's translation unless the text seemed to warrant a somewhat different wording. Except on one or two points I have made no references to particular expositors or commentators. My love for Spinoza goes back to my student days half a century ago; but, with much else claiming attention, anything I have hitherto written on his philosophy has been confined to class lectures and an address delivered to a Jewish community on the occasion of the Spinoza Tercentenary in 1932. What follows aims at giving a concise statement on the subject immediately concerned.

[4] *Ethics* I, Def. 1.

"By substance I understand that which is in itself and is conceived through itself." [5] "It pertains to the nature of substance to exist." [6]

The first definition of Spinoza's *Ethics* lays the foundation for his whole system of philosophy. It expresses his fundamental intuition— that of the unity of all reality—in the idea of an ultimate or absolute reality as the necessary cause or ground of all that is. This alone is truly substance or self-subsistent reality. It is the absolutely self-dependent, on which all else depends, and is therefore at once the ultimate in being or existence and in thought or knowledge.

To the objection that a self-causing cause is logically inconceivable the appropriate answer seems to be that the term "cause of itself" (or "its own cause")—like Plato's "self-mover" and Aristotle's "unmoved mover," which have likewise been called wholly unintelligible—seeks to apply the most fitting idea available to what is in actual fact not fully expressible. Reality is not unknowable: on the contrary, it is just what is known in all knowledge; but no terms are wholly adequate to its being and nature. Again, to the criticism[7] that Spinoza's idea of substance, *causa sui,* is a substantiation or hypostatization of logic and of logical necessity, and gives no real or ontological necessity, one may perhaps reply that the defect, if such there be, lies in the method rather than in the significance of Spinoza's philosophy, and that the whole tenor of his doctrine implies that the logical is only one aspect, though an essential aspect, of the real or ontological. For Spinoza there is an inherent relation between thought and being such that what is found to be necessary for thought can be taken as true of existence.[8]

Spinoza's method of exposition of his philosophical principles is particularly open to criticism in that he seems to begin from an abstract concept of being, which makes impossible his ever reaching the concrete reality whose nature and action it is his purpose to disclose. But what he wants to affirm is a reality that is not indeterminate but fully determinate and therefore the determinant of all lesser or derivative forms of existence. Such reality is not the negation of all characters and relations but their totality or correlation.

[5] Def. 3.
[6] Ibid., Prop. 7.
[7] Made, e.g., by Jacques Maritain in one of the essays in his volume entitled *Redeeming the Time.*
[8] This conception is expressed, e.g., in his statement that "it is of the nature of the mind to frame true ideas."

Accordingly the infinite is not the mere negation of the finite, it is the finite that is the negation of the infinite; or rather, each is the necessary counterpart of the other.

Another deficiency, or another aspect of the same deficiency, in Spinoza's mode of statement is that he seems from the outset to assert the unity of reality in a way that involves denial of all real difference or diversity. That this is not Spinoza's intention, even if his exposition be faulty, is shown by the principles he affirms in the subsequent parts of his great treatise. It is seen especially in his doctrine of the self-maintaining or self-realizing impulse, which is the very essence of each particular being, and by virtue of which every creature strives after the preservation and fulfilment of its own nature. Spinoza's whole philosophy has this implication of diversity along with unity, although the unity may throughout be overstressed. Indeed it has been said that Spinoza's philosophy is one of the greatest efforts in the entire history of human thought to give adequate expression to the principle of unity in diversity as the fundamental character of reality. Unity and difference are meaningless apart from each other, and an infinite unity must be realized or expressed in infinite variety. This principle of individuality and self-persistence will be treated more fully in a later section.

God as the One Reality

"By God I understand a being absolutely infinite, that is, consisting of infinite attributes, each of which expresses eternal and infinite essence." [9] God, or substance consisting of infinite attributes, necessarily exists.[10] "Besides God no substance can be or be conceived." [11] "Whatever is, is in God, and nothing can either be or be conceived without God." [12]

The ultimate reality, which he has initially posited, Spinoza forthwith identifies with God. He does so because to it must pertain all fullness of being and completeness of nature, and because God must be conceived as eternal, infinite and perfect being. If God is to be all that is truly meant by God, nothing else will suffice; since anything

[9] *Ethics* I, Def. 6.
[10] Ibid., Prop. 11.
[11] Prop. 14.
[12] Prop. 15.

less than this falsifies the divine nature by turning it into something finite and therefore imperfect.

God, so conceived, necessarily exists, because existence is involved in the very nature of the being thus defined. Or, as Spinoza expresses the same principle in a somewhat less abstract form, the more perfection and therefore the more reality anything has, the more has it power to exist and therefore necessarily exists.[13] This is Spinoza's version of the ontological argument for the existence of God, or rather his substitute for it.[14] For Spinoza, therefore, nothing is surer or can be surer than the existence of God. That anything exists at all involves the existence of infinite and perfect being, since otherwise the finite and imperfect would have more power or capacity to exist than the infinite and perfect.

In identifying God with the one substance or ultimate reality Spinoza is neither merely using conventional language nor forcing his terminology upon a principle or conception to which it is inappropriate. He is expressing his insight into the real meaning of the concepts concerned and is convinced that he is not misinterpreting but reinterpreting common thought and usage. Taking the accepted definition of substance as that which needs nothing else for its conception or its existence and the customary idea of God as an infinite and absolutely perfect being (*ens perfectissimum*), he shows that there can be only one such substance and that this can only be God —or God can only be this.

Objection may be taken to the use of the word "God" unless it expressly connotes a personal being as the creator and ruler of the world. But it is Spinoza's supreme merit that he takes the bold step of identifying the God of religion with the ultimate reality which philosophical thought compels him to affirm, and thereby makes possible the union of the quest of truth and the worship of the living God. It may be that the God of true religion is more properly to be conceived as superpersonal, if not as impersonal,[15]

---

[13] Cf. I, 11, Dem. and II, Def. 6 ("By reality and perfection I understand the same thing").

[14] As his alternative proofs taken together show, Spinoza's demonstration combines the ontological and the cosmological arguments; and it may also be said to accord with the logical principle that all necessity is hypothetical inasmuch as it takes the form: If anything exists, God exists.

[15] Cf. "At all times and in every part of the world mystics of the first order have always agreed that the ultimate reality, apprehended in the process of meditation, is essentially impersonal" (Aldous Huxley).

rather than as personal. But whatever be the solution of this theological or metaphysical problem, Spinoza's doctrine is in principle
indefeasible. If religion is to be defined as the sentiment of the holy,
or the sense of the numinous, then what alone can ultimately satisfy
the need concerned is not any finite object of awe or reverence, but
assuredly the perfect and sublime as revealed in the infinite whole of
reality.[16]

Spinoza's conception of God as the only true substance or the one
reality implies, further, the identification in some sense of God and
Nature, or of God with the world which is commonly spoken of as
his creation. This is signified by the expression "God or Nature." [17]
But he adopts from Scholastic philosophy the distinction of *natura
naturans* and *natura naturata*[18] to denote a certain self-differentia-
tion in the absolute reality implying two distinguishable though inseparable aspects or characters. In terms of Spinoza's fundamental
principle, *causa sui*, the former is God as self-*cause* or ground of all
existence, the latter is God as self-*caused* or consequent, that is, his
manifestation in all existence. To the one belong the infinite attributes of God, such as thought and extension; to the other the infinitude of diverse modes under each of these, namely all bodies as
particular modifications of infinite motion and rest and all thoughts
or ideas as comprised in infinite intellect.[19]

It may be held that any such self-diremption of the one substance
or reality cannot be made intelligible on his logical principles as an
actual significant element in Spinoza's system. But the spirit of his
philosophy, if not its logic, involves a duality-in-unity which may
be expressed by distinguishing between the divine activity in all the
processes of nature or the work of creation (not at one point of time
but as continuous action) and the relative passivity of facts and
things as they are made or have become.[20] Without this aspect of
differentiation or self-negation in the infinite reality there could not

---

[16] Cf. Spinoza's own statement of his quest and problem in *De Intellectus Emendatione*, I. One may also recall Carlyle's fine saying: "This Universe . . . is a
living thing—ah, an unspeakable, godlike thing; towards which the best attitude for us . . . is awe, devout prostration and humility of soul; worship if not
in words, then in silence" (*Heroes and Hero-Worship*).
[17] IV, Pref.
[18] I, 29, Schol.
[19] The further distinctions are not necessary for my present purpose.
[20] This is what is properly signified by the opposition of "spirit" and "nature."

be the complementary self-affirmation or reaffirmation implied in the progressive becoming or perfecting of the finite.[21]

God the Only True Cause

Causi sui, when the implications of the principle are unfolded, involves the conception that God or infinite and perfect being, is not only the one real substance but also the one real cause. What are commonly called causes can only be the conditions under which, in accordance with the nature of reality, this or that particular finite expression of its being comes into existence. Moreover, the term "cause of itself," duly interpreted, already indicates that the causal relation of the infinite to the finite differs from that of one finite being or thing to another. Spinoza's explicit statements concerning the divine causation may be considered under the headings: (1) God's causality is immanent causality; (2) God alone is a free cause; (3) God does not act for an end.

(1) *God's causality is immanent causality.*—"From the necessity of the divine nature must follow an infinitude of things in infinite ways." [22] "God is the efficient (or active) cause of all things. . . . God is absolutely the first cause." [23] "God is the immanent, and not the transient (or transitive) cause of all things." [24]

As is implied in what has already been said, God is the first cause, or creator, of the world or cosmos, not as existing and acting externally to it, but as its indwelling power or activity, its inmost reality. God is not the remote cause of any thing or event in the sense of being removed from it in time with intermediate causes coming in between. The reciprocal relations of different finite things or beings to one another are seen as an endless series of causes and effects, each of which conditions and is in turn conditioned by that which precedes or follows it.[25] But the infinite is related to the finite not as one particular thing or individual is to another but as the universal ground or common basis of all existence. This relation cannot be expressed in terms of time or succession; it is in the nature of a timeless fact or eternal truth. Further, God is the efficient cause of all

[21] Cf. below.
[22] I, 16.
[23] Ibid., Corol. 1 and 3.
[24] I, Prop. 18.
[25] Prop. 28 and Schol.

things, not as being only the cause of the beginning of their existence and not also of their persistence or continuance in existence; for the nature or essence of particular things does not in itself involve either existence or duration, since it is to the nature of God alone that existence necessarily pertains.[26]

Spinoza's doctrine of immanent causation is doubtless connected historically with the mechanical conception of nature associated with the names of Descartes and Hobbes. Consequently the action of the world-ground is expressed in terms appropriate to mechanical causation and to the concept of the conservation and transformation of energy. But the philosophy of Spinoza does not involve acceptance of the mechanist principle as the last word in the explanation of natural events. It is rather an attempt to interpret this in conformity with other and more fundamental concepts. The essential significance of the doctrine is that everything is connected both existentially and causally with everything else, and that all action and reaction are ultimately dependent on the underlying nature of the eternal reality.

(2) *God alone is a free cause.*—"That thing is called free which exists from the necessity of its own nature alone, and is determined to action by itself alone." [27] "God acts from the laws (or the necessity) of his own nature only." [28] "The will cannot be called a free cause, but can only be called necessary." [29] "Things could have been produced by God in no other manner and in no other order than they have been produced." [30]

The term "cause of itself," besides expressing the ultimate identity of essence and existence, also indicates the true unity of freedom and necessity. That God is the only fully free cause follows from the fact that his nature alone essentially involves existence. And the same principle implies that God's activity is a necessity of his nature, or rather that his nature and his activity are one and the same thing. What follows from the existence and nature of God may be called the expression of his will, but not in a sense that would make this will arbitrary or anything less than his whole being. Hence there is no real distinction between the truly necessary and the actually pos-

[26] Prop. 24.
[27] Def. 7.
[28] Prop. 17.
[29] Prop. 32.
[30] Prop. 33.

sible;[31] for whatever has power or reality enough to exist does exist and with the degree of perfection involved in its own nature.

Further, since all things are determined to existence and action by God as following from the necessity of his nature, there is nothing that exists or happens in the world which does not result of necessity from determinate causes or conditions.[32] Along with all other finite things and creatures man's activity is thus necessitated. But none the less the finite individual shares in the freedom of God, so that his action is free in proportion as it is determined from within by his own proper nature and not merely by conditions external to himself.

Spinoza thus denies free will in the sense of an indeterminism that implies the "liberty of indifference," [33] or an absolute power of choosing between alternative courses of action altogether independently of the agent's dispositions and beliefs and the bearing upon these of the conditions involved in his relations to other beings and things. Freedom and necessity are ultimately one, and the only valid opposition between them is that of the relative predominance of internal or of external factors in the determination of any particular action or course of action. An act is free just in so far as it is the expression of the agent's innermost being. There is nothing, therefore, in Spinoza's denial of absolute freedom of will that is inconsistent with his conception of the liberating power or influence of "adequate ideas," or the entrance into the human mind of the truth that makes men free. The one principle is indeed the complement of the other.

---

[31] Leibniz's conception that God in creating the universe acts in accordance not with the only possibility but with his choice of the best—which is regarded as uniting efficient and final causation—shows the distinction between abstract and concrete possibility, but cannot be taken to express a wholly different principle from that of Spinoza. Cf. the statement: "The divine perfection . . . could also be manifested through other creatures in another order" (Johannes Stufler —following Thomas Aquinas—in *Why God Created the World*), which is likewise tenable only if it precludes the idea of an arbitrary volition.

[32] I, 26–29 and II, 48.

[33] The stress laid by Descartes upon the influence of will on judgment—like a similar principle in Bacon's philosophy—concerns the need of suspense of judgment, or the avoidance (as he puts it) of "precipitancy and anticipation" in judgment through bias or undue haste, and does not properly involve the liberty of indifference. But Spinoza expressly rejects an antithesis of will and intellect in so far as it suggests that volition and judgment do not depend essentially on ideas. ("There is in the mind no volition or affirmation and negation save that which an idea as such involves." II, 49 with Corol. and Schol.)

(3) *God does not act for an end.*—"There is no cause, either without or within himself, that moves God to act except the perfection of his own nature." [34] "It is commonly supposed that God directs all things to some determinate end. . . . This doctrine does away with God's perfection. For if God acts for the sake of an end, he necessarily seeks something of which he stands in need." [35]

Spinoza's argument here is that action for the sake of an end is a mark of a finite and imperfect being, whose existence can only be maintained or whose true nature can only be realized by seeking and attaining a goal beyond actual fulfilment. Such a conception, implying as it does a lack or want in the agent concerned, is meaningless in reference to an infinite and perfect being whose nature is eternally complete. If we are to speak of a divine purpose at all, it can only be in the sense that it belongs to the perfection of God's nature that he should manifest himself in the creation of finite beings who can share in that perfection according to the degree in which they attain self-realization. This signifies not any external but an immanent end.

Spinoza's doctrine on this point is linked with his denial of final causes in nature. Man habitually acts for some end and devises means to its attainment, and he thinks that the same is true of nature or creation generally. More particularly, he thinks that God has made all things for the sake of man—to serve the ends and purposes of human beings—and that things and events in nature can be judged to be good or bad according as they do or do not further the fulfilment of these ends. But "the perfection of things is to be judged by their own nature and power alone." In the infinite fullness of his being there is nothing wanting to God "for the creation of everything, from the highest down to the lowest grade of perfection"; and things have no other reason than the expression of his being.[36] As products or manifestations of the divine nature and power they have no end external to themselves, since their being is actualized in the maintenance and development of their own natures, albeit also in the service of all other things in the pursuit of like ends.

[34] I, 17, Corol. 1.
[35] I, Append.; cf. Prop. 33, Schol. 2 *fin.*
[36] Ibid.; cf. IV, Pref.

Causation as Self-Expression of the Eternal Reality

"God's omnipotence has been actual from eternity, and to eternity will remain in the same actuality." [37] "By eternity I understand existence itself, so far as it is conceived to follow necessarily from the definition alone of the eternal thing. Such existence cannot be explained by duration or time, even if the duration be conceived as without beginning or end." [38] "It is of the nature of reason to perceive things under a certain form of eternity." [39] "We feel and know (or experience) that we are eternal." [40]

The various aspects of Spinoza's doctrine of causation, when taken together, give the fundamental principle indicated by the above citations. That God's causality is immanent causality, that it is alike free and necessary, and that it has no external purpose signify that the causality concerned is the self-expression of the ultimate reality, or *causa sui,* as the eternal ground of all existence. Such causality must be conceived after the fashion or on the analogy of necessary truth, or of the relation of ground and consequent rather than temporal succession.[41] It implies an order or sequence of which relations in time are only the symbol or outward semblance.[42] The fundamental order in terms of which the relations of things must ultimately be understood is that of different essences or individual natures and different levels of existence as determinate expressions of the being and nature of God.[43]

Spinoza's doctrine seems at first sight to be altogether incompatible with the reality in any sense of time or duration.[44] But the dis-

[37] I, 17, Schol., where the necessity with which things follow from the existence and nature of God is illustrated by reference to "necessary" or "eternal" truth.
[38] I, Def. 8 and Expl.
[39] II, 44, Corol. 2.
[40] V, 23, Schol.
[41] Joachim points out that the categories of ground and consequent, cause and effect, whole and part are all inadequate to express the immanence of God in the universe (*The Ethics of Spinoza,* pp. 118–119).
[42] Cf. Plato's definition of time as the "moving image of eternity."
[43] My statement in this section owes much to Prof. H. F. Hallett's article on "Spinoza's Conception of Eternity" in *Mind,* vol. xxxvii, n.s., No. 147. I have not at hand for reference his *Aeternitas* in which the subject is treated at length.
[44] Time is distinguishable from duration—which Spinoza defines as "the indefinite continuation of existence" (II, Def. 5)—as its measurement by means of a comparison of durations, or, as Aristotle puts it, "the numbering of motion"; though common usage tends to identify them.

tinction of eternity as the character of true reality from mere ever-lastingness or endurance throughout all time does not imply timelessness in the sense of being that is out of all relation to time. It means rather that eternity is the *truth* of time, as freedom is of necessity or as spirit is of nature or matter. Time or duration must be explained through the nature of eternity and not contrariwise. Duration may be defined as the process of change or transition from a lower to a higher or a higher to a lower degree of perfection, and it presupposes the eternal actuality of perfect being.[45]

Further, eternity or eternal life must be understood as a quality rather than a quantity of existence,[46] and as participated in by finite beings according as they rise above mere conditions of time and place. For eternity can have no meaning for us unless it can in some degree enter into our experience here and now. There are, indeed, experiences in life in which one feels that the moment is itself eternal, that eternity is *in* the experience in such wise that time and change can never make it really pass away. To see things thus "under the form of eternity," that is, as having, each in its own time and place, an eternal existence and significance, and to live in the spirit of such insight, is to possess something of the perfection and joy of true being.

The *Nisus* Towards Perfection or Self-Realization

"Each thing endeavours to persevere in its own being." "The effort by which each thing so endeavours is nothing but the actual essence (or nature) of the thing itself." [47] "Desire is the very essence of man in so far as determined to any action by any affect whatsoever." "Joy is man's passage from a less to a greater perfection." [48] "The actions of the mind arise from adequate ideas alone, but the passions depend alone upon those which are inadequate." [49]

As already said, the principle of differentiation along with the unity of reality is expressed, in Spinoza's philosophy, more especially in terms of the self-maintaining or self-realizing impulse (*conatus in*

---

[45] Cf. Aristotle's principle of the primacy of actuality, which I endeavoured to set forth in the article mentioned above.

[46] For Spinoza's opposition of eternity and duration in reference to the question of immortality, see V, 34, Schol.

[47] III, 6 and 7.

[48] Ibid., Definitions of the Affects or Emotions.

[49] III, Prop. 3.

suo esse perseverare). It has also been noted that it belongs inherently to the finite and imperfect to aim at a goal or ideal beyond actual attainment. The essential character, therefore, of the finite—in its quest of the infinite and perfect, which is at the same time the presence of the infinite in it—is found in striving, endeavour, or desire. Desire, being the impulse to satisfy a want or need, is essentially for self-fulfilment. Such desire or aspiration is the efficient cause whereby the end or ideal goal is in any measure realized. Here, therefore, efficient and final cause are one.

Further, the sense or feeling of attainment is experienced as joy or happiness, which is the sign of upward as against downward tendency. In general, any affect or emotion ceases to be a mere passion and becomes action in proportion as it is controlled or sublimated through the power of adequate ideas, more particularly a true knowledge of oneself and of the causes of the emotions. Herein lies the road from bondage to liberty, and thereby to participation in some small measure in the blessedness of God. This impulse in virtue of which the finite individual aspires to its own perfection is, indeed, the self-affirmation of God in us, and is at once the affirmation of the individual self as a unique expression of the infinite divine nature and its negation as a self-centred or self-sufficient unit.

The Intellectual Love of God

"Whatever we apprehend by 'intuitive knowledge' brings us the greatest satisfaction of mind (or acquiescence), and so the greatest joy, accompanied with the idea of God as its cause. . . . From this kind of knowledge, therefore, necessarily springs the intellectual love of God." [50] "He who loves God cannot seek that God should love him in return." [51] "The intellectual love of the mind towards God is part of the infinite love with which God loves himself. . . . Hence the love of God towards men and the intellectual love of the mind towards God are one and the same thing." [52]

These propositions must suffice to indicate the significance of the culminating phase of Spinoza's philosophy. According to his distinction of different kinds or stages of knowledge,[53] as the mind rises

[50] V, 32 and Corol.
[51] Ibid., Prop. 19.
[52] Prop. 36 and Corol.
[53] II, 40, Schol. 2.

from the mere particulars of time and circumstance as apprehended in sense-perception and memory (*imaginatio*) through the universals of thought or reason (*ratio*) to what he calls intuitive knowledge (*scientia intuitiva*), that is, an intellectual intuition or insight which apprehends particular things and events in all their concrete reality as features of the universal order and therefore as necessarily following from the being and nature of God, it comes to acquiesce in that order not merely as the only possible one but also as an order of love. For, rightly apprehended, it is such as reveals a being that is at once supremely powerful and supremely wise and good, and so meets all the needs of the human spirit. This, then, is that "infinite and eternal object" [54] in the contemplation of which the mind is alone filled with a love that yields lasting joy and happiness.

Putting together the several strands of Spinoza's philosophy one sees that, whatever may be its deficiencies of logic and method, its essential import is not in doubt. What it teaches is that it is of the very nature of an infinite and perfect being to be manifested in finite individuals who can seek and find their true good in union with their immanent cause and end—a union which is at the same time that of each with all. This relation of the finite and the infinite implies that the divine activity creating, sustaining and controlling all things is not that of mere external power and compulsion but rather the inspiring and persuasive power of infinite love. The response of the finite individual has at its highest level the character of a rationally grounded and disinterested "love towards God" as the supreme reality made manifest in the whole universe of being. Thus the movement or process of the finite towards the infinite and the boundless self-giving of the infinite to the finite are one and the same fact. As the theologian expresses it, "Our opening and His entering are one moment."

[54] *De Int. Emend.,* I, 10.

Spinoza's Conception of the Attributes of Substance*

A. Wolf

§ 1: Foreword

As THIS IS THE two-hundred-and-fiftieth anniversary of the death of Spinoza, it is but right that the Society should devote the evening to the consideration of some aspects of his philosophy. This is all the more desirable in view of the difference of opinion, not to say confusion, still prevalent about the interpretation of his works. It may seem amazing that two hundred and fifty years after the author's death his works should still be subject to very different, inconsistent interpretations. But so it is. Even more surprising, perhaps, is the fact that criticism of Spinoza's philosophy has not been delayed thereby. Or is this the explanation of the Babel of interpretations? Are people in such a hurry to criticize Spinoza that they do not take the necessary time and trouble to understand him? It certainly does seem strange that after two-and-a-half centuries of study the very foundations of Spinozism should still be subject, not merely to conflicting *criticisms* or *estimates,* but to conflicting *interpretations.* No doubt Spinoza is an uncommonly difficult writer, and his use of terms in senses rather different from their then usual meaning, to say nothing of their present meaning or meaninglessness, helps to complicate matters. Moreover, he was a recluse with entirely insufficient incentive to make himself easily intelligible. After all, there are lots of professional teachers who remain unintelligible, even after decades of daily contact with searching undergraduates. No doubt also his thoughts are difficult, quite apart from their expression. But when all such allowances have been made, it still seems to me that some of the misinterpretations of Spinozism are really inexcusable. They are largely due to a certain lack of

* An address delivered to the meeting of the Aristotelian Society on February 21, 1927, to commemorate the 250th anniversary of the death of Spinoza.

patient determination to find out what Spinoza really meant, a proneness to view his philosophy through Cartesian, Kantian, Hegelian, or other coloured spectacles, and, above all, to an excessive haste to criticize.

In the present paper I propose to deal briefly with a few misinterpretations, all of them relating mainly to Spinoza's conception of the Attributes of Substance, which is the very foundation of his philosophy. It is obvious that once the fundamental ideas of a system of philosophy are misunderstood, the rest is inevitably distorted. Yet, putting aside for the moment the question whether the fundamental conceptions of Spinoza do or do not commend themselves to us, it seems to me that there is no real reason for regarding them as obscure, or for justifying some of the interpretations which have been put upon them and which still have considerable vogue.

§ 2: The Relation of the Attributes to Substance

I begin with one of the less prevalent misconceptions concerning the relation of the Attributes to Substance. The elucidation of this point may be helpful in connection with the subsequent topics, but need not detain us long.

Spinoza's real view seems sufficiently clear. Substance (or Nature or God) is the unified totality of Attributes. This seems clear from such passages as *Ethics* I, IV, Dem. ("substances, or, what is the same thing, their attributes"), and I, XIX ("God is eternal, or, in other words, His Attributes are eternal"). In his earlier writings (*Letters* II, IV, IX) he defined Attribute in the same way as Substance, and a survival of this usage is met with in *Ethics* I, XV, Schol. ("extended substance is one of the infinite attributes of God"). The only difference between the Attributes and Substance is that our intellect can by an act of abstraction think of one of the Attributes apart from the rest, whereas in reality all the Attributes are inseparably together.

Unfortunately, for some of his readers, Spinoza had an interest in etymologies, and occasionally went out of his way to give the etymology of the word Attribute. *Attributum*, he explains, is connected with the verb *tribuere*, and an *attribute* is so called because the intellect *attributes* it to substance as one of its characteristics (*Ethics* I, IX, etc.). These etymological excursions have given rise to a kind of Kantian interpretation of the Attributes. According to J. E. Erd-

mann (*Grundriss der Geschichte der Philosophie,* Band II, Edition
1878), the Attributes were not regarded by Spinoza as real, objective
characters of Substance, but only as our (subjective) ways of conceiving it. This kind of interpretation may seem plausible so long as
one confines his attention to *Ethics* I, Definition IV ("By attribute I
understand that which the intellect apprehends of substance, as
constituting its essence"). But it loses every vestige of its plausibility
the moment one takes other passages, and Spinoza's other doctrines,
into account. According to Spinoza, the intellect (unlike the imagination) gives real knowledge, or knowledge of the real. It is therefore entirely unwarranted to read into Spinoza the distinction between what a known Attribute is *realiter* and what it is *in intellectu.*

The question may, of course, be raised whether Spinoza was really
justified in conceiving all the Attributes as constituting one only
Substance. There is, however, no reasonable doubt that he did so
regard them.

But it is unnecessary to elaborate this point, as hardly any English
writer has adopted Erdmann's Kantian interpretation of Spinoza's
Attributes. Assuming, then, that for Spinoza *Substance* and *the
totality of Attributes* were identical, we may pass on to the next
problem, which is much more serious.

§ 3: The Alleged Logico-Mathematical Character of the Attributes

One of the commonest and most serious misinterpretations of Spinoza's thought is that which maintains that ultimate Reality (i.e.,
God or His Attributes) was regarded by Spinoza as logico-mathematical in character, not dynamic. In other words, it is maintained
that when Spinoza speaks of causes and effects he really means
grounds and consequences. This interpretation owes its vogue mainly
to W. Windelband, who finds the essential feature of the philosophy
of Spinoza in its *mathematical* pantheism. Windelband's view that
Spinoza conceived of the Attributes as non-dynamic in character
seems to be shared more or less by all English expositors of Spinoza.
Yet it seems to me entirely unwarranted, a sheer travesty of Spinozism.

The unsophisticated reader of Spinoza cannot fail to be impressed
by the dynamic terminology to be found throughout his writings.
For example, Spinoza maintains that it is as impossible for us to

think that God does not *act* as that He does not exist, and God's essence is accordingly identified with the *power* by which He and all things are and *act* (*Ethics* I, xvii, II, iii, etc.). Similarly with the Attributes. Already in the *Short Treatise* (pp. 34 and 120 of my Translation) we find Thought and Extension described as *powers,* and the same view is expressed in the *Ethics* (II, i, vii and xxi). In fact, throughout his writings Spinoza lays stress on the identity of essence or reality with power or activity. To quote but two passages, let me give one from the *Short Treatise* (p. 146) and one from the *Ethics* (V, xl):—"The more essence a thing has, so much more has it also of activity"; "the more perfect a thing is the more reality it possesses, and consequently acts more."

Prima facie Spinoza's philosophy is essentially and characteristically dynamic. Yet Kuno Fischer appears to be almost the only important exponent who interprets the Attributes as *Forces;* and even his interpretation of the relation of the Attributes to Substance is not satisfactory.

When we pass from God (or Substance or the Attributes) to the Modes (from *Natura naturans* to *Natura naturata*), then Spinoza's dynamic conception is so undeniable that extremely few have ever seriously ventured to interpret it otherwise. This fact might have made people pause to re-consider their non-dynamic (or purely logico-mathematical) interpretation of the Attributes. But no, the fact is only made an additional reason for adverse criticism, for the critics naturally cannot see how Spinoza could conceive of a dynamic world of finite objects or events as emerging out of merely logico-mathematical Attributes!

Now to my mind, the purely logico-mathematical interpretation of Spinoza's Attributes is a gross misinterpretation, and is unjust to Spinoza in two ways. It cheats him (unintentionally, of course) of one of the most original features of his philosophy, and having committed one blunder, it caps it with another, by accusing him of inconsistency in deriving dynamic modes from non-dynamic Attributes.

Needless to say, the interpretation in question is not a wilful misinterpretation. There are reasons for it. But I will endeavour to show that the alleged reasons do not really bear out such a non-dynamic interpretation.

The reasons by which the logico-mathematical view is defended are two in number, so far as I know. They are these: (1) In a num-

ber of passages (e.g., *Ethics* I, xi; IV, Preface) Spinoza uses the
phrase *cause or reason* (*causa seu ratio*); (2) Spinoza's illustrations
of causal connections are mainly geometrical in character (the properties of the triangle, circle, etc.). From the first of these (1) it is
argued that for Spinoza *cause* was synomymous with *reason*. From
the second point (2) it is urged that just as the interrelations between the properties of geometrical figures are not really causal, but
logico-mathematical, so the cosmic relations, which Spinoza tried to
illustrate with the aid of the geometrical examples, must have been
conceived by him as standing in logico-mathematical, not in causal
relations.

(1) Now, the first of the above reasons seems to me to be almost
frivolous. There are plenty of occasions when the strongest believer
in dynamic causality may correctly use the phrase "cause or reason."
After all, the knowledge of any causal relationship may function as
a reason—any *causa essendi* or *causa fiendi* may become a *causa
cognoscendi*. So that the use of the phrase *cause or reason* does not
necessarily imply that the writer intends to abolish the distinction
between a dynamic cause and a logical reason. I can see nothing in
Spinoza's use of the phrase to warrant the view that he meant to identify the terms *cause* and *reason*. Take, for instance, *Ethics* I, xi, in
which the phrase occurs several times, though one example will serve
our purpose. He there says: "For everything there must be assignable a cause or reason why it exists or does not exist." This simply
means that if anything exists then there must be, or have been, conditions which produced it, and if something does not exist, then
there must be conditions which prevent its existence; and, of course,
if we know these causes, then we have the reasons, though there are
also reasons which are not causes.

(2) I turn to the second of the reasons given in justification of the
logico-mathematical interpretation of the Attributes, namely, the
frequent use of geometrical illustrations. The assumption invariably
made is, that the relation between the properties of geometrical
figures can by no manner of means be regarded as causal. The very
suggestion of another view would probably be enough to shock most
teachers of philosophy. I propose to say something on this head
presently. But let us suppose, for the moment at least, that the usual
assumption is correct, that the properties of geometrical figures
stand in so-called logico-mathematical relations to each other, not in
causal relations. Even so, I would maintain that Spinoza's use of

geometrical illustrations does not warrant the conclusion that he recognized no other relations, more particularly causal relations. It is a familiar fact that illustrations, like metaphors, must not be pressed too closely, because they are usually only intended to bring out some special point or points, and are not meant to resemble in every respect that which they are used to illustrate. This is only too obvious in the case of metaphors, but metaphors are only a kind of illustration. It is necessary to be cautious not to read too much into illustrations, or to deduce too much from their use. Now Spinoza's geometrical illustrations, I venture to say, always have a very real significance, even if we ignore entirely their alleged logico-mathematical character. What he usually wants to illustrate with their aid is the prevalence of necessary law (as distinguished from arbitrary caprice or contingency), or of immanent causality (as distinguished from transeunt causality), and the like. I can see no reason for supposing that he intended them to illustrate logico-mathematical relationship as opposed to causal relationship, and that he meant to deny the reality of causal relationships. The trouble which he took in the *Short Treatise* and in the *Ethics* to explain the different kinds of causes rather tends to show that he did not really propose to swamp them all in the logico-mathematical relationship.

I conclude, accordingly, that the case for the logico-mathematical interpretation is "not proven," and that there is no valid ground for explaining away Spinoza's dynamic terminology. It appears to me that the philosophy of Spinoza is essentially dynamic in character, that is to say, his conception of Reality is emphatically that of a dynamic Reality. This is a very original and very important feature of his philosophy. And it is only the rather persistent, wrong-headed attempt to make him a mere Cartesian that is largely responsible for the misconception or neglect with which this side of Spinoza's philosophy has met.

§ 4: The Dynamic Character of Reality according to Spinoza

That Spinoza regarded the universe as something essentially dynamic is made particularly clear if we compare his conception of the nature of Extension with the Cartesian conception of it. It is too commonly assumed that, because Descartes and Spinoza both used the same term (Extension), therefore they both meant the same thing. But that is a grave mistake. For Descartes, matter was essentially Extension, and nothing else. Matter as he conceived it was inert by nature. One result of this conception was that he had to invoke a *deus ex machina* not only to create matter and to maintain it in existence by incessant re-creation, but also to impart motion and rest to it, and to keep this motion and rest constant in quantity. Altogether, the Cartesian philosophy not only treats God like an outsider, but works Him terribly hard in keeping this sorry scheme of things together. Essentially the Cartesian philosophy is like any of the familiar cosmogonies of the historic theologies, and is addicted to incessant miracles.

As a philosophy, Spinozism is, in my humble opinion, incomparably superior to Cartesianism. To Spinoza, the incessant cosmic wire-pulling by an external God did not appear to conform to the rules of the game, if I may say so. Spinoza endeavoured to conceive the universe as a self-sufficient, autonomous, and perfectly rational system, free from external interference, and free from arbitrariness or caprice. Accordingly, he strongly criticized the Cartesian conception of matter as mere extension and entirely inert. From such matter, he maintained (*Letters* LXXXI and LXXXIII), the material universe could not possibly evolve. True, as Tschirnhaus reminded him, Descartes supposed that God added the necessary motion and rest to set things going; but the assumption of such miraculous external interference was just what appeared unphilosophical to Spinoza. Spinoza's conception of matter was dynamic from the very outset. He retained the Cartesian term Extension because the name indicated the difference between Matter and Thought, which Spinoza likewise conceived dynamically. What Spinoza means by Extension is really what may be called Physical Energy, which expresses itself in the infinite mode of Motion and Rest, which consequently need not be introduced miraculously from outside the material world. It may be pointed out here that the dynamic interpretation of Extension makes the relation of Motion and Rest (or energy of motion and energy of position) to Extension intelligible; the logico-mathematical interpretation makes nonsense of it. For how can Motion be logically derived from Extension? Motion implies Extension; but Extension does not imply Motion. If, therefore, Spinoza admitted only logico-mathematical relations, then Motion should have been the Attribute and Extension its mode. Presumably he knew what he really meant, and said it. And what he did say, already in the *Short Treatise* (p. 120), was that Extension is "the power to produce" Motion and Rest (or kinetic and potential energy, as we might say).

The subsequent history of science has abundantly justified Spinoza's dynamic or kinetic conception of matter as against the inert conception of matter held by Descartes and all his contemporaries as well as some of the most distinguished successors. Descartes, for instance, could only explain the movements of the planets by invoking, not only the aid of God, but also the machinery of æther vortices to carry the planets. Even Newton could not do without the æther, and for much the same reason. But after Newton's formulation of the law of universal gravitation, a marked change came about in the scientific world. In spite of Newton's opposition to it, the view generally accepted, and actually advocated by Cotes in his Preface to the second edition of the *Principia,* was that gravitation is inherent in matter as such, so that the motion of matter need not be accounted for by reference to external agencies; only changes of motion (in direction, etc.) need be accounted for in that way. Since then till the present day, the kinetic conception of matter has grown so much in favour that "matter" has almost been displaced by energy or "fields of force," an expression that may well remind us of Spinoza's conception of a dynamic Extension. Of course, I do not for a moment desire to claim for Spinoza the credit for the new physical conceptions. But I think that he deserves great credit for having suggested so long in advance a metaphysical basis for these modern ideas in Physics.

The other Attribute or Attributes were likewise regarded by Spinoza dynamically. He repeatedly refers to Thought as a power (*potentia*). It is, one might say, Mind Energy, just as Extension is Physical Energy. This naturally involved a dynamic conception of the modes of Thought. And so we find Spinoza protesting against the view which prevailed in his time and long afterwards that ideas are like "mute pictures on a tablet" (*Ethics* II, xlix, Schol., and compare Def. iii, Expl.), and maintaining, on the contrary, that they are active thoughts or assertions. Having regard to the *tabula rasa* view, and the passive sensationalist psychology, which dominated European thought over such a long period after the time of Spinoza, it was surely no small matter that by his insight he anticipated the dynamic tendency of present-day psychology as well as of present-

day physics. In my view Spinoza's consistently dynamic conception
of Reality is one of the most remarkable and most creditable features of his metaphysics.

This brings me to the consideration of a point to which allusion
has already been made before, namely, the significance of Spinoza's
use of geometrical illustrations. I contended before that even if the
usual conception of the purely logico-mathematical relations between the properties of geometrical figures were the only one conceivable, so that Spinoza could take no other view of them, even
then it would not follow that Spinoza intended his illustrations to
be interpreted as a denial of causal or dynamic relations. But now
I would go a step farther and maintain that his favourite way of regarding things dynamically manifests itself even in his attitude
towards geometrical figures. His favourite way of defining such
figures was by means of *genetic* definitions, that is, descriptions of
their construction, and such definitions are essentially dynamic. This
is perfectly clear from his account of the best definition of a circle
in Letter LX, where he says that "a circle is a figure described by a
line one point of which is fixed while the other is revolving." And
he says that he prefers this definition to other possible definitions
just because it expresses the *efficient cause* of the object defined.
(Compare the *Treatise on the Improvement of the Understanding*,
near the end.) We may suppose, accordingly, that a triangle was
regarded by Spinoza as the figure produced when three straight lines
(of which any two are greater than the third) are joined in such a
way as to enclose a space. By moving these lines about (actually or
in imagination) it could be shown that the sum of the three angles
must be equal to two right angles, and so on. In so far as Spinoza
thought of geometrical figures after this fashion, his use of geometrical examples, instead of confirming the logico-mathematical interpretation of his philosophy, would rather tend the other way.

§ 5: The Number of the Attributes
according to Spinoza

The Attributes of God, or Substance, are, according to Spinoza, not
only each infinite in its kind, but they are also infinite in number,
although only two of them (Thought and Extension) are known to
human beings. Spinoza's argument is, briefly, this. Only nothing has
no attributes. To be real a thing must have attributes; and the more

reality it has, the more attributes it must have. Consequently, God or Substance, the Infinitely Real, must have infinite attributes.

Commentators, not unnaturally perhaps, speak of the *innumerable* Attributes of Substance, according to Spinoza. And they are not at all happy about this infinity of Attributes. It is commonly regarded as spoiling the harmony or parallelism of the whole scheme. If all the Attributes are concurrent or parallel natures of one and the same Substance, which they constitute, then *prima facie* each mode might have been expected to manifest this infinite-sidedness, as a manifestation of the infinity of Attributes. But that does not appear to be the case. Even human beings appear to express and to know only two Attributes—Thought and Extension. Then, again, in the *Short Treatise* (Appendix II, p. 159), Spinoza maintains that not only has each mode of Extension its mode of Thought, or soul, but the modes of every other Attribute (that is, other than Extension) have each its soul or idea (that is, a mode of Thought). If so, then the Attribute Thought appears to have a privileged position among the Attributes: instead of being parallel with one Attribute (like Extension with Thought), it seems to be co-extensive with *all* the other Attributes.

Such are the difficulties which the commentators feel about the infinity of Attributes which Spinoza alleges. The critics feel that Spinoza was logically compelled to assume an infinity of Attributes, for the reasons briefly indicated above, and that, nevertheless, it does not fit into his scheme, but creates difficulties.

Now, in the first place, I do not attach any importance to the alleged difficulties. Spinoza nowhere speaks of the parallelism of the Attributes, and even if he did, it would surely be a gross instance of abusing a metaphor to suppose that he intended any sort of spatial co-extensiveness of the Attributes, whatever that may mean. All that he insists on is that each Attribute is infinite (that is, complete) in its kind, and it is surely absurd to try and measure the infinities of different Attributes against each other. Nor, again, can I see any cogent reason for supposing that an infinite-sided mode must needs be self-conscious of its infinite-sidedness. Man, for instance, might be more than he knows. I may return to this point presently.

But what I want to bring out more particularly is that in my view the whole doctrine of an infinite number of Attributes has really been misconstrued by all the commentators and expositors. It is true, of course, that Spinoza does speak of God or Substance as "consisting of infinite Attributes" (*Ethics* I, xi, for instance), and that "infinite" in this phrase refers to the number of the Attributes, and not merely to the fact that each Attribute is infinite in kind in itself. But it is a sheer blunder to translate Spinoza's *infinite* by *innumerable*. And it is this mistranslation that is at the root of the trouble. By *infinite* Spinoza means *complete* or *all*. Again and again Spinoza insists on his positive use of the term *infinite*; and again and again he uses *perfect* (i.e., complete) or *all* as the equivalent of *infinite*. Thus, for example, in the *Short Treatise* (I, ii, p. 21) he describes God as "*a being of whom all or infinite attributes are predicated.*" Now, nobody could think of describing two attributes as *innumerable* attributes, but they may well be *all* the attributes. What I contend is, that Spinoza did not posit innumerable attributes at all. He only knew of two Attributes, and as a cautious thinker, he had, of course, to allow for the possibility of other Attributes unknown to man, since Spinoza did not regard man as the measure of all things. He accordingly posited "infinite or all the attributes," in the sense of "certainly two, possibly more." My interpretation of Spinoza's meaning is, I think, borne out to some extent by what he says in *Ethics* III, ii, where, referring to the mutual relations between the modes of the different Attributes, he says: "The body cannot determine the mind to think, nor can the mind determine the body to motion or rest, nor to anything else if such there be." The expression "anything else" may refer to some mode of extension other than motion and rest. But the last part of the sentence may be a rather awkward way of stating that the mode of no other Attribute can be determined by a mode of Extension or of Thought, just as a mode of Extension and a mode of Thought cannot determine each other. In any case, whether this latter interpretation of *Ethics* III, ii, be possible or not, there can be no doubt about Spinoza's use of the term *infinite,* on which I base chiefly my view of his conception of the number of Attributes.

For Spinoza, then, as I understand him, there *may be,* but there need not be more than two Attributes, and what he says about the limitation of each mode of Thought to the apprehension of the mode of only one other Attribute (Extension, for instance, in our case), has reference to the possible case of there being other Attributes. In other words, if there really are other Attributes than Extension and Thought (Spinoza may be understood to say), then the fact that our mind apprehends only its own Attribute and that of Extension, and not the modes of any of the other (to us unknown) Attributes, must be due to the fact that each mind (or idea) is so constituted as only to know one other Attribute besides its own, namely, the Attribute of its *ideatum*, which may be a mode of a different Attribute in different cases.

§ 6: Afterword

This paper gives but a brief account of some of the interpretations of Spinoza's fundamental concepts which seem to me to be palpable misinterpretations. The account may suffice to show the need of a really close study of Spinoza, and the advisability of postponing criticism until we can be tolerably sure of the accuracy of our interpretation of him. I think that a close study of Spinoza is eminently worth while. Unless I am very much mistaken, the philosophy of Spinoza is more in harmony with present-day scientific thought, to say nothing of social and political thought, than any other philosophy since his time.

Spinoza's Definition of Attribute

Francis S. Haserot

THE SCHISM that cuts deepest into the interpretation of Spinoza is that concerned with the status of the attributes. Are the attributes subjective and hence essentially forms of cognition, or are they objective and inherent characters of substance? No exposition is needed to show that these views are opposite and give fundamentally different conceptions of Spinoza's meaning. The preponderance of opinion among commentators, I believe, is on the side of the objective interpretation. But whatever the truth with regard to this may be, it is evident that the question itself is primary. I here propose to treat this question by a direct examination of the definition of attribute.

Spinoza defines attribute as follows: "Per attributum intelligo id, quod intellectus de substantia percipit, tanquam ejusdem essentia constituens" (*E*, I, Def. 4).[1]

In this definition lie three ambiguities, ambiguities that have aroused essential difficulties for the interpretation of Spinoza. They have, together, thrown discord into the whole interpretation of *natura naturata,* or things that follow from God, and they have raised the dispute as to whether Spinoza is a mystic on the order of Maimonides or a rationalist after the general manner of Descartes. By an analysis of these ambiguities we may discover the possible versions that can be assigned to the definition.

The first ambiguity attaches to the word *intellectus.* Spinoza employs this term with two references. First, he refers to the "infinite intellect of God" (*intellectus infinitus Dei*); second, to the finite intellect, the intellect of such finite beings as men. The infinite intellect of God is the infinite range of adequate ideas compresent within

---

[1] References to the *Ethics* will be made as in the following example: *E*, II, 7, refers to *Ethics*, Pt. II, Prop. 7. Latin quotations are from the text of Carl Gebhardt; English quotations are from the translation of W. H. White.

the attribute of thought. Every idea in God's intellect, moreover, is rationally co-ordinated with the whole system of adequate ideas. In contrast to the infinite intellect, the finite intellect is limited in scope. Like the infinite intellect it is constituted of adequate ideas, but it does not contain the entire nexus of these ideas, and hence is not cognizant of the total range of attributes and their respective modes. Its extent is restricted, whereas that of the infinite intellect is unlimited; its cognition is partial, that of the infinite intellect complete.

The second indeterminancy of reference pertains to the relation between the phrase *tanquam ejusdem essentiam constituens* and the three elements: *intellectus, id quod,* and the term *percipit* in the clause *quod intellectus de substantia percipit.* Grammatically the phrase may modify any one of them. But, though this is true grammatically, evidence from the text indicates that the phrase containing *constituens* cannot intelligibly be taken to modify *intellectus.* For if it did, the intellect would then be identified with the essence of substance, as may be seen by the substitution of this relation in the definition. The definition would then read: "By attribute I understand that which the intellect, as constituting the essence of substance, perceives of substance." But the intellect, whether finite or infinite, is a mode (*E,* I, 31, Dem.), and it is clear that a mode cannot constitute the essence of substance. This follows from the definition of mode: "By mode, I understand the affections of substance, or that which is in another thing through which it is conceived." No version therefore that identifies the intellect with the essence of substance is acceptable, and this circumstance reduces the ambiguity in the present case to that which joins the phrase *tanquam ejusdem essentiam constituens* either with *id quod* or with *percipit.* In the one case the definition tells what the intellect perceives as the attribute; in the other, the way in which the attribute is perceived. The readings for these different assignments will be given below.

Last, there remains the ambiguity attaching to the adverb *tanquam. Tanquam* may mean either "as if," suggesting apparency as compared with fact, or "as," suggesting a real state.[2] *Tanquam* has

---

[2] It is to be noted that "as if" is itself ambiguous. It may mean (1) "as if, and maybe in fact," or (2) "as if, though not in fact." If I say, "I perceive this line as if constituting the diameter of a circle," the "as if" can mean "as if, and maybe in fact" or "as if, and also in fact." If I say, "I perceive this polygon as

this dual use in Latin, and some writers contend that the proper translation, with corresponding meaning, is "as if." [3] But if "as if" means "as if and also in fact," then this translation would be misleading as compared with the simple "as," and would obviously imply not the subjective, but the objective interpretation.

Aside from his use of *tanquam* in the definition, Spinoza employs the word twenty-nine times in the *Ethics*. In twenty-six of these the word clearly means "as." With respect to three—namely, *E*, I, 33, Schol. 2; *E*, II, 49, Schol. (Sec. 1 of last paragraph); and *E*, V, 31, Schol., the contention might be raised (though with some question) that Spinoza employs the term with counterfactual reference. Hence, though the weight of usage favors "as," the argument will not here be invoked that, on purely grammatical grounds, the counterfactual usage is excluded. In any case however it is evident that the translation of *tanquam* as "as if" conforms to the subjective interpretation of the attributes; the translation of it as "as" to the realistic interpretation.

Spinoza's meaning, it appears, attained ample clarity in his own mind, and he saw no reasonable probability that readers would discover an equivocality in the definition. That he left these ambiguities intentionally is scarcely to be supposed.

We come now to the possible versions which, through translation, can be given to the definition. I shall indicate these first in symbols, to show their relations, and thereafter give them in verbal translations, and in that form discuss them.

Let the letters from a to f represent the indicated meanings: a, *intellectus finitus;* b, *intellectus infinitus;* c, *tanquam ejusdem essentiam constituens* as referring to *id quod;* d, *tanquam ejusdem essentiam constituens* as referring to the verb *percipit* in the clause *quod intellectus de substantia percipit;* e, *tanquam* translated "as if"; f, *tanquam* translated "as." Now the following combinations—all pos-

---

if constituting a circle," the "as if" means "as if, though not in fact." According to the context, the "if" in the term "as if" implies either uncertainty as to the factual character of the predication or certainty as to its counterfactual character. But the term "as if," in the manner here used, must mean the latter, i.e., "as if, though not in fact." Otherwise the conditional "if" would have no determinant bearing on the interpretations of the definition, and the expression "as if" would be indistinguishable in meaning from "as."

[3] Harry Austryn Wolfson, *The Philosophy of Spinoza* (Cambridge, Mass.: Harvard University Press, 1934), I, 146, 153.

sible with these meanings—may be noted: ace, acf, ade, adf, bce, bcf, bde, bdf. This gives eight versions of the definition. I shall now state these in words and for convenience of discussion examine them in the following order: 1, acf; 2, adf; 3, ace; 4, ade; 5, bce; 6, bde; 7, bdf; 8, bcf.

1. By attribute I understand that which, as in fact constituting the essence of substance, the finite intellect perceives of substance.

This version is at once recognized as invalid, that is, as incompatible with the text, since it means: that, and *that only,* which a finite intellect perceives of the essence of substance, is to be identified with the attribute. The *definiens* is too narrow. If the infinite intellect perceived something of the essence of substance that a finite intellect did not perceive, then, according to this version, that character could not be an attribute. But the attributes are infinite in number, and no finite intellect can perceive an infinite number of attributes. If, by supposition, an intellect were conceived to do so, it would by necessity be conceived as infinite (*E,* II, 1, Schol.). Hence this version cannot be sustained.

Were the following proposition asserted: "That which, as in fact constituting the essence of substance, the finite intellect perceives of substance, is an attribute," the proposition would be true, but it would not constitute a definition of attribute.

2. By attribute I understand that which the finite intellect perceives of substance as constituting its essence.

This version is excluded for the same reasons that apply to Version 1. The finite intellect cannot apprehend an infinity of attributes. If it cannot, there are attributes which it does not perceive. But this contradicts the sense of the present version.

3. By attribute I understand that which, as if (though not in fact) constituting the essence of substance, the finite intellect perceives of substance.

This version is plain nonsense. It states that there is something that is not the essence of substance but which exists as if it were that essence, and that this item is what "the finite intellect perceives of substance." Now it is clear that the attributes, in this case, cannot constitute the essence of substance. This, however, is incompatible with the text (*E,* I, Def. 6).

4. By attribute I understand that which the finite intellect perceives of substance as if (though not in fact) constituting its essence.

This version interprets the attributes as constructions of the finite mind. It is a form of the subjectivist view. That it is not valid, however, is evidenced by a number of reasons.

First, the term "finite intellect" cannot, in this version, refer to the human intellect, since the human intellect perceives two attributes only. But any other finite intellect, as we have seen (Version 1), would likewise be limited as to the number of attributes it could perceive. The attributes, however, are infinite in number. It follows that the term "finite" in the present version is unsustainable.

Second, the attributes are comprehended, whether by the infinite or the finite intellect, only by adequate, therefore true, ideas. But the *ideatum* of a true idea necessarily is (*E*, I, 30, Dem.; *E*, II, 34). Hence in this case the attribute, as actually pertaining to substance, necessarily is. But then an attribute is not subjective to the finite intellect. It would be impossible, that is, contradictory, for the finite intellect to conceive an attribute adequately, "as if, though not in fact, constituting the essence of substance," since an attribute, to be adequately conceived, must be conceived as it is. It cannot be conceived, in the rational sense of the term "conceived" here used, as if it were something that is not. To suppose that, in the definition of attribute, Spinoza disregarded this point would be to put forward a very dubious assumption. Spinoza is too explicit about the ontological reference of a true idea to leave any plausibility to such a view.

If, however, in spite of this the present version were to be maintained, the thesis would have to be adopted that the attributes are not simply inadequately perceived but that they are, in their true natures, nothing but inadequate ideas of the finite mind. But such a construction is too incongruous with the text to require serious consideration.

Spinoza repeatedly says that the finite intellect has an adequate idea of God. By this he means that it perceives God adequately through those attributes that it comprehends. But the attributes are known by the intellect alone, not by external perception or imagination, that is, inadequately.[4] And it is to emphasize this that Spinoza associates knowledge of the attributes with conceptions of the intellect and frequently refers to the one in relation to the other. His whole critique of the representations of God through images or

---

[4] The imagination yields inadequate ideas only (*E*, II, 28; *E*, II, 41).

imaginative analogies is that such representations, rather than revealing God through His attributes, that is, as in reality infinite, inevitably characterize Him through predicates that involve finitude, and hence in fact misrepresent Him.[5] From Spinoza's point of view, to believe that we can know God, or what is the same, His attributes, through the imagination, is basically mistaken. It is mistaken because, if we so believe, we cannot attain the attitude toward God described in Part V of the *Ethics*. If we do not conceive Him rightly, we cannot have the right attitude toward Him, or at least we cannot understand what this attitude is. Hence the importance for Spinoza of the thesis that the attributes are perceived by the intellect alone. But if the attributes are perceived by the intellect (in contradistinction to the imagination), they are perceived adequately, and hence they are; that is, they are objectively.

It is evident that no version of the definition that interprets the term "intellect" to mean the finite intellect is reconcilable with the text. And this excludes *a fortiori* any view that identifies the attributes with constructions of the human intellect.

5. By attribute I understand that which, as if (though not in fact) constituting the essence of substance, the infinite intellect perceives of substance.

As in Version 3, the phrase, "as if (though not in fact) constituting the essence of substance," gives little other than nonsense. In any case it is manifest (1) that in this version what the infinite intellect perceives of substance does not constitute the essence of substance, and (2) that this item which does not constitute the essence of substance is identified with attribute. As regards both points the version is invalid.

6. By attribute I understand that which the infinite intellect perceives of substance as if (though not in fact) constituting its essence.

This is a form of the subjective interpretation. It conceives the attributes as distinctions originating in the infinite intellect, and not referable as such to substance in its real nature. The invalidity of the version, however, is evidenced in its statement. The infinite intellect can perceive things only as they are. It could perceive nothing "as if (though not in fact) constituting the essence of substance." Otherwise it would be passive and subject to inadequate ideas. This, however, is not compatible with the nature of the infinite intellect,

[5] *E*, I, 15, Schol.; *E*, I, 17, Schol.; *E*, II, 3, Schol.; *E*, IV, Preface.

which can be subject to no inadequate ideas, and least of all to
make-believe. According to this version, moreover, only that portion
of what the infinite intellect perceives of substance that is *not* constitutive of the essence of substance is to be identified with the
attributes. This is absurd.[6]

No force, moreover, attaches to the present version unless it is
taken as rendered, that is, "By attribute I understand that which the
infinite intellect perceives of substance as if (though not in fact)
constituting the essence of substance." For if the term "as if" in the
version were taken to mean "as if, and also in fact," then the prepo-
sition "if" would have no force; "as if" would then mean "as," and
this version would not be distinguishable from the one that follows.
The emphasis here lies, therefore, on the phrase, "though not in
fact." That this construction jars with Spinoza's meaning is at once
evident. Thought is an attribute. The infinite intellect is a modification of the attribute of thought (*E*, I, 31). The attribute then, according to this view, is nothing but a thought of one of its own
modifications. But this, again, is absurd.

Further, in terms of this version, God or substance, in His real
nature, is unknowable and ineffable. His nature transcends ideas.
The whole world of *natura naturata* then is, in its relation to God,
inexplicable; in fact it is entirely phenomenal, and whatever reality
exists lies beyond the horizon of thought. But if this is the status
of *natura naturata,* what becomes of the primal thesis (*E*, II, 7)
that the order and connection of ideas is one with the order and
connection of things? What are the things to which the ideas pertain and which have the same order and connection as the ideas?
On this interpretation these questions remain unanswered.

[6] Cf. *E*, I, 19, Dem.: "Again, by attributes of God is to be understood that which
(Def. 4) expresses the essence of the divine substance, that is to say, that which
pertains to substance." Also, *E*, I, 20, Dem.: "The same attributes of God, therefore, which (Def. 4) manifest the eternal essence of God, at the same time manifest His eternal existence, that is to say, the very same thing which constitutes
the essence of God [i.e., the attributes] constitutes His existence. . . ."

It is to be noted that both of these passages point back to Def. 4, the definition of attribute, and are explanatory of that definition. It may also be noted
that Spinoza here says that the attributes constitute the existence of God. This
assertion should be considered in respect to any form of the subjective interpretation. If the attributes are subjective, i.e., phenomenal, or perceptions of the
mind, then God's very existence is constituted of perceptions of the mind. This
however is obviously impossible, and would clash directly with the conception
of God as *causa sui.*

Again, if the things thus referred to are phenomena and phenomena only, then they are dependent on thought. Spinoza, however, tells us that they are modes of another attribute, that each attribute is absolute, is infinite in its kind, and is therefore independent of the other attributes. The things then are not dependent on thought. This, however, is incompatible with the present version.

7. By attribute I understand that which the infinite intellect perceives of substance as constituting its essence.

The meaning of this version is identical with that of the version which follows.

The infinite intellect is a mode of thought. And what the infinite intellect perceives, that is, has adequate ideas of, is given in nature (*E*, I, 30 Dem.). Therefore, since the attributes are among the things perceived by the infinite intellect, the attributes are, that is, are objectively. Nor can the attributes be merely perceptions of the infinite intellect, for then they would be nothing more than modes of a mode of thought. But the attributes are independent, one of another; hence they cannot be modes of a mode of thought. Or, in other words, they cannot be perceptions of the infinite intellect in contradistinction to the things of which those perceptions are perceptions. They are, in short, not perceptions of the infinite intellect but "that which the infinite intellect perceives [i.e., has adequate ideas of]." Then, however, the meaning of the present version is identical with that of the next version.

8. By attribute I understand that which, as in fact constituting the essence of substance, the infinite intellect perceives of substance.

We have already seen why the versions previous to Version 7 are invalid. The meaning of Version 7 and that of the present version coincide. It remains to indicate why this last version is valid.

The primary but not the sole reason for this lies in the term "infinite intellect." What the infinite intellect perceives must include anything that the finite intellect perceives. Also what the infinite intellect perceives, that is, comprehends through adequate ideas, must be in nature. No finite intellect, as we have seen, could perceive all of the attributes. Nevertheless all the attributes are attributes of substance. Hence the term "intellect" in the definition as given in the *Ethics* cannot refer to the finite intellect. To adjust the definition to the specification of infinite attributes, we must assume that the term "intellect" refers to the infinite intellect. The infinite intellect alone can perceive an infinite number of infinite attributes.

And since, according to the text, the infinity of attributes is what
the intellect perceives, the intellect that perceives it must be the
infinite intellect. That Spinoza, moreover, in composing the definition of attribute, had in mind the infinite intellect is indicated explicitly in *E*, II, 7, Schol., in which he says: "Everything [i.e., the
attributes] which can be perceived by the infinite intellect as constituting the essence of substance pertains entirely to the one sole substance only. . . ." [7]

Now in the light of this it is scarcely necessary to raise the question: Are the attributes nevertheless merely perceptions or constructions of the infinite intellect and not real aspects of substance?
The answer to this has already been given in the discussion of Version 7, where it was pointed out that the attributes would then be
modes of a mode of thought, which is prima facie impossible.

But to neglect nothing that Spinoza considered relevant, I shall
refer to a group of statements that bear directly on the point. First
comes the definition of God: "By God, I understand Being absolutely infinite, that is to say, *substance consisting of infinite attributes,* each one of which expresses eternal and infinite essence." [8]
Here Spinoza says as simply and straightforwardly as possible that
God is substance consisting of infinite attributes. Are we to suppose
that he did not mean this as here stated, or that he was not fully
aware of what he was saying, particularly in the most central definition of the *Ethics?* Or are we to suppose that this was, as it were,
a manner of speaking, and that by the expression "consisting of" he
did not mean that the attributes are inherent in the essence, or that
by the term "infinite" he did not mean a plurality of attributes but
a single ineffable and uncharacterizable attribute? If we argue that
Spinoza like Maimonides admitted no distinctions of any kind in
the essence of God [9] and if this is what he in fact meant, then he
could have selected no language more perfectly calculated to suggest
a meaning directly opposed to his real meaning, especially when he
could have given the latter plainly in words adjusted to it. But such
a dubious use of language does not appear to be customary with
Spinoza, and he repeats the assertion made in the definition of God
in different words but no less specifically in *E*, I, 29, Schol.: "For,

---

[7] For the relation of this passage to the definition of attribute, see Lewis Robinson, *Kommentar zu Spinozas Ethik* (Leipzig: Felix Meiner, 1928), p. 274.
[8] Italics supplied.
[9] Wolfson, op. cit., pp. 115 ff.

from what has gone before, I think it is plain that by *natura natu-rans* we are to understand that which is in itself and is conceived through itself, or those attributes of substance which express eternal and infinite essence, that is to say . . . God in so far as He is considered as a free cause." But these reflections notwithstanding, we are urged, in drawing conclusions from Spinoza's reconstructed medieval background, to consider the definition of God as meaning that there is not *extra intellectum* a plurality of attributes, and that the attributes as a plurality are not in fact constitutive of the essence of substance.[10] In view of the explicit character of Spinoza's statements, this interpretation must appear doubtful.

Further, in *E*, I, 16, Dem., Spinoza makes the following assertion, in no way construable in a figurative or nonliteral sense: "But the divine nature possesses absolutely infinite attributes. . . ." And in *E*, I, 19, Dem., he says: "Again, by the attributes of God is to be understood that which (Def. 4) expresses the essence of divine substance, that is to say, *that which pertains to substance*. It is this very thing, I say, which the attributes themselves must involve." [11] Moreover, in *E*, I, 4, Dem., he says: "There is nothing therefore outside the intellect by which a number of things can be distinguished one from another, but substances (or which is the same thing by Def. 4) their attributes and their affections." Here he asserts not simply that the attributes exist outside the intellect, but that they, with their modifications, are the sole things that do exist outside the intellect. Now pointed as this is, if nevertheless it is yet not sufficiently explicit, we may turn to *E*, I, 10, Schol.:

> For this is the nature of substance, that each of its attributes
> is conceived through itself, *since all the attributes which sub-*

---

[10] Ibid., pp. 118 ff. Note also a statement of the medieval view attributed to Spinoza: "First, all the attributes of God are in reality one attribute, and, whatever difference there may appear to exist between them, they do not affect the nature of God . . ." (p. 120). In this account the supposition that Spinoza might have exercised any independence of judgment seems to be taken as unthinkable. *Ethics* I is considered a restatement, scarcely more than a summary, of the conceptions of his medieval predecessors.

[11] Italics supplied. It must be borne in mind that on the subjective interpretation the attributes do not pertain essentially to substance, and are not characters of substance, but are ways in which the perceiving mind envisages substance. Take away the perceiving mind, on this view, and you take away the attributes also, although you leave substance intact—intact, that is, as an undifferentiated and attributeless substratum.

stance possesses were always in it together, nor could one be produced by another; [extension, for example, or extended things could not be produced by thought] but each expresses the reality or being of substance. It is far from being absurd, therefore, to ascribe to one substance a number of attributes, since nothing in nature is clearer than that each thing must be conceived under some attribute, and the more reality or being it has the more attributes it possesses expressing necessity or eternity or infinity.[12]

In Spinoza's view, to be conceived is to be conceived adequately, that is, rationally, and to be conceived adequately is to be in nature.

How, it may be asked, could the infinite intellect perceive, that is, have adequate ideas of, *ideata* that were not as they are perceived? How could it have true ideas of distinctions that have no ground in the nature of things? The answer is that it could not. If the infinite intellect has adequate ideas of the infinite attributes, then, to use Spinoza's terms, the infinite attributes exist formally as well as objectively,[13] or generally in our terms, objectively as well as subjectively. They could in no way be characterized as existing subjectively but not objectively, for "a true idea must agree with that of which it is the idea." If a true idea is present, then it must have an *ideatum*. Further, "All ideas which are in God [that is, in the infinite intellect] always agree with those things of which they are ideas (Corol. Prop. 7, pt. 2) and therefore (Axiom 6, pt. 1) they are all true" (*E*, II, 32, Dem.). One conclusion alone follows from this: the attributes are real, that is, objective, for they are *ideata* of adequate ideas in the infinite intellect. And if this reasoning is valid, then the so-called subjective interpretation of the attributes must be relegated to the sphere of fiction.

A final comment with regard to that interpretation is now relevant. The gist of the subjective interpretation is that it removes any plurality of attributes from the essence of substance. The essence of substance, it avers, contains no differentiation of any kind. "Substance is thus to Spinoza, like God to the medievals, absolutely sim-

---

[12] Italics supplied.

[13] *E*, I, 30, Dem.: "Idea vera debet convenire cum suo ideato (per Axiom. 6), hoc est (ut per se notum) id, quod in intellectu objective continetur, debet necessario in natura dari . . . ergo intellectus actu finitus, aut actu infinitus Dei attributa, Deique affectiones comprehendere debet, et nihil aliud."

ple, free from accidental as well as essential attributes. . . ." [14] Then from whence arises the predication of an infinite plurality of attributes? It must arise, according to this view, from the forms of cognition native to the intellect, but not applicable to substance. The infinite plurality of attributes is thus an invention of the mind.

If this is the case, however, the question arises as to how the intellect could invent or engender from within itself a multiplicity of forms whose prior rational possibility was not already given. From whence could this possibility issue? It must come from substance itself. But this places the plurality or differentiation right back in its source, that is, the essence of substance, from which it was supposed to be removed. The proposed solution not only does not solve the problem but generates further problems quite as formidable as the one it purports to resolve.

Now the intellect that invents the infinite plurality of attributes cannot be the finite intellect; it must be the infinite intellect of God. The infinite attributes thus invented are not in God as God is in reality; they are forms of cognition of the infinite intellect. If God were perceived or apprehended as He is in reality, all distinctions between attribute and attribute would vanish, and His essence would be revealed as a unique attributeless or characterless nature. No character such as an attribute could be distinguished in it, for the essence is posited as free from distinctions of any kind. On this interpretation, the plurality of attributes is unreal; only the one undifferentiated essence is present, with no attribute and no plurality of attributes. The plurality of attributes is a contribution of the intellect.

The term "subjective" is used to indicate this status of the attributes. It means that any distinction between attribute and attribute is the outcome of the mind's envisagement and is, in fact, inapplicable as such to reality. Thought, in its real nature, is literally extension, and extension is literally thought, and so on for the other attributes. There is no difference or distinction of any kind between them as they are in themselves. But this hypothesis encounters important difficulties. If the attributes are identical in this absolute sense, then to know one as it is in fact, that is, to have an adequate idea of one, is to know all, for there is no distinction between them. But the human intellect, as exemplifying the finite intellect, knows

[14] Wolfson, op. cit., p. 116.

only two. Now if the finite intellect in knowing one or a limited number does in fact know all, then there is no distinction between it and the infinite intellect. The hypothesis of the real indistinguishability or absolute identity of the attributes removes any ground for the distinction of finite from infinite intellect, for the scope of the one, in that case, becomes identical with the scope of the other, namely, the total range of the attributes. Nor could the one have a more comprehensive knowledge of the essence of God than the other.

But the difficulties do not end here. If the attributes are one and indistinguishable in their real nature, then they cannot be respectively ultimate and infinite in their kinds, that is, they cannot be independent. In what way could forms or characters the same to the point of identity be independent one of another, and possess natures such that each, to be conceived at all, must be conceived through itself? The implication of this is that either the attributes are not constitutive of the essence of substance (which is posited as free from internal distinctions of any kind), or they are not independent one of another (for in that case they are distinct). However, both of these positions are rejected by Spinoza and, as we have seen, run contrary to the sense of the *Ethics*.

Nevertheless, in accordance with the subjective view, there is, aside from the invention of the intellect, no distinction between the attributes. They are not many but one, and the one thing that they are taken to be is the essence of substance. This essence is qualitatively neutral but is viewed by the intellect in an infinite number of ways, and the ways in which it is viewed are considered to be the attributes. If the intellect were by hypothesis taken away, there would be no infinity of attributes but simply one ineffable and undifferenced essence.

This interpretation, though it effaces all distinctions from God's nature, threatens gravely the intelligibility of Spinoza's philosophy and the rational method it professes to follow. It makes Spinoza a pure mystic, with no available explanation of the modes, for the modes, as we have seen, cannot be taken as inventions of the intellect, since if they were they would be simply modifications of thought. Such a view, moreover, does not conform with Spinoza's exposition.[15] The world then truly becomes such stuff as dreams are

---

[15] The modes are distinguished fundamentally from one another by the attributes. "Omnia, quae sunt, vel in se, vel in alio sunt . . . , hoc est . . . extra intellec-

made of, but why the dream should occur is a point sunk in impenetrable mystery. How an absolutely undifferenced substance, as thus posited, could have any modes at all, not to say be the logical origin of an infinite world of modes, lies beyond the power of rational explanation. Spinoza could not then validly deduce things from God or explain things in terms of God, nor could he intelligibly say as he does in *E*, I, 17, Schol.:

> But I think I have shown with sufficient clearness (Prop. 16) that from the supreme power of God, or from His infinite nature, infinite things in infinite ways, that is to say, all things, have necessarily flowed, or continually follow by the same necessity, in the same way as it follows from the nature of a triangle, from eternity and to eternity, that its three angles are equal to two right angles.

For from a blank or an Absolute Indifferent nothing can be deduced.

It is true that if Spinoza is to be considered a mystic seer, essentially irrational or overrational in character, then the subjective interpretation, in spite of its discordance with the *Ethics*, would have the greater appeal. God becomes, on this view, a fathomless depth that somehow contains all things, yet without harboring within itself the slightest trace of difference. God, moreover, since He is manifested to the intellect only through the infinite attributes, is, in this view, unknowable even to Himself, that is, to the infinite intellect; a conclusion which at least one commentator has not hesitated to draw.[16] But the conclusion lacks any credible support in the *Ethics*.

---

tum nihil datur praeter substantias, earumque affectiones. Nihil ergo extra intellectum datur, per quod plures res distingui inter se possunt praeter substantias, sive quod idem est (per Defin. 4) earum attributa, earumque affectiones" (*E*, I, 4, Dem.).

[16] Lewis Robinson, op. cit., p. 66 n.: "Eine solche Folgerung hat indessen einen modernen Spinoza-forscher, G. Huan (*Le dieu de Spinoza*, 1913, p. 161) nicht aufgehalten. Spinoza, versichert er, *n'accorde en aucune façon que l'entendement, même infini, puisse avoir de la substance une connaissance absolue, une connaissance de ce qu'elle est en soi*. In wirklichkeit aber schreibt Spinoza eine absolute, adäquate Kenntniss der göttlichen Substanz nicht nur der Gottheit selbst, sondern auch dem menschlichen Verstand zu (S. Eth. II Prop. 47; vgl, auch Theol.-polit. c. 13: intellectualis Dei cognitio ejus naturam prout in se est considerat)."

If, however, in contradistinction to the subjective interpretation, Spinoza is taken to be a rationalist, then the attributes can be construed only as distinct but inherent and mutually inseparable characters of substance. In this case God's nature, though indivisible, contains the ground for all possible differentiation in the world. God and the world are not separate but constitute a single ultimate, rationally coherent, and all-inclusive system. And this is, in fact, the metaphysical basis of Spinoza's determinism.

Williamsburg, Virginia

Spinoza and the
Status of Universals[1]

Francis S. Haserot

THE QUESTION of the status of universals constitutes, because of its pervasive implications, an essential problem for Spinoza interpretation. If Spinoza is a nominalist his philosophy is one thing; if he is a realist it is another, and quite different, thing. The latter interpretation can have little in common with the former. Spinozists are one in name only. According as they represent one interpretation or another they represent one philosophy or another. At their extremes these philosophies are opposites. Unfortunately Spinoza's words are not unambiguous. Some support may be derived from the texts for contrary or incompatible views. Clarification, if it is to be reached, must be attained (1) by considering the demands of consistency that follow from the philosopher's basic theses, and (2) by comparing verbally opposed statements in the text for the purpose of distinguishing whatever primary tendency may be present. Both of these methods will here be applied.

Before proceeding to this a note as to the specific bearing of the topic should be added. The question of the status of universals is connected with the problem of the nature of the attributes. The attributes, although not modes, are common properties of their respective modes. They are, as common properties, universals—using the term "universal" in its present-day sense—and if Spinoza is interpreted as a nominalist the attributes must be considered as *entia rationis,* that is, as subjective. In this case the word *tanquam* in the definition of the attribute will be translated "as if" rather than "as," or the word *constituens* will be taken to modify *intellectus* rather than *quod.*[2] God becomes inherently unknowable and the whole

---

[1] Read before The Virginia Philosophical Association at Roanoke College, Salem, Virginia, October 27, 1949.

[2] *Ethics,* Pt. I, Def. IV. *Per attributum intelligo id, quod intellectus de substantia percipit, tanquam ejusdem essentiam constituens.* Cf. Lewis Robinson, *Kommentar zu Spinozas Ethik* (Leipzig, 1928), p. 64.

philosophy of the *Ethics* takes the form of a mental construct in accordance with which we conjecture a reality that, in its true nature, lies beyond our ken. The attributes become primary categories of the understanding, and philosophy, on this interpretation, becomes essentially epistemology, for ontology is impossible.

As opposed to this, if Spinoza is considered to be a realist on the ground that he admits certain kinds of universals, then the definition of an attribute can, at least, possess objective reference; the word *tanquam* can be considered to mean "as" and the term *constituens* can be construed as referring to *quod*. The attribute, in this case, becomes an ontological character of substance; God or reality is conceived as knowable; the attribute is a common property of its respective modes; the second and third kinds of knowledge yield objective truth, and the *Ethics* becomes an ontology based on logical presuppositions. The two views are *toto caelo* different.

The problem of the status of universals has thus direct relevance to any general interpretation of Spinoza. For to hold that Spinoza is a nominalist is not compatible with the premise that the attributes have real as compared to mental existence. The sole way to escape this circumstance is to deny that common properties are universals; but this is scarcely intelligible. The one thing that the nominalist rejects is the notion of common properties. Otherwise no point attaches to his position. Occam's razor cuts off common properties as unnecessary entities, and in their place substitutes similarities or likenesses. One red rose has nothing in common with another red rose; one circle has nothing in common with another. The redness of the one rose is a particular redness of its own, and is merely *like* that of the other rose. And the same relation pertains to the circles. Each circle is unique; and, although different circles are similar, they have no form, or, for that matter, anything else in common. To the nominalist, words other than proper nouns can be signs for things only as a consequence of the likenesses of the things; but, in point of accuracy, such words refer to nothing common in the things, and the classes they supposedly represent are *entia rationis*. Since this is the case, there can be no joint assertion of nominalism and common properties. If one is affirmed, the other is, by definition, denied.

With these remarks I shall pass to the first method of investigation, that is, the method of consistency. Are the views historically

associated with nominalism, or those that follow as logical consequences of it, consistent with Spinoza's basic conceptions? This question must be answered by an inspection of these views and a comparison of them with Spinoza's conclusions. To this we may turn.

Since for nominalism particulars alone exist, and logical generali-
zations are subjective constructs, the chief topics of concern for
nominalism are those of knowledge and truth. Its main problem is
concentrated in the question: how is knowledge possible? From this
point on, nominalism is primarily an epistemology. Its one existential dogma, namely, that particulars alone exist, having been sum-
marily reached by the use of Occam's razor (itself an epistemological
consideration), nominalism is henceforth exercised with the problem as to how we can know anything at all, particular or universal.
Since all propositions except those whose subject and predicate are
singular have general connotations (and even these are scarcely
meaningful without such connotations) the question becomes: how
can language as a system of conventional signs signify things and
thus yield truth? Nominalists, following their native economical
bent, find in language a means for economizing mental activity.
Language provides a mechanism whereby the endless number of
singular things can be thought of in relatively few terms. Language
is an instrument of simplification. But the fact is always recognized
that real things are complex. They possess all the diversity of their
particular determinations. Hence, though language may be simple,
things are not. How then are particulars to be initially apprehended? Here a priori knowledge is inapplicable, and the cognition
of particulars, in so far as it can occur, is understood to be a matter
of the senses—inner or outer. Sense perception is the origin of all
knowledge, and nominalism leads directly to empiricism.

But a branch of the nominalist school, while recognizing the foregoing conclusions, affirms another source for knowledge of particulars, that is, for knowledge of any kind, namely direct intuition.
Sense perception is incomplete and external. How then do we apprehend the inner and real nature of individual things? The answer is:
by direct intuition, and here nominalism passes into mysticism.

Although nominalism may thus develop into mysticism it perhaps
more frequently takes another course. Since all logical universality is
ens rationis, a thing of the mind, and finds its expression in words or
signs that may, but that in no sense necessarily do, apply to existence, and since sense perception is relative, incomplete, and essen-

tially private, the consequence becomes evident that all avenues to real particulars are cut off; confirmable knowledge is impossible; truth is relative, and all knowledge, such as it is, is nothing more than probable. In other words there is no knowledge—simply opinion. Belief cannot be based on knowledge; if it arises it must rest on faith. Nominalism here passes from empiricism to skepticism, which is perhaps its most natural outcome.

One might suppose that this typal series had now reached an end, and that the final consequences of nominalism are either mysticism or scepticism. Such however is not the case. The contingencies of life persist regardless of philosophy, and the will to believe asserts itself whether it has grounds to do so or not. Since universals are relegated to the mind or to language, and since all laws of logic are universals, there is not the least necessity of supposing that such laws have anything whatsoever to do with existent things. The sole basis on which we have a right to assume that existent things are rational, on this view, is an empirical one; and empirical information, being forever incomplete, can give us no such report. No imperative to believe that reality, whatever it may be, is rational either is or can be established. From scepticism nominalism reasons itself into irrationalism. The world may be anything. The mind knows no limits to possibility. No grounds can be affirmed to take the world as an analogue of reason; we must take it as we sense it, or as we feel it. As such it is a perpetual flux dominated by an inner urge, an urge frequently designated by the generalized term "will."

Will—the inner activator both of things and of men—makes truth as it makes the world. The will is not limited by reason but it creates reason along with other things, and reason or intellect becomes its instrument. The primacy of will is taken to be complete; the surge of the will is time itself, which is the incessant creation of novelty; the changeless logical structures of reason vanish as mirages into the flux; the present is a spontaneous eject of the self-transforming will, and the future is an indeterminate manifold of unpredictable contingencies. The will is not led, but leads; it sets up its own objectives or ideals and changes them according to its own inner fluxions. There is no final direction to its path or to the path of change. Reality is never complete but is perpetually becoming; its partial consummation occurs only in its moment-to-moment self-realization. Thus from irrationalism, nominalism passes to voluntarism, to temporalism, and to indeterminism.

From this point of view the postulated objective truth of the intellect is an *ignis fatuus*. Values, in the form of transistory aspirations or desires, take precedence over any such hypostatized truth. Knowledge is never disinterested, and truth is interpreted in terms of value rather than value in terms of truth. Truth is relative, changing; it is made by separate valuing subjects. Ideas are not cognitive but instrumental, and their truth, that is, in the sense of their value, is determined by their effectiveness in controlling the flux and attaining self-engendered ends. Truth is interpreted in terms of usefulness; and nominalism, through voluntarism and irrationalism, passes into pragmatism and instrumentalism. On this view metaphysics as ontology is professedly abandoned, for there is no independent and transpersonal truth about any objective reality. The very terms *world, universe, reality* have illicit connotations of unity supported by no experiential evidence. The so-called world is an endless aggregate of particulars more or less conjoined, but if conjoined, then merely by external relations. There is no connected whole, but rather a loosely joined congeries of essentially independent individuals. Pragmatic nominalism favors pluralism as an essential hypothesis. The world outside the mind is and remains a question mark, and its significance is known only as it bears on human life through experience. The primary question becomes: how may this world be controlled for human ends set up at an historical human moment? The answer is to be found in science, for it is science that most patently gives control over nature.

What, however, is science? It is not the discovery of rational laws in things, for such laws are universals and have long been discarded. Science is a set of formulae, essentially verbal, by which the more orderly sense-data can be described and partially predicted. By giving empirical interpretations to symbols, the symbols can be so combined as to yield propositions that are verifiable by experiment or observation. But the logic and the mathematics through which the symbols are combined are pure inventions of the mind and have no inherent relevance to the objective world. They are conventional rules only. In spite of this, however, and for no reason in the nature of things, they happily find exemplifications in experience and are hence serviceable in describing the behavior of sense-data. Scientific laws are of a like nature; and, although they are verbal or symbolic forms, they are forms that, for the time being, find content in the immediate presentations of sense. Such laws represent the maximum of human knowledge; and with this conclusion nominalism finds a consistent resting place in positivism.

The purport of this whole development is as follows: when universals are excluded from existent items, reason or rationality is removed from things; it is relegated to the mind. Once it is enclosed within that confine it is in an epistemological prison from which it can never escape. The world is made unknowable; metaphysics is reduced to futility, and man, whatever he may be, is and can be guided only by faith or practicality.

Now the object of this account of the transformations of nominalism is not to give a criticism of it, but to show its bearing on the thought of Spinoza. Not only does Spinoza not profess any of these consequences but he is diametrically opposed to every one of them. Scarcely a thinker could be found who rejects them so completely.

That reality is rational is, for him, axiomatic. Truth is one, absolute, and unchanging. Epistemology is not primary; it is deduced from ontology. Part II of the *Ethics* is unintelligible without Part I. Empiricism is successful only in producing inadequate ideas. It is not conclusive even in science. Nor is Spinoza an empirical mystic. If he is a mystic at all, his mysticism is rational. What is, is intelligible ; but what he does not know, as the infinite attributes beyond thought and extension, he does not pretend to know. There is, in his conception, a rational intuition of essence, but no suprarational intuition. He rejects skepticism as a general epistemological position and affirms it only in regard to those things about which the nominalists are inclined to deny it, namely, the data of sense perception. So far as knowledge of God or reality is concerned he not only affirms such knowledge but goes so far as to say that everyone has an adequate idea of God. That his rejection of irrationalism is absolute and complete requires no exposition. And as to voluntarism he denies that the will, either divine or human, is anything distinct from the intellect. It is constituted simply by the affirmation or denial inherent in ideas themselves.[3] Nothing is produced by will, and the notion of free will is a natural fiction arising from ignorance of causes. The correlates of voluntarism, that is, temporalism and indeterminism, are both expressly rejected. Time and determinate duration are ways of imagining things, results of inadequate ideas. Things cognized in their true being are seen *sub specie aeternitatis* and this applies even to individuals. This being so, indeterminism is

[3] *Ethics*, Pt. II, Prop. 49 and Corollary.

wholly excluded, and chance is held to be simply another name for ignorance.

Values, as interests or desires, are not the determinants of truth but are a primary cause of its obfuscation. Value for man is derived from truth, not truth from value—in fact, it is by attaining truth that man attains value, and if he is to reach beatitude at all it is through the vision of God. An idea is not true because of its use but because of its intrinsic rational nature. And the most significantly useful ideas are so because they are true. Truth moreover is neither many, relative, nor changeable; nor is it dependent on the motives of individuals. No man ever strove so single-mindedly to rid his thought of anthropomorphism in any of its aspects. Thus Spinoza's philosophy represents the antithesis of pragmatism. And since (for Spinoza) the world has a fully integrated rational structure, things can be known by their essences, and the objects of nature can be known by their common properties; and, since true definitions are real, not nominal, the order of nature is ever present to be discovered whether it is so discovered at any historical moment or not. Logic is not a verbal invention, science is not an essentially hypothetical or mental construct, and nature is not an occult and unknowable mystery. As a consequence, however true or false these premises may be, they are sufficient to indicate that Spinoza is not a positivist. Nor can he be considered a pluralist for, as it is unnecessary to explain, this view is rejected in Part I of the *Ethics*.[4]

It would appear then that all of the basic views either implied by nominalism or most closely associated with it are not simply rejected by Spinoza but are directly and emphatically disavowed. It follows that if all, several, or any one of them can be held to be logical consequences of nominalism then Spinoza is not a nominalist. This circumstance together with the fact that there is an obvious incompatibility between nominalism and rationalism (since rationalism presupposes that logical laws are inherent in reality, and such laws are universals)—this circumstance creates the strong presumption that whatever language Spinoza used (and he was not obliged to use the language of Plato) he was not a nominalist. We cannot argue indubitably from what appear to us to be considerations of consistency to what Spinoza actually thought, as psychological indeterminates always play a role in surmises of this kind; but it is doubtful whether, in the present case, such evident incompatibilities could be over-

[4] Ibid., Pt. I, Prop. 14.

looked, and reasons which show that they were not will shortly be
examined.

At this point we may pass to the second and main part of our inquiry, namely, that concerned with textual interpretation. In accordance with this, evidences derived from Spinoza's text, and from
theses therein contained, will be compared, with a view to determining his real position. References purporting to deny universals
will be considered first; thereafter, those that imply universals.

In regard to the former it may be said that not less than twelve
significant passages that have an apparently nominalistic ring might
be indicated in Spinoza's writings.[5] These passages possess a fairly
close resemblance and it is not necessary here to treat them separately. In lieu of so doing I shall select one only for consideration—
one however that contains the gist of the others, and that also gives
the fullest available account of Spinoza's argument. This passage is
found in the well-known Scholium to Prop. 40, Part II of the *Ethics*.
It reads as follows:

> But not to omit anything which is necessary for us to know, I
> will briefly give the causes from which terms called Tran-
> scendental, such as *Being, Thing, Something,* have taken their
> origin. These terms have arisen because the human body,
> inasmuch as it is limited, can form distinctly in itself a certain
> number only of images at once. (For the explanation of the
> word *image,* see Schol. Prop. 17, pt. 2.) If this number be ex-
> ceeded, the images will become confused; and if the number
> of images which the body is able to form distinctly be greatly
> exceeded, they will all run one into another. Since this is so,
> it is clear (Corol. Prop. 17, and Prop. 18, pt. 2) that in propor-
> tion to the number of images which can be formed at the
> same time in the body will be the number of bodies which the
> human mind can imagine at the same time. If the images in
> the body, therefore, are all confused, the mind will confusedly
> imagine all the bodies without distinguishing the one from

---

[5] *Short Treatise on God, Man, and His Well-Being,* Pt. I, ch. vi; ibid., Pt. I,
ch. x; *Cogitata Metaphysica,* pars I, cap. i; ibid., pars II, cap. vii; *Tractatus de
Intellectus Emendatione,* ed. Van Vloten and Land (The Hague, 1914), p. 16;
ibid., p. 24; ibid., p. 30; *Ethica,* pars II, Prop. XL, Scholium I; ibid., pars II,
Prop. XLVIII, Scholium; ibid., pars IV, Praefatio; *Epistolae,* ed. Van Vloten and
Land (The Hague, 1914), Epistola II, p. 6; ibid., Epistola LVI, p. 192.

the other, and will include them all, as it were, under one attribute, that of being or thing. The same confusion may also be caused by lack of uniform force in the images and from other analogous causes, which there is no need to discuss here, the consideration of one cause being sufficient for the purpose we have in view. For it all comes to this, that these terms signify ideas in the highest degree confused. It is in this way that those notions have arisen which are called *Universal*, such as, *Man, Horse, Dog*, &c.; that is to say, so many images of men, for instance, are formed in the human body at once, that they exceed the power of the imagination, not entirely, but to such a degree that the mind has no power to imagine the determinate number of men and the small differences of each, such as colour and size, &c. It will therefore distinctly imagine that only in which all of them agree in so far as the body is affected by them, for by that the body was chiefly affected, that is to say, by each individual, and this it will express by the name *man*, covering thereby an infinite number of individuals; to imagine a determinate number of individuals being out of its power. But we must observe that these notions are not formed by all persons in the same way, but that they vary in each case according to the thing by which the body is more frequently affected, and which the mind more easily imagines or recollects. For example, those who have more frequently looked with admiration upon the stature of men, by the name *man* will understand an animal of erect stature, while those who have been in the habit of fixing their thoughts on something else, will form another common image of men, describing man, for instance, as an animal capable of laughter, a biped without feathers, a rational animal, and so on; each person forming universal images of things according to the temperament of his own body. It is not therefore to be wondered at that so many controversies have arisen amongst those philosophers who have endeavoured to explain natural objects by the images of things alone.[6]

[6] *Ethics*, Pt. II, Prop. 40, Scholium I, translation by W. H. White in *Spinoza Selections*, edited by John Wild (New York: Charles Scribner's Sons, 1930). I am indebted to Charles Scribner's Sons for permission to quote this, and other passages from this book, used in the present paper.

Spinoza here makes clear what he means by "universals" or, as he elsewhere calls them, "species." [7] He employs these terms to refer to composite images derived by abstraction from inner or outer perception. On the mental side "universals" or "species" are not composed of ideas, since ideas, in Spinoza's sense of the word, are conceptions of the mind and are not images. "Universals" or "species," for Spinoza, are made up of confused images. They are, as it were, simulacra of the individual thing, reduced and emaciated by the perceptive process. Moreover they are not conceived alike by all minds, but differently by each mind. They are private impressions rather than common principles of reason. And again they are not, as here considered, essences, or the elements of essences, nor are they common properties. They are extracted from things not by reason or rational intuition but by imagery and mnemonic blending.

Spinoza took the expressions *notiones Universales* and *termini Transcendentales* from the scholastics. In using these expressions he makes it clear toward whom he is directing his criticism. He rejects Universal notions and Transcendental terms as "intelligible species" derived by abstraction from sense perception. Since they are thus derived they can have, for Spinoza, no ultimate ontological connotations. They are not obtained from real definitions nor are they deduced from proximate causes, that is, anterior principles. They have therefore no rational ground. Spinoza's own theory of sense perceptions, namely, that perceptions are simply affects recording the immediate modifications of one's own body, required him to reject the scholastic conception of "intelligible species"—the conception on which universal notions were based—as well as the inductive method employed to reach these mental constructs. It likewise required him to reject the scholastic contention that knowledge originates in sensation. His objection to "intelligible species" is precisely that they are derived from sensation and are in fact not true concepts but are only confused perceptual pictures. Further, they are not held together by any inherent logic; they are not connected by any deductive linkage. The logic invoked to give them order is the inductive logic of external classification and of the syllogism, employed by the scholastics—a logic which, as Spinoza conceived, discovered nothing, but merely arranged what was already given it by perception into an abstract, relative, and subjective order. To this logic

[7] For example, *Cogitata Metaphysica,* pars I, cap. I; Epistola LVI.

Spinoza was opposed, and in place of it he recommended an intensional logic of mathematical deduction, a logic of concepts, as described in the *Tractatus de Intellectus Emendatione*. From these dual conditions then, that is, the inadequacy of "intelligible species" as forms of generalization, and the limitations of the logic that goes with them, derive the grounds for Spinoza's rejection of scholastic universals. What Spinoza is in effect saying is that if universals are constituted by so-called "intelligible species" and thus are abstracted from perception, then they must be recognized as fictions.

Such universality, as is plain, for Spinoza, is invalid. There is, however, another kind of universality, a kind that is valid. This is rational universality. That Spinoza's system incorporates—in fact, requires—this kind of universality is evidenced by his most central teachings. Imbedded in these are the premises that affirm universals. To these elements of his thought I shall now turn, distinguishing them as they appear in the doctrines of essence, attribute, mode, substance, and man.

With regard to essence the primary question is: can an essence be embodied in two or more things? If it can, then here is a point where universality is posited. Now in an important passage in the Scholium to Prop. 8, Part I of the *Ethics* Spinoza uses language that unequivocally implies that the same essence pertains to several particulars. Here Spinoza is showing that from an essence or nature no definite number of individuals can be deduced. He says: "The definition of a triangle, for example, expresses nothing else than the simple nature of a triangle, but not a certain number of triangles." From this and from what he later says it is clear that any number of individual triangles can exemplify the same nature. This same conception is applied to man, and, by implication, to any finite things that may have essences. Here rational universality is plainly posited. But this is not all. Previously in the same scholium he points out that true ideas may be had of the essences of nonexistent things:

> By modifications, however, [men should understand] those things that are in another thing and whose conception is formed from the conception of the thing in which they are; whence it follows that we can have true ideas of nonexistent modifications, since although these modifications do not actually exist outside of the intellect, their essence nevertheless, is

so comprehended in another thing that through this thing
they can be conceived.[8]

Here we not only have *universalia in re* but *universalia ante rem,*
not only universal form in things but form subsisting without actually existent exemplifications. This view is suggested also by Spinoza's example of a true idea:

> . . . a true idea is distinguished from a false one, not so much
> by its extrinsic object as by its intrinsic nature. If an architect
> conceives a building properly constructed, though such a
> building may never have existed, and may never exist, never-
> theless the idea is true; and the idea remains the same
> whether it be put into execution or not.[9]

Now the idea here referred to is derived from the eternal laws or
principles of nature. *That* is what gives it its truth. Although the
architect may be concerned with the construction of a single house
the house must embody these principles. The idea is true because a
house, to be a house, must conform to these principles, that is, any
house must embody them. Spinoza is here referring to a rational, as
opposed to an imaginative, universal essence—and not merely this,
but to a universal *ante rem.* A more clear-cut expression of Platonism would be difficult to find.

Passing now to the Scholium, Prop. 17, Part I of the *Ethics,* we
find the same conception not simply repeated and confirmed but set
forth with the added specification that essences are eternal.

> For example, one man is the cause of the existence but not of
> the essence of another, for the essence is an eternal truth;
> and therefore with regard to essence the two men may exactly
> resemble one another, but with regard to existence they must
> differ. Consequently if the existence of one should perish,
> that of the other will not therefore perish; but if the essence
> of one could be destroyed and become false, the essence of the
> other would be likewise destroyed.

Here it is stated: (1) essences are eternal; (2) several individuals can
agree in the same essence; (3) if the essence is removed the individuals are removed (the individuals are dependent on the essence and
without it are impossible); (4) if the individuals are removed the

---

[8] *Ethics,* Pt. I, Prop. 8, Scholium. My translation.
[9] *Improvement of the Understanding,* in *Spinoza Selections,* p. 26.

essence is not affected (the essence is not dependent on its individual representations). Three further items only are requisite to make Spinoza's Platonism complete: (1) the essences are not dependent on mind; (2) they are not perceived or known by the senses; (3) they are the objects of all real knowledge. The first point, that is, that the essences are not dependent on mind, scarcely needs elaboration. The attributes possess a one-to-one correspondence in their modifications but they are, in themselves, independent. That is, thought is independent of extension. The essence of an extended thing is not an idea although it is known by an adequate idea. And the same is true, for the infinite intellect, of the essences of modes in any other attribute. Essences are things known and, for finite minds, things discoverable, but they are not simply ideas. The second point, that is, that essences are not perceived by the senses, is affirmed in so many words by Spinoza himself: . . . *nam experientia nullas rerum essentias docet.*[10] On the third point, that is, that the essences are the objects of real knowledge, the passage in Scholium 2, Prop. 40, Part II, concerning the third kind of knowledge, namely, intuitive science, is explicit: "Besides these two kinds of knowledge, there is a third, as I shall hereafter show, which we shall call intuitive science. This kind of knowing advances from an adequate idea of the formal essence of certain attributes of God to the adequate knowledge of the essence of things." Elsewhere Spinoza explains that by an idea he does not mean a perceptual image: "For by ideas I do not understand the images which are formed at the back of the eye, or, if you please, in the middle of the brain, but rather the conceptions of thought." [11] From these references it is clear that essences involve logical universality and that they are the objects of knowledge. The assertions stand in direct opposition to the thesis of nominalism and if negated would reduce Spinoza's philosophy to sensationalistic empiricism.

At this point however two considerations bearing on the universality of essences arise which cannot be passed over. They refer (1) to Spinoza's definition of what pertains to an essence, and (2) to his expression of the view that each singular thing has an unique and singular essence.[12]

[10] *Epistolae,* ed. Van Vloten and Land, Epistola X.
[11] *Ethics,* Pt. II, Prop. 48, Scholium.
[12] *Short Treatise on God, Man, and His Well-Being,* in *Spinoza Selections,* pp. 76, 83.

The definition indicated is stated: "I say that to the essence of anything pertains that, which being given, the thing itself is necessarily posited, and being taken away, the thing is necessarily taken; or, in other words, that, without which the thing can neither be nor be conceived, and which in its turn cannot be nor be conceived without the thing." [13] This appears to say that the essence is dependent on its object and to contradict the statement above that if the individuals are removed the essence is not affected, that is, that the essence is not dependent on its individual representations. The opposition here is verbal and not real. It is dependent on a dual sense that Spinoza attributes to the term "existence." Existence is real as it follows from God; durational as it is apprehended by the imagination.[14] An essence does not imply existence in the second sense; it may have being and yet not have any perceptual exemplification. Essences are eternal and hence independent of the duration of their objects. In what sense this is to be understood may be seen from Spinoza's account of nonexistent modes. In Prop. 8 of Part II Spinoza refers to ideas of nonexistent modes as also in Corol., Prop. 24, Part I. If however there are ideas of nonexistent modes there are essences of nonexistent modes and the being of the essence, though related to, is not dependent on the existence of the modes. The point is that the nonexistence here referred to is durational, not real, nonexistence. In this sense essence and existence may be separate. If real existence however is contemplated, that is, existence as constituted by implication in God's nature, then essence and existence are compresent. But here also the essence is not dependent on the existence of the mode. Both the essence and the real existence of the mode follow from the nature of God and are dependent on that nature, not on one another. This was the first point.

As to the second, namely, that of the being of unique essences of single individuals, for example, of Peter or Paul, it is to be said that these essences do not preclude essences relating to several individuals

[13] *Ethics*, Pt. II, Def. 2.
[14] Ibid., Pt. II, Prop. 45, Scholium: "By existence I do not understand duration, that is, existence considered abstractly as if it were a certain kind of quantity, but I refer to the nature itself of existence which is attributed to singular things because from the eternal necessity of the nature of God infinite numbers of things follow in infinite ways (Prop. 16, Pt. I). I mean, I say, the true existence (*ipsa existentia*) of singular things in so far as they are in God" [my translation].

as is seen from the references given above and as will be further evidenced in considering the elements of universality in Spinoza's conception of man. A sense may be designated in which everyone is a unique example of himself but this does not imply that no essences subsist except those confined to singular things. For if this were the case the essence of one man could be removed without affecting the essence or existence of another, and, as the individuals were separate and disconnected, so likewise would be their essences. This however is incompatible with Spinoza's own account.

The study of essences leads us next to the conception of method as revealed in the *Treatise on the Improvement of the Understanding* and the *Ethics*, since this method is the method of definition and definitions are the expressions of essences: ". . . the true definition of any one thing neither involves nor expresses anything except the nature of the thing defined." [15] The object of the method is to apprehend essences, to express them in real definitions, and to deduce from the definitions the properties of the things and other essences implied by them. If such a deduction could be carried to its completion it would embrace an implicative network of definitions that would include all possible things, and all things would be viewed logically *sub specie aeternitatis*. This emphasis on definition is another Platonic parallel in Spinoza. The method here indicated is mathematical and synthetic. It employs a logic of intension that must cover in its application any things subsequently amenable to extensional logic. For Spinoza it is a productive as contrasted with an exclusively receptive logic. The logic of extension merely receives its classes ready made and fixes them in an order of inclusion. Intensional logic does not receive its elements from without but, by its own inherent process, discovers them. Extensional logic is basically a matter of induction or perception. Intensional logic—or the logic of concepts and definitions—is a matter of reason or deduction. Spinoza rejects definition by genus and differentia[16] since it is an extensional definition and is not productive of further knowledge. He advocates (in the case of all things except substance) definition from proximate cause,[17] that is, definition from an immediately

---

[15] *Ethics*, Pt. I, Prop. 8, Scholium.

[16] *Short Treatise on God, Man, and His Well-Being*, Pt. I, ch. 7, in *Spinoza Selections*, p. 79.

[17] *Improvement of the Understanding*, in *Spinoza Selections*, p. 37.

anterior essence or definition. A more rigorously deductive method
could hardly be conceived, and the method, to be applicable, must
postulate an objectively deductive linkage of essences.

But here we are in the presence of another primary element of
universality in Spinoza's philosophy, and one that is of necessity
inherent in any rationalist world view, namely the laws of logic,
that is, the laws of consistency and implication. These laws are universals and are implicit in the nature of things. Nominalism cannot
postulate these laws as in things without contradicting itself, and as
a result it is channeled into semantics and positivism. Logical laws,
for it, are exclusively conventions. As such they can be used rigorously but they can tell you nothing necessary about the existential
world. Now our purpose here is not to give a criticism either of the
one view or the other but simply to determine the nature of Spinoza's philosophy. For Spinoza, both on the score of consistency and
that of his own words, the laws of logic are absolutely and unexcep-
tionally universal.[18] If this is denied his method of the deduction of
essences is meaningless and his thought, instead of having the absolute ontological validity that he posits, is simply a *jeu d'esprit* with
his own ideas—which from a nominalistic point of view any rationalist philosophy must be.

Our results so far then are that some essences at least are universals (in the present-day sense) and that the laws of logic are universals. Here, however, we are confronted with another element of
universality in Spinoza's system. The liaison of essences resulting
from their implicative interconnections establishes for the modes of
any attribute an inherent order and connection. Every one of the
infinite sets of modes of each of the infinite attributes has its own
order and connection. But is the order and connection of each modal
system different and distinct from that of each of the others? No. It
is one and the same. We have here one formal order common to all
of the infinite attributes: many realms but one order in them all. If
this is called nominalism, whose distinguishing mark is that it
denies any one in the many, any single form in a plurality of instances, we may reasonably abandon any attempt to find a distinction between nominalism and realism. The acceptance of this
conception as nominalistic would simply be the admission that nominalism itself is inconceivable without the postulation of universals,

---

[18] *Ethics*, Pt. I, Axioms II, III, IV; ibid., Pt. I, Prop. 11, Demonstration. Here the
law of sufficient reason is stated categorically. Ibid., Pt. II, Prop. 40.

in other words, that nominalism implies its own opposite. This is one major reason why the nominalist interpretation of Spinoza demands the subjectivity of the attributes. Without such an assumption its case is lost.

Turning now from the general doctrine of essences to that of attributes, we may ask whether the attributes themselves possess characters of universality, and it seems clear that they do. An attribute, as previously remarked, is not a thing nor is it the sum total of the modes subsumed under itself. Such sum totals of modes, in their respective organizations, are mediate infinite modes, not attributes.[19] Then what are the attributes? They are ultimate and irreducible natures, of which their modes are respective modifications. They are, in other terminology, the ultimate categories of being. Spinoza asserts that the essence of an attribute is the attribute itself, that is, that an attribute is itself a nature or essence. It follows that the modes of an attribute are modes of that attribute because they possess the attribute in common as a common nature.[20] The attribute is not sufficient to constitute the essence of any one of its modes, but without it the essences of the modes would be impossible. Again we have the case of one nature in many things and the attribute is a universal even though it may be conceived as a universal *in re*. In the rational order of things the modes cannot escape their attributes nor the attributes their modes.

The attributes moreover must be considered in their relation to substance as well as to the modes. In this respect the simple observation becomes relevant that though each attribute is different from the others they all nevertheless have this in common, namely, that they are all attributes. They are infinite in number but they all possess this universal feature of identity, and without it their intelligibility vanishes. The matter is not one of mere resemblance, nor is it reducible to a sign or vocable. It is an objective meaning, and the meaning *attribute* is the same for each of its infinite exemplifications. Otherwise they could be subject to no single definition. In this case also the presumption of universality can be avoided, and then but speciously, only on the assumption that the attributes are subjective.

Now directing attention primarily to the modes, one might suppose that here if anywhere nominalism, were it Spinoza's essential

[19] *Epistolae*, ed. Van Vloten and Land, Epistola LXIV; *Spinoza Selections*, p. 463.
[20] *Ethics*, Pt. I, Prop. 25, Corol.; ibid., Pt. II, Prop. 13, Lemma 2.

view, would assert itself with maximum emphasis. Every mode would be particular, unique, separate, and discontinuous in respect to other things. It might bear similarities to, but it could have nothing in common with, other modes. There could be no one nature in many things. But, as is well known, the modes are inconceivable without common properties, which are not only in the whole but in the part. The language is Spinoza's own.[21] The properties referred to are no more in one mode than in another but are equally shared by all modes of a given attribute. They constitute the only avenue between the finite mind and the world at large, and without them every subject would be shut into a tight solipsism of his own inadequate ideas. And it may be inferred that under such a circumstance, since all our ideas are associated with internal conditions of the body, we could have no ideas, adequate or inadequate, in common with any other individual; communication, linguistic or otherwise, would be cut off as an impossibility. According to Spinoza, however, these common properties are the points of origin of our initial adequate ideas;[22] they form the basis of public as compared to private knowledge; they are adequately perceived by everyone and are the grounds for scientific knowledge. We can know other bodies in so far as we have properties in common with them, for knowing the properties in ourselves we know them everywhere and they give us the power to discover general laws of nature.

Such laws are causal laws, since physical or existential causation is not only possible but logically necessary in Spinoza's view. It is possible because things have something in common. On this condition and only on this condition can causation pertain. It is necessary because things participate in a common order. Causation and implication for Spinoza are correlative; and existential or particular causation is simply one form of implication. It involves the same necessity as that which holds between premise and conclusion. Such causation is necessary because the possible relations or interactions of things follow necessarily from their essences; and from the interrelations of eternal essences follows an interconnected complex of eternal laws which constitute the common order of nature.[23] We are thus once more in the presence of the one in the many, the common form in the multitude of instances, continuity within differentiation.

[21] *Ethics,* Pt. II, Prop. 38, Demonstration and Corollary.
[22] Ibid.
[23] Cf. *Ethics,* Pt. II, Prop. 13, Axiom I following Lemma 2.

The laws of nature are universals. They are the existential principles that determine the interrelations of the modes.

From these observations concerning the topic of universality as it applies to modal nature we may now turn to that of universality as it pertains to substance. Substance possesses logical universality not as a common form but as an all-inclusive individual. All things have this in common that they are in substance as logical derivatives; they are expressions of substance. And substance commands universality as the common origin of all things. But a further universality issues from the fact that, as we have seen, substance implies the same order and connection in all attributes.[24] If, by an impossible assumption, an attribute subsisted that did not attach to substance or that pertained to a supposedly different substance, then by no necessity would the order and connection of modes of such an attribute be the same as that of the other attributes. Identity of order in the modal systems of the attributes is a consequence of the unity of substance and this order and connection implies, in turn, that things, of necessity, are as they are. Hence substance, as an ultimate individual, determines the nature of all its infinite and finite products. And substance, though not a formal universal, expresses its nature universally in all the modes.

Leaving now the doctrine of substance we come to our last topic, that is, the nature of man. This is a primary topic in the *Ethics* and one which, in the conception of Spinoza, cannot be treated apart from a consideration of man's relation to God. Said in another way, Spinoza considers that a philosophical anthropology must be derived from ontology. The question may therefore be asked: was Spinoza's conception of man nominalistic? In his book on Plato, A. E. Taylor is confident that it was, basing his interpretation on the Appendix to Part I of the *Ethics* and the Preface to Part IV, and also on the contention that, in Spinoza's view, Nero is as good an example of man as anyone.[25] The notion of man, on this ground, is not recognized to involve ethical perfection, whereas Taylor believes that in Plato's view it must. If this was Spinoza's thought, a case could well be made for the thesis that, even on a realistic basis, Spinoza would be right. If there is any such thing as the form of man, an object cannot participate in it by degrees. A thing cannot be more or less a man with any greater meaning than it can be

[24] Ibid., Pt. II, Prop. 7, Scholium.
[25] A. E. Taylor, *Plato: The Man and His Work* (London, 1926), p. 197.

more or less a triangle. If the thing is an example of man at all it possesses the whole form of man and is as good an example as any other. If the point is raised as to whether Nero is an example of a *good man,* it might well be answered in the negative; but that, it is clear, is another matter.

Let us take up directly, however, the question as to whether Spinoza's conception is or is not consistent with nominalism. In not one place alone but in a number of places Spinoza has referred to *humanity* in contrast to individual men and has either explicity or by implication deprecated the term as an *ens rationis,* a confused imaginal universal, and a mere nothing.[26] Again in the much quoted Scholium to Prop. 40, Part II of the *Ethics,* he designates the concept Man (as well as that of Dog or that of Horse) as an example of fatuity in thinking. He not only does this but shows why he does it, namely, because the generalized Man, in the sense here meant, is an intentional species, an abstraction derived from the fortuitous impressions of this or that person. It is not an *intima essentia rerum.* It is distinguished from other things in different ways by different definers and is characterized by means of external and accidental features. Any such designation, Spinoza asserts, is trivial, since it shows nothing about the true essence of man. *Man,* in the rejected sense of the term, is simply another case of empirical generalization. Does this mean therefore that Spinoza's account is nominalistic (as Taylor asserts) and that it foregoes any elements of rational universality?

Some reasons occur to believe that it does not. In the first place there is the statement, previously mentioned, in Scholium, Prop. 17, Part I of the *Ethics,* that if you take away individual men you do not take away the essence of man, which is eternal. But if you take away the essence of any man you take away the essence of all. This is scarcely nominalism. Next there is the Axiom at the beginning of Part II: Man thinks (*Homo cogitat*). What does this axiom mean? It means that if anything is a man it thinks, or thinking is involved in the nature of man, or thinking is common to men. The implication of universality is not obscure. *Homo cogitat,* it is to be noted, is not a comment by the way; it is an axiom. Had Spinoza so desired he could have said: *Homines cogitant.* Had he done so however his meaning would have been different.

[26] Cf. *Ethics,* Pt. II, Prop. 40, Scholium; ibid., Pt. II, Prop. 48, Scholium; Letter II, *Spinoza Selections,* p. 406.

Again in Prop. 10, Part II, we find a designation, somewhat surprising for a nominalist, namely, "the form of man," *formam hominis*. The proposition is stated as follows: *ad essentium hominis non pertinet esse substantiae, sive substantia formam hominis non constituit*. Later in the Scholium he says : *Cum autem plures homines existere possint, ergo id, quod hominis formam constituit, non est esse substantiae*. Now we are not here concerned with the denial that the being of substance pertains to the essence of man. What is evident is that a common form pertains to a plurality of men. The realistic implication is manifest. In the Corollary Spinoza adds: *hinc sequitur essentiam hominis constitui a certis Dei attributorum modificationibus*. Even if the *essentiam hominis* were interpreted to mean : all the unique essences of all men—in which case the essence of one man could be removed without removing either the essences or existences of other men—even in this case all of these essences would have something in common, namely, that they are all modifications of the same attributes, which in itself is the undoing of nominalism.

These considerations, however, are subsidiary. We may more justly approach the central feature of Spinoza's conception of man, that is, his treatment of the intellect and the emotions. In Part II of the *Ethics* Spinoza has given us an account of man's intellect. The imagination engenders inadequate ideas; the intellect, adequate ideas. And no possibility subsists that two different adequate ideas may refer to the same essence. Corresponding to each essence there is a single adequate idea. Truth is one. The intellect however is constituted by adequate ideas. It follows that, is so far as men have adequate ideas, the minds of all men are the same. Spinoza's conception of truth and adequacy conflict with a nominalistic interpretation of man.[27]

[27] The same is true of reason which is itself a rational universal and is the same for all men or reasoning beings, i.e., it is the same in all of its manifestations. Cf. *Ethics*, Pt. IV, Prop. 26, Demonstration. Indeed, if reason were not the same in all men there would be no grounds to assert that it would lead universally to the same results, i.e., adequate ideas. This is one of the conditions that makes nominalism and rationalism incompatible.

In Scholium, Prop. 18, Pt. IV, Spinoza endeavors to show the principles, common to men, which reason prescribes:

"It remains for me now to show what it is which reason prescribes to us, which affects agree with the rules of human reason and which . . . are opposed to these rules. . . . I should like to set forth here these dictates of reason in

But let us turn to Part III in which the emotions are deduced. We begin with an inherent tendency to persist, not only common to all men but to all bodies.[28] And being a common property it is adequately known. This character, as known, is, in man, the *conatus* and is the actual essence of man, hence something common to all men. It follows that as a man knows it is in himself he knows it in others. Every man may feel his *conatus* differently according to the nature of his own body, but it is the *conatus* that he feels. The *conatus* follows from the nature of body itself and for this reason cannot be equated to a mere vocable—nor to a species abstracted from a manifold of images. Now from the *conatus* as aided or opposed, that is, from pleasure, pain, and desire, Spinoza deduces the whole mechanics of the emotions. It is not necessary here to go into his deduction. There is a logic of the emotions. The emotions are determined by laws which, since they spring from the *conatus,* are continuous with the natural laws of bodies. Man's nature is not a separate domain isolated from the rest of nature; it is logically incorporated in nature. The emphasis here is upon law, that is, the one principle in the many instances, and the emotions have a nexus of laws which are continuous with other natural law. Now wherein lies the descriptive power of this deduction of the emotions? Is it a fiction imagined by the mind and applicable to nothing, or is it a true deduction of properties from an essence, and applicable to all individuals that possess this essence? Were it the former Spinoza would never have taken the trouble to make the deduction. The essence of man and his properties are true universals, that is, rational universals, and constitute the significant features of "the form of man" as contrasted with the accidental superficialities of his durational existence. In fact, durational existence can do nothing more than elicit or exemplify these laws in particular circumstances. And the laws are common to all men. For if they are not, the path to

order that what I have in my mind about them may be easily comprehended by all. Since reason demands nothing which is opposed to nature, it demands, therefore, that every person should love himself, should seek his own profit, . . . should desire everything that really leads man to greater perfection, and absolutely that every one should endeavor, as far as in him lies, to preserve his own being." If reason were not a rational universal, i.e., the same in all men, how could it prescribe these common rules for them? But as is evident, reason is not one thing for one man and another for another.

[28] *Ethics*, Pt. III, Prop. 6.

salvation, the love of God arising from the third kind of knowledge, and its consequent and causal effect on the emotions, must be different for different men and there can be no single or absolute path to beatitude. If there were a million men there would be a million such paths—or none; or every man would find his salvation, if at all, in a way peculiar to himself. But the laws of emotion and the laws of knowledge, and the laws of relation of emotion to knowledge are universal and invariable; the path to salvation, the way to freedom, is, for all rational beings, one and the same. What remains of the hypothesized nominalism in Spinoza's conception of man may be left to the reader to judge for himself. On such an interpretation the philosopher's language relinquishes intelligibility.

A man can be a man, in Spinoza's view, without being a good man. But even here Spinoza advances a conception that implies universality. Goodness and badness for man are, like man himself, deductive prolongations of the logical structure of nature. What is good for man depends on his nature and consists in what is useful to him in terms of that nature. But his nature follows from a larger nature as do the laws determining what is useful and what is noxious to it. Spinoza's ethics are naturalistic but are not therefore relative to, and dependent on, individual determination or private judgment. They apply equally to all men. The notion of the good man can be expressed through an exemplar which itself follows from the conditions of *man in nature* and is not one thing for one individual and another for another. Men exist in a variety of differences but wherever and however they exist the exemplar is the same, namely, that of man under the guidance of reason. Spinoza's words are as follows:

> If anybody asks, What if the highest good of those who follow after virtue were not common to all? Would it not thence follow that men who live according to the guidance of reason, that is to say men in so far as they agree in nature, would be contrary to one another? We reply that it arises from no accident, but from the nature itself of reason, that the highest good of man is common to all, inasmuch as it is deduced from the human essence itself, in so far as it is determined by reason, and also because man could not be or be conceived if he had not the power of rejoicing in this highest good. For it

pertains to the essence of the human mind to have an adequate knowledge of the eternal and infinite essence of God.[29]

With this passage, which is hardly susceptible to misconstruction, I will conclude this examination of Spinoza's conception of man. It is doubtful whether additional reference could manifest more distinctly the realistic implications of that conception.

In conclusion, we have now distinguished the following elements of logical universality in the philosophy of Spinoza: essences common to a plurality of individuals, the laws of logic, the order and connection of modes in relation to their respective attributes, the attributes themselves, the common properties of the modes, the laws of modal nature, the nature of man as a finite mode, and the common origin of all dependent things in substance. Without these elements of universality Spinoza's world would either be pulverized into an unending aggregate of discontinuous particulars or else collapsed into a blank, logically sterile, and undifferentiated substance. In either of these extremes universality would be eliminated, but at the cost of intelligibility. In the first case reality would be an indefinite multiplicity without any unity, which, being devoid of the last shred of rationality, the nominalists find so ineffably congenial. In the second case reality would be nothing but the simon-pure abstract being that Spinoza himself characterized as the final distillation of ideational confusion. Nominalism, in short, would be the *reductio ad absurdum* of his philosophy. Unsolved problems, it must be granted, remain for Spinoza interpretation, but this, I think, cannot be counted as one of them. No philosopher either does or can finish his philosophy down to the last dot, nor can any philosopher attain perfect verbal, as compared with real, consistency. Spinoza did not complete the details of his ontology or of his epistemology. If he had, the question of nominalism in his thought could scarcely have arisen. He is not aware that the universal validity of reason can constitute a problem, but rather, as his axioms show, presupposes it as the common ground either of thought or of existence.

Spinoza is not a William of Occam nor is he a modern semantic positivist. The philosopher to whom he is closest both in his method and in his ontology is Plato. Certain features of Platonism he would not have accepted, for example, Plato's cosmology, but so far as the

[29] *Ethics*, Pt. IV, Prop. 36, Scholium.

eternity and immutability of the elements of rational universality are concerned, the two philosophers are one. Spinoza did not refer to these elements in the same language, or always with the same special applications, as did Plato, but that they are present in his conceptions is a consequence implied in the rational character of the conceptions themselves.

Williamsburg, Virginia

Spinoza and Time

S. Alexander

Spinoza's Conception of Time

THE TROUBLE IS that there is very little to say about Spinoza's conception of Time. It stands for the general character which things have of existence: they exist for a longer or a shorter time, according as they are determined by other things. Thus the momentary closing of a current produces a flash of light; if the current remains switched on, the light endures. But when we speak thus we are, according to Spinoza, not using the language of philosophy but of imagination. We are comparing one duration of time with another in our sensible world, and we may even conceive of these bits of time as limitations of an indefinite duration. But neither the bits of duration nor the indefinite duration are true realities. We are but using relative measures of duration; because we are considering things as if they were separate from one another and had an independent existence, whereas they are but manifestations of the one reality which is God. Now just as Newton contrasts what he calls the relative measures of time with absolute Time, we might expect Spinoza to contrast these pieces of duration with Time or Duration as such. This is what he does when he considers Space or Extension. There too, when we speak of lengths and figures of things, we are not dealing with reality except in the confused manner of imagination. There are no separate lengths and figures, but only Space as such, which is God under a certain attribute, and is indivisible into lengths. But Spinoza does not contrast durations with duration as such, but with eternity, and eternity is not Time, but is timeless. When he declares that there is something eternal in the human mind, which lies at the basis of our experience that we are immortal, he does not mean that we are immortal in the sense of indefinite continuance after death. To be eternal is to be comprehended in the

nature of God, and things are real in so far as they are thus comprehended and are seen in the light of eternity, *sub specie quâdam
aeternitatis*. Thus times are not contrasted with Time as bits of
space with Space, but with timelessness. Had he treated Time as he
treats Space, Time would have been an attribute of God. As it is,
Time is no more than a character of finite things. I am proposing
to explain what difference it would make to Spinoza's philosophy
if, to make an impossible hypothesis, he had treated Time as an
attribute of God.

It is not so much to be wondered at that Spinoza has failed to conceive the relation of finite times to infinite Time with the same
clearness as he has conceived that of finite spaces to infinite Space.
Time is indeed thoroughly perplexing, in a way in which at first
sight Space is not. For bits of space can be kept together before our
minds at once, and though we cannot imagine Space as a whole, but
only an indefinitely large space, we can readily think of it. But we
cannot do this with the parts of time. For Time is successive; there
is no sense in a duration which is not a duration that is passing
away, and when you experience a moment of time, the immediately
preceding moment is gone. Otherwise Time would be a kind of
Space. No doubt we do experience Time as not merely a succession
but as a duration, as something that lasts: the moments of time are
not discontinuous, but are as much continuous as the points of
space. But how can we in our thoughts reconcile the persistence of
Time which we experience, with its habit of dying from one moment to another? You will say the past is preserved for us in memory, in which the past and the present are before our minds together, just as the parts of space, distant and near, are before our
eyes together. But now comes Mr. Bergson and says that when we
thus conceive Time we are spatializing it, turning it into Space, and
urges that the Time we thus spatialize is not real Time.

There are more ways than one of meeting these difficulties. One
was the naïve answer of Descartes, to which we shall recur, that
things are conserved and endure, because they are being re-created
by God at each moment. This is the very *ne plus ultra* of the conception that I alluded to, that things are extended, and that Time
happens to them. Another way is to show that Space and Time are
not independent of each other, but as the mathematicians say, are
but aspects or elements of Space-Time. Spinoza takes neither one

view nor the other, yet he gives us indications which stimulate the
reflecting mind to pass from the one to the other.

The Infinite Mode of Motion and Rest

Let me first remind you of the main outlines of Spinoza's metaphysical doctrine. Spinoza is a pantheist, not in the superficial sense that
God is a spirit which pervades all things, but in the truer sense that
all things are in God and are modifications of him. There is and can
be but one being which is entirely self-dependent, needing no other
being for its explanation; this being is Substance or God or Nature:
it is the universe as a whole, not as an aggregate of things, not even
as a whole of parts in the sense in which you and I who are organic
are wholes of parts without being mere aggregates, but as a unitary
being from which all its so-called parts draw their nature and in the
end their existence. In themselves these parts, or as Spinoza calls
them, modes, have no being except in God. Only our fancy, as I
have noted, assigns them in what he calls the common order of
nature a fictitious independence. God is the unity of all his modes
conceived in their interrelation with one another and in their eternal, that is, ultimate and timeless, effluence from himself; and Spinoza tries steadily to think of God as the positive comprehension
of all things, though, as his commentators have pointed out, he
sometimes falls into the mystical conception which defines God by
the negation of all positive predicates.

For him the finite is the negation of the infinite, and not the infinite the negation of the finite, however much he may drop into the
other way of thought. In truth, for Spinoza and Descartes and the
men of their day the infinite was conceived positively as prior to
the finite, as it is in modern mathematics, and in fact it is only by
negativing the infinitude of God that we can arrive at the notion of
quantity at all. To apply the idea of quantity to God were to make
him not infinite but indefinitely large. Most of our modern difficulties have arisen from trying to reconcile the notion of infinity with
that of quantity, and the reconciliation has been accomplished in
present mathematics.

Now, Substance or God presents itself to intellect, not to our intellect alone, but to intellect of every sort, under the form of attributes. They are not constructions of the intellect nor forms of it
in the Kantian sense, but what intellect discovers in the Substance,

so that so far there is in Spinoza no suggestion of idealism. God as
infinite possesses infinite such attributes or aspects, but only two of
these are discoverable to the human intellect, namely Extension and
Thought. How we are to understand the infinite other attributes is
a longstanding puzzle in the interpretation of Spinoza to which I
shall advert later. These attributes reveal the whole of God's nature
or essence; and the great forward step which Spinoza took in philosophy consisted in this doctrine. For it follows that since God is
perceived completely either as Extension or as Thought or Thinking, Extension and Thought are not two different realities, but two
forms of one and the same reality.

It follows further that since modes are modifications of God, each
of them is alike extended and a thought. Hence in the first place our
thoughts and our bodies are not two different things, but the same
mode of God under two different attributes. This is the way Spinoza
would answer the question whether brain-processes and their corresponding thought-processes accompany each other or act upon each
other. For him they are the same thing twice over; there is neither
correspondence nor interaction between them, but identity of essence. This he expresses by saying that an idea or thought is the idea
of a certain condition of the body, which varies with the object
which provokes this bodily condition. I only wish there were room
for me within the limits of my subject to develop his famous proposition which really follows from this conception, that the idea which
I have of the table informs me rather of the state of my body than
of the table, or in other words the table reveals itself to me in so far
as it induces in me a certain process of body (we should say of the
brain) which is identical with what we call the thought of the table.

Next it is a consequence of the truth that every mode exists under
both attributes that not only our self but every extended mode is
also a thinking one, and that all things are 'in a manner animated.'
The importance of this we shall see later on.

So much is simple and clear. But now I have to turn to one of the
most difficult and at the same time most fascinating parts of the
doctrine. Between God as perceived under the attribute of extension
and the finite extended modes which are singular bodies there intervene infinite modes which as it were break the fall from Heaven to
earth. Spinoza touches them only lightly, enough for his immediate
purpose of explaining the constitution of our bodies, yet it is about
these that what I have to say centres. The 'immediate' infinite mode

of extension Spinoza calls motion and rest. The first step in breaking
up the unity of God's infinite extension into multiplicity (a multiplicity still retained within the unity) is its manifestation as motion
and rest. The next step is the 'mediate' infinite mode, in which
God's extension is the whole system of bodies as reduced to terms of
motion and rest; and the finite modes or singular things are but the
parts of this 'face of the whole universe,' when those parts are considered, as they must be for science, in their relation to the whole
—as varying modifications of motion and rest. These are the gradations in the specification of God as extended. The corresponding
gradations between God as a thinking being and finite thinking
things or thoughts are harder to identify, and I need not refer to
them further.

These immediate and mediate infinite modes of motion and rest
take us back to the doctrine of Descartes in the second part of his
Principles. Spinoza takes it as axiomatic, speaking first of uncom-
pounded bodies, that they are all either in motion or at rest, and
move either more quickly or more slowly. Rest seems to be regarded
as something positive, not the mere absence of motion, and a slower
motion is as it were the blending of motion with rest, much as
Goethe later regarded colour as a blending of light and darkness.
Descartes apparently, perhaps only apparently, has the same notion.
Compound bodies, what we ordinarily call bodies, are constituted
of these simple bodies impinging on one another and communi-
cating their motions in a certain proportion. Such an individual
body remains the same when the proportion of its component motions is undisturbed, and the whole "moves altogether if it moves
at all," and hence, though affected by other bodies in many ways,
it may retain its own nature. The individual changes if this proportion is disturbed. The dissolution of our body at death is a case
in point, occurring in a very composite body composed of many
individual bodies which are its parts.

The Transition from Extension to This Mode

The details do not concern us so much. After all, vague as it is, the
picture is but the familiar one that in the end bodies are complexes
of motions. I would fain linger on its consequences for the theory of
science. Motion and rest being the common characters of bodies,
their laws are the ultimate and simplest conceptions for science,

which Spinoza contrasts with such vague and confused conceptions as being, thing, something, which he calls transcendental terms. Motion and rest would be the true universals, in contrast with what are vaguely called universals, such as man, tree, etc. But I must not be tempted away from my immediate topic.

For us the question is by what right Spinoza can pass from God's attribute of extension to the infinite mode of motion and rest. That he deliberately faced the problem is clear from his attitude towards Descartes. Bodies for Spinoza are intrinsically complexes of motion and rest. For Descartes body was nothing but extension, figure, size, in three dimensions. Extension without body, that is empty space, was nothing. An empty space between two bodies or in the pores of a body meant only the presence of some other body; hence, in the famous illustration, if a vessel could be completely emptied of body, the sides of the vessel would be in contact. Motion, according to Descartes, was a mode or state of body, and it was imparted to body by God. Spinoza protests in explicit terms in two letters to his friend Tschirnhaus against the Cartesian view and denies that the variety of the universe can be deduced *a priori* from extension alone. Descartes' view that motion is imparted by God is in fact a confession that body in motion is not mere extension, if extension is conceived as by Descartes as created, not as by Spinoza as being an attribute of God. Matter, says Spinoza, must necessarily be explained through an attribute which expresses eternal and infinite essence. This attribute he found in Extension, which he conceived to manifest itself immediately as we have seen in the infinite mode of motion and rest.

Spinoza is thus aware of the problem; and it is a great advance upon Descartes to see that body or matter is intrinsically motion and rest, and not bare extension into which motion is introduced by the creative act of God. But has Spinoza solved the problem? The answer must be, I think, that he has failed because he has omitted Time. It seems to him indeed that matter is motion because extension expresses God's essence, or as Mr. Joachim puts it, expresses God's omnipotence. Substance, this admirable interpreter urges, is not lifeless, but alive, and doubtless this was at the bottom of Spinoza's mind. But life and omnipotence are undefined ideas, transferred from our experience to describe metaphorically the being of God which is held to be behind and beyond the things of experience. Life implies change and so does omnipotence; and change implies time. Yet Time is excluded from the eternal nature of God,

who comprehends Time indeed, but only, to use a paradoxical
phrase, in its timelessness.

If, therefore, motion is to be the infinite mode of God's extension,
it must be because Time has been slipped into Extension out of the
undefined activity of God. We might be tempted to say that extension includes not only extension in space but duration in time. This
would make extension a double-faced attribute. It would solve Spinoza's problem, but there is no word of it in Spinoza and could not
be. On the contrary, such a supposition would make existence of
which Time is the general character an attribute of God, which for
Spinoza it is not. God's essence and his existence are, he says, one
and the same thing.

The truth appears to be that Spinoza could pass so easily from
extension to motion because motion was conceived as it were statically. Nothing seems so obvious to us as the proposition that motion
takes time and is unintelligible without it. But Descartes certainly,
and it would seem Spinoza as well, conceives motion as change of
place. Motion Descartes describes as 'the transference of a part of
matter or body from the neighbourhood of those which are touching
it immediately and which we consider as at rest to the neighbourhood of some other bodies.' This conception of motion makes it
something geometrical instead of physical. Consistently with this
conception Descartes could think of motion only as an impulse given
to matter from God. Spinoza's insight was a deeper one. Extension
being an attribute of God reflected the activity of God's nature, and
therefore the modes of extension were intrinsically motion, to correspond with the activity of God. He did not see that this implied
Time also as an attribute. The activity of God could not translate
itself into motion, when motion was conceived as more than a
change of place, except God's activity was expressed by Time. In
other words, if motion and rest is the infinite mode of extension,
that extension must be not Space but Space-Time. By insisting that
bodies are intrinsically complexes of motion, Spinoza, though he has
rather stated the problem than solved it, has put us upon the way
of solution.[1]

---

[1] I have omitted to notice minor difficulties in Spinoza's doctrine of motion and
rest, such as the question how simple bodies come to have variety of motion.
(See Camerer, *Die Lehre Spinozas*, 1877, pp. 61 ff.) For an admirable account of
the difficulties of Descartes' treatment of motion, see N. Kemp Smith, *Studies in
the Cartesian Philosophy* (London, 1902), pp. 75 ff.

Time as an Attribute of God:
Consequences of This Hypothesis

Let us ask then what changes are produced in Spinoza's doctrine if we regard Time itself as an attribute of the ultimate reality. In what remains I propose to offer these consequences as a gloss upon Spinoza's teaching, remarking explicitly that they are a gloss and not a commentary. A commentary must be historically true, but for Spinoza it was impossible to think of Time as an attribute. Slight as the change may seem verbally, it leads to a remodelling of the whole. Yet unhistorical as the procedure is, I venture upon it before an Historical Society because the real greatness and spirit of a man may often be best appreciated by asking not what he said himself but what he may lead us to say.

(1) In the first place the ultimate reality would be something which in one aspect, under one attribute, is Space, under another, Time. It would be Space-Time or Motion itself. I dare not yet assume that Time in this conception replaces Thought as the second attribute which our intellect perceives. It might still be true that Thought is a third attribute. It will appear, however, presently that Thought is not an attribute at all, but is an empirical or finite mode.

The ultimate reality or Space-Time ceases also to be Substance in Spinoza's sense, still less is it identifiable with God, which is for Spinoza the only substance. It is rather identical with the infinite immediate mode of motion and rest, or if we rid ourselves of the perplexing idea of rest as something positive, with the infinite mode of motion. It is still infinite and self-contained and the ground of all finite modes. But it is not so much the Substance of which things are modes as the stuff of which they are pieces, the material out of which they are made. It is comparable rather to the Space which in the Platonic *Timæus* is that which receives definite character through the ingression (I borrow the word from Mr. Whitehead) of the Forms or Ideas. The difference from Plato is that the material which thus receives form is in the *Timæus* purely spatial, and contains intrinsically no time. For Plato Time comes into being with the creation of things and is but the shadow of eternity. In our gloss upon Spinoza the ultimate reality is full of Time, not timeless but essentially alive with Time, and the theatre of incessant change. It is only timeless in the sense that taken as a whole it is not particularized to any one moment or duration, but comprehends them all.

For Spinoza the ultimate reality was necessarily conceived as Substance, as the one self-dependent, self-contained or infinite, self-caused, being; this distinguished it from the finite things which were its modes. The very difference and advance which he made upon Descartes was that created things, which for Descartes were in a secondary sense substances, became for Spinoza mere modes of the one Substance. And at least it is clear that if the ultimate reality is described as Substance, finite things, which in the words of Locke "are but retainers to other parts of nature for that which they are most taken notice of by us," cannot be substances in the same sense. But in fact substance, causality and the like are categories applicable in the first instance to finite things, and only transferred to infinite reality by a metaphor in which their meaning is changed; and it has now become a commonplace since Kant to declare that the categories of finite things are not applicable to the ground of finite things. And when once Time is regarded as an attribute of ultimate reality, the contrast of the Spinozistic Substance and its modes falls away. Reality is Space-Time or motion itself, infinite or self-contained and having nothing outside itself; and the vital contrast is that of this infinite or *a priori* stuff of the Universe and the empirical things or substances which are parts or modes of it. For this reason I speak of the ultimate reality of motion not as substance but as stuff.

Before passing to these empirical modes let me observe that the conception of Space-Time or Motion as the stuff of the Universe is not in all respects the same as that taken of it in the theory of relativity. That theory is a physical and not a metaphysical theory, and, properly, as a physical theory it begins with bodies. Space-Time for it is perhaps best described as an order or system of relations that subsists between bodies. Whether this is to be accepted as an ultimate statement for philosophy is just one of those matters to which I alluded at the beginning, on which discussion has yet to do its work. I may merely note in passing that one pronounced supporter of the relativity theory in this country maintains that when it is said that Space-Time is wrinkled or warped in the presence of matter this means that matter is the very wrinkle in Space-Time. From this to the proposition which I have taken as included in our gloss upon Spinoza, namely, that Space-Time is the stuff of which matter is made, is but a step.

(2) I pass to the singular things which in their totality constitute

the *facies totius universi*. As with Spinoza, they are modifications of
the ultimate reality which has now become Space-Time. But there
is now no ditch to jump between the ultimate ground of things and
things themselves; for things are, as Spinoza himself would say, but
complexes of motion and made of the stuff which the ultimate or
a priori reality is. In this way the danger is avoided which besets
Spinoza's doctrine, the danger that the modes or things should be
engulfed in an ultimate being which purports to be the positive
ground of its modes, but always is on the point of slipping into bare
indefiniteness.

This danger I have noted already, but it may be well to revert to
it here by way of pointing out the source of the difficulty. The
modes for Spinoza determine each other into existence within the
modal system in a chain of causation. But they follow, considered
in the light of eternity, from the nature of Substance or God, who is
their cause or ground. This causal issuing from God is, however, not
the physical relation of cause and effect, but the geometrical one of
ground and consequent. The modes follow from God as the properties of a triangle follow from the nature of the triangle. This being
so, the ultimate Substance being the ground of the modes must be
a positive reality which accounts for them, of which they are, in
modern phrase, the appearance. But then, we have to urge, the
modes are not properties of Substance, but are things.

On the other hand, if we ask for the ground of these things which
are modes, and are told that they follow from the ground, but that
the characters which things possess in the common order of nature
are the confused deliverances of our imagination, how can we conceive the ground otherwise than as something or other, we know
not what except that it is their ground? The case is different if
things are regarded as modes of the stuff which is Space-Time. Their
relation to their ground is no longer that of the properties of a
triangle to the triangle, but rather that of the two triangles which
compose an oblong to the oblong. They are involved in the oblong;
and in like manner the valley and the mountain are both contained
in that configuration of nature which we call a valley or a mountain,
but the valley does not follow from the mountain geometrically in
the sense in which the properties of the triangle follow from the
triangle.

But if the reality in its barest character is Space-Time, the face of
the whole universe is the totality of all those configurations into

which Space-Time falls through its inherent character of timefulness
or restlessness. The stuff of reality is not stagnant, its soul's wings are
never furled, and in virtue of this unceasing movement it strikes out
fresh complexes of movements, created things.

(3) This leads us directly to a third consequence. All things as in
God are alike perfect; they are what they are and cannot be other.
Yet there are grades of perfection amongst things, the one has more
reality than another. On this subject, as I cannot express Spinoza's
sense so well myself, I will transcribe a page from Mr. Joachim's
book:[2]

"God, as the necessary consequent of his own free causality, is
Natura Naturata—an ordered system of modes, following with coherent necessity from Natura Naturans.[3] But, though all things follow with the same inevitable necessity from God's nature, they differ
from one another in degree of perfection or reality; and indeed the
difference is one not only of degree but also of kind. 'For although
a mouse and an angel, sadness and joy, depend equally on God, yet
a mouse cannot be a species of angel, nor sadness a species of joy'
(Ep. 23). 'The criminal expresses God's will in his own way, just as
the good man does in his; but the criminal is not on that account
comparable with the good man. The more perfection a thing has,
the more it participates in the divine nature and the more it expresses God's perfection. The good have incalculably more perfection than the vicious; and therefore their "virtue" is not to be compared with the "virtue" of the vicious. . . .' (Ep. 19.)

"It is in 'natura naturata,' the eternal system of modes, that these
degrees of perfection or reality are exhibited. For there is an order
in the sequence of the modes from God's nature, and on that order
their degree of perfection depends. The order is not a temporal, but
a logical one. There is no before and after, no temporal succession,
in the relation of the modes to God; all modes are the eternal consequence of God's causality. But there is a logical priority and pos-
teriority; and on this their degrees of reality depend. 'That effect is

[2] H. H. Joachim, *A Study of the Ethics of Spinoza* (Oxford, 1901), p. 73.

[3] For the distinction of natura naturans and naturata, see Eth. I, 29, Sch. God as
free cause is natura naturans; natura naturata is all the modes of God's attributes, so far as they are considered as things which are in God and which cannot
either be or be conceived without God. See Mr. Joachim's note 1, p. 65. Mr.
Joachim adds that "Natura naturata is not the world of sense-perception, but
the universe in all its articulation as a perfect understanding would grasp it,
if that understanding apprehended it as the *effect* of God's causality."

the most perfect which is produced by God immediately; and the more mediating causes which any effect requires, the less perfect it is.' (Eth. I, App.)"

Now directly Time has become an attribute of the ultimate reality, this order ceases to be merely a logical one, and becomes temporal. The grades of modal perfection are no longer a 'static' series of forms, but a hierarchy produced in the order of time. The idea of evolution is introduced, and from matter or from before matter there have grown up in time the modes of physical existence, and thence the forms of life and finally of mind. Existence is stratified, level upon level with each its distinctive quality, and the strata are not barely superposed, but each higher level is the descendant in time of the lower. Hence, for instance, living things are not merely alive, but their life is a differentiation of physico-chemical body, and that body is but a particular complexity of mere matter. Upon what particular basis bare matter depends is a question not for the philosopher but the physicist to decide. If the old doctrine of the *Timæus* should be true, according to which solid matter is composed of elementary figures in space, we should have the notion here suggested as flowing from our gloss upon Spinoza, that the primary modes are the mere differentiations of bare Space-Time. But all the particular history of this long descent (or call it rather ascent) to higher levels of perfection amongst the modes is to be traced empirically under the guidance of science.

(4) The last level of things accessible to our senses would be that of minds, or as Spinoza would call them thinking things. Thought, therefore, upon our gloss becomes not an attribute of the ultimate reality but the distinguishing quality of the highest level of empirical things. We are left with Space and Time as the two attributes which our intellect perceives, and Time displaces Thought in the Spinozistic scheme. And yet we arrive also at a conclusion which seems to repeat Spinoza's view that thought is a universal feature of things, only with a difference. All things for him are in a sense animated, they are all in their degree thinking things. For us things which are not minds, which are merely alive or are inanimate, are no longer minds, but they do bear an aspect, or contain in themselves an element, which corresponds to the aspect or element of mind in a thinking thing. That aspect or element is Time.

We may express the relation between the orders of modes in two different ways. We may say that life is the mind of the living body,

colour the mind of the coloured material body, matter or material-
ity the mind of the spatio-temporal substructure of a material body.
In doing so, we are humouring our propensity to construe things on
the pattern of what is most familiar to us, our own selves, in which
mind is united with a living body; and are just comparing one set of
empirical things with another. The other way penetrates more
deeply into the nature of things. It starts with a piece of space-time,
in which there are the bare aspects of its space and its time, and it
construes thinking things after the pattern of this. One portion of
the living thing, let us say its brain, is at once a peculiarly differentiated portion of space and correspondingly and inevitably a peculiarly differentiated complex of time. Were it not for the peculiar
complexity of the brain, we should have the brain a merely living
structure; as it is, when living matter is so differentiated as to be a
brain, its time element becomes mind, or rather the character of
mentality. It is as if we had a clock which not only showed the time
but was the time it showed.

According, then, to the one method all things are, as Spinoza says,
thinking things, and in the end, paradoxical as it sounds to say so,
Time is the mind of Space. According to the other, mind is the time
of its brain, life the time of the living parts of the living body and
the like. On either method we realize the same truth that all the
world and everything in it are constructed on the same plan, which
betrays itself most plainly in our thinking bodies. But the Spinozistic method is a comparison of the modes with one another; the
other method views the modes in the light of the ultimate or a priori
reality from which they derive.

The same result is reached from a different consideration. Thinking things know, they have ideas. The idea of a tree which I have
when I see one is for Spinoza the thought-aspect of the bodily condition into which I am thrown by the action of the tree upon my
bodily senses. Or as we should say nowadays, it is the inner side of
the brain-process. What is a brain-process under the attribute of extension is an idea or thinking process under the attribute of thought.
To think of the tree means to have an idea or a bodily process which
would be different if the tree were replaced by a table; and accordingly if for some reason or other this bodily condition recurs in the
absence of the tree I still have the tree before my view as an image.
Whether this is or is not a true account of the knowing process is

under some discussion at the present moment among philosophers.
But that does not concern us here. What does concern us is that it
applies in its degree to all things alike whether minds in the empirical sense or not. The stone knows its surroundings in the same
way as we know ours, though of course not to the same extent. Now,
if this is so, it would seem again, that thought or knowing is a universal character of things and might claim therefore to be an attribute. Yet once more, thought as knowing is in truth merely a
relation among the modes. In so far as my mind or the stone is
affected by other things, it knows them. Accordingly knowing, being
an affair of modes *inter se,* is not an attribute. For an attribute is
not a character which arises out of the interrelation of modes, but
every mode intrinsically possesses a character in so far as it is considered under an attribute. We again arrive at the conclusion that
thought is empirical, not *a priori* or ultimate; and so far Space and
Time are seen to exhaust the attributes of reality.

Spinoza's Infinity of Attributes[4]

What then becomes of the infinite other attributes which the ultimate reality according to Spinoza possesses in virtue of its infinite
perfection? The answer to this question will illustrate the tenor of
the foregoing remarks. For we shall see that these supposed attributes are otiose and unnecessary; but what is more important, we
shall see that Spinoza's justification of them, to my mind successful,
depends for its force not upon the view that Thought is an attribute,
but on the empirical character of particular minds.

This matter is the standing unresolved puzzle of interpretation of
Spinoza to which I have alluded above. For we are faced with a
dilemma. All the attributes are in a metaphorical phrase co-extensive, and accordingly my mind is identical not only with my body
but with modes under all the other attributes—let us take one of
them for short and call it the *x*-attribute. Why then do I not perceive my *x*-ian mode as well as my body? I do not, and Spinoza
insists that I cannot (Ep. 64). But if so, there must be thought-modes
which correspond not only to body-modes, as they do, but to

[4] A reader not interested in Spinoza scholarship may be recommended to pass
over this section.

x-modes, that is (to quote Mr. Joachim[5]), "there are modes of Thought which are *not* the thought-side of modes of Extension, and the 'completeness' of the Attribute of Thought is more full than the 'completeness' of any other Attribute," or as Tschirnhaus put it, the attribute of Thought is much wider than the other Attributes —is in fact coextensive with them all.

Even Mr. Joachim regards the difficulty as insoluble. One commentator, Sir F. Pollock, in his excellent book,[6] reminding us that an Attribute is what intellect perceives in Substance as constituting its essence, has accepted this last result and given Spinoza's doctrine a kink in the direction of idealism. Yet exactly the same kind of reflection might with proper changes be applied to Extension, which would then be wider than all the other attributes, and Spinoza might thus receive a kink in the direction of materialism. Spinoza himself answers Tschirnhaus briefly, and perhaps a little impatiently, in a letter which I will quote (Ep. 66): "In answer to your objection I say, that although each particular thing be expressed in infinite ways in the infinite intellect of God, yet those infinite ideas, whereby it is expressed, cannot constitute one and the same mind of a particular thing, but infinite minds; seeing that each of these infinite ideas has no connection with the rest (and he refers to Eth. II, 7, and Sch. I, 10). If you will reflect on these passages a little, you will see that all the difficulty vanishes."

It may be doubted whether a little reflection is enough or all difficulty vanishes; but I believe that Spinoza upon his own principles is right and that his thought is clear, with a little indulgence for his language. I cannot perceive x-modes because I am a body, and I can only perceive those objects which my body enables me to apprehend. Remember that when Spinoza says that a mode of thought, my idea, has for its *ideatum* a condition of my body, he does not mean that in the usual sense of the word I *perceive* that condition of body. The body is expressed (objectively he says, subjectively we should say) as the idea, but what I perceive is the tree, whose existence is implied in my bodily condition, because that condition varies with the perceived object. We perceive extended things, and we may also perceive our body, though the perceiving of my body is of course not the same idea as corresponds to the con-

[5] Op. cit., p. 137.
[6] *Spinoza, His Life and Philosophy*, 2d ed. (London, 1899), p. 162.

dition of my body when I perceive the table. Thus I can be said to perceive Reality under the attribute of extension, and in like manner I may be said to perceive the attribute of Thought because I apprehend thought in my own person, although it must be admitted this statement raises certain difficulties.

Now there is an x-mode corresponding to the idea and bodily condition I am in when I perceive the table. But I cannot perceive an x-mode because my particular sort of mind which is united to a particular sort of body has no means of perceiving x-modes. My bodily organs are affected in the world of motion and rest by the extended table, but I do not perceive the x-mode of the table but only its extension-mode, and consequently though my idea has a corresponding x-mode I cannot perceive it, because I do not perceive x-objects exterior to my body.

It may be answered: granted that I do not as a matter of fact perceive the x-mode of the table, the question is still, why not? Does not the x-mode of the table affect the x-mode of my body or mind and throw it into a condition parallel to the condition of my extended body which has for its mental correlate the idea of the table? The answer is that interaction between a thing like the table and my body is intelligible only within the infinite mode of motion and rest; but we cannot speak of x-modes in such terms. We cannot therefore be sure that the x-correspondent of my idea of the table gives me the perception of the x-table. It might, for instance, be possible that in order to have perception of the x-table there was needed another body composed say of half my body and half yours, or of my body and a stone. The x-correspondent of my body in perceiving the table may be only a part of the x-mode which is necessary for the perception of the x-table, which perception consequently would belong to a quite different mind from mine. In other words, a different distribution of matter or rather of motion may be required for the purpose than is afforded by that particular distribution which constitutes my human body.

I can now return more immediately to Spinoza's own words in his letter. A different kind of mind is required to apprehend things as x-modes, and so it is only such minds which can perceive x-modes, for example, the x-table, and can consequently perceive themselves also as x-modes. The infinite thought-mode includes every possible empirical variety of mind, some of which may overlap ours. Such

minds would of course have extended bodies, but it is easy enough
to conceive that they might apprehend x-modes but fail to apprehend modes of extension, for want of the proper means. I take it
that when Spinoza says that each particular thing may be expressed
in infinite ways in the infinite understanding of God he means that
in that infinite understanding there are minds enough to perceive
the x-mode and every other mode of my body or mind; and that he
uses the word 'express' with some looseness or inaccuracy, and does
not mean that the x-mode of my mind or body has a different mind
for its *correspondent,* but only a different mind for its *percipient.*
This being granted, there is no further difficulty in Spinoza's reply
to the question of Tschirnhaus and his modern critics than is implied in the habitual ambiguity with which he speaks of an idea
sometimes as the idea of the bodily condition which is its correspondent mode of extension, sometimes as the idea of the object.

Spinoza's critics have therefore, I plead, forgotten that what we
humans can perceive in the ultimate substance depends on the
empirical character of our bodies, on our particular distribution of
motion and rest, and correspondingly of thought.

At the same time, good as Spinoza's defence may be made, consistently with his presuppositions, the defence is only necessary because he has taken thought to be an attribute of reality instead of
merely an empirical character of certain complexes of space-time
or motion. Substitute Time for Thought, and the whole edifice of
infinite other attributes is otiose and unverifiable. It is founded
indeed on the notion that Substance being the ground of all things
must not only have attributes which characterize infinite modes but
an infinite number of such attributes. With our gloss, we can be
content to note that mind belongs to certain things in the world
and not to others. There may indeed be other minds than ours, with
bodies different from or more perfect than ours. And it is legitimate
enough to suppose that such minds may apprehend other characters
of things than we do. Why should colour, taste, etc., be the only
secondary qualities of things? But there is no reason why we should
assume that the objects perceived by such minds should be other
than material or quasi-material objects like ours, and like them
modes of extension or rather complexes of motion. The usefulness
of other minds is in probing to the full the riches and variety of the
facies totius universi. Perfection we shall find not in the arbitrary
imagination of attributes which cannot fall within our human ken,

but in the hierarchy of the verifiable qualities of the real world, culminating in the quality characteristic of God.

What remains of Spinoza's doctrine upon our gloss is not that there are infinite attributes but that there are infinite levels of the modes, that there is no end to the hierarchy of qualities amongst finite things.

Personal Identity
in Spinoza

Ruth L. Saw

Spinoza's avowed aim is to discover and present the essential stages in achieving the life of human blessedness. The most important element in this progression is knowledge, of one's own nature as man, and of one's place in the universe. Utility as opposed to truth of belief will not serve Spinoza's purpose. Spinoza assumes the unity of the human individual without question, and it is doubtful whether this assumption is justified on his own principles. The concept of the human individual is examined first as a system of modifications of substance under the attributes of extension and thought, then as enduring and finally as an agent. The conclusion is reached that unity and self-identity are illusions, but the question then arises: Who or what could be under such illusions? The possibility of false claims to self-identity is examined and found to be difficult to accept.

Nevertheless, if Spinoza is taken as speaking suitably at varying levels of discourse, he has enlightening things to say about the human person, even though from one point of view his enterprise may be seen as self-stultifying.

AT FIRST SIGHT, this is an odd topic to choose to write upon in connexion with Spinoza. The problem of personal identity does not seem to have presented itself urgently to Spinoza as it did to the British Empiricists, nor to have received the attention which Leibniz gave to it. Nevertheless, Spinoza's metaphysical system can be so viewed that it is seen to provide a place in the universe for the uniqueness of individuals if for no other of the attributes usually thought to belong to them. Moreover, it cannot be doubted that Spinoza was not only vitally concerned with the well-being of Peter and Paul, but that he was also firmly persuaded that as objects of knowledge, they were vastly superior to that more usual object of knowledge, MAN. This may be thought odd in a mathematician and metaphysician, but it is my contention that these are just the people from whom we may expect a satisfactory account of individuality, if not of personality.

At first sight, this is a ridiculous statement. Are not mathematicians and metaphysicians of all people the most concerned with the universal, with vast spatio-temporal schemes in which the individual appears to be lost? This cannot be denied, but there is a saving peculiarity belonging to the objects of mathematics. They are undoubtedly universal in a sense, but if there are any universals that are at the same time individual, it is triangles, squares, circles and so on. The enemy of the individual is the general, not the universal. 'What is for the most part' is a miserable notion compared with what is here now on the one hand, and with what must be universally on the other. Man, plant, mineral, all these are readily thought of as figments of the mind, formed to help us state general truths and having no other status, but it is far other with triangle, square, circle and so on. We have not formed the notion of triangularity from observation of many instances, but see it complete in each exemplification. That most determined of empiricists, John Stuart Mill, declared that the man who could explain why in some cases a single instance was enough to produce conviction, while in others a thousand would not suffice, would have solved the problem of induction. The answer to this is that if one case is genuinely enough to produce conviction, as in mathematics, then induction in Mill's sense is not involved. Critics of art and literature sometimes reverse the foregoing manner of speaking about universals and particulars, and speak for instance, of Falstaff, that great example of individuality, as a universal, though a universal of himself. Equally, Guernica is seen as a universal of outrage at the manifestations of tyranny upon the life of ordinary people.

A very natural objection may be raised at this point. It may be said that the reason for the difference between the general notion 'man' and the universal 'triangle' is precisely that men can and do develop all kinds of personal idiosyncrasies, while triangles are simply three-sided, together with all that follows from three-sidedness. This is true, but it is also true that there is variety even in triangularity. Triangles are infinite in number, each 'individual universal' differing from those nearest to it by an infinitely little from the scalene through the isosceles to the equilateral, and so on. I admit that this is not the kind of variety that we ordinarily desire for persons, but it provides a model for ordered variety among examples which are individual in a sense. Rationalist philosophers are faced with this insoluble problem, if they wish to say with Spinoza, that 'our highest knowledge is of the individual'—they wish to say both that knowledge progresses by rational reflection upon our 'common ideas', and that the actual bearers of the properties which are the objects of rational knowledge are the this-here-now. Leibniz made the most determined attempt upon this combination with his 'concept of an individual', each named by its own unique name from which one might read off all the properties of the individual named if one were gifted with complete understanding. Only one person has this complete understanding, the Perfect Being, God. The difficulty of combining knowledge by acquaintance of individuals and their properties with the possibility of the rational unfolding of these properties is nicely illustrated by the efforts of biologists to combat food shortage in World War I. They tried to treat grass in such a way that it would nourish human beings directly, without having first to have gone through the digestion of a cow. The calculations of food values and the transforming of substances was simple: what could not be deduced in any way was the plain fact which emerged when the calculations had been acted upon. All the products were so horrible to the taste that no human being could swallow them. In a rational account of the universe, we must be content with a scheme which 'places' individuals, and not look for a rational account of their peculiarities of flavour.

Not only do Spinoza and Leibniz accept individuals as objects of knowledge alongside mathematical objects, they accommodate them also in their metaphysical system, Leibniz more adequately than Spinoza, partly, perhaps, because he had seen the inadequacies of Spinoza's treatment. They share the notion of the whole of nature as a vast all-embracing system, in which all happenings are interconnected. For both, human beings lie within the network of change, completely determined, by causal factors for Spinoza, for Leibniz 'inclined to action' by their partial understanding of and sometimes deliberate co-operation with the purposes of God. The two systems diverge sharply at this point, but both agree in the respect which is of interest to us here. For both Spinoza and Leibniz, every happening in the universe is inescapably in its unique spatio-temporal place, timelessly and eternally individuated by its place in the network of the modal system for Spinoza, and by the pre-established harmony of mutually mirroring substances for Leibniz. For both, knowledge of the individual is to be increased by growing knowledge of its context. For Spinoza, this will be knowledge of causal sequences expressed most satisfactorily in mathematical terms, which lead to the particular concatenation in which we happen to be interested, and leading on to further causal sequences. In practical terms, that is, in the terms in which a scientist will usefully theorize, the processes for the two philosophies are essentially the same, though in metaphysical terms, as we said before, what Spinoza characterizes as causally determined will be described by Leibniz as jointly fulfilling the purposes of God. For neither will the process of growing in knowledge be the Aristotelian one of subsuming the particular under its appropriate universal, but of completing our knowledge of its environment. It is in this sense that Spinoza says: 'Our highest knowledge is of the individual.' A long-treasured and wish-fulfilling belief of mine has finally disappeared—the belief that Spinoza was promising us an account from which we might draw Peter in all his particularity as the object of our highest knowledge. It is not Peter as a person that we are given, but Peter, the unique system of converging finite modifications of substance under the attributes of extension and thought occurring in its own place in the spatio-temporal scheme of *natura naturata*.

We must, then, accept this situation. Spinoza has placed before himself as his most important and highest endeavour the increasing of human happiness, and the setting out of the steps which a reasonable man might follow and find himself set free from the constant self-frustrating of his own desire for happiness, and the constant spoiling of the happiness of others, even of those he believed himself to love. On the other hand, we also have to accept that the Peter and Paul, so set free, would seem to themselves and to others, not as Peter and Paul, but as 'rational men', very far indeed from the passionately loving, hating, impetuous persons they had believed themselves to be. Rightly or wrongly, most people believe that their individuality is most strongly displayed in their emotional and even passionate involvement with their fellows, and that if they rightly believe themselves to be eternal, they will rejoice in that a life apart from this one promises them a re-uniting with their beloved companions.

We may now go on to the actual account which Spinoza gives of human beings. Men are enminded bodies, or embodied minds, but Spinoza treats very completely of men as physical organisms, and very sketchily of men as thinking beings. This does not, of course, apply to the reasoned account of the appraisal of conduct, of the emotions and of the power of the human intellect, but only to the theoretical foundation given to, or rather, lacking from, the whole structure of the thinking side of the system of finite modes making up the human person.

The human body, like any other, is to be thought of as a complex of complexes of simpler and simpler bodies, coming finally to the 'simplest bodies'. Considered as bodies, men are to be described most truly in the scientific terms which allow for the complete understanding of their manner of functioning. At the basic level, these descriptions are appropriate to inanimate as well as to organic bodies. Spinoza's treatment of these descriptions appears in a number of axioms and lemmas after 2P13.[1] Here he distinguishes between 'simplest bodies', that is, bodies distinguishable from one another in respect of motion and rest, speed and slowness alone, individuals composed of these simplest bodies and distinguishable from one another by their hardness and softness, these qualities arising from the manner of compounding the simplest bodies, and finally, composite individuals composed of bodies of the second order. These are distinguishable from one another by the complexity of the ways in which the second-order individuals are combined, and by the efficiency with which they maintain their unity along with the varying degrees of their internal change. There is no reason why we should not conceive of this process of compounding individuals, producing more and more complex bodies, until we arrive at the notion of the whole of nature as an individual with an infinite number of changes in its parts, yet itself unchanging. The essence of individuals is said to be their *conatus,* the endeavour with which each persists in its own being. It is one of the paradoxes of Spinoza's position that *conatus* can belong only to the derived, dissoluble,

[1] In the references to the *Ethics* in this paper '2P13' is to be read as: 'Part 2, Proposition 13'. For further comments on this notation, see the notes to the article of G. Fløistad in this volume.

and in a sense, illusory individuals, and not to the only true individual, God or Substance, nor to the next in metaphysical order, the simplest bodies. The essence of God involves existence, and he could not possibly *not* persist in his own being. As for the simplest bodies, they do not endure, so that they could neither persist nor not persist in their own being.

Having been given this very complete account of the way in which the description of men as physical beings may be reached from the basic level, we suddenly come upon 2A1: 'Man thinks'. This is the first appearance of the 'whole' concept 'man', though we have been given, so to speak, all the ingredients of men as bodies. If we are to accept 'man thinks' as axiomatic, we should have been given grounds for his unity as a thinking being. What we have been given so far is infinite substance, infinitely modified under its known attributes of extension and thought, an account of the unity of man as a bodily being, and nothing whatever of his unity as a thinking being. If, on the other hand, we are to accept 'Man thinks' as an empirical statement, we are engaged in quite a different enterprise from the one initially presented to us. We could have embarked straightaway on an empirical account of men's life of wrong-headed attachment to unsuitable objects with all the unhappy consequences, without the apparatus of substance infinitely modified under its two attributes of extension and thought, and so on.

It might be thought that I am embarking here on a perverse course of criticism. Men are embodied minds, or enminded bodies, and just as we may accept without question, 'Men move', why may we not also accept without question, or as axiomatic 'Men think'? There are several different kinds of answer here. First, as a matter of fact, we were not given as axiomatic, 'Men move', but simply given a detailed exposition of their moving. More importantly, not only have we been given no comparable account of the terms in which the thinking must be described at the basic level, but it is difficult to see how we could even begin to work out such a description. In later books there are descriptions of mental events, but then, as is suitable, the descriptions are in terms of association, of coincidence of ideas and feelings with the consequent building up of more complex states of mind. This would be all very well if the preliminary work had been done. Spinoza criticizes Descartes in the preface to Book V in terms which seem to me equally destructive of his own basic position. He says:

What does he understand, I ask, by the union of mind and
body? What clear and distinct conception has he of thought
intimately connected with a certain small portion of matter?
I wish that he had explained this union by its proximate
cause.

We may equally well wish that Spinoza had given us a way of speaking of the infinite modifications of thinking comparable to the passage from the infinite attribute of extension to the simplest bodies.
When we are speaking about morals we may allow ourselves to
speak of man as a thinking being, but if we have made Spinoza's
claims, we must ensure that the description given of him at a deeper
level justifies the higher-level way of speaking.

Superficially, there is an easy answer to this criticism. The two
infinite attributes, extension and thought, belong equally to infinite
substance, and if there were any grounds for speaking of God's
body, we could similarly speak of God's mind. Similarly, the moving together of the 'parts' of a man's body, and their maintaining
their proportion of motion and rest entitle us to speak of the whole
system as one, with its thinking side, consequently, also as one. The
conatus presumably is neither physical nor mental, nor is it exactly
both. It is rather the principle of unity thought of as belonging to
both sides of man's nature. But this will not do, for several reasons.
First, it is doubtful whether we ought to say 'God thinks' if by this
we mean that this is comparable to saying that man thinks. Secondly, the moving together of the bodily parts must not be allowed
to engender the unity of the mind, nor even of the total organism.
(1A5: 'Those things which have nothing mutually in common with
one another cannot through one another be mutually understood,
that is to say, the conception of the one does not involve the conception of the other.') The unity must be explained independently on
both sides. Moreover, there are bodily unities other than human,
but we do not say that planetary systems think. If it be objected
that we must say precisely this if we are to take seriously Spinoza's
claim that there is a thinking side to every part of the modal system
of extension, then we must also admit that this obscures rather than
clarifies the nature of 'thinking man'. The final objection is that it
is very difficult to complete the process of establishing the elements
of thinking as we did for extension. 'The thinking side of the simplest bodies' has no content, but if we are to interpret 'thinking

side' differently for complex and for simple bodies, we should have been told so. The attribute of thought is infinitely modified, but into what? We know by experience, finite thoughts, fragmentary thoughts, but we have no terms for the simplest elements of thinking, nor any experience of them.

It may be objected that we are equally unacquainted with the simplest bodies, and this of course is true. We may be under an illusion when we think that we can conceive of them, but we certainly feel at no loss when we entertain the thought of some such process as indefinitely continuing division, yielding something similar to the bodies we already know. We cannot think of this process as even beginning in the case of thought. Even if we could make anything of the notion of the 'simplest thought', we should still not have made the necessary connexion with 'the thinking side of the simplest body'.

Let us now pursue another line of criticism. We are to take 'Man thinks' as compatible with the account of man as a complex bodily organism made up of simpler and simpler bodies standing in varying relations to one another. These organisms are together 'one' in that they move as a whole, maintaining the internal relationships of their simpler elements. But this will not do as an account of their oneness as thinking beings. Either we must take their oneness as given and inexplicable on Spinoza's own grounds, or we must deny their oneness. No collection of thinking beings can constitute a thinking being. If we drop the notion of a collection of thinking beings and substitute a number of thoughts, we are no better off, for a collection of thoughts does not make up a thinking being. Moreover, one thought cannot be the 'owner' of the other thoughts, and what is the relation of the thoughts to one another? It is difficult to avoid the conclusion that having stayed strictly within his own lines in describing men as modifications under the attribute of extension, Spinoza then forgets all that he has said so far and starts afresh with men as we know them, both from the inside and the outside. If it were not for our inside knowledge as human beings, *conatus* would be no more than gravitation as applied to bodies.

Even if we grant the unity of the human being as a system of modifications under both attributes, there is still a serious obstacle. Spinoza might have said, 'Man endures' equally with 'Man thinks', for if a man does not endure, he cannot think. Yet Spinoza rejects the notion of identity throughout duration in favour of continuity

of life history, so long as there is enough similarity maintained
through the parts of the history. He says:

> This body of course had a different proportion of motion and
> rest when it was an unborn embryo; and in due course, when
> we are dead, it will have a different proportion again.

In between birth and death the human body maintains its proportion of motion–rest to a degree great enough to allow the body to be
called 'the same' body. Its elements are different from moment to
moment, what remains is the pattern in which the sets and subsets of
elements form and reform, the whole sustained by the all-embracing
system of nature, 'the face of the whole universe'.

Now if the change from the last moment of life to the first moment of death is so decisive, the changes of proportion in motion–
rest determining that the individual has lost its identity, then I
cannot help thinking that earlier changes, less violent it is true,
must also be described in terms of loss of identity. More importantly, if in terms of the ultimate entities, the simplest bodies, there
is no carry-over from one moment to the next, then not only must
we conceive of the human being, body and mind, as atomistically
in space, but also in time. If the embryo is not identical with the
child and the man, then the man of now is not identical with the
man of a moment ago, nor of a moment to come. If we may identify
the man of now with the man of a moment ago, then since identity
is a transitive relation, we could reach the embryo in a series of steps
and establish its identity with the man. It may be argued that empirically speaking, it is clear that the embryo is different enough
from the man, and the man in his successive stages alike enough for
us to disclaim the first identity and accept the second. This is true,
but we were not going with Spinoza on these empirical grounds. It
seems clear, in any event, that Spinoza is genuinely wishing to claim,
on a *priori* grounds, that identity through duration is not possible,
and so we may go on to point out that if he is right, we cannot give
a satisfactory account of the human person. Let us consider again,
'Man thinks'. This must mean that men can follow through an argument, consider what is proposed to them and draw out its implications. But if a man is a series of momentary states, far from being
able to follow an argument, he could not even state its first premiss. Not only is the man who propounds the first premiss of the
syllogism, 'All men are mortal, Socrates is a man, so Socrates is

mortal', not identical with the man who follows with the second premiss and draws the conclusion, the man who says 'all' is not identical with the man who says 'men', and so on. It follows, then, that 'Man thinks' is not only not axiomatic, it is an empirical statement which cannot be true on Spinoza's own grounds.

It may be objected that I am confusing thought as a process with the content of thought. It is true that I begin to think and come to an end, while *what* I am thinking does not pattern step by step the process of thinking. Suppose I reach a startling conclusion, and say very slowly: 'Parallels may meet at infinity.' All these words belong together in a timeless whole, even though the utterance took time, and when I say 'infinity', 'parallels' has gone. To say that the *content* of thought is timeless does not help us; it simply means that this timeless whole was present at each stage of the temporal utterance, which seems odd, to say the least of it. I do not mind accepting it as an absurdity; it would simply mean for me that man as a thinking being is not to be described wholly in spatio-temporal terms, as Spinoza would claim. 'Man' for him, is a transient, shifting complex system of elements, enduring and maintaining no identity throughout the temporal stages.

The next objection will certainly be that I have forgotten memory. Here again, a similar line of argument may be followed. If 'I now' am not identical with the 'I of ten years ago', my present memories are no more memories than if I had annexed the past of a neighbour. A memory is said to be genuine if it were really 'of' something that happened to me. But if the remembering belongs to the me of now, and the remembered belongs to the me of ten years ago, then the test of genuineness cannot even be applied, for there is nothing with which to compare it. The test of genuineness presupposes the fact of memory, and if this is challenged, there is no test to be applied. Memory, then, cannot help in the theoretical binding together of the 'parts' of an individual life. All the talk about the continuity of history is irrelevant. Of course, if we were to be engaged in an empirical inquiry into the 'feeling' of being an individual, then memory experiences would be of the utmost importance, but if this is what Spinoza is doing, then we have been sadly misled, and the largeness of Spinoza's metaphysical speculation with all its attraction for his followers has gone.

Thirdly and lastly, Spinoza's human individual is not an agent. Nobody can deny that Spinoza absolutely rejects the notion of free

will, but if there is no *free* will, then there is no meaning to 'will'.
It is true that Spinoza stresses the importance of the distinction between activity and passivity, but the distinction is not to be made
in terms of will. It does not therefore yield the notion of the 'active'
man as agent. Man is passive when what he 'does' is to be explained
largely in terms of his environment, circumstances, and so on. He is
active when what he 'does' (and here we need the inverted commas
just as much as for the passive man), when what he 'does' is largely
explainable in terms of his own properties. The explanation in both
cases is causal. I am aware that for Spinoza causal explanation is
what philosophers in general describe as ground–consequent explanation, but I think that this makes no difference to my argument. If
all causal explanation is in reality ground–consequent explanation,
then nothing turns on the difference between the two.

The fact of the matter is that Spinoza has no account whatever to
give of the 'I' who does anything at all. At this point, we may remember that Leibniz said that if it were not for the monads, Spinoza
would be right. The monads do just this: they supply the beings
who actively *do* this, that and the other thing. If Spinoza *had* said
that men acted freely, then he would have had to revise most if not
all of what he had already said about human beings. In this sense,
what he says is all of a piece.

At this point, we must notice what is to me a strong temptation,
and to most people a common-sense course to pursue. It may be said
that if we allow Spinoza to speak of persons, to use the pronouns
'we' and 'I' without discussion, and to say of 'us' that 'we feel and
know ourselves to be eternal', even though it is in opposition to
everything that follows from his own basic principles, we are merely
allowing him a way of speaking that is useful in bringing it about
that people act in a way that is conducive to happiness. The first
answer to this objection is that Spinoza insists on knowledge as the
most important element in the life of blessedness, and consequently,
on the importance of the truth of our beliefs. He nowhere considers
the usefulness of a belief in contrast to its truth. But we must also
remember his reply to his landlady, when she asked him whether
she might be saved in her religion. He replied that her religion was
a 'good one'. It might be that Spinoza found himself obliged to bear
in mind the unsuitability of some truths for some minds, and had to
concede that the sternest truths must be kept for the strongest thinkers. If so, we ought to have been told of this concession.

The second reply is that if it were really the case that Spinoza was concerned with the usefulness of the belief in individuality, we should expect him to demonstrate this usefulness. (He shows the harmfulness of accepting this usefulness.) He shows the harmfulness of accepting the illusion of free will, but though he does not speak of the usefulness in the good life of assuming our separate and personal identities, neither does he speak of its harmfulness. We might connect such an illusion with our mistaken belief that God loves each one of us, but Spinoza does not make this connexion.

We must not confuse the notion of speaking in a manner that is suited to some intellects and not to others, with the different and legitimate notion of speaking differently at different levels of discourse. In conversation, moral and political discussion, it is suitable to speak of men and institutions, tables and chairs, dogs and trees, and not of these objects as describable in terms of spheres and triangles, molecules and atoms, points and straight lines. In mathematics it is suitable to speak of points and straight lines and not of natural objects. In mechanics, we speak of mass and inertia, in metaphysics we speak of whatever entities we take to be ultimate, in Spinoza's case, of the one infinite substance, infinitely modified under its infinite attributes, each infinite in its own kind. We must insist, however, that the way of speaking at each level is allowed for at the other levels, even, for Spinoza, that the way of speaking at any level other than the ultimate must be shown to follow from the earlier. Otherwise, we are simply not taking him seriously. Berkeley and Hume allowed themselves to 'think with the learned and speak with the vulgar'. We may allow them this privilege since they had not insisted upon the importance of knowledge for human happiness, but we may not allow a similar license to Spinoza.

To sum up: A human being is an embodied mind whose body maintains a precarious and unstable unity of 'parts', is not self-identical through time, and is only a unity of its contemporary parts in that they move together. Correspondingly, the mind which is the inner side or the idea of this body, is also such an unstable and precarious unity. It is not self-identical through time, and hardly a contemporaneous unity. In fact, 'properly understood', the human person is not a person in the ordinary sense of the word. We have the illusion, even, if we may borrow a Leibnizian term, 'the well-founded illusion', of being self-identical in all our spatial parts, and through time, but it remains an illusion. But it is precisely these illusory beings whose welfare is so important for Spinoza. They can achieve their 'proper' blessedness only by being shown their true nature as illusory beings. Here, however, we reach the crowning absurdity: how is it possible for anybody, or perhaps we should say, anything, to be under any illusions at all, to say nothing of being under the illusion that it is a person? We could not allow a nonperson to say truly that he thought, and he certainly cannot be allowed to say that he is a person. If a being makes a genuine claim to be a person—I say 'genuine' to rule out utterances of parrots, gramophones, etc.—then it must be a justified claim. If we read more into 'being a person' than self-identity through time and through a certain portion of space, then difficulties arise. Suppose in the very moment of changing from Dr. Jekyll into Mr. Hyde, this 'individual' was saying: 'Yet I am still an individual', or even: 'I am still Jekyll', he might begin in a despairing tone and end with a snarl. What has been demonstrated would be that it is the same person whose properties vary enormously from one moment to the next. Mr. Hyde's contempt would be for what he had been, and Dr. Jekyll's despair for what he was becoming.

Just as Spinoza said after he had finished all that had to be said about 'this life', that 'nevertheless we feel and know that we are eternal', I should like to add, 'nevertheless, we feel and know that we are persons'. It is 'nevertheless', for Spinoza, because the eternity that is allowed for in Spinoza's system is the same for modes under both attributes. Just as it is timelessly and eternally true that a given 'material' modal system was in a certain place at a certain time, this may be said also of 'minds'. The eternity which we 'feel and know' ourselves to possess is more than this eternal place in the universe. To know is to know that we know, and to know adequately is to become part of the complete system of knowledge which is God's knowledge, so that to be eternal is to be aware of ourselves as such a part. This is not to have eternal life in the sense in which it is usually hoped for, but neither is it to be absolutely and utterly temporal and ephemeral. Not to be ephemeral is to have a certain kind of personal identity, though even this may be more than is strictly allowed for in Spinoza's own system. We need not preface 'We feel and know that we are persons' by 'nevertheless' in quite this way. It is not to be thought for one moment that any finite modal system other than human beings could possibly be persons. The 'nevertheless' must remain because our feeling that we are persons is *in spite of* whatever Spinoza may be thought to have shown as to our ephemeral and fragmentary nature.

Before bringing this unsatisfactory and unsatisfying paper to a conclusion, I must notice a way of treating Spinoza which I find very congenial but which I cannot bring myself to follow. There is a way of presenting Spinoza, or perhaps of elaborating on what he has said, or even of first paraphrasing it and then enlarging upon it according to which all that I have said is wrong-headed and misleading. In the face of Spinoza's plain warnings, I have spoken as if substance could be divided under both its attributes of extension and thought. I have not forgotten that Spinoza has said: 'No attribute of substance can be truly conceived from which it follows that substance can be divided.' (1P12) It seems to me, however, that we take a metaphysician seriously only by relating his utterances in his metaphysical system with what he believes to be useful ways of speaking in other fields. I cannot be satisfied to speak of modifications of extension and thought without working out their bearing on what must be said of bodies and minds. When, then, I come upon passages such as the following, I admire them, and rejoice to meet the mind of someone steeped in Spinoza and moved to eloquence, even though I could not for one moment be led to attempt anything similar.

The human body in the midst of nature, is, indeed, very roughly analogous to an instrument in an orchestra: its contribution is a part of the whole symphony, but it also *sotto voce* contributes a reproduction of the whole; each instrument takes its part with the others in the whole, but a very acute ear would detect it playing its own responsive, and therefore selective, version of the whole in a normally undetected undertone. To bodily responsiveness in extension there corresponds an appropriate relation in Thought, and it is because nature (both psychical and physical) is a whole of responsive parts, parts which as capable of adequate response are more than mere sections—are indeed, relative wholes, that complete knowledge is an ideal for man, or in truth, that knowledge for him is possible at all.[2]

[2] H. F. Hallett, *Aeternitas; a Spinozistic Study* (Oxford: The Clarendon Press, 1930).

Thinking cannot be divided. Thoughts are processes, not events, having no definite beginning or end, rising and mutually connected and merging like waves of the sea, a few crashing or lapping on the shores of human consciousness. Thought runs through all things without a break; all things always think. There can never be any lapse from cogitation even for the butterfly or the Sphinx. Again, and more paradoxically, extension cannot be divided.[3]

It is possible to enter into the thoughts and feelings of a philosopher so completely that one speaks in his language, and, in explicating difficulties, produces more utterances in the same tone. This way of exposition is admirably fitted to display a system in all its inner consistency, and to induce in readers a frame of mind similar to that of our philosopher. It is to apply one very important test to a metaphysical system, to exhibit its inner harmony, but this needs to be complemented by another test, the confrontation with fact, or at any rate, with our ordinary ways of referring to facts.

[3] P. H. Nidditch, 'Spinoza', in D. J. O'Connor, *A Critical History of Western Philosophy* (Glencoe: The Free Press); (London: Collier-Macmillan, 1964), p. 195.

Notes on the Second Part
of Spinoza's *Ethics* (I)

H. Barker

§ 1

THE FIRST PART of Spinoza's *Ethics* seems to have attracted an undue amount of attention as compared with the Second Part. The First Part may be said to work out a set of formal determinations applicable to reality as a single whole, without much concern as to what, in actual fact, reality consists of. But as soon as we begin to consider how the actual contents of experience fit into this formal scheme, we have to transfer our attention from generalities about substance and attribute and mode to the actual natures of the two attributes which, according to Spinoza himself, are the only ones we have any acquaintance with. We have to ask what do we find to be the actual facts about these attributes and their modes and about the relations of these attributes and modes, and we then find ourselves involved in questions about knowledge and mind, and the relation of knowledge to its object, and of mind to body, and so on. Now it is the answers that we see ourselves compelled to give about the only two attributes which are known to us, that must determine whether the formal scheme of Part I has any solid basis in experience. It is no use, for example, for Spinoza to lay down the proposition (I, 10) that each attribute *"per se concipi debet"*, if, as soon as we consider the two known attributes, we see that this proposition is not true of them, since thinking and knowledge, as we actually experience them, are directed upon an objective world and depend upon it for their content and existence, while conversely the only extended world known to us is that with which we become acquainted in perception. The doctrine of the complete independence of the attributes is simply not true as regards the only two attributes with which we are acquainted, taken as we actually experience them. It may be objected that to say this is to beg the question against

101

Spinoza, since he conceives the relation of thinking or knowing to
the extended world otherwise. The answer is that Spinoza apparently did not examine for himself this relation, as it is actually
found to be in experience, but simply took over Descartes' dualism
of thought and extension, while we, on the other hand, are not
committed to this dualism, and must examine for ourselves whether
Spinoza's assertions in Part II are true of our actual experience. If
they are not, we must conclude that the formal scheme of Part I,
so far as it cannot be true if they are not, must also be rejected with
them. Thus the philosophical value of Spinoza's metaphysical system really turns much more upon Part II than upon Part I. If Part
II is seriously at fault, much of Part I becomes a mere formal exercise in the working out of the mutual relations of more or less
arbitrary concepts.[1]

The student who tries to arrive at a clear understanding of Spinoza's account of the human mind in Part II has to encounter formidable difficulties; and, if I may judge from my own rather limited
acquaintance with the literature of the subject, he cannot always ob-
tain from the commentators the kind of assistance he needs. In
these Notes I propose to state some of the difficulties as they have
presented themselves to myself. To give a connected criticism of
Spinoza's account one would have to be fairly confident of being
able to take his point of view and see things as he saw them. I am
not confident of being able to do this, so I have preferred to leave
my paper in the form of notes on the difficulties as these arise in
Part II.

It may be objected against this procedure that we cannot profitably discuss one Part of the *Ethics* without reference to the other
Parts or one proposition without reference to the connected series
of propositions to which it belongs. What is true in this objection is
that we cannot profitably discuss Part II without reference to Part
I, or—to state the point in the most definite way—we cannot profitably discuss any later proposition unless we are prepared to take
account of any earlier proposition on which the proof of the later
one depends, and again of any still earlier one on which the proof

---

[1] A very little consideration of the definitions of Part I is enough to show us that,
e.g., the concepts *causa sui, substantia,* and *res libera* reciprocate, while *causa
sui,* etc., and *modus* are mutually exclusive. From such relations between a few
concepts strings of propositions may be derived, as may be seen in the essay
of Avenarius on Spinoza's pantheism, § 18.

of that earlier one depends, and so on, until at last we come, if necessary, to definitions and axioms. But no more than this is required. It is a plain implication of the geometrical method that no later proposition can 'modify' any earlier one in the sense of 'correcting' it[2] and requiring it to be altered; for the earlier one was proved independently of the later one, and therefore the truth of the earlier one cannot be affected by anything which the later one asserts. If we care to use the word 'modify' in the sense of 'substituting more precise statements for vaguer ones'—a substitution which may of course be justified by proving a new proposition—then, no doubt, later propositions may be said to modify earlier ones. A geometer may speak of lines passing through a point in the circumference of a circle, and then show that one and only one of these is a tangent: he can then speak of *the* tangent at that point. Similarly, Spinoza may speak in earlier propositions about substances in the plural, although in a later proposition he claims to show that there is only one substance, namely, the substance which he calls Deus. But his statements about substances or substance-in-general would not be made erroneous by the fact that there was only one thing to which they actually applied. A work such as the *Ethics* in which the geometrical method is used is different in logical character from a modern philosophical work such as Bradley's *Appearance and Reality*, and makes, or implies, assumptions which the modern writer would not make. By adopting the geometrical method Spinoza in effect assumes (1) that certain conceptions applicable to reality can be defined once for all with complete clearness; (2) that certain self-evident truths (e.g., the axioms of Part I) can be stated, and certain unquestionable matters of fact (e.g., '*homo cogitat*', II, axiom 2).[3] In other words, he assumes that he is in possession of premisses so clear and certain in themselves that no other knowledge (and, of course, no consequences deduced from the premisses themselves) can in any way affect their truth. A writer who does not make these assumptions is entitled to say to the reader: "The subject-matter which

---

[2] Joachim (*op. cit.*, p. 123) uses the expressions 'modify' and 'modified form' in a way which seems doubtful.

[3] I do not see that the use of the geometrical method commits Spinoza to anything more than this, e.g., it does not necessarily commit him, as Caird and Joachim seem to think it does, to applying geometrical categories to a non-geometrical subject-matter. By such application of geometrical categories is presumably meant something more than the use of definitions and axioms.

I have to deal with is very complex, and all the parts of it are more or less closely inter-related, but I cannot deal with everything at once. I must start with one part and ignore its relations to some of the others for the time being. Hence my earlier statements must be taken as provisional and liable to qualification, and my final view will only appear in proportion as we are able to survey all the parts of the subject-matter and see them in all their relations to each other". But Spinoza cannot say anything like this, for to say it implies that the geometrical method is not applicable to such a subject-matter.

Spinoza, so far as I can see, takes his geometrical method quite seriously, and does not regard it as a mere expository device. The remark that he used it in expounding views of Descartes with which he did not agree, seems to be sufficiently answered by the consideration that by stating another person's views in such a way as to show the premises from which they would follow Spinoza did not in any way commit himself to accepting these premises themselves. But the fact that he took the trouble to state the views of Descartes in the geometrical method does seem to indicate that he regarded the method as the best way of exhibiting the logical structure of any system of doctrine. That he himself had the fullest confidence in the method as used in expounding his own views seems to me to be shown by the difference in the way in which he replies to different types of objection and criticism on the part of his friends and correspondents. When he thinks that it is popular ideas and prejudices that stand in the way of a right understanding of his views, for example, about the will and freedom, he is willing to explain and argue at great length. But when it is a question about some particular point in the argument of the *Ethics,* he is very ready to assume that his critics have overlooked, or not sufficiently studied, some part of the demonstration, and therefore to content himself with a brief reference back to previous propositions. One may thus easily get the impression that it is the most competent and philosophical of his critics whose difficulties he takes least pains to deal with. Indeed, he seems at times not to see the point, or at any rate not to appreciate the force of their objections; and where this is the case, it is natural to attribute his failure to do so to an over-confidence on his part in the logical strength of his chain of demonstration.

If it ought not to be necessary to study later propositions in the

Ethics in order to understand earlier ones, then *a fortiori* it ought
not to be necessary to go outside the *Ethics* altogether and study
Spinoza's other writings in order to understand the *Ethics*. When
the commentators think it necessary to do so, they are admitting
that Spinoza has not made his meaning clear in the *Ethics*—an admission which he himself was by no means ready to make. There
are two cases, however, in which the expediency of having recourse
to his other writings can be open to no doubt, and in which Spinoza
himself could not but have approved of our doing so. One is the obvious case of the letters in which Spinoza answers difficulties and
criticisms in regard to the *Ethics* put before him by correspondents.
The other case is where Spinoza uses phraseology which might be
clear enough to his contemporaries but is not so to us, and where he
has himself explained it elsewhere, for example, the distinction between *esse formale* and *esse objectivum,* which is explained in the
well-known passage in *de Intellectus Emendatione.*

§ 2: Definition of Adequate Idea (Def. 4)

This definition, left as it is without any explanation, can hardly
but surprise the reader, especially if he remembers that it was an
axiom of Part I that a true idea must agree with its ideatum (I, ax.
6). Here, on the contrary, in defining an adequate idea we are to
consider it in itself apart from its relation to its object. The agreement of the idea with its object or ideatum is disparaged as an extrinsic character, and the adequacy of the idea is made to depend
on the possession of the intrinsic properties of a true idea—by which
properties Spinoza means, no doubt, the clearness and distinctness
of an idea or again the certainty which it carries with it. But it is
difficult to accept these properties as infallible guarantees of truth
or adequacy. It may be true that a false or inadequate idea cannot
really be clear and distinct and cannot *really* carry certainty with it,
but then an idea may *seem* to be clear and distinct when it really is
not, and we may *feel* certain and yet be wrong.

How did Spinoza come to take the view expressed in the definition? There were, it seems to me, two causes, and these acted in
combination: (1) his confused and inconsistent view of the relation
of idea to ideatum; (2) his metaphysical view about the independence of the attributes.

His view of the relation of idea to ideatum is expounded in the passage in *de Int. Em.* already referred to (ed. Bruder II, p. 16, §§ 33 ff.). He there insists that a true idea[4] and its ideatum are two distinct entities; the idea is *diversum quid a suo ideato—omnino diversum,* as he says a little further on. The idea is the *essentia objectiva* of the ideatum, but it is also *in se quid reale* and has its own *esse formale.* Now to say that an idea and its object, idea and ideatum, that is, the having of an object before the mind and the object which the mind has before it, are two distinct entities, of which the one is *omnino diversum* from the other, is against the natural use of language and at once involves us in difficulties; for idea and object, idea and ideatum, are obviously correlatives, the two elements or constituents of a single fact, namely, the ideating or apprehending of an object. To have an idea is to think about an object, to ideate an ideatum. Take away the object or ideatum, and there is nothing left for the ideation to be about. The ideation cannot take place *in vacuo.* An idea is just the ideating of an ideatum, and therefore *not* a *second* entity over and above *its own* ideatum. Spinoza's argument for the distinction in the case of his example of the circle is, that the idea of a circle has not a circumference and a centre as the circle has. This kind of argument has been often repeated since his time, and it may seem, at first sight, profound and convincing, but in reality it is merely confused. What is meant here by the idea? Is it the ideating, the mental event or act or process? But then it is pointless, and indeed absurd, to say that *that* has not a circumference and a centre, for it is not a figure in space at all. On the other, is it the ideatum that is meant, the ideatum which is ideated in the mental act? But *that* is the circle itself and *has* a circumference and a centre, and unless the ideating were the ideating of something that had a circumference and a centre it would not be the ideating of a circle at all.

But it may be objected that the real ground for regarding the idea and the ideatum as two distinct entities is not shown by this case, and can be more easily seen by taking Spinoza's second example. The geometrical circle is an object of thought, and may perhaps be regarded as having no existence outside or apart from thought,[5] but Peter certainly has an existence apart from anybody's idea of him, hence if a person S thinks about Peter, S's idea of Peter

[4] It is important to notice that he is speaking of a *true* idea, for we are thus saved from any complications that might be introduced by error.

[5] Although Spinoza himself speaks of the 'circulus in natura existens' in II, 7 S.

is not Peter himself. Idea and ideatum are clearly two distinct entities here, and the *esse formale* of the idea is by no means the same as the *esse formale* of Peter. The answer to this objection is to be found in recognising that just as the word idea was being misused before by taking it apart from its correlative, the ideatum, so the word ideatum is being misused now by taking it apart from its correlative, the idea or ideating. Peter is not an ideatum in the strict sense of the term, except in so far as he is the object of somebody's ideation. If, then, we want to avoid confusion, we must distinguish between Peter as he is in himself whether anybody is thinking about him or not, Peter as a *res in se* we might perhaps say, and Peter so far as he is the object of somebody's ideation, Peter as a *res ideata*. Then we can say quite truly that S's idea of Peter, that is, what S thinks about Peter, for example, that Peter is a tall man, is precisely identical with Peter as *res ideata*, that is, Peter's being a tall man. On the other hand, if without drawing any distinction we speak of Peter as the ideatum of S's idea, and think at the same time, as we may very naturally do, of Peter rather as *res in se* than as *res ideata*, then of course we must say that S's idea of Peter is *omnino diversum ab ipso Petro*. This way of speaking is very natural for the purposes for which it would ordinarily be used, but the results of using it in psychology and philosophy are disastrous. For, if the ideatum is identified with the *esse formale* of Peter and separated from the idea, we must have a new ideatum (the *essentia objectiva*) to be the immediate or internal object of the idea; for the idea is not bare ideating, and cannot be left empty. The *essentia objectiva* is then a mental duplicate of the *essentia formalis* (or of part of it) and, as Spinoza himself says, it must *omnino convenire cum sua essentia formali*. It is *diversum quid* in so far as it is a mental entity and Peter a bodily one, but in every other respect there must be a point to point correspondence between the *essentia objectiva* and the *essentia formalis*, otherwise the idea will not be true.[6]

The doctrine of the attributes may now conveniently be brought in. The sharp separation which Spinoza has made between the es-

---

[6] I need hardly dwell on the inconsistencies in which Spinoza is thus involved. Suppose the circle of the first example to be a circle drawn on paper. The *essentia objectiva* cannot be something drawn on paper, but, contrary to what Spinoza affirmed, it must have a circumference and a centre, otherwise it will not be the *essentia objectiva* of a circle, and thus there must be an extended image in the mind to represent the extended figure on the paper.

sentiae objectivae of extended things[7] and the extended things themselves connects at once with the view that they belong to different attributes and can have no relation to each other but that of correspondence. To know an extended thing can no longer mean to have it immediately present to the mind's apprehension; the meaning can only be that in the mind there is an *essentia objectiva* to which the *esse formale* of an extended thing in the attribute of extension corresponds. The existence of the extended thing is really inferred in virtue of the doctrine of attributes: we have in unextended thought the *essentia objectiva* of an extended thing—a mystery which may here be passed over—and *therefore* there must exist in the attribute of extension the extended thing itself which corresponds to the idea; as Spinoza says in I, 30: *id quod in intellectu objective continetur debet necessario in natura dari.* We can now see how Spinoza is compelled to define an adequate or true idea by means of some intrinsic character. An idea is an affair of thought and is shut up in that attribute; it cannot wander out and compare itself with its extended ideatum; it can only try to make sure that it is as clear and distinct as possible in itself, and, if it is certain of itself, it will then be entitled (or inspired) to be certain of the existence of its extended ideatum.[8]

It may be worth while, even at the cost of a little repetition, to consider shortly a re-statement of Spinoza's view about idea and ideatum by a recent writer who appears to be a wholehearted follower and defender of the philosopher. "If we use the terms 'subject' and 'object' in their modern sense", says this writer,[9] "we may say that Thought 'includes' Extension and Extension 'includes' Thought only in the sense that Extension is the ultimate 'object' (= *ideatum*) of all *our* Thought and Thought the essential 'subject' (= *essentia objectiva*) of Extension. . . . But from this it cannot follow that Extension is *existentially* included in Thought, for so Thought would not *know* its object, but would contain or possess

---

[7] I am not concerned here with the *essentia objectiva* of an idea (the *idea ideae*), but of course Spinoza—consistently in one way, inconsistently in another—does not make a sharp separation in that case.

[8] Spinoza seems thus to be involved in circular reasoning. Before he can assert the correspondence between ideas and extended things, he must know that the extended things which are the *ideata* of the ideas exist *in natura,* and yet he knows this only because he assumes that ideas must have *ideata* corresponding to them.

[9] Hallett, in his book, *Aeternitas*, pp. 291 ff.

it; [nor] that Thought is *existentially* included in Extension, for so Extension would have no 'subject' or correlative consciousness; and in each case knowledge would be impossible". In the first sentence the writer puts the word 'includes' in inverted commas—presumably in order to warn us that it is being used metaphorically; but he unfortunately continues to use it (without even the inverted commas) instead of substituting some less misleading phrase. What could be meant by speaking of Thought as included in Extension I do not know;[10] but if we speak of Extension as existentially included in Thought, what we ought to mean is simply that extended things can be and are present to the mind as its immediate objects.[11] If this is denied, then some other immediate objects must be provided to take their place as proxies, by means of which the not immediately present extended things are 'known' (or from which they are inferred). Accordingly we find the writer going on to say: "the object which is *included in* knowledge[12] (i.e., the 'objective content' of the idea) cannot be identical with the object (i.e., the thing) which is *known through* knowledge". What precisely this 'objective content' is we are not told, but it must be involved in the same difficulties as Spinoza's *essentia objectiva*. If existentially different from the thing known (*diversum quid*) it must none the less be qualitatively similar (*debet omnino convenire cum sua essentia formali*), for example, it must have an extensional character, otherwise it could not be the means through which we know the extended things that are not experienced by us, not 'included in' knowledge, not the immediate objects of knowledge. Finally we are told that there is no "third real *interpositum*" between the thought or knowing and the thing known. The "object *contained* by thought is an abstract *ens rationis* (= objective content of thought) and is no real separate existent, being real only in its relation to the equally abstract act of knowing (= subjective content of thought), by which relation

[10] The two cases of 'inclusion' are treated as if they were parallel, but they are not. Thought must include an object of some sort, otherwise it would be empty and null; but there is no *obvious* reason why an extended *res in se* should be the object of a mind or consciousness. *We*, of course, must start from *res ideatae*, but we have to recognise that there may (and in a sense, must) exist *res* which are *non-ideatae*, so far as we are concerned. Whether these last can be shown to be necessarily *ideatae* by some other mind or minds than ours is a question which can hardly be decided by Spinoza's methods.

[11] Not 'ultimate' objects—whatever that means.

[12] 'Included in knowledge' = known?

concrete thought is constituted; it thus falls on the side of the subject." It is not necessary to comment in detail on these statements,[13] for the real point is the 'objective content' or 'object contained in thought' is a useless duplicate of the object known. We may as well apprehend the thing itself immediately as apprehend it by means of another object 'contained in thought'. When we remove the metaphorical phrase 'contained in thought'—which really adds nothing to the word object, if the object is contained *as an object*—then it is plain that two objects are said to be before the mind when in fact it is aware only of one.

§ 3: *Cogitatio* and *Res Cogitans* (II, 1–3)

The first two propositions of Part II assert that *Cogitatio* and *Extensio* are attributes of Deus or that Deus is both *res cogitans* and *res extensa*. It is unfortunate (though perhaps unavoidable) that Spinoza should have used the word Deus as he did; it is still more unfortunate that his translators and commentators have acquiesced in his misuse of the word by using the ordinary equivalent of it in their own language; for the 'Deus' of Spinoza is not the 'God' of ordinary linguistic usage. Whether Spinoza himself was able to use the Latin word without being in any way influenced by its ordinary associations, I will not undertake to say. But I think it is extremely difficult for the English reader (even, for that matter, when he is using the Latin text) to avoid being influenced and really misled by the ordinary associations of the word 'God'; for example, being accustomed to the notions of the divine mind and divine omniscience he will be apt to accept corresponding expressions in the *Ethics* without inquiring as closely as he ought to do into their meaning and warrant on Spinoza's view, or, to put the same point in another way, he will be less critical about the notion of Deus as *res cogitans* than he is about the notion of Deus as *res extensa*. For this reason I propose to avoid the words Deus or God as much as possible, and to use the word Natura, which Spinoza himself uses as an equivalent for his Deus. It may be objected that we shall then be misled by the associations of the English word 'nature', which so often means the

---

[13] The writer seems to be modernising. Spinoza does not distinguish an objective and a subjective content, though he thinks of ideas as formed by the mind's action (II, def. 3). His *essentia objectiva* is *in se quid reale,* and can be itself the object of another idea as its own ideatum is an object for it.

material world only. But we do often use the word 'Nature' (with a capital N) in a much wider sense, and indeed in a sense which is comparable with that in which Spinoza uses 'Natura', and, perhaps, by using always the Latin form of the word we may be sufficiently reminded that it is the 'Natura' of Spinoza that we are dealing with.

Our two propositions, then, will now be expressed in the form that *Cogitatio* and *Extensio* are attributes of Natura or that Natura is both *res cogitans* and *res extensa*. The proof of the propositions runs on the following lines: Particular things such as *cogitationes* and *corpora* are modes of the one substance Natura. Hence, corresponding to each distinct type or class of modes there must be in Natura some fundamental type of being of which the modes of that type are the particular modifications—in Spinoza's language, an attribute, the conception of which is involved in the modes, or in terms of which they must be conceived. Now the application of this proof to the case of Extension raises no difficulty. Particular material bodies are configurations in space: they presuppose the space which they fill and cannot be conceived except as occupying space.[14] Space itself has a nature of its own apart from those particular configurations in it: it is continuous, infinite, and three-dimensional. Space, then, is that in which the particular configurations become possible, the ὕλη to which they give specific forms.

But when we attempt to understand the proof in its application to *Cogitatio*, difficulties present themselves at once. In II, ax. 3 Spinoza asserts that the idea or, as we may say, 'ideation',[15] is the primary *modus cogitandi*: it may be the *whole* content or process of *cogitatio* and can stand alone, whereas all other modes, such as *amor* and *cupiditas* and in general the feelings (*affectus*) imply and depend upon the ideas of their objects. It will simplify our argument, then, if we consider *cogitatio*, in the first instance, as if it consisted of ideas or ideation alone, since, according to Spinoza, it might do so. Now when we consider *cogitatio* as ideation, we see that there is nothing which stands to particular ideas in a relation similar to that in which space stands to particular bodies. There is no entity *Cogi-*

---

[14] I do not mean that Spinoza's Extension is to be simply identified with space; but it is that, whatever more it may be, and space is enough for the purpose of the argument.

[15] 'Ideation', not in the modern psychological usage in which it is connected specially with imagery and contrasted with 'perception' and 'intellection', but as the correlative of Spinoza's 'idea'.

tatio or ideation of which the particular ideas are the specific forms. Ideation is merely a general term for the having of ideas. We have Spinoza's own authority for saying so: for in II, 48, S, he insists that *intellectus* (= our ideation) is related to this or that idea as *lapideitas* is related to this or that stone and *homo* to this or that man. But if *Cogitatio* or ideation is only a general term, it is not a real entity, not an attribute (or *substantia,* as Spinoza would at one time have called it). It may perhaps be objected that there *is* a fundamental common character in all ideations, namely, awareness, the awareness of an object. The answer is that awareness is nothing in itself, it must be an awareness 'of' something, of some object. When you take away the particular configurations from space, space itself remains. But when you take away particular objects from awareness, nothing remains, for there cannot be an awareness which is an awareness of nothing, nor is there any object-in-general of which particular objects are the specific forms. We are dealing again with mere general terms, not real entities.[16]

The above criticism was put quite clearly to Spinoza by de Vries (Ep. 26 in Bruder II = VV. 8). *"Remotis ab ea* [i.e., *a cogitatione*] *omnibus ideis, cogitationem destrui necessum est,"* he says. Spinoza seems to have completely missed the point of the criticism. Obviously what de Vries meant was, that if you take away ideas from *Cogitatio,* there is nothing left; *cogitatio* is not anything substantive of which ideas are the modes. But Spinoza seems to have thought that de Vries was trying to think about *cogitatio* without using ideas, to think with an empty mind: *dum tu,* he says, *res scilicet cogitans, id facis* [viz., think about *cogitatio*], *omnes tuas cogitationes et conceptus seponis. Quare non mirum est, quod ubi omnes tuas cogitationes seposuisti, nihil postea tibi cogitandum supersit.* But de Vries,

---

[16] In a letter to Arnauld (quoted in Robinson's *Kommentar zu Spinozas Ethik,* p. 37) Descartes compares *Cogitatio* with *Extensio,* and, strangely enough, affirms in so many words the very points in which the comparison does *not* hold good: "Ut enim extensio, quae constituit naturam corporis, multum differt a variis figuris sive extensionis modis, quos induit; ita cogitatio, sive natura cogitans, in qua puto mentis humanae essentiam constituere, longe aliud est, quam hic vel ille actus cogitandi. . . . Per cogitationem igitur non intelligo universale quid, omnes cogitandi modos comprehendens, sed naturam particularem, quae recipit omnes illos modos, ut etiam extensio est natura, quae recipit omnes figuras." It would have been interesting to be told exactly what was meant by the "longe aliud etc." and the "naturam particularem".

of course, was not trying to think with an empty mind, but trying to think what would be left of *cogitatio* if *it* were emptied of ideas, and the answer is: nothing, therefore not an attribute or a substance. In I, 5 Spinoza invites us to consider a substance *'depositis affectionibus'*, which we can do, he says, because substance is *prior natura suis affectionibus*. Now an attribute is in the same sense prior to its modes, and we can therefore state the difficulty which de Vries felt by saying, that he found *cogitatio, depositis affectionibus et in se considerata,* to be simply nothing at all. It was not the case that de Vries had put away all *his* ideas, for he was thinking about *cogitatio* and *its* relation to *ideae,* and therefore had quite definite things to think about. His point was that when he did think about *cogitatio,* and tried to think what would be left of it when all particular ideas had been removed, he found that nothing at all would be left. There was *nihil cogitandum* left, not because he had emptied his mind of ideas, but because *cogitatio* without any object of cogitation is a nonentity.[17]

So far we have been considering *Cogitatio* as if it consisted of ideation only, but we have now to take account of feeling, and it may be said that, since *Cogitatio* covers both ideation and feeling, we must translate the term by some English term, such as 'consciousness', that covers both, and it may then be argued that consciousness in relation to the modes of *cogitatio* is what space is in relation to the modes of *extensio,* the ὕλη of which particular ideas and feelings are the specific forms. In other words, consciousness is a sort of mental stuff, of which ideas and feelings are the two kinds. But this notion of consciousness as the common basis of ideation and feeling is

---

[17] It may be objected from Spinoza's point of view that there cannot be modes which are not the modes of an attribute (i.e., of something substantive). But this objection assumes that the notion of attribute can be applied in exactly the same sense to *Cogitatio* as to *Extensio;* and this is plainly not the case, since *Cogitatio* consists primarily in a *knowing* of *other* attributes, e.g., *Extensio,* whereas *Extensio* is a kind of being that is not a knowing, i.e., does not involve any reference to other attributes; and therefore it may be substantive in a sense in which *Cogitatio* may not be. It is a radical error on Spinoza's part that he tries to treat *Cogitatio* as if it were exactly like any other attribute, although he cannot really ignore the quite peculiar cognitive function which is of its very essence. He treats it sometimes as if it were mere being (like *Extensio*), sometimes as if it were a being that is a knowing, and thus involves himself in radical inconsistency.

due simply to the ambiguity of the word. When we speak of ideation as consciousness, we mean by this latter term consciousness 'of'
something, awareness of an object, but when we apply the term to
feeling we mean merely that the feeling *is felt,* not that it is the feeling *'of'* something. Where the feeling is related to an object, there,
as Spinoza rightly says, an idea is present; in *amor* and *cupiditas*
there must be the idea of what is loved or desired. If feeling is taken
in abstraction from all ideas, it may be regarded as a mental stuff;
but then it simply exists or is felt. But ideation or awareness of
objects is not a mental stuff: the stuff of ideas is their objects. Why
is it, then, that psychologists and Spinoza (when he is talking about
the *esse formale* of ideas) regard ideas as a mental stuff? In the case
of the psychologists it is because they either in effect accept a doctrine of representative perception, or else start from a confused kind
of realism, in which they think of *objects* as first existing apart from
'consciousness' and then entering into consciousness or having it
added to them, so that the total mental fact is consciousness + its
objects. Whereas the real state of the case is that we start from the
awareness of objects and are driven to think of the objects (or some
of them) as things that still exist when they are not objects present
to our minds. In Spinoza's case, it is because he starts from a rigid
dualism of the attributes, and therefore must give the ideas an *esse
formale* of their own, and must hold a representative doctrine of
perception.

When ideas are regarded both as knowledges of objects and as a
mental stuff, or rather, when they are regarded sometimes as the one
and sometimes as the other—for it is not really possible to regard
them at one and the same time as both—we are naturally involved
in a serious confusion, and this confusion, it seems to me, is one of
the difficulties in the way of understanding how exactly Spinoza conceived his *Res Cogitans.* But before going on to discuss this latter
question, the second proof of Prop. 1 has still to be considered. We
are able to conceive, says Spinoza, an *ens cogitans infinitum,* and
since Deus or Natura (by definition) includes all the attributes or
infinite types of being, this *ens cogitans infinitum* must be one of
them. Is Spinoza entitled to assume so easily that we can conceive
an *ens cogitans infinitum?* No doubt we can think of the cogitation
of a finite *ens cogitans* being indefinitely extended, in proportion
as it *plura potest cogitare,* but the step from *plura* to *infinita* surely
needs to be taken with more caution. In I, 17 S Spinoza, according

to the interpretation which so far saves his consistency,[18] argued that, *if* we hold intellect (and will) to belong to Deus as *attribute,* then we must also admit that such intellect must be quite different from our own. For our intellect is usually conceived as receptive, that is, as posterior to the things it apprehends, whereas an intellect that belonged to the very essence of Deus, to *Natura naturans,* would be creative. Now surely such an argument applies just as well to *cogitatio* as to intellect; in fact, it is difficult to see how Spinoza is able to distinguish *cogitatio* from *intellectus* in the case of Deus, since Deus is *expers passionum*—in the demonstration of I, 31 Spinoza seems to have overlooked this—and in our present Scholium to II, 1 it is surely intellect he has in view when he uses a phrase like '*quo plura ens cogitans potest cogitare*'. On his own showing, then, the step from *plura* to *infinita* is not so simple as he here represents it to be, for it may involve a qualitative difference, not a mere quantitative extension. But what he does not seem to see, even in I, 17 S, is that the qualitative difference may amount to the disappearance of intellect or knowledge *as intellect or knowledge* altogether, since the ground which the finite intellect has for distinguishing between its knowledge and the things it knows—namely, the fact that the things known are known only incompletely and therefore have an existence that extends beyond their existence as known objects—is removed in the case of an infinite intellect. Such an intellect could not distinguish between what was known to it and anything else, since there would be nothing which it did not know. And for the same reason it could not distinguish between what was known to it and its knowledge, for there would be no point at which, for it, the distinction between being in itself and being as known could arise. And again for the same reason we must dismiss the *idea Dei*[19] of Props. 3 and 4 regarded as an idea standing side by side, so to speak, with its ideatum; for in the nature of the case there would be no means of distinguishing here between *esse objectivum* and *esse formale.* The idea would contain 'objectively' the whole of Natura and nothing but Natura and therefore could not distinguish itself from Natura; nor is it possible to see by what addition Natura could be given a 'formal' existence beyond its 'objective' existence in the

[18] See Robinson, *Kommentar,* ad loc.
[19] We are not here concerned with any distinction between the *idea Dei* and the *intellectus infinitus* other than that the latter is the faculty of which the former is the object.

idea. In the case of Natura to think and to be would have to be the same thing.[20]

We are thus brought again to the difficulty of understanding how Spinoza did conceive his *Res Cogitans*. As I cannot profess to have made out satisfactorily how he did, I cannot, in discussing the topic, distinguish clearly between the question of fact or interpretation and the question of what is tenable or would have been reasonable for Spinoza to hold. As we have just seen, his view of the *Res Cogitans* seems far from consistent. He distinguishes it from the *intellectus infinitus,* although knowledge seems the only kind of cogitation appropriate to it. And he relegates the *intellectus infinitus* to *Natura naturata,* although the *Cogitatio* of *Natura naturans* could then, it would seem, be only a power of generating the contents of the *intellectus infinitus,* this so-called 'power' being an empty expression which tells us nothing. One cannot altogether avoid subtleties of this sort, but I do not wish to refer to them more than is absolutely necessary, and will therefore treat *Res Cogitans* and *intellectus infinitus* for the most part as equivalent expressions, although strictly they are not so for Spinoza himself. I will now state three views of the *Res Cogitans* any one of which might be taken at first sight to be a possible view, but all of which seem to involve serious difficulties either in themselves or when compared with definite statements of Spinoza's.

1. Part II is concerned with the human mind and, as is obvious from ax. 2, regards it as an *ens cogitans.* Therefore when Spinoza speaks of *Deus* as *ens cogitans infinitum,* it is natural to think of the *Res Cogitans* as a divine mind analogous to the human mind, but freed from the finite limitations of the latter. Now when we think of a human mind, we think of its ideas or knowledges as the knowledges of an individual, a psychological 'subject', a person who is aware of his own unity and identity in his mental life as he lives it. The ideas or knowledges are the ideas or knowledges of a thinker or knower, and this subject or person is always implied even when not expressly referred to. In like manner, when we think of a divine mind, we can preserve the analogy with the human mind only if we

[20] The phrase *idea Dei* as used by Spinoza necessarily introduces an ambiguity into the term *Deus.* For we can say that the *idea Dei* (1) is itself *in Deo* (2). Here *Deus* (1) = the attributes *other than* Thought, but *Deus* (2) = the one substance with all its attributes, but regarded *with special reference to* the attribute of Thought.

think of the divine mind as implying a subject or personal centre of unity. Did Spinoza think of his *Res Cogitans* in this way? I suppose it would be pretty widely agreed that he did not. (Indeed, it might even be questioned whether he thinks of the human mind itself in this way, although he could not but use language which ought to mean that he does.) We regard a man as being essentially a psychological subject or person, but Spinoza's Deus or Natura is expressed indifferently in all the attributes alike. Hence his Deus is described by one commentator as the active inner force[21] which generates, or expresses itself in, all the manifold particular contents of the infinitely many attributes. This description may not convey Spinoza's view accurately, but it suggests the important point that Natura is not pre-eminently a mind or person. Natura is just as much *Res Extensa* as *Res Cogitans*. Again, particular *cogitationes* are all modes of the one attribute *Cogitatio*, but we could hardly say that they are all the thoughts of a single person. The *Res Cogitans* or *intellectus infinitus* may rather be said to generate, or to include, the particular *cogitationes*. According to Spinoza's own statement (II, 11 C) the *intellectus infinitus* includes human minds as parts of itself. We must add that for that very reason it cannot be a mind in the sense in which they are minds; for the parts of an individual mind are thoughts, not other individual minds. This consideration seems to be decisive, though I do not say that it would have been a decisive consideration for Spinoza. We should probably express Spinoza's view better by saying that in any sense in which the *intellectus infinitus* is a unity or whole, human minds cannot be genuine unities or wholes, since they are mere parts of the *intellectus infinitus*. But on either way of stating the matter the analogy between the human mind and Spinoza's *Res Cogitans* or *intellectus infinitus* breaks down, and it was upon that analogy that our first view of the *Res Cogitans* turned.

Perhaps I ought to explain more fully why I say that finite minds cannot be existentially parts of an infinite mind. I do not mean that the contents of a mind are necessarily private to it. There is no reason why two minds should not apprehend the same thing, and no reason why an omniscient mind (if such a mind exists) should not

---

[21] Camerer, p. 2: 'Naturkraft', 'die innere Lebenskraft der Welt und nichts weiter.' Avenarius, p. 56, is even stronger in his expressions; the God of the *Ethics* is 'ein blindes Wesen, das ohne Willen und ohne Verstand einzig nach dem starren Gesetz seiner Nothwendigkeit wirkt.'

apprehend all that finite minds apprehend. The point is that just because an infinite or omniscient mind, in apprehending what the finite mind apprehends, apprehends it *in relation to all other knowledge,* its apprehension can never coincide with the finite apprehension. The infinite mind may apprehend the same objects but must apprehend them as modified by their relation to all other objects. The infinite mind may even apprehend the way in which the finite mind must apprehend *its* finite objects, but the infinite mind cannot *exist* in the finite state of apprehension, since it cannot empty itself of its other knowledge. We do not get rid of this existential difference by saying that finiteness is merely negative; for the point is that, for lack of the knowledge which it does not possess, the finite apprehension is other than it would be if that knowledge were present. The same line of reasoning is, of course, equally fatal to what I suggested as the more Spinozistic way of stating the matter. The only way in which we can have both finite minds and an infinite or omniscient mind is by taking them as distinct existences, and Spinoza could not do this; even an omniscient mind would not then be infinite in his sense of the term.

It would seem that Spinoza cannot escape the above difficulty on any view of his *intellectus infinitus.* For in the human mind there are inadequate or false ideas, whereas in the *intellectus infinitus* there are only true ideas. To say that all ideas are true, *quatenus ad Deum referuntur* (II, 32) is a mere evasion, since it means that an inadequate idea *taken otherwise than it is in the mind that thinks it* is true, or, in other words, that its inadequacy is causally necessitated (cf. reference to II, 7 C), though not seen to be so.

It should also be observed that the difficulty does not arise in the case of *Res Extensa,* for space is everywhere the same in character; smaller spaces differ from larger ones only in magnitude, and there is nothing to prevent us from regarding all spaces as parts of one infinite space.

2. It is a familiar criticism upon Spinoza that he confuses the relation of cause and effect with that of ground and consequence, or that he resolves the former into the latter, or even that he ignores or rejects the former altogether.[22] Now it may be admitted that he does not sufficiently distinguish the two relations. But it is to be re-

---

[22] Joachim (p. 54 n) goes so far as to say: "the term 'causa', in its more ordinary meaning, has no place in Spinoza's Philosophy, nor does he intend it to be understood in a sense implying temporal sequence."

membered that they do have something in common; they are both forms of *necessary* connection. Moreover, causal connection, however obscure it may be to us, might be *seen* to be necessary by an intelligence not subject to the limitations of our finitude. In the case of geometrical entities—of which Spinoza speaks as if he attributed to them existence *in natura* (e.g., II, 7 S, I, 11 dem. 2)—even we have insight, for example, into the connection of the properties of a triangle with the nature or definition of the triangle. Nevertheless Spinoza was quite well aware that we cannot see directly how a given finite mode is connected with the attribute to which it belongs. What we can assert (I, 28) is that any one finite mode must be determined as regards its existence and operation by another finite mode, and so on *in infinitum*. Now, when Spinoza had in view this series of finite modes, each coming into existence, lasting for a time, and then ceasing to exist, he surely must have thought of the relation of cause and effect in its ordinary sense. The determination of finite modes in such a series is a necessary determination, but the necessity is for us unintelligible, since we are referred back from mode to mode indefinitely and can never see, with full comprehension, *how* any particular mode is necessitated to be what it is. I suppose Spinoza would have allowed that we can be confident as a matter of experience that a particular effect in the physical world was determined by a particular cause; but such empirical assurance would for him be very different from an insight into the dependence of that particular determination on the structure of the physical world as a whole. We must say, then, it seems to me, that Spinoza was aware of the difference between the apprehension of a causal relationship without insight into its ultimate nature and the apprehension of, or insight into, the way in which a consequence follows from its ground. The physical world is known to our finite minds by means of the former kind of apprehension, not the latter; consequently it is *for us* a mere chain of causes and effects or a complex of such chains.

Now did Spinoza think of minds or a psychical world in the same way? According to the doctrine of the parallelism of the attributes he ought to have done so, and he does expressly repeat in II, 9 as regards ideas the proposition which he laid down in I, 28 as regards finite modes in general. In that case the connection between ideas would be a mere connection of cause and effect, as unintelligible to us in the world of mind as the connection of the corresponding physical modes is in the physical world. Ideas (and minds) would be bits of a mental stuff as the physical modes are of a physical stuff, and the pattern of the mental stuff would copy or be identical with the pattern of the physical stuff. We have to remember also that Spinoza boldly asserts in II, 13 S that *omnia (individua)*—not merely human *individua*—*quamvis diversis gradibus animata sunt,* that is, all bodies, not merely human or animal bodies, have minds. All these minds would presumably be (like human minds) parts of the *intellectus infinitus* or *Res Cogitans,* which would thus consist of an infinite continuum of mental stuff corresponding to the infinite continuum of corporeal stuff which makes up the content of *Extensio* or *Res Extensa.* Can such a construction represent Spinoza's conception of the *Res Cogitans?* I can hardly believe so.

But it must be allowed that some of the obvious objections which *we* should bring against such a view, objections based on our ordinary interpretation of our experience, would not have weighed with Spinoza. One such objection is that we have no reason to believe that *all* bodies have minds; on the contrary, there are manifest differences between those bodies to which we attribute minds, and bodies which are not endowed even with life, while even among living bodies we attribute mind to animals only and not to plants. But Spinoza was not the kind of thinker to be troubled by the lack of empirical evidence, as we may see from his assertion that Natura has an infinity of attributes, although by his own admission only two are actually known to us. A second objection is even more formidable. In the case of the minds about which we know most, human minds, there appears to be no such complete continuity as Spinoza's theory demands. Such mind as a human being may have in his earliest infancy is nothing to boast of; judged by behaviour, his mind would appear to be in the merest beginning of existence, and it grows gradually. On the death of the body the mind, to all appearance, ceases altogether to exist. That is to say, the human mind appears not to be continuous with any mental existence outside its own term of life. The materials of the body continue to exist after its death, but to suggest that anything analogous happens in the case of the mind would seem to be using language without meaning. Even within its own term of life the existential continuity of the mind's actual 'cogitation' is interrupted, for example, in deep sleep and other unconscious states. Moreover, its continuity is constantly being interrupted by new sense experiences which are not caused by anything in the immediately preceding mental state. Finally, one mind is not in any direct continuity with other contemporary minds, since minds communicate with each other only by the instrumentality of their bodies. Of some of these facts Spinoza, so far as I know, takes no account, but to judge from the little he does say in his *Short Treatise* about the first mentioned ones (KV, II, Praef. note 10) he would be quite ready to override the apparent facts with *a priori* speculations.

But there is another kind of objection which can find a basis in Spinoza's own doctrine. In treating the mind as so much mental stuff we have eliminated or denied its cognitive function. Mental stuff (e.g., mere feeling) may exist, but it cannot be true or false, and if an idea is merely a copy in mental stuff of a pattern existing in physical stuff it is not a knowledge: to possess a photograph of an ancient MS. or inscription is not to be able to read it. Moreover, the degree of accuracy or inaccuracy in the copy or photograph can be judged only by a knowing mind able to compare them with their originals. One copy may be defective and another complete, but the defects of the defective copy will be visible only to a mind that has fuller knowledge and is able to see them.[23] Now there is far too much in Spinoza about knowledge and the truth and falsity of ideas to allow us to be satisfied with a conception of the *intellectus infinitus* or *Res Cogitans* which makes these things simply impossible.

3. Are we, then, to reverse our procedure, start from truth and knowledge, and try to interpret the *intellectus infinitus* by reference to them? Can we regard the *intellectus infinitus* as the complete system or whole of truth, while finite minds are those fragmentary parts of it which at a given time actually exist (i.e., are being thought) in the same way as the corresponding finite bodies are those parts or configurations of the attribute of Extension which actually exist at that time? Such a view may seem strange to us, but it might not have seemed so strange to Spinoza. For it may be questioned whether he distinguished as sharply as we do between truth and existence. In the case of existence that is not subject to temporal

---

[23] In the place (II, 43 S) where Spinoza insists that *veritas* is *norma sui et falsi* he also repudiates the copy view and says that an idea is not like a picture; to have an idea is to apprehend or know. But is the *essentia objectiva*, then, a mere act of apprehension, or is it *in se quid reale* as we are told in *de Int. Em.*? In II, 43 S *idea* = *intelligere*, in *de Int. Em. idea* = *per se aliquid intelligibile*. Which is it?

limitations he is ready to describe such existence as an eternal truth, and we may perhaps infer that eternal truths (properly so-called— see Ep. 28 in Bruder II = VV, 10) in some sense exist.[24] The ideas of things that are subject to temporal limitations exist (i.e., are thought) only so far as the things exist; but then these ideas are fragmentary and, at least in some measure, defective or erroneous, and it is only what is true in them[25] that is really included in the *intellectus infinitus*. Some parts of Spinoza's doctrine seem to be better understood on such a view, for example, II, 8. Its strangeness to us is probably due to the fact that we come to it with preconceptions. We think of truth as existing only in the true thoughts of particular thinkers or minds, whereas Spinoza seems to think of eternal truths as having some higher or more real existence; and again, we think of the knower or mind as the really existing thing and his true thoughts as mere states of his mind, whereas Spinoza seems to resolve the mind into ideas, and, when he wants to speak of it as a unity or whole, calls it the idea (in the singular) which constitutes (or is) the human mind.

I do not say, however, that this third view is Spinoza's, for, in the first place, it conflicts with the conception of the sequence of ideas as a mere causal sequence of events parallel to the sequence of bodily events. A sequence or connection of knowledges must be in some manner a logical sequence, and Spinoza does sometimes imply, however inconsistently, that the sequence of ideas is logical. Secondly, the view involves a dualism within the attribute of *Cogitatio* between truth and psychical existence, and the *intellectus infinitus* would seem to be either not wholly actual or else actual in two diverse ways. I suppose questions about eternal and temporal existence might come in here, but if so I cannot discuss them.

I am unable, then, to make out what Spinoza's own conception of the *Res Cogitans* really was, and can only suggest that he must have thought on the lines, sometimes of the second view, sometimes of the third, without realising their inconsistency.

(To be continued.)

[24] 'Unter einer ewigen Wahrheit versteht Spinoza nicht bloss einen ewigen Gedanken, sondern auch eine ewige Realität'—Camerer, p. 24.

[25] II, 43 S at end: *mens nostra, quatenus res vere percipit, pars est infiniti Dei intellectus*. We are referred to II, 11 C, but there the limiting clause *quatenus,* etc., does not appear, and in II, 32 and 36 we are told that *all* ideas, *quatenus ad Deum referunter,* are true. The question of consistency must in the meantime be passed over.

Notes on the Second Part
of Spinoza's *Ethics* (II)

H. Barker

§ 4: Parallelism of the Attributes (II, 7)

O N ANY INTERPRETATION of Spinoza's metaphysical doctrine
the seventh proposition of Part II is a proposition of the highest
importance, but on the interpretation which I believe to be, on the
whole, the right one, the seventh proposition becomes the most
important proposition in the whole book. Spinoza at one time, as we
know, used the term substance to denote what in the *Ethics* he calls
attribute, so that, instead of saying that the one and only substance
has infinitely many attributes, he could then have said that Natura
consists of infinitely many substances. Robinson takes this earlier
phraseology as the clue to the interpretation of the metaphysical
doctrine of the *Ethics,* and insists again and again that Spinoza's
doctrine is not an Identitätsphilosophie; that is to say, the one and
only substance has no *underlying identical nature,* which is only
manifested in different ways in the attributes, but, on the contrary,
its whole nature is contained and expressed in the different attributes, and the unity of these different expressions consists solely in
the sameness or parallelism of the *order and connexion* of the modes
of the several attributes: the unity of substance or Natura consists in
this, that a single Weltgesetz or order prevails throughout all the
infinitely many attributes.

Now there is one obvious merit of this interpretation: it gets rid
of a contradiction in the language used by the commentators about
the substance and attributes of the *Ethics* which cannot but strike
us as soon as our attention is called to it. The commentators have to
say that the substance is one and the same, that the attributes are
entirely different from each other, and yet that the attributes constitute the essence of the substance. How one and the same substance
can have infinitely many different essences is a puzzle indeed. The
trouble goes back to Spinoza himself. In the scholium to II, 7 his

123

language parades the contradiction before our eyes: *substantia cogitans et substantia extensa una eademque est substantia, quae jam sub hoc jam sub illo attributo comprehenditur.* Even if this statement is not to be taken as asserting that two substances are one and the same substance, it does at any rate assert that the substance which cogitates is one and the same substance as that which is extended, although he has said in the immediately preceding proposition that the attributes are wholly distinct, while by definition, as we know, *each* of them *constitutes* the essence of substance. Wherein can the *identity* of the *substantia cogitans* and the *substantia extensa* consist? Not in an identity of *essence,* for the two essences are wholly distinct. In what, then? Further on in the scholium the identity is apparently asserted to consist (as Robinson maintains it does) in the *ordo* or *connexio causarum.*

When the commentators follow, as it is only natural they should do, the emphatic language used at the beginning of the scholium, they are involved in the same inconsistencies and straining of language. For example, Pollock (ed. 2, p. 152) says: "If we think of Spinoza's Substance as distinct from and underlying the Attributes . . . we shall certainly go wrong." But next he says, "Substance is indeed manifested in the Attributes"; only, however, to retract the word 'manifested' by adding that "The manifestations are themselves the reality". Again, he suggests 'aspect' as the least unsatisfactory description of an attribute, whereas one would think that that word suggests the very ideas he wants to reject, namely, that the distinction between the attributes is superficial, due to the spectators' point of view, and that there is no real plurality in the substance itself. On page 156 he speaks of the attributes as expressing 'the very same reality', but as 'differing in kind', though repeating 'the same order and sequence'. Joachim (p. 25) says: "It is one and the same Reality which manifests both characters (i.e., Thought and Extension)"—a phraseology which would naturally suggest some distinction between the Reality and the 'characters' which it 'manifests'. But we are told later (pp. 66–67) that "The Attributes . . . are not consequences of God's nature—they *are* that nature: and each Attribute expresses the whole nature of God under some one of its ultimate characters". It is surely obvious to remark that, if the attributes *are* that nature and are *all equally* 'essential to Reality' 'necessary to its being' (p. 26), no *one* of them can express the *whole* nature of God or Reality.

I have thought it worth while to give these quotations in order to show into what straits the commentators are brought when they attempt to expound a combination of three inconsistent doctrines: (1) that the substance consists of the attributes, (2) that the substance is one, (3) that the attributes are many and all wholly different from each other. No ingenuity and no straining of language are equal to the task. The other interpretation, whatever criticism it may itself be open to, does not at any rate land us in a situation which is quite obviously hopeless.

I will take one more quotation, because it may be used to bring out a new point. On page 148 Joachim says: "an idea is at once identical with its 'ideatum', and absolutely distinct from it". How was it possible to make a statement that appears to be flatly contradictory? The explanation is, of course, that we are here concerned with two relations which are not being clearly distinguished either by Spinoza or by his expositor: (1) the cognitive relation of the idea to its object, (2) the existential relation of two modes in different attributes. The attribute of Thought has a quite exceptional function, namely, that it 'knows'—and for Spinoza this really means 'reproduces' or 'copies'—the contents of the other attributes; it has thus a double status, it exists on its own account and it knows the other attributes. If we think of an inscription on stone being copied on paper, we can see at once how a statement like that above quoted, which seems on the face of it so absurd, becomes merely ambiguous, for the identity and the distinctness are not asserted in the same sense. The literary content of the copy and of the original inscription is the same, but the paper copy is a different entity from the stone original. Spinoza is taking advantage of this ambiguity when he says in the scholium: *modus extensionis et idea illius modi una eademque est res, sed duobus modis expressa.* The *modus extensionis* and the *idea* cannot both be the thing of which they are different expressions. But for the fact that we are dealing with idea and ideatum this would be more obvious, and on Spinoza's view of idea and ideatum—namely, that they belong to different attributes—they should not be called one thing at all: existentially they are quite distinct.[1] The fact that one of the two known attributes has (on

---

[1] If we were speaking, not of idea and ideatum, but of mind and body, a further confusion would be apt to come in. Mind and body are spoken of as one being, in the sense that they make up one being; but here again Spinoza has strictly no right to use that language.

Spinoza's view) this double status helps, I think, to conceal the inconsistencies on which I have been commenting.

I think, then, that, notwithstanding our scholium, Robinson's interpretation of Spinoza's doctrine is the right one, or, at the least, that it gives the doctrine which Spinoza ought to have held—further reasons for thinking so will be given presently—but it seems to me that he does not fully bring out (perhaps he was not concerned to do so) the extent to which our whole view of Spinoza's metaphysics must be affected by this interpretation. He admits (p. 163) that Spinoza's earlier mode of statement is in many respects preferable to the later one, that is, that there are advantages in speaking, not of a single substance, Deus, and its attributes, but of Natura and the *substantiae* of which it consists. But I think we must go far beyond this and say that the later mode of statement is quite inconsistent and misleading. It is evident that if, as I, 10 says, an attribute *per se concipi debet,* then the so-called attribute *is* a substance, for substance is defined as that which *per se concipitur.* The definition of substance also says that substance is that which *in se est;* but this must apply to attribute also, for if the attribute were *in alio* it would be a mode and could not be conceived *per se.* In the scholium to I, 10 Spinoza asserts the exact contrary, namely, that we cannot conclude that, because two attributes are conceived as *realiter distincta* (i.e., conceived without any reference to each other), they are therefore two different substances. But his argument really begs the question. *Id enim est de natura substantiae,* he says, *ut unumquodque ejus attributorum per se concipiatur.* No doubt that is so, *if* a substance *can have* more than one attribute or essence.[2] But the question at issue is precisely whether the supposition that one substance can have two (or more) attributes is not self-contradictory, since it virtually asserts that one substance can be two (or more) substances. To say that Natura contains, or consists of, infinitely many wholly different substances might (provisionally) pass muster, but to say that the one substance, Deus, has infinitely many totally different essences is to say what is incomprehensible. But in any case, whether we speak of Natura or Deus or Substantia, the same problem

---

[2] No wonder that de Vries objected that this had not been proved (Ep. 26 in Bruder II—VV 8). The proofs which Spinoza gives in his reply, using the vaguer word *ens* instead of *substantia,* seem to beg the question as much as ever, if he means to distinguish *substantia* from *attributum*; but a little later he says the two words denote the same thing.

emerges, namely, Wherein does the unity of this entity consist, seeing that the entity itself is said to consist of infinitely many wholly different substances or attributes?

Several of Spinoza's correspondents (e.g., Oldenburg and Tschirnhaus) pointed out to him that the totally different substances or attributes become so many different worlds, which have no connexion with each other. Oldenburg and Tschirnhaus, at any rate, would hardly get much satisfaction from such answers as they received. Spinoza himself had already stated the difficulty in a note in the *Short Treatise* (KV, I, 2—p. 26, n. 1 in the Suppl. to Bruder's ed.): If there were different substances, *quae non ad unicum quoddam ens referrentur*, then the kind of unity which we see, for example, of mind and body in man, would be impossible, since *cogitatio* and *extensio* as different substances have no *communio inter se*. But what is the *unicum ens*? It is here postulated rather than explained. And what could it be, if the substances in Natura are all different and have no *communio inter se*? Natura lapses into a mere aggregate. Later critics, of course, have found the same difficulty in seeing how the unity of Deus is to be reconciled with the infinite plurality of attributes totally different from each other. Joachim, for example, says (p. 104): "The unity of Substance which seemed so absolute . . . resolves itself into a mere 'togetherness' of an infinite multiplicity".[3] "Die Einheit der Substanz angesichts der Bestimmungen über die Attribute", says Camerer (p. 9), "bleibt ein unvollziehbarer Gedanke".

Now Robinson thinks that on his interpretation he escapes this difficulty. After quoting a number of statements about the difficulty similar to those I have given he says the difficulty is "nur ein Scheinproblem". The unity of Spinoza's Absolute is "keine gleichartige Einheit, sondern Einheit des Ungleichartigen" (p. 286). But of course it is just this 'Einheit des Ungleichartigen' that is the problem. He goes on: "Dass die verschiedenen Attribute, aus denen Gott besteht, keine separate Welten bilden, offenbart sich lediglich durch das Walten in ihnen allen eines und desselben Weltgesetzes". The

---

[3] In the next sentence he says: "The Reality falls apart into a substratum without character, and characters which have no principle of coherence in a substratum." This introduction of a 'substratum' is inconsistent with what was quoted before from pp. 66–67, and shows how necessary it is to keep to one version of Spinoza's doctrine. The 'principle of coherence' might lie in the depths of the 'substratum', and Spinoza could fall back on the plea of our ignorance.

unity consists solely in the singleness and sameness of the *ordo sive connexio causarum*. Now whether the sameness of the *connexio causarum* in totally heterogeneous attributes is really more intelligible than a more substantive kind of unity I need not inquire. For the point I am at present concerned with is that this interpretation makes the stability of Spinoza's metaphysical system depend wholly on II, 7, and the question becomes all-important, whether this foundation is secure. Has Spinoza in this proposition proved what is required by the demands of his theory? It seems to me that he has not.

In the first place, he has certainly not proved that the proposition can be generalized so as to assert that the same *ordo* prevails throughout *all* the attributes. In the proposition itself he does not even assert a thoroughgoing parallelism of this sort: he asserts only a parallelism of *ideae* and *res*. The scholium extends the parallelism to all the attributes, but in a rather casual way and without attempting a proof, which indeed it would be rather difficult to give since all the attributes but the two he has already referred to are unknown. Joachim says, (p. 126, n. 3): "In ii, 7 Spinoza is thinking primarily of Extension and Thought; but of course the doctrine holds of all the Attributes". Why 'of course'? That Spinoza means the doctrine to apply to all the attributes I do not doubt, but that the doctrine 'holds' of them all is totally unproved and totally incapable of proof. Let us make the utmost concession to Spinoza which we are entitled to make. If we accept his *a priori* assertion in II, 1 and 3 that the *intellectus infinitus* contains ideas of the whole contents of Natura, then there will be a parallelism to this extent, that to each of the attributes there will correspond a part of, or set of ideas in, *Cogitatio*. Thus, if we symbolize Extension by E and our part of *Cogitatio* by C_e, we can symbolize an unknown attribute by X and its part of *Cogitatio* by C_x. The attributes other than *Cogitatio* and the parts of *Cogitatio* will then 'run in pairs', as Caird puts it (p. 156),[4] with a part of *Cogitatio* as one member of every pair. E will be parallel to C_e and X to C_x. But this state of things has not the least tendency to prove that E and X will be parallel. The fact is that the case of *Cogitatio* is a quite special case and we cannot generalize from its relation to the other attributes to the relation of these other attributes *inter se*. The special character is that it has

[4] J. Caird, *Spinoza* (Edinburgh and London: Wm. Blackwood and Sons, 1910).

no independent content of its own. Its ideas or knowledges only repeat *objective* what exists in the other attributes *formaliter*. Consequently a correspondence between *Cogitatio* and the other attributes is implied in the very character assigned to *Cogitatio*. But there is no reason to suppose that any comparable relation holds between the other attributes. The presumption is surely rather against it. A simple illustration will bring out the point. Suppose there were English translations of the whole of French literature and again of the whole of German literature, there would be a correspondence between each literature and its translation, but there need not be any between the two literatures. And it will not do *now* (i.e., on the interpretation we have adopted) to fall back on Spinoza's assertion that all the attributes express the same substance, for we must then ask wherein this sameness consists, and if the answer is, In the sameness of the *ordo,* we are going round in a circle.

Thus, if the unity of Natura consists in the sameness of the *ordo* there is no proof for it and a certain presumption against it. And it should be observed that the same kind of difficulty will be repeated within the attribute of *Cogitatio,* whose parts will have no more connexion with each other than the corresponding attributes have.

The only way to save the situation would be to abandon the doctrine of the infinitely many attributes. But it may be surmised that Spinoza would have been anything but willing to do so, and his expositor seems to be of that mind also, for he calls the doctrine 'eine Grundsäule des spinozistischen Monismus' (p. 112). An infinite pluralism a 'Grundsäule' of monism! How can that be? Because "in diesem Pluralismus findete der (cartesianische) Dualismus seine Überwindung, indem die Grundverschiedenheit des Denkens und der Ausdehnung nur zum Spezialfall der unendlich mannigfaltigen Verschiedenheit wird, die innerhalb des absolut Unendlichen statt hat". But what we found was that the relation between *Cogitatio* and *Extensio* is a 'Spezialfall', not in the sense that it is only a special case of a relation that holds between any two attributes indifferently, but in the sense that it holds *only* between *Cogitatio* (or parts of it) and the other attributes, so that, instead of having overcome the Cartesian dualism, the doctrine of the infinitely many attributes merely repeats that dualism *ad infinitum*.[5]

---

[5] We must therefore agree with Lotze when he says (deutsche Philosophie seit Kant, Diktate, p. 9): Die Sonderbarkeit, dass zwei ausdrücklich für unvergleichbar anerkannte Attribute in dem Wesen der absoluten Substanz vereinigt sein sollen,

When we next consider the proof of the proposition, we may well complain (with Tschirnhaus) of Spinoza's brevity. He simply says: *Patet ex ax. 4, part.* 1. *Nam cujuscumque causati idea a cognitione causae, cujus est effectus, dependet.* The axiom itself says: *Effectus cognitio a cognitione causae dependet et eandem involvit;* and Spinoza quotes the axiom in his reply to Tschirnhaus (Bruder, Suppl. p. 317 = VV 72) in the form: *Effectus cognitio sive idea a cognitione sive idea causae pendet.*

From this meagre material—the variations of form can hardly have any significance—it is very difficult to infer Spinoza's meaning with any certainty; and what adds greatly to *our* difficulty is the fact that Spinoza himself seems to see none. The natural meaning of the axiom is either (*a*) that when we know B *as an effect* (of A) we must know its cause (A)—a proposition which is not merely axiomatic but tautological—or (*b*) that in order to know B adequately we must see it as an effect, that is, see how it was produced by its cause A. With (*b*) we may compare a statement in *de Int. Em.* (Bruder II, p. 36, § 92): *revera cognitio effectus nihil aliud est quam perfectiorem causae cognitionem acquirere.* But neither of the meanings seems to suit II, 7, for that proposition applies to ideas in general, and we cannot say that all ideas are ideas of things as effects, nor again that in the case of all things that we know we have an insight into the cause of their production. In the axiom as quoted in the letter, if it stood alone, the addition of *sive idea* to *cognitio* might suggest that the axiom means that the idea of B—since B is an effect of A—must depend upon the idea of A in the same way as B depends upon A. From that statement the proposition would certainly follow at once, but the statement would hardly be axiomatic in the way in which (*a*) and (*b*) are; it really involves propositions that are proved in the *Ethics*, as will appear immediately.

But the meaning of the so-called demonstration can hardly be anything very profound or obscure in itself, since Spinoza himself regards the proposition as practically self-evident. The best I am able to do in the way of interpretation is the following: We know from I, 28 that every finite mode is determined by another, and that other by a third, and so on; and we have just been reminded in II, 5 and

---

auf deren Einheit das grösste Gewicht gelegt wird, verdeckt Spinoza nur unvollkommen durch die Vermutung, die unendliche Substanz habe nicht nur diese zwei, sondern unzähliche positive Attribute, von denen nur diese beiden uns bekannt seien.

6 that the causal series within each attribute is self-contained. Let ABCD be a causal series in the attribute of *Extensio,* and $\alpha\beta\gamma\delta$ a causal series in the attribute of *Cogitatio,* and let $\alpha\beta\gamma\delta$ be the ideas or knowledges of ABCD: then the causal order of $\alpha\beta\gamma\delta$ must reflect, or be identical with that of ABCD, otherwise $\alpha\beta\gamma\delta$ would not be the ideas or knowledges of ABCD. In other words, the proposition is simply the axiom *Idea vera debet cum suo ideato convenire* (I ax. 6) *applied to the causal order.* How far $\alpha\beta\gamma\delta$ would contain an insight into the causal relations of ABCD would depend upon the degree of adequacy of the ideas. To such an interpretation, however, it may be objected, that Spinoza does not refer to the propositions and axiom here quoted, whereas he usually seems rather anxious to drag in all the propositions involved in a demonstration. The interpretation would in fact involve that Spinoza is reading into axiom 4 of I far more than it originally meant.

In view of the uncertainty as to Spinoza's meaning I will not deal further with the proof itself, but will rather go on to say something about the assumptions underlying the proposition. In doing so I shall have to refer to questions which I have already touched on, but at this stage in Spinoza's argument they become more pressing. If I have also to refer to questions that are familiar in the history of philosophy, that can hardly be avoided.

The proposition assumes, first, that there is an *idea* for every *res,* and conversely. This assumption may be taken as guaranteed by II, 1 S. and 3. Second, the examples in the scholium imply that the only case actually before us is that in which the *res* are modes of Extension, and the *ideae* are the ideas of these modes. This assumption may be taken as guaranteed by II, 1 and 2 taken along with ax. 5. In the discussion of the early propositions of II, Spinoza (and his reader) may appear to be regarding the two known attributes from a superior or neutral point of view, contemplating both attributes equally, and affirming the correspondence between them. But strictly this is not of course the case: the thinking of the philosopher falls within the attribute of *Cogitatio.* We were told long ago (I, 10) that each attribute *per se concipi debet;* from which it follows that two attributes (like the hypothetical *two* substances of I, 2) *nihil inter se commune habent.* But it has now been further impressed upon us in II, 5 that the *Res Cogitans* produces the ideas which are its modes solely by its own action, and without any action upon it by the *Res Extensa.* It is at the same time assumed that the ideas

know the corresponding modes of Extension; for in II, 5 Spinoza
uses the expressions *ideata, res perceptae, ideae objectum,* and in II,
7 the *ideae* are obviously meant to be the *ideae* of which the *res* are
the *ideata.* But surely we must now insist on some justification for
this assumption and the use of these expressions. For, if we state the
bare existential facts of II, 5 and 7, we must say that there is a self-
contained causal series of modes of *Cogitatio* and a self-contained
causal series of modes of *Extensio,* and that the *ordo* of the two
series is the same. But we surely want some explanation of the *additional* relation between the two series, that the modes of *Cogitatio*
know the modes of *Extensio.* In the case of attribute X and Extension there would be no such relation. Are we not, in fact, in danger
of going round in a circle or involving ourselves in a contradiction,[6]
since the correspondence of the two series seems to depend on the
cognitive relation between them? We surely at least require some
explanation of *how* the cognitive relation is *possible,* when the two
attributes are absolutely disparate and independent.

The Spinozist may say the answer is obvious: it is simply the nature of an idea to know its ideatum; for Spinoza it is an axiom that
a true idea *debet cum suo ideato convenire.* As to the first statement
our reply must be, that it is precisely this nature or property of an
idea whose possibility we find it difficult, *on Spinoza's view,* to understand, since the idea belongs to one attribute and the ideatum to
another. As for the axiom, its natural meaning is, that an idea must
agree with its ideatum *in order to be true,* and this naturally implies
that the truth or falsity of the idea can be tested or verified by comparing the ideatum as ideated in the idea with the ideatum known
in some further way, as when a person A, who has been asked
whether B is in, says, No, I don't think so, but I'll go and see.

The Spinozist may say, This way of taking the axiom won't do;
for Spinoza rejects the notion of an external criterion; according to
him, the truth or adequacy of an idea is a property internal to it,
as def. 4 of II clearly indicates. True, we may reply, but this only
makes our difficulty the more obvious. We ask now, How is it possible that an idea or *essentia objectiva,* no matter what properties it

---

[6] A circle, if we use the cognitive relation to establish the correspondence and
then the correspondence to explain the cognitive relation; a contradiction, if we
affirm a cognitive *relation* between things that are *wholly independent* of each
other.

may have in itself, can reveal, or assure us of, the existence of an *essentia formalis in another attribute*?

It is worth while to return for a moment to the passage in the *de Int. Em.* quoted in § 2, for our difficulty comes up there in the immediate sequel, and we see Spinoza wavering (whether he realized it or not) between two quite different views of an idea. In the passage quoted we were told that the idea is an *essentia objectiva et in se quid reale*. But a little later we are told that *certitudo nihil est praeter ipsam essentiam objectivam; id est, modus quo sentimus esse formale est ipsa certitudo*. Now surely *certitudo* cannot at once be a mere *manner* of perceiving the *esse formale itself* and also an *essentia objectiva* which is *in se quid reale*. What Spinoza no doubt means to say is that in the case of a true idea the *essentia objectiva* brings with it an assurance of knowing the *esse formale*. But our difficulty is precisely to understand how it is able to do this, when it has no access to or communion with the *esse formale*, which exists as a mode of another attribute.

Now in the early propositions of II the conception of the idea or *essentia objectiva* as *in se quid reale* has been greatly strengthened. The *essentia objectiva* can hardly now be regarded even for a moment as a mere manner of perceiving. It is a mode of an attribute, a particular thing, an *esse formale* which is the effect of a second *esse formale* and presumably the cause of a third. But if the existence of an idea is wholly confined to the attribute of *Cogitatio*, and the idea is at the same time a knowledge of an object, then the immediate object of that knowledge must also be contained in *Cogitatio*—in other words, the *essentia objectiva* is not a manner of perceiving, but an object perceived, the immediate object of the idea as a knowing,[7] and this immediate or immanent object somehow carries with it a belief or assurance of the existence of a transcendent thing that is a mode in the attribute of Extension.

The Spinozist may say, You are misrepresenting Spinoza's doc-

---

[7] That existentially the idea is one thing and the ideatum another, and also that the *essentia objectiva* is the immediate or internal object of the idea, is clearly implied in II, 5. For there Sp. asserts that every idea is caused by the agency of the *Res Cogitans*, i.e. (as II, 9 says), by another idea, and he at the same time denies that the idea is caused by its ideatum. Now, if the *ideatum* were really the internal *object* of the idea it would be meaningless to suggest or to deny that it is or could be the *cause* of the idea. Some modern psychologists are guilty of such a gross confusion, but we need not charge Spinoza with it.

trine here, and begging the question against him: his doctrine is that the idea *exists* in the attribute of *Cogitatio* but *knows* a mode of Extension. There are two difficulties in this answer. (1) The *essentia objectiva* is a particular thing, which has a content of its own; we can see how this content should *correspond to* or *copy* the content of the *esse formale*, but we cannot see how it can be said to *know the esse formale*.[8] (2) We cannot see how an idea should know immediately what exists in a wholly separate world which has no communion with that in which the idea exists; such knowledge would be miraculous, and is Spinoza of all people to ask us to accept a miracle?

Let us take it, then, that Spinoza's doctrine must be stated in the form that the *essentia objectiva* is the immediate object of knowledge and somehow carries with it a belief or assurance of the extramental existence of an extended thing, and let us ask once more how this is possible. Obviously the *essentiae objectivae* do not come with letters of introduction explaining that they are the *essentiae objectivae* of extended things. The *essentiae objectivae* must somehow reveal in themselves the character and independent reality of the extended things of which they give us the knowledge. How can they reveal the extended character of extended things? Only, we must answer, by being themselves extended. How can they reveal the independent reality of the extended things? Only, we must answer, by themselves behaving as if they were independent things. In other words, we can explain the knowledge of extended things only by transporting them in effect into the ideas and enabling them to be known directly, and, if this is so, the assertion on their behalf of an extra existence over and above their known existence becomes unmeaning. When the extended things are known by us as existing, it is the extended thing themselves that are the immediate object of knowledge, not mere copies of them. We are brought, in short, to recognize that Spinoza's absolute separation of the two attributes, of knowledge and reality, is untrue and makes knowledge impossible. If knowledge is to be possible, to have indeed any meaning, there must be some sort of direct apprehension of reality from the very beginning, for example, we know extended things by directly perceiving them.

How did Spinoza get himself into the impossible position in

---

[8] I.e., to know that copy is a copy, or to be aware of itself as being a copy.

which we have found him to be? Because he accepted Descartes' dualism of Thought and Extension in an even more rigid way than Descartes himself had asserted it, and then had to reconcile it with his own metaphysical-religious belief in the unity of Natura or Deus. Descartes, starting in a more psychological way from the *Cogito*, felt the difficulty of understanding how a knowledge of the extended world was possible, and did his best by rather roundabout methods to solve it. He started from the standpoint of the Erkenntnistheoretiker; but Spinoza was primarily the metaphysician, and, accepting the dualism of Thought and Extension apparently without difficulty, and having knowledge before him as a fact, he had to find some metaphysical way of combining the dualism and the fact. His way of doing so was to assert an existential *correspondence* between idea and thing, and at the same time to substitute the notion of the *adequacy* of an idea for the ordinary notion of its truth. But the significance of the substitution is partly concealed by the assertion of the correspondence. On Spinoza's as well as on the ordinary view the idea agrees with its ideatum, but on the ordinary view, interpreted as I have suggested it should be, the agreement is *seen* to hold in virtue of an actual comparison made either by the person himself, or else by some one whose knowledge is fuller than his own, as Mr. Cargill's ideas about distances in Palestine were corrected by Touchwood who had been there. On Spinoza's view it is impossible that the agreement should be *seen*; it is metaphysically *inferred* from the adequacy of the idea (its truth in Spinoza's sense) on the principle that *id quod in intellectu objective continetur debet necessario in natura dari* (I, 30)—a principle which simply inverts the ordinary meaning of the axiom that *idea vera debet convenire cum suo ideato*.

§ 5

Spinoza, as I have already remarked, seems to have had a boundless confidence in *a priori* reasoning, the obvious example being his assertion of an infinity of attributes when experience shows us only two. In this case his assertion is of purely speculative interest. For, since the attributes other than the experienced two are unknown to us, and unknowable by us, and since all the attributes are quite independent of each other, it is wholly immaterial, so far as our experience is concerned, whether the alleged but not experienced attributes do or do not exist. If they do exist, they might as well not exist so far as we are concerned, for their existence can make no difference to our experience. But when Spinoza comes to apply his *a priori* reasonings within the field of experience itself the case is very different, for his reasonings may then conflict with experience, and yet his confidence in them be so great as apparently to blind him to the most evident facts. Our difficulty then is to explain how this was psychologically possible. The only explanation would seem to lie in some serious confusion of thought on his part, and he has accordingly been charged with it. This charge, I need hardly say, is one not to be brought lightly against a great philosopher, and, if there was the least possibility that the charge was due to a wrong interpretation of Spinoza's view, we should be bound to go upon that assumption and to try to discover where our error lay. But when he lays down a proposition in terms which seem to admit of no interpretation but one, we must simply accept that interpretation and try then to discover the nature of Spinoza's own error.

Such a case presents itself in II, 13. Spinoza there says, in terms which seem to admit of no dubiety, that the *object* of the mind's knowledge is the body, *and nothing else than the body*.[9] It is, of course, the last part of this assertion that occasions the difficulty. That in all (or nearly all) conscious states there is some awareness of the body, however vague, is true enough, but that there is no awareness of anything else is manifestly not true—it is contradicted by Spinoza's own statements, for example, in 16 C 1 (where he says that the human mind perceives *plurimorum corporum naturam una cum sui corporis natura*),[10] and in 17 (where he says that, when the

---

[9] Cf. the opening sentence of 19: *mens humana est ipsa idea sive cognitio corporis humani.*

[10] Robinson commenting on this corollary says: "Die Seelendefinition der Ethik will nicht besagen (auch eine derartige Missdeutung ist in der Spinozaliteratur zu treffen) dass der Mensch beständig an seinen Körper denkt, sondern bedeutet, dass der Mensch, indem er die Aussenwelt zu erkennen glaubt, in der Regel nur verworrene Ideen von den Zuständen seines eigenen, durch äussere Körper affizierten Körpers hat." This explanation of the definition seems to me to be explaining it away. Spinoza does not say that the object of the human mind is "as a rule" the body. And there is no warrant for the 'nur'. What Spinoza himself says in 16 C 2 is that our ideas of external bodies *magis nostri corporis constitutionem, quam corporum externorum naturam indicant;* and in 38 he says of the *omnibus corporibus communia* that the mind necessarily perceives them *adequately* when it *suum vel quodcumque externum corpus percipit.* The difficulty of the definition is precisely that Spinoza does not qualify his assertion in

body is affected by an external body, the mind *idem corpus externum ut actu existens vel ut sibi praesens contemplabitur*). How, then, could he assert the *et nihil aliud* of 13? Again, if the mind's knowledge of the body is necessarily a knowledge of it as *actu existens*, that is, if the mind's object is always an actually or presently existing thing, this would seem to exclude memory, which may be of something that no longer exists at all and is certainly of things that do not now exist in their past state; yet Spinoza, of course, elsewhere recognizes memory as a fact.

There must, then, it would seem, be some serious confusion in Spinoza's thought, if his assertion of our proposition is to be explained. Among the commentators Pollock frankly recognizes this, and charges Spinoza with using the one word idea to denote two quite distinct relations; others, for example, Caird and Joachim, are unwilling to admit that Spinoza could be guilty of such confusion, but their own explanations of what Spinoza means when he speaks of the mind as the idea of the body are far from clear. The gist of Pollock's criticism can be given in a couple of sentences. After remarking that the human mind is spoken of as the idea of the body he says: "Now a man can easily think of his own body, but he is not always doing so, and when he does his thought will not be accurate unless he has learnt something of physiology. And even if every human being were an accomplished physiologist, the constant relation of the mind as a whole to the body as a whole would still be something different from the relation of the knowing to the known" (ed. 2, p. 124).[11] As regards the first sentence I think it is preferable to emphasize, not so much the negative statement that we are not always thinking of our body, as the positive one, that, unless something is wrong with the body, we do and must think a great deal more about other things. But it seems to me that Pollock's criticism is substantially right. As he is content, however, to state his criticism quite briefly, it may be worth while to give a rather fuller statement,

---

any way, but on the contrary adds the emphatic *et nihil aliud*. If, then, a man's body is the only object of his mind, surely he must think of it whenever he does think.

[11] Caird, *op. cit.* (pp. 197–199) comments on these sentences, and, unless his reader had the sentences actually before him, the comments would almost certainly suggest that Pollock had asserted that Spinoza was logically bound to maintain that "every human being must be an accomplished physiologist." The suggestion would, of course, be quite false: Pollock says 'even if'. I will refer to Caird's defence of Spinoza later.

and also to preface it by a brief statement of what seems the true view of the distinct relations in which the mind stands respectively to its objects, and to its body and external bodies considered not as objects of, but as conditions of, perception.

When the mind, or knower, K, perceives an object in the external world, for example, the sun, two relations between the mind and the thing (the sun) are involved: (1) the cognitive relation between the mind as knowing and the thing as object, (2) an existential relation between the thing and the embodied mind as existents. The latter relation needs a little explanation. The sun as a cause sets up light waves which travel to the earth, affect the body or eye, and so initiate a physiological process which causes a brain change, in virtue of which, as a condition, perception of the sun takes place. The series of events that starts from the sun and has its physical (or physiological) termination in the brain is in its earlier stages a causal series, but in its last stage, namely, that in which perception takes place, and in which the brain functions as the organ or instrument of the mind, we had better describe it by another adjective such as 'instrumental,' for the relation of mind to body or brain is so intimate that the notion of causal action seems inappropriate. I propose to call the cognitive relation the C-relation, and the existential or causal-instrumental process the E-process. Now it is all-important to see and to keep in mind that the relation and the process are quite distinct from each other. For, in the first place, the E-process is always prior in time. In our example of the sun the interval between the start and the termination of the process is about eight minutes, since light takes that time to travel from the sun to the earth, and it is only when the process reaches its termination that perception takes place. The sun as thing is both object and cause, but its causal action is always 8 minutes ahead of its status as visible object; if the transmission of light were instantaneous the sun in the morning would be a visible object 8 minutes earlier. In the case of things close at hand the time interval is practically negligible, but it is theoretically important, because, if we keep it in mind, we shall be prevented from confusing object with cause and from supposing that the E-process intervenes between the *object* and the mind. If anything intervenes between the mind and its object, that is, if perception involves a process, the process must be psychical, not physical. In the second place, the E-process is an inferred, not a perceived process, and more especially so as regards K himself. The point is not merely that much of it is not, and cannot, be perceived *in point of fact,* for example, the brain processes, but that *theoretically* even if they could be perceived, and in some magical way made perceptible to K himself, yet whatever brain processes he perceived they could never be the self-same brain processes as those which conditioned his perception, since there would always be the time-interval between eye and brain-change: object and cause or stimulus could never be absolutely coincident. In actual fact, of course, K does not perceive the E-process at all: it belongs to science and not to the world of ordinary perception.

If we ask ourselves the question which Spinoza answers in his way in II, 13, namely, What is the object of K's knowledge (or external perception) as a whole?—we cannot possibly answer it as Spinoza does. It is a plain fact that we perceive much more than the body. For example, if I turn and face the window of the room in which I am writing, I see not only my own hand and arm, but part of the room and its furniture, part of a garden, houses in the village, and a range of hills. What K knows or perceives is not his body only, but the whole field of objects that come within his knowledge or perception, among which his own body is only one, though for him a constant and very important one. But a difficulty may suggest itself here—it no doubt influenced Spinoza. How is it that, if perception is immediately conditioned by brain processes which are wholly within the body, we are nevertheless able to apprehend things that exist altogether apart from the body and only act upon it externally? It may be for us impossible to answer this question. It is conceivable that the brain processes might have had for their concomitants on the mental side merely sensations and feelings that would have indicated nothing but the state of the body itself: the mind of animals, or at any rate of the lower grades of animals, is often supposed to be of that type. But such is not the case as regards the human mind. Human brain processes are the condition of a knowledge, not only of the body, but of things that exist altogether apart from the body; while of the brain processes themselves nothing is known except by science, and then only in a vague and inferential way. It would be a serious blunder, then, to use the scientific doctrine that perception is conditioned by brain processes to throw doubt upon the directness or value of our knowledge of external things. The E-process is itself a fact of *knowledge* and presupposes on the part of the man of science that very apprehension of external things which it would have been used to throw doubt upon.

Consider now Spinoza's doctrine in relation to the foregoing statement. He asserts, of course, a cognitive relation between the mind and its object; he denies an instrumental relation of body to mind, for they belong to different attributes which have no *communio inter se;* but he asserts a correspondence between events in the two attributes, an identity of the *connexio causarum.* But now II, 13 throws all our previous ideas on these points into confusion. If we follow the epistemological doctrine of the *de Int. Em.,* the cognitive relation is the relation of the *essentiae objectivae* in the mind to their *essentiae formales,* and when these latter are extended things it seems obvious to suggest that the knowledge is at the same time a correspondence between ideas and things, whether the correspondence is to be explained on the ordinary view that the mind experiences and apprehends the things, or on Spinoza's metaphysical theory that the ideas and the things are parallel events in wholly separate attributes. The so-called correspondence does in fact hold between ideas and 'objects' in the strict sense of the latter term as meaning things considered *so far as known only;* for then, as we have seen, the case is really one of identity, and not of correspondence. But it does not hold between things ἁπλῶς and ideas, for we can know that our ideas of the things are incomplete. Still the cognitive relation and the relation of correspondence can, on Spinoza's view of ideas, be plausibly identified, especially if we are at liberty to assume that the incompleteness of *our* ideas is somehow compensated in the *intellectus infinitus.* And it will be remembered that on this general view Spinoza, strictly speaking, should argue from ideas to things by means of the *a priori* assumption *id quod in intellectu objective continetur, debet necessario in natura dari.* But now we are told that the mind's one and only object is the body. We are now to regard cognition and correspondence from a quite different point of view. We are to start, as the proof of II, 13 shows, from the empirical fact stated in axiom 4: *Nos corpus quoddam multis modis affici sentimus*—a fact which, as so stated, seems hardly consistent with the total independence of the attributes. We are to treat the correspondence, not as a general one between ideas and the things which are their objects, but as a much more special one between bodily states and their psychical correlates. We are to limit the object of mind accordingly and say it is the body only. And we are in effect to surrender the doctrine of the independence of the attributes by treating the mind as if it were really determined, in respect both of cognition and correspondence, by the body.

Camerer (p. 77) says of II, 13: "Dass die Ideen von den Affectionen des Körpers im menschlichen Geiste sind, wird hier mit der Erfahrungsthatsache bewiesen, dass wir die Empfindung von jenen Affectionen haben, welche selbstverständlich eine Empfindung des eigenen Körpers ist". I think that Camerer here gives us the right clue to Spinoza's reason for asserting the proposition. External bodies can make us aware of their existence only by affecting our own body, and it is these affections of our own body which alone *we* experience; consequently, it would seem, our own body is the mind's only object. The fallacy of this reasoning lies in the ambiguity of the expression 'affections of our own body', Spinoza's *ideae affectionum corporis,* Camerer's 'Empfindung des eigenen Körpers'. No one would wish to dispute that *affectiones* occurring in any other body can make no difference to us; it is only when *affectiones* are excited in our own body that we experience anything. But this is not to say that what we experience, the object of our experience, is these *affectiones* themselves. The *ideae affectionum* are ideas which depend upon, or are conditioned by, the *affectiones*, but they need not be ideas which have these *affectiones* for their objects.[12]

---

[12] There is an ambiguity here which should perhaps be noticed more particularly, in order to prevent misunderstanding. An *affectio* may be (α) a bodily fact of which we are aware, and so in the technical sense an 'object', or (β) a physiological process of which we are not aware at all; and our awareness of α is always conditioned by β. But there are cases of α in which the bodily fact is so vague, and so internal to the body, as it were, that the description of it as an object seems unnatural, and these vaguer experiences may tend to confuse the really clear distinction between α and β. Suppose a person is being taught to play the violin. The teacher may take his pupil's hand and place it in the correct position for bowing. Here the pupil sees his own hand and the teacher's hand equally as objects by means of the same visual β; he has also the tactual experience of his hand being touched and moved, but in ordinary talk we should be less ready to describe this experience as experience of an object, yet of course the touch and movement are objects of awareness in a sense in which the β on which the awareness of them immediately depends is not. And we may have bodily experiences of a much vaguer kind, vague bodily pains and discomfort, which we can perhaps hardly localize at all. If the β process is disordered it may itself give rise to pains, e.g., eye-strain may cause headaches, but such pains are not an awareness of the β process. Thus the distinction between

The *affectiones* upon which the ideas or perceptions *immediately* depend are in fact physiological processes, which the *body* may be said metaphorically to 'experience', but which *we*, strictly speaking, do not experience at all and which are objects only for the physiologist. Hence, although the *affectiones* are the *affectiones* of our own body, we must not conclude that the *ideae* corresponding to, or conditioned by, them have necessarily our own body for their object. When we perceive external bodies this is plainly not the case; and, when we are perceiving external bodies, we very often do not even think of our own body as being affected by them at all, though we may do so, for example, when we are dazzled by a too bright light. The danger of confusion and fallacy is all the greater when a single word may be used, like Camerer's 'Empfindung' and our 'affection' above or 'sensation', to denote both process and object. Spinoza uses *affectiones* to denote the bodily processes or facts, and speaks of the *ideae affectionum,* but he fails apparently to see that the *ideae* which occur in the mind when the *affectiones* occur in the body need not have the *affectiones* or the body for their object. *Ideae affectionum* may mean either ideas which correspond to the *affectiones,* or ideas which are aware of or know the *affectiones,* but Spinoza apparently identifies the two meanings, that is, identifies correspondence and cognition, but now from a physiological rather than an epistemological point of view.

In 17 S. he says *corporis humani affectiones, quarum ideae corpora externa velut nobis praesentia repraesentant, rerum imagines vocabimus, tametsi rerum figuras non referunt: et quum mens hac ratione contemplatur corpora, eandem imaginari dicemus.* Here, it might seem at first sight, he is certainly distinguishing between the so-called *'imagines'* in the body and the objects of the *mentis imaginatio* which are *corpora externa.* But then he has in view in this scholium the case in which the external bodies are *not* actually present and are not being *really perceived.* So it is to be feared that he would find it even easier in this case to say that the mind is expressing in its ideas only something that occurs in the body; and it might indeed be suggested that it is in the light of this case that we should interpret the case of perception itself, so that we should thus regard II, 13 as asserting that the mind's object is the body in the

---

an *affectio* of the type α, however vague the awareness may be, and an *affectio* of the type β, where there is no awareness whatsoever, remains absolute. The *imagines* of II, 17 S. belong, I take it, to type β.

sense that (where we should ordinarily say that the mind's object is external bodies) the mind is only expressing by means of ideas of external bodies *affectiones* which are occurring in its own body. But if Spinoza was thinking on these lines he would surely have stated 13 in a different way and made his meaning clear; and even then he would still be interpreting his correspondence in two ways, epistemological and physiological, without clearly recognizing that he was doing so. I think, then, that we must agree with Pollock that, when Spinoza speaks of the mind as *idea sive cognitio corporis,* he is confused and is using the word *idea* in a new and strange way.

Caird denies the confusion, and endeavours to defend Spinoza against Pollock, but unfortunately he makes much of the reference to physiology which is quite incidental in Pollock's criticism, and on the really important points merely repeats Spinoza's own confusion. Thus he asks, "What can be the special object of the idea which is a particular mode of thought if not the particular mode of extension which corresponds to it?" (p. 198). Let the idea be an idea (or perception) of the sun. Surely there can be only one answer to the question, What is the special object of that idea? What, then, does Caird mean by his vague phrase 'the particular mode of extension which corresponds to it'? He goes on to say, "Outside of itself, there is nothing for the individual mind to think, nothing that for it immediately exists, save the individual mode of extension which is the obverse, so to speak, of itself". By the obverse he means, of course, the body. Now the body *as organ* is intimately connected with the mind in a way that nothing else is, but the body *as object* is only one object among other objects, and there is no justification for saying that there is no other object 'for the individual mind to think', and no other thing that 'for the individual mind immediately exists'. The body is normally perceived in an environment of other bodies, and the individual mind may at a given moment be much more intent upon one of these bodies than upon its own body. Finally we are told that "In being the mental correlate of the body the mind *thinks* the body". What is meant by this obscure expression 'thinks the body'? Joachim also uses this phraseology (p. 71): "God, in being the 'soul' of a thing, thinks the thing, whose soul his act of thought is". On the same page he says: "The intelligence of God is one and the same as its objects: it is the soul-side of them, and is thereby, for God, the reflection or apprehension of them". The first half of the sentence, as an exposition of Spinoza's view, is obviously expressed loosely; in the second half 'soul-side' suggests an existential part or concomitant, 'apprehension' should mean cognition, 'reflection' is somewhere between the two, an existential copy. Later (p. 125) we are told, in like manner but with special reference to the finite body and soul, that "Every body is an idea, and its ideal side is at once its 'soul' and the apprehension of its body". Strictly speaking, no body *is* an idea: Spinoza's own statement (II, 7 S.) is that the *res* is one and the same but the modes are *two* (and therefore not the same). And here, too, 'ideal side', 'soul', and 'apprehension of its body' are equated like the similar expressions above. It may seem pedantic to insist on such points, especially if the quoted sentences are read in their (unquoted) contexts, but I do so in order to justify the remark that expositions of Spinoza which merely repeat his own confusion and obscurity do nothing to answer criticism like Pollock's.

The general charges against Spinoza, then, in the part of II which I am now to examine in more detail are (1) that he confuses the cognitive relation with the existential correspondence asserted by him in II, 7 and now to be taken in the sense of a correspondence between mind and body, (2) that, in consequence of that confusion, he asserts the body to be the sole object of the mind's knowledge, and (3) that, in spite of his denial of any *communio* between the attributes, his argument repeatedly suggests that he is really thinking of the mind as determined by the body, so that, not parallelism, but epiphenomenalism, would be the word to describe the real tendency of his thought.[13]

(*To be concluded.*)

[13] Robinson (pp. 273–274) puts this predominance of the extended world over thought rather quaintly. For Spinoza, he says, "die bloss gedachte Welt ist der wirklichen nicht ebenbürtig. Wenn die realitas objectiva, wenn das Attribut des Denkens sich so weit wie die äussere Realität . . . erstreckt, so ist doch die intramentale Realität nicht mit der extramentalen zu vergleichen, ihr spezifisches Gewicht ist sozusagen nicht gleich Eins, sondern zwischen Null und Eins zu setzen." Such a view is quite at variance with II 5, which insists that the *esse formale* of ideas depends solely upon the *Res Cogitans,* or attribute of *Cogitatio,* and does not involve the conception of any other attribute; the proposition is evidently intended to assert the complete equality of the attribute of *Cogitatio* with the other attributes.

Notes on the Second Part
of Spinoza's *Ethics* (III)

H. Barker

§ 6: Mind and Body (II, 11–15)

In 11 SPINOZA SAYS *idea primum est, quod humanae mentis esse constituit: at non idea rei non existentis; nam tum (per 8c) ipsa idea non posset dici existere.* Here the use of *idea* in the singular is a first source of confusion, for the preceding part of the demonstration with its reference to ax. 3 shows that *idea* here does not mean one idea in the ordinary sense of that phrase, but *the totality* of the ideas which together make up the primary content of the mind. Now the ideas have not one object, as the use of *idea* in the singular suggests, but many objects, and of these objects some are thought of as things that do not now exist but existed in the past. Spinoza could not, of course, have denied that an existing idea may ideate a non-existing thing. What he means to deny is that the mind can be the mind of a non-existing body. But instead of using the word mind he uses the word *idea* in the singular, which he has no right to do, since def. 3 says *per ideam intelligo mentis conceptum, quem mens format.* Using *idea* in the singular he can then speak of its ideatum as *res singularis* and argue that since the mind exists its existential correlate must also exist. But in truth the mind has not one ideatum but as many ideata as it has ideas, and if we want to express the fact that these ideata form in some sense one whole corresponding to the unity of the mind, we must speak, not of the body, which is only one ideatum among others, but of the world so far as known to the individual knower K, K's known world.

The use of one and the same word *idea* to denote sometimes *conceptus*, sometimes *mens*, is objectionable and unfortunate, for, though the human mind is not a substance in any sense that Spinoza could admit, it is nevertheless an independent entity in a sense in which the particular idea *which it thinks* is not. Spinoza

145

may have thought of the mind as related to particular ideas in a manner comparable with that in which a larger space is related to the smaller spaces contained in it, but if so, his thought was not true, for the mind is not merely a marked off part of an indefinite and homogeneous continuum that exists all at once and unchanged, as space does, but an individual being that develops in time and is characterised by a certain unity and continuity amidst change. Again, the double use of *idea* makes it very difficult to know how to interpret II, 9, a proposition of which Spinoza makes frequent use. If *idea* there means a particular idea, the causation spoken of will be an intra-mental process, the causation of one particular idea by another;[1] but if idea means a mind—and in 11 the phrase *idea rei singularis actu existentis* does mean a mind—then the statement in 9, *idea rei singularis actu existentis Deum pro causa habet . . . quatenus alia rei singularis actu existentis idea affectus consideratur* is one to which it is difficult to attach any meaning.

Prop. 12 supplies another instance of the boldness with which Spinoza follows out his *a priori* reasonings in defiance of experience. It asserts that if the *res singularis* which is the object of the idea that constitutes the human mind is the body, then *nihil in eo corpore poterit contingere, quod a mente non percipiatur*. Now even when we allow (in accordance with 11 C) for the fact that such perception is *ex parte* and inadequate, this assertion seems astounding. The proposition does not assert merely that whatever goes on in the body will, directly or indirectly, make some difference to what goes on in the mind, but that whatever goes on in the body is actually apprehended in some manner, however partial and inadequate the apprehension may be. Thus either we must say that the assertion is simply false, being in flat contradiction with experience, or we must, without any empirical warrant, enormously expand our conception of the mind and say that it contains innumerable ideas[2] of which there is no consciousness and has never been any consciousness, and which are in no effective continuity with the ideas of which the individual is conscious—a view which seems in conflict with the later

---

[1] Of course, even then, the regress cannot go on *in infinitum*, since an individual human mind has a beginning—according to our ordinary notions, whatever Spinoza may say.

[2] That the mind is composed of very many ideas is stated in II, 15, but it is not explained there that the great bulk of them are unconscious, so far as the individual is concerned.

doctrine of the *idea mentis,* and, for that matter, in conflict with the very notion of an idea as cognitive. If, however, the ideas exist as conscious ideas, then surely we must say that they exist in some *other* mind.

Joachim, expounding or inferring Spinoza's view, states it as follows (p. 131—my quotations are incomplete): "The mind of man *in God's complete knowledge* would thus be the soul-side of all the modes of Extension which constitute his body; and, as their soul-side, it would be the complete apprehension of them all. But what we call our 'mind' falls far short of this, though it may approximate to it in various degrees . . . an infinite number of the constituents of our 'mind' never *for us* enter into, or form part of, our soul-life at all. They form no part of the 'mind' of an actually existing man, either for himself or for the ordinary observer." On the last two sentences I would remark, that surely at any given time all the parts of the mind must be actually existing parts just as the parts of the body are, and, since the essential constituents of the mind are ideas, I do not see how ideas that we don't think can be constituents of our minds at all. The reference to God's complete knowledge is presumably introduced to mitigate the conflict between Spinoza's doctrine and the empirical facts, but it does not help us with II, 12, for what Spinoza says there is that a *cognitio* of whatever happens in the body is *in Deo quatenus naturam humanae mentis constituit,* and this is not God's complete knowledge, but the mind of man considered by itself and apart from anything else.[3]

In the demonstrations of 12 and 13 reference is made to 9 C. Since the demonstration of this corollary is peculiarly difficult to follow, it is fortunate that Spinoza says that 12 can be understood more clearly as following from 7 S.

We have now to return to 13 and consider some of the details. As I have said, the clause which occasions difficulty is *et nihil aliud.* The proof of it is as follows: *si praeter corpus etiam aliud esset mentis objectum, quum nihil (per I, 36) existat, ex quo aliquis effectus non sequatur, deberet (per II, 11) necessario alicujus ejus effectus idea in mente nostra dari. Atqui (per II, ax. 5) nulla ejus idea*

---

[3] Joachim, *op. cit.,* p. 130 seems to connect the phrase 'God, so far as he is expressed by the nature of the human mind' (which is the same as 'so far as he constitutes the nature of the human mind') with *adequate* knowledge, whereas I take 11 C to connect it with *inadequate* knowledge, a knowledge or perception which is ignorant of causal connections (cf. Camerer, p. 68, and see e.g. 28 dem.).

datur. What is the point of introducing the argument about a thing producing effects? It would surely be sufficient to say that, if there were any other object, there would be a corresponding idea of it in the mind (by II, 7). Does Spinoza mean that the object would produce an idea, as an effect, in the mind? Elwes and Robinson translate as if he did: Elwes says "there would necessarily have to be in our mind an idea, which would be an effect of that other object"; Robinson says "so müsste es notwendig . . . eine Wirkung dieses Objekts in unserer Seele geben" (nach Prop. 12—which he says is the correct reference). But to say that an object in another attribute must produce an effect in the mind would contradict the doctrine of the independence of the attributes. I take it that Spinoza must have meant that, if there were another object of mind than the body, there would have been in the mind ideas of the *affectiones* of that object as well as of the *affectiones* of the body.[4] But if so, the reference to ax. 5 (should the reference have been to ax. 4 again?) is of no use for proving his point. For ax. 5 is quite general: it merely says that the only particular things of which we are aware are *corpora* and *modi cogitandi,* and from this it does not follow that we perceive no other body than our own. In point of fact we have, of course, ideas of other bodies. Since Spinoza uses our proposition in proving to Tschirnhaus (Ep. 66 in Bruder II = VV 64) that *Cogitatio* and *Extensio* are the only attributes we can know, it might be tempting to suppose that *et nihil aliud* means 'nothing other than body', that is, no other kind of entity, but the phrase *certus extensionis modus* (in the enunciation), the corollary and scholium, the quotation of our prop. in 19, and even the language of Ep. 66 itself, are too strongly against the supposition to allow us to entertain it.

Spinoza, as I have already suggested, must be assuming that, since sensations as sensory processes (*affectiones*) are bodily processes, perceptions or sensations as cognitive (*ideae affectionum*) must have the body for their object.

In the opening sentence of the scholium Spinoza claims that we can now understand what is meant by the union of mind and body, and the commentators seem inclined to endorse his claim and to think that in his doctrine of body and mind he has made a great advance upon the other Cartesians. I cannot see that he deserves

---

[4] For the meaning of *effectus,* cf. ax. 1 after Lemma 3. The *modi* there spoken of are *effectus* of the two bodies. And cf. *de Int. Em.,* § 21, Clare percipimus nos tale corpus sentire et nullum aliud.

these praises. The statements that the mind is the idea of the body and the body is the one object of mind do not really throw any light upon the relationship—naturally, since they are not true. And the confusion of correspondence with cognition is simply misleading. The scholium itself supplies further evidence of confusion. If the scholium is taken along with the proposition—and in the first half Spinoza uses the language of the proposition—the argument becomes tautologous. For, if knowledge of the body constitutes the very being of the mind, it is needless to tell us that we cannot know the mind without knowing the body and that, the more there is in the body to know, the more there will be in the mind that knows it. But in the sentence that begins, *Hoc tamen in genere dico,* he is evidently thinking of the body as the organ of mind or indeed as determining it, and the stress he lays on a prior knowledge of the body as the key to an understanding of the mind then takes on a different significance. But in so arguing he is inverting the true order of inquiry. We cannot use our knowledge of the body in dealing with the mind until we have first learned how to connect the relevant parts of the body (the bodily organs) with the types of mental experience to which they are instrumental. We know in general that the eyes are the organs of vision by the experiences we have when we open or shut them, and as regards the more special qualities and defects of vision the oculist had first to learn to connect them with the structure of the eyes before he could know how to remedy the defects by artificial aids or surgical operations.

In spite of the doctrine of the independence of the attributes and the express statement in III, 2, we can hardly doubt that in this scholium, in the statements about body and the human body that intervene between this scholium and prop. 14, and in the use he makes later of physiological hypotheses, Spinoza is really thinking of the body as determining the mind. We may say, if we prefer it, that he is thinking of the mind as merely reflecting what goes on in the body, but the essential point is that he really gives a priority or predominance to the body, in spite of his professed doctrine of the complete independence and equality of the attributes. The obvious tendency of the scholium to III, 2—in spite of what the proposition itself asserts—is to glorify the body at the expense of the mind. Joachim (p. 154) says: "As a rule, the bodily changes are most conspicuous, and mental changes are therefore most readily 'explained' as 'effects' of a chain of bodily changes. Really, they are effects of a chain of mental changes which we cannot exhibit, but of which the bodily side is clear to us. We must bear Spinoza's general position in mind, and interpret occasional obscurities and lapses simply *as lapses*: as survivals from his earlier mental history, partly caused, no doubt, by the influence of those popular notions of the relation of body and soul which in his explicit theory he has rejected." The intention of this passage is, of course, to do justice to Spinoza by not laying too much stress on verbal inconsistencies, but I question whether it does not err on the other side by not recognising that there really are at work in his mind different tendencies of thought, and that the tendency to give priority to extension is possibly more potent than the professed doctrine of the independence and equality of the attributes. The vehemence of Spinoza's antagonism to any kind of freedom of the will seems to indicate that he is only too ready to misrepresent mental facts in order to make them conform to the laws of the physical order. It would perhaps be out of place to comment on the statements of fact in the passage quoted from Joachim, since he may be merely expounding, and not endorsing, Spinoza's view. But the second sentence raises a difficulty even as exposition. Why the lack of detail on the mental side, if bodily and mental changes really correspond? And, if the body is the mind's object, and the bodily side is clear to us, what more than the clear apprehensions of the bodily series can the mental series consist of?

Prop. 15 connects closely with 13. The mind, being the idea of the body, is precisely as complex as the body; there is necessarily an idea in the mind corresponding to each part of the body. This proposition, with its references to II, 7 and 8 C shows again that we cannot evade the conflict between Spinoza's doctrine and the actual facts of mental experience by speaking as if the unexperienced ideas existed, not in the actual consciousness of the individual, but 'in God's complete knowledge'. Spinoza asserts, in spite of actual experience, that the mind of the individual is composed of as many actual ideas as there are actual parts of the body. Let the ideas of the parts be ever so inadequate—and that inadequacy also raises difficulties—yet there must be an actual idea for every actual part. Pollock's reference to the physiologist is not without its justification.

§ 7: External Bodies (II, 16 and 17)

In the enunciation of prop. 16, one would have expected Spinoza to say, not *Idea . . . involvere debet naturam corporis,* etc., but rather *involvere debet ideam corporis* or *ideam naturae corporis.*

The demonstration starts with saying that, when our body is affected by an external body, the *affectio* depends upon the natures both of the affecting and the affected bodies—which, of course, is obvious. Spinoza then infers that the *idea affectionis* necessarily involves the natures of both bodies, and refers us to I, ax. 4, which says that the cognition of an effect depends upon a cognition of the cause. We have already seen that there is an ambiguity in the application of this axiom, and here there is a similar ambiguity in the present inference. An effect, *known as an effect,* of course implies a knowledge of the cause, and similarly here the idea of an affection, *as an affection by an external body,* of course implies ideas of the affecting and affected bodies. But it is possible to be aware of a bodily state without connecting it with the action of any external body, for example, a person might be ill without knowing anything about the cause and might then learn from the doctor that the illness must have been due to some external infection. Now Spinoza told us in 13 that the body is the only (immediate?) object of the mind. Therefore in this proposition he is surely guilty of a most serious omission. He ought to have shown (i) why we are led to refer a state of our own body to the action of an external body at all, and (ii) how, when we know only our own body, we can know anything about the nature of the external body. An answer of some sort might perhaps be given to these questions. In answer to (i) we might say that, when something happens in the body which is not to be accounted for by anything in the preceding bodily state, it must be attributed to an external cause, and as regards (ii) we might perhaps be able to infer vaguely from the nature of the effect that the cause must have been of such and such a kind, although any precise knowledge of the nature of the cause would imply a knowledge of external bodies which could not be assumed without a logical circle.

Now in our proposition and the first corollary Spinoza shows no consciousness of these difficulties at all. One who read them without reference to 13 would naturally suppose that Spinoza thought that we can perceive our own body and external bodies equally, and can perceive the former being affected by the latter. True, he says in C 2 that the ideas we have of external bodies *magis nostri corporis constitutionem, quam corporum externorum naturam indicant,* but the examples (in I Appendix) to which he refers us, seem to show that the corollary means, not that we do not perceive the external bodies themselves, but that we do not sufficiently distinguish between qualities which belong to the bodies themselves and descriptions used by us which merely express the ways in which we feel about the bodies.

To maintain consistency with 13 Spinoza would be bound to hold that our knowledge of external bodies is wholly inferential. Did he hold this? Prop. 26 would seem at first sight to assert it plainly, for it says, *Mens humana nullum corpus externum ut actu existens percipit, nisi per ideas affectionum sui corporis.* But when we read the demonstration the first sentence makes only the obvious and harmless assertion that, unless the external body affected our body in some way, the mind could not be aware of the existence of the external body; and the second sentence refers us back to our present proposition, 16. But 16, as we have seen, simply assumes, without any explanation, that we have ideas of our own body as being affected by other bodies.

Joachim (p. 158) speaks of the inferential character of our ideas of external bodies, but the passage is not altogether clear, and I am not sure that he distinguishes sufficiently between the things that Spinoza ought to have said and the things he does say. I will quote a few sentences. "No doubt the idea, which gives us an external body as actually existent, involves an inference. It is primarily the idea of a state of our own body, and only secondarily an idea of an external body, *viz.* only in so far as the idea of the cause is involved in that of the effect." But "the inference . . . is not recognised by the mind in the state of imagination, and is in any case very inadequately performed. In 'imagination' we 'picture' states of our own body and interpret them as external bodies acting upon or modifying our own body." The language of the first two sentences seems to me not to express correctly what Spinoza says in 16. The 'idea which gives us' is of course an *idea affectionis.* Now, when Spinoza says this idea 'involves' the natures of both bodies, I don't think he means that it is primarily the idea of the one and secondarily (or inferentially) the idea of the other; I think he means that the *idea affectionis* necessarily includes ideas of both bodies, that is, cannot be thought without thinking these ideas. This is certainly the meaning of *involvere* as explained in the demonstration of II, 49, where he says that the assertion that the 3 angles of a triangle = 2 right angles involves the idea of a triangle. Moreover, our C 1 with its *una cum* does not suggest any inference. In the last sentence of the quotation, the statement that "in imagination we picture states of our body and interpret *them* as external bodies acting upon our body" is to me unintelligible.

A passage[5] in Camerer (pp. 72–3) dealing with the *ideae affectionum*, and taking us over to prop. 17, may usefully be quoted here. These *ideae*, he says, "bestehen darin, dass 'solange der menschliche Körper in einem bestimmten Zustand sich befindet, auch der menschliche Geist diesen Zustand schaut, das heisst, dass er einen äusseren Körper als wirklich existerend oder als gegenwärtig schaut'. Den Zustand seines eigenen Körpers also, wie er durch die Einwirkung eines äusseren Körpers hervorgebracht worden ist, erkennt der menschliche Geist dadurch, dass er jenen äusseren Körper, der dem menschlichen Körper seine Spuren eingedrückt hat, als gegenwärtig schaut, dass er ihn vor sich sieht. Die Thätigkeit des menschlichen Geistes, vermöge deren dieser die Ideen von den Abdrücken oder Abbildungen der äusseren Körper im menschlichen Körper gewinnt, nennt Spinoza das Gestalten von Bildern, die Imagination." In the first sentence the phrase 'in einem bestimmten Zustand', used in translating a sentence of 17 dem., is not sufficiently precise, for Spinoza's *sic affectum est* means the state of being affected by an external body. The second sentence is difficult. It says that the mind knows the Zustand of its own body 'dadurch dass er jenen äusseren Körper . . . als gegenwärtig schaut'. How can the mind be said to know a state of its *own* body by perceiving an *external* body as present to it? Does Spinoza say this? Again, it would seem as if the Zustand was distinguished from the Spuren, although these also are *affectiones*. This ambiguity is present in our proposition itself. In the demonstration Spinoza says *tam diu mens humana hanc corporis affectionem contemplabitur*, but in the scholium he says *corporis humani affectiones, quarum ideae corpora externa velut nobis praesentia repraesentant, rerum imagines vocabimus, tametsi rerum figuras non referunt.* Now the mind does not

---

[5] Which Joachim may be partly following.

perceive the *imagines,* which (II, 48) may be *in fundo oculi* or *in medio cerebro,* yet in the sentence just quoted he speaks of the *imagines* as being *affectiones quarum ideae corpora externa velut nobis praesentia repraesentant.* Thus he is using the terms *affectiones* and *ideae affectionum* in two quite distinct senses. The *affectiones* (with which we are here concerned) may be perceived or unperceived; and in the former case they are objects, in the latter physiological correlates, of the *ideae affectionum.* And we see once more that Pollock's statement about the ambiguous use of *idea* is justified. Camerer himself, if I understand him rightly, achieves consistency by identifying the *affectiones* exclusively with the *imagines*—in which case the phrase *affectionem contemplari* cannot have its natural meaning—and regarding the *ideae affectionum* as ideas of external bodies produced spontaneously by *Cogitatio* when the *imagines* are reproduced in the body. Possibly he had in view only the ordinary case of vision, where we simply see external bodies without being aware of any affection of our own body. But I see no reason to suppose that Spinoza had this case alone in view. He may quite well have had in view the cases, for example, of seeing a fire and feeling its heat, or of seeing a friend and hearing his voice as contrasted with thinking about him after he has gone. Some of the phrases he uses certainly suggest awareness of the *affectio* itself, for example, *affectionem contemplari, corpus affici sentimus, corpus prout ipsum sentimus, percipere* applied in 16 C 1 equally to external bodies and our own body, and, of course, the *objectum est corpus* of 13. Oddly enough Camerer appeals (p. 74) to 13 as providing an assurance that 'die Bilder im Geist den Bildern im Körper genau entsprechen'. If the 'Bilder im Körper' are the *imagines* which *rerum figuras non referunt,* the exact correspondence must be that of an idea to its physiological condition; yet one would hardly take this meaning from the immediately succeeding statement that 'die Ideen in der Form des Denkens darstellen und wiedergeben, was im Körper körperlich sich vollzieht'. This latter statement would rather suggest such a case as thinking one had cut one's finger when one had actually done it.

   Some of the above difficulties may be partly due to the fact that Spinoza gives no sufficient *psychological* account of the nature of, and differences between, perception, memory, and imagination; he prefers to rely on physiological hypotheses of a conjectural kind. These are of no interest for us, except in so far as they seem plainly to imply that mental process is determined by bodily process. To say that *x* merely corresponds to, and is not determined by, *y* (as Spinoza insists in III, 2 is the case with mind and body) is idle, if what happens in *y* is used to account for what happens in *x*.

The scholium to 17 is interesting because it contains the passage which Pollock uses (pp. 124–125 and 182–183) in explaining his criticism of the double use of the word *idea*. But the confusion is really greater than might appear from Pollock's reference to it. The word *idea* in the phrase *idea Petri* is used to mean (α) *mens Petri*, (β) *conceptus (Petri) in mente Pauli* (γ) this same *conceptus* or *mentis imaginatio* regarded as the *idea* which corresponds to, or expresses, the *image* of Peter in Paul's body or brain. Now if we take α on the one hand and βγ on the other, the word *idea* is being used to denote facts which are not of the same dimension at all, as I have pointed out already. According to Spinoza's own definition an *idea* is a *mentis conceptus quem mens format;* the mind, there-fore, cannot be an idea in this sense. Again, if we take β on the one hand and αγ on the other, what we have in view in β is the cogni-tive relation, whereas what we have in view in αγ is the existential relation between mind and body, or again between a particular mental process and its physiological correlate. Also it certainly seems as if Spinoza was thinking of the mind's 'imaginations' as deter-mined by processes going on in the body. The *ideae affectionum,* then, are ideas which (1) know or represent external bodies as well as our own body, (2) correspond to the *imagines* in our own body and somehow express them, and (3) are apparently determined by them. It seems unlikely that Spinoza would have used the one word *idea* so freely, if he had clearly recognized these complications.

§ 8: The Mind's Knowledge of Body and of Itself (II, 19 and 23)

Prop. 19 presents a peculiar difficulty. There appears to be a glaring verbal contradiction between statements which occur within a few lines of each other. The reader cannot fail to find it a stumbling-block, yet Spinoza shows no consciousness of its presence. The enun-ciation (abbreviated) says *Mens humana ipsum humanum corpus non cognoscit . . . nisi per ideas affectionum,* that is, the mind knows the body but only through the ideas of the *affectiones*. The first sentence of the demonstration speaks of the mind as the idea or *cognitio* of the body. We are then told that the knowledge of the body is *in Deo, quatenus plurimarum rerum ideis affectus est,* for the body will be known (by the *intellectus infinitus*) in its dependence upon other bodies. But what about *Deus, quatenus naturam humanae mentis constituit?* We expect to be told how a knowledge of the body is *in Deo* considered in that way, but instead of that we are told that *in Deo* so considered, that is, in the human mind, there is *no* knowledge of the body, *mens humana corpus humanum non cognoscit,* and not a word of qualification is added. Yet the demonstration goes on to argue that the *ideae affectionum* are *in Deo quatenus humanae mentis naturam constituit,* that is, that the human mind perceives the *affectiones,* and to that extent perceives the body. The word *'percipit'* is used here, but *'cognoscit'* is used in the enunciation, as it is in the statement which says *'non cognoscit'.*

The simplest explanation would be to suppose that something has been omitted from the text after the words *non cognoscit,* namely, some qualifying phrase, and the reference to 11 C suggests the phrase *nisi ex parte sive inadequate,*[6] and with this agrees the statement at the end of 13 S that of our body we have *non nisi admodum confusam cognitionem.* But a difficulty in the way of this solution is that our proposition is quoted in 23, and there again it is said without any qualification that *mens humana ipsum corpus non cognoscit, hoc est, cognitio corporis humani ad Deum non refertur, quatenus essentiam mentis humanae constituit.* Is Spinoza, then, using the word *cognoscere* sometimes in a looser, sometimes in a stricter, sense in the same proposition without a word of explanation? This too would surely be strange.

Two of the commentators expound the proposition, and their expositions imply that, in reading the proposition, the reader has himself to supply the qualification required to avoid the contradiction. Camerer (p. 68) says "der menschliche Geist erkennt den menschlichen Körper nicht (an sich)". Here 'an sich' is used apparently as the contrast to *per ideas affectionum,* but what Spinoza opposes to *per ideas affectionum* is *'per plurimarum rerum singularium ideas'.* The German phrase 'an sich' seems to me to suggest a quite wrong idea. Robinson also uses the phrase 'an sich' but at the important point in demonstration gives a different explanation (p. 325): "Gott hat die Idee oder Erkenntnis des menschlichen Körpers, sofern

---

[6] Cf. the reference to 11 C at the end of 24. What is denied there is not *cognitio* in general, but *adaequata cognitio.*

er von vielen andern Ideen affiziert ist, nicht aber sofern er bloss die Natur der menschlichen Seele ausmacht . . . Daher erkennt die menschliche Seele (auf diesem direkten Wege) den menschlichen Körper nicht (sofern sie nämlich sinnlich erkennt, sofern sie imaginiert)". This may be what was in Spinoza's mind—though 'direkt' seems hardly the right word: it is what one would have expected him to say, but the trouble is that he does not say it, never gives even a hint of it.

The same kind of difficulty recurs in prop. 23. In the enunciation and at the end of the demonstration it is said that the mind does possess a certain *cognitio* of itself, namely, through the *ideae affecttionum,* yet in the middle of the demonstration we are told without any qualification—for *eatenus* there means merely that the human mind is being considered in itself and not as known to the *intellectus infinitus—mens humana se ipsam non cognoscit.*

§ 9: *Idea ideae* (II, 20 and 21)

There seems to be a considerable amount of agreement among the commentators in thinking that the doctrine of the *idea ideae* or *idea mentis* is Spinoza's equivalent for self-consciousness and is important for him as securing the unity and continuity of the mind. I cannot see myself how it can serve this purpose, for there can be no more unity and continuity in the *idea mentis* than there was in *mens* itself, for the *idea mentis* is simply a reflective awareness of what is in the mind; in other words, reflective knowledge can only become aware of, not create, any unity or continuity there is in the mind. I question also whether it is not misleading to identify the *idea ideae* with our notion of self-consciousness. Camerer (p. 55) goes so far as to say: "Das Selbstbewusstein besteht für Spinoza darin, dass eine Idee selbst wieder Object einer Idee wird; ausserdem wäre jene Idee eine bewusstlose". This last statement is surely either ambiguous or wrong; a 'bewusstlose Idee' seems a contradiction in terms. It may be doubted whether Spinoza had any carefully thought-out conception of the self, or had the psychological problem of self-consciousness before his mind at all.

He is not content to take reflective knowledge as an empirical fact but gives an *a priori* deduction of it. This deduction seems to be open to two criticisms. (1) He argues that, *cogitatio* being an attribute, there must necessarily be *in Deo* an idea of it and all its modes (by II, 3). But this argument seems to overlook the fact that *cogitatio* is itself the idea of the *other* attributes which are its objects, that is, it has no independent content of its own which could be the object of another idea. We are back, of course, at the false separation of *idea* from *ideatum*. (2) Even if we put aside this objection, yet *in Deo* as omniscient or infinite intellect there can be no *reflective* knowledge, for there is no need or room for it. *We* reflect on the operations of our mind and on the relations among its contents, because our mind is finite, acquires its contents gradually, never has them all before it at once, and has to reflect in order to take stock of itself. But none of this can be attributed to the infinite intellect, to which all truth is eternally manifest: its knowledge must be completely direct. And once more we have the difficulty of seeing how, in view of this difference between the human and the infinite intellect, the former can be a part of the latter.

At the end of 21 S he refers to what he takes to be an empirical fact and had already stated in *de Int. Em.* § 34, namely, that when we know any object we also know that we know it, and know that we know that we know it, and so on *in infinitum*. This infinite series must surely be dismissed as being, not a fact, but a mere absurdity.[7] It is easy to go on expanding the verbal formula that we know, that we know, that we know and so on, but to these repetitions no real thought, no real distinction of stages, corresponds; we could distinguish one stage from another only by counting the number of times the word 'know' recurs in the verbal formula. But the fundamental error goes back to the very beginning of the series, to the first repetition of the word 'know'. Spinoza seems to think that the whole series of 'knowings' can take place in relation to the one original and self-same object. But he apparently fails to see that we can distinguish one knowing from another only by reference to their respective objects. We cannot distinguish even the second knowing from the first, unless we can make some distinction between their objects. Nor would it be of any use to answer that the object of the second knowing is the object of the first knowing + the knowing of it, for (1) an *object* is, as such, a *known* object; you cannot separate the knowing from it and still have it as object; (2) the knowing is not a second object that can be known apart from its own object; it is not anything added to the *known object,* hence, if we have nothing

[7] Although, strangely enough, a psychologist of so high standing as Ward seems to give some countenance to it (*Psych. Princ.*, p. 372 n).

more than the first object before us, we have no means of distinguishing the second knowing from the first. The fact is, of course, that reflective knowledge consists, not in a senseless repetition of indistinguishable knowings in relation to one single object, but in the recognition of relations between the original object and other contents of mind. How, for example, do I know that I know Euclid, I, 47? Because I remember the figure, the construction, the general method of proof. The second knowing must always bring something additional to confirm the first, otherwise the assertion 'I know that I know' would be indistinguishable from a mere repetition such as, 'Yes, I do know'.

Spinoza's error is shown again in 21 S when he says *mentis idea et ipsa mens una eademque est res, quae sub uno eodemque attributo, nempe cogitationis, concipitur,* for this leaves us with no means of distinguishing between two ideas which are after all one and the same idea. Nor can he really help himself by saying that the *idea ideae* is the *forma ideae, quatenus haec ut modus cogitandi absque relatione ad objectum consideratur,* for an idea *absque relatione ad objectum* is nothing at all, not an idea of anything, and therefore not an idea. Any such *idea mentis* as actually exists in the mind of a reflective human being, any self-consciousness, is not, and cannot be, simply identified with the mind, and in fact the word mind in this connection is necessarily being used ambiguously, for mind as a whole includes (α) direct activities and knowledge, (β) reflection upon these, but when we speak of *idea mentis,* that is, β, *mens* must then mean α only. In a human being β gives only a partial and imperfect knowledge of α: the distinction between α and β is in fact only a special case of the distinction between knowledge and the things it knows. On the other hand, if we are thinking of the *idea mentis* as it exists *in Deo,* in the perfect knowledge of the *intellectus infinitus,* then there is no difference at all between *mens* and the *idea mentis,* for there is no way of distinguishing between the object of perfect knowledge and the thing itself.

§ 10: Truth and Error—Finite and Infinite Intellect (II, 32–36)

It is unfortunate that the examples which Spinoza uses to illustrate his doctrine of error are all, as stated by himself, open to objection. There are two in 35 S and another in IV, 1 S, where 35 S is referred to. The first is that men erroneously think themselves free, and do so because they are ignorant of the causes that determine their actions. This statement may be met by a simple denial. Men think themselves free because they are aware of the plain distinction between action (or movement) under compulsion (as when a man under arrest is marched to the police office by policemen) and action (proper) in which a man does what he himself wills to do. And since a man usually has some reason for doing what he wills to do, he is not ignorant of the cause of his action. The second example is that we 'imagine' the sun to be only about 200 feet distant from us. How Spinoza could make this statement is beyond me, for everybody surely has often seen the sun setting at the far horizon. If a person ignorant of the true distance of the sun were asked, say at midday, how far away he thought the sun to be, I should think he would answer in some such way as this, 'I can't really say, it looks a long way off, but there is no means of judging how far'. And if, apart from astronomy, we have *no* definite ideas about the sun's distance, we can hardly be in error about it. This example also, then, is not of much use to us. And the additional one given in IV, 1 S is, in itself, not much better. When the sun is reflected in water, *eundem perinde, ac si in aqua esset, imaginamur; tametsi verum ejus locum noverimus.* If we know the reflection to be a reflection of the sun, we surely cannot even 'imagine' it as the sun itself. But from the context Spinoza presumably means that, even although we know that the real sun is in the sky, we do not cease to *see* a 'reflected sun'. And this is also his point at the end of 17 S, to which we are here referred, namely, that the *mentis imaginatio* considered in itself contains nothing erroneous.

The enunciation of prop. 33 says: *Nihil in ideis positivum est, propter quod falsae dicuntur.* The demonstration depends on 32, which will be more conveniently discussed later, but we may usefully consider the assertion in the enunciation by itself for a moment. What we should rather have expected Spinoza to say is that there is nothing *in the reality* which can justify what is false in the false idea; the false idea is false precisely because it asserts what does *not* hold good in reality, for example, asserts something to exist which does not exist. But surely the assertion of what is false, the thought that the non-existent thing does exist, is something positive. The idea cannot surely be called false on account of something that is not in it, on account of something that it does not assert. And, if so, we must also reject the assertion of prop. 35 (proved by means of 33) that falsity *consists* in a privation of knowledge. Falsity may be *due to and explained by* a privation of knowledge in this sense, that, if the knowledge had been present, the error would have been prevented, but the falsity *consists* in the positive assertion or thought which was not prevented. It would seem, then, that Spinoza's doctrine of error is not satisfactory, in so far as (1) it does not take sufficient account of the positive assertion or thought which makes the idea erroneous, and therefore (2) fails to give a complete explanation of error; for it will hardly do to say that the error occurred merely because it was not prevented. It may be said in reply that he does try to explain the psychical fact of the *mentis imaginatio* considered merely in itself. But then he himself tells us that in the *imaginatio* considered in itself there is no error. The error consists in a wrong assertion based on the *imaginatio*, a wrong interpretation, and he does not account for that. The interpretation asserts something to exist which does not in reality exist, and Spinoza does not deal at all with the ancient puzzle, how we can think τὸ μὴ ὄν.

Falsity or error is, of course, a defect or vice in an idea, but Spinoza much more frequently uses another term to characterise the defectiveness of defective ideas, namely, inadequacy. How are the two terms related to each other? In a letter to Tschirnhaus (Bruder 11, Ep. 64 = VV 60) Spinoza himself says that there is no difference between a true and an adequate idea, except that when we characterise the idea as true we are thinking of its agreement with its ideatum. Presumably a corresponding statement would apply to a false and an inadequate idea. And it seems obvious enough that, on the one hand, a false idea cannot be adequate, and, on the other, an inadequate idea cannot be true, if, at any rate, it professes to be adequate. Spinoza, of course, introduced the definition of an adequate idea in II, because, in view of the complete independence of the attributes he wished to insist that there is a wholly internal criterion of the truth of an idea, namely, its clearness and distinctness, its self-evidencing quality. But, as we have seen, he does not really escape the external reference of ideas, for (1) they know their ideata, (2) they correspond to their ideata in the respect that the order and connection of ideas is the same as that of their ideata.

What, then, is the internal mark of character of inadequacy in an idea? Since adequacy is shown by clearness and distinctness, we should expect inadequacy to be shown by confusion, and this is the expression which Spinoza most frequently uses as an equivalent for inadequacy, but it is not the only one. In 11 C inadequacy is equated —in the phrase *rem ex parte sive inadaequate percipere*—with partiality or incompleteness; and, from the corollary itself and the use made of it, the incompleteness would seem to consist in this, that a thing known only *ex parte* is a thing not known in relation to its cause or ground.[8] For, as ax. 6 of I tells us, knowledge of an effect depends upon knowledge of its cause, or, as Spinoza says in II, 28, when speaking of the *affectiones,* things not known in terms of their causes are like *consequentiae absque praemissis.* Are we, then, to regard 'incompleteness' and 'confusion' as equivalent? Spinoza himself seems to do so, for, for example, after the phrase just quoted from 28 he adds *hoc est (ut per se notum) ideae confusae,* and he couples together *confusa et mutilata cognitio* in 28 C, and speaks of ideas as *inadaequatae sive mutilatae et confusae* in 35. Busolt (p. 37) takes the opposite view: "Irrthum ist nicht Unvollständigkeit, sondern Widerspruch in der Vorstellung". But this is hardly Spinoza's way of putting the matter, and the various considerations which Busolt advances in the context in support of his statement do not seem to me to justify it. He says: "Wenn man sich der unvollständigen Vorstellung als solcher bewusst ist, so irrt man sich nicht". But the knowledge that *imaginationes* are inadequate belongs to a higher kind of knowledge than *imaginatio* itself, namely, to the knowledge expounded in some of the propositions of II. Next, he refers to the statement in 17 S that the *imaginationes* regarded merely in themselves contain nothing erroneous. But then it is only when the *imaginationes* are taken as cognitions of external realities that the question of error arises at all. Finally, he says that it is only when the *imaginationes* are taken as cognitions of existing things at a time when the things have ceased to exist, that there is a 'falsche Vorstellung', and I suppose he would say that there is then 'Widerspruch in der Vorstellung'. But what Spinoza himself says in 17 S is that the error lies in the fact that the mind is without the

---

[8] As Busolt, *Die Grundzüge der Erkenntnisztheorie und Metaphysik Spinozas* (Berlin, 1875) (p. 35) puts it: "Kein Einzelding ist durch sich selbst da . . . sein Dasein und sein Wesen hängt von andern Dingen ab. Der Körper ist nur ein Glied . . . in dem unendlichen Causalnexus, welcher den Zusammenhang der Natur der Dinge ausdrückt . . . Nur als Glied dieser unendlichen Reihe von Ursachen und Wirkungen wird ein Einzelding in adaequater Weise begriffen."

idea that would prevent it from taking the *imaginationes* as cognitions of existing things; in other words, the error consists, as 35 says, in a *privatio cognitionis*. In 11 C Spinoza is not explaining error but only thinking of inadequacy as consisting in an ignorance of causes, but in 35 S error itself is imputed to an ignorance of causes. Thus I think we must regard Spinoza as holding that the partial or incomplete character of 'imaginative' knowledge necessarily involves it in falsity.

It would seem, then, that we have to interpret Spinoza's statement in 35 that *falsitas* consists in a *privatio cognitionis*, not in the sense that what looks like error is only partial knowledge, but in the opposite sense that knowledge that is only partial necessarily involves error or misrepresentation of the reality, that is, the false idea does not merely omit some features contained in its ideatum, but, owing to the lack of fuller knowledge, misrepresents and falsifies its ideatum. And the examples in 35 S (freedom and the sun's distance) bear this interpretation out, for they seem clearly meant to be examples of ideas that are in conflict with fact. They are ideas which could only exist in a mind ignorant of the actual facts, and in that sense their falsity depends upon a privation of knowledge, but they are ideas which do not correspond to, but misrepresent, their ideata. In the case of the sun's distance, the sun, according to Spinoza, looks quite near, but it is to our ignorance of the true distance and of the cause of the near appearance, and not to this appearance itself, that he imputes the error. The ignorance of privation of knowledge is held responsible for the error; the near appearance is innocent, for it remains even after we know the true distance.

However much, then, Spinoza may insist that error depends on a privation of knowledge, so that, given the knowledge, error would disappear and cease to exist, yet, so long as the privation continues the error will continue, and the false idea will be a real idea existing in its falsity. There can, of course, be no false ideas in the *intellectus infinitus*, for in that intellect there is no privation of knowledge. How, then, is the human intellect with its many false ideas related to the *intellectus infinitus* in which there are no false ideas? Spinoza's utterances on the subject are *prima facie* not consistent. In 11 C he says without any qualification that the human mind is part of the *intellectus infinitus*, but in 43 S, although he refers to 11 C, he inserts a qualification; our mind, *quatenus res vere percipit*, is part of the *intellectus infinitus*. But is our mind, then, so far as it does *not* perceive things truly but has false ideas, *not* part of the *intellectus infinitus?* Some real difference between the human mind and the *intellectus infinitus* as existents there must surely be, if the one contains false ideas and the other does not. But if the human mind were, as respects any part of it, outside the *intellectus infinitus,* the latter would not be infinite in Spinoza's sense of the term. We must be careful here not to confuse our present difficulty with a more general difficulty about the application of the notions of part and whole to the relation between the finite and the infinite. There is on Spinoza's view no difficulty in saying that *true* ideas are parts of the *intellectus infinitus.* Spinoza does not hold that no truth short of the whole truth can be in itself completely true; his view about truth is not Bradley's. The *intellectus infinitus* can have ideas that are true of their specific objects in the same way as its knowledge as a whole is true of reality as a whole, and the human mind can attain to some of these true and adequate ideas. It is the existence of false ideas in the human mind that seems to make it impossible that that mind should be part of the *intellectus infinitus.*

It would seem that there are only two possible solutions of our difficulty, and neither of them is such as Spinoza, in view of other parts of his doctrine, could easily accept. Either the human mind and the *intellectus infinitus* are distinct psychical existents, and in that case infinite is being used in the sense of omniscient but *not* in the sense of *in suo genere infinitus,* or the *intellectus infinitus* is not a psychical existent at all, but an expression signifying the totality of truth.

The foregoing difficulty arises within *Cogitatio* taken by itself, but there is the further difficulty of a conflict with the fundamental doctrine of the correspondence of the order and connection within the attributes as stated in II, 7. False ideas misrepresent their ideata, whereas according to II, 7 the order and connection of ideas is the same as the order and connection of things. How, then, is the existence of false ideas possible?

Prop. 32, which we have so far passed over, makes a startling and puzzling assertion. After reading a whole series of propositions about inadequate ideas it is startling to be told that *all* ideas, *quatenus ad Deum referuntur,* are *true.* How can inadequate and false ideas be made adequate and true by being referred *ad Deum?* We have just been urging that only true ideas can be so referred. Pollock (p. 183) says roundly: "The proposition amounts to saying that every mental state is in one sense *true,* inasmuch as it really exists". Similarly Busolt (p. 37) says of *imaginationes* that they "involviren an sich noch keinen Irrthum, denn sie sind als Bilder[9] etwas Wirkliches, also die Ideen von ihnen als solchen wahr". To say, however, that Spinoza in this proposition is simply equating the truth of ideas with the existence of mental states seems too rough and ready a way of disposing of the proposition, and in any case does not solve the difficulty how false mental states come to exist at all, if II, 7 is true. Important as the proposition obviously is, Spinoza himself, certainly, gives us little help in understanding it. The demonstration occupies three lines, and there is no further explanation. The first words of the demonstration are *Omnes ideae quae in Deo sunt,* a phrase which might suggest that there are some ideas which are not *in Deo.* But this cannot be Spinoza's meaning, for, as he says in prop. 36, *Ideae omnes in Deo sunt (per* I, 15)—naturally, since they have nowhere else to be. He then goes on *et, quatenus ad Deum referuntur, sunt verae (per* 32). Here a distinction is apparently drawn between the phrases *in Deo* and *quatenus ad Deum referuntur,* and *in Deo* is the wider expression, but in 32 the two phrases must be used as equivalent. Why, then, are all ideas, *quatenus ad Deum referuntur,* said to be true? We are referred both in 32 and 36 to 7 C, which says in effect that ideas as produced by the *Res Cogitans* have the same *ordo et connexio* as their *essentiae formales,* and therefore (as 32 says) agree entirely with these their *ideata,* and so are true.

The expression which in 36 is contrasted with *quatenus ad Deum referuntur* is *quatenus ad singularem alicujus mentem referuntur,* and as so referred ideas may be inadequate and confused. In what sense are such ideas nevertheless *in Deo?* From 11 C we may infer that it is *quatenus [Deus] per naturam humanae mentis explicatur, sive humanae mentis essentiam constituit;* and the *humana mens* here is of course the same as the *singularis mens* of 36, that is to say, it is the mind of the individual man, taken by itself, and apart from its place and connections within the *intellectus infinitus.*

Prop. 34 tells us further that there may be ideas which are adequate and true even in us, that is, *in Deo quatenus nostrae mentis essentiam constituit.*

To sum up what we learn from props. 32, 34 and 36:—all ideas

[9] = *Imagines?* (Busolt does not keep the distinction between *imagines* and *imaginationes* clear.) Strictly the *imaginationes* are neither true nor false.

are *in Deo* in a wide sense of that phrase; but they may be (α) *in Deo* and referred *ad Deum* without qualification, or (β) *in Deo* and referred *ad Deum, quatenus tantum humanae mentis essentiam constituit.* When ideas are considered as referred in one or other or both of these ways, it is asserted: (1) that all ideas are adequate and true when referred in manner α, (2) that some ideas are adequate and true both when referred in manner α and when referred in manner β, and (3) that other ideas are adequate and true when referred in manner α but not when referred in manner β.

Two difficulties are raised by this summary of results:—first, as regards the double reference in 3, according to which the same ideas are true in one way and false in another; and, second, as regards the inconsistency of (1), proved as it is by 7 C, with the existence of any false ideas whatsoever.

The two parts of (3) are not openly contradictory, for there is a distinction in the mode of reference of the ideas. But is the distinction between *Deus* unqualified and *Deus* qualified, which professes to be only a distinction between two ways of regarding *Deus,* anything more than a slight disguise for the fact that *Deus* qualified is not *Deus* but man? We are back, of course, at our previous difficulty about the *intellectus infinitus.* Does the *Res Cogitans* exist in two ways, as *intellectus infinitus* knowing everything adequately, and as finite minds knowing many things inadequately; as at once one and infinite with the characteristics of an infinite mind, and also as many finite minds with the characteristics of finite minds? To put the difficulty in another way, the ideas which are inadequate in man must surely undergo a change in order to become adequate in the *intellectus infinitus*; and the change will not consist in the mere filling up of that lack of knowledge in which the privation consisted; it requires also the giving up of that erroneous part of the idea which the knowledge would have prevented from coming into existence. Or, conversely, ideas which are adequate in the *intellectus infinitus* must undergo a change in order to have a place as inadequate ideas in the mind of man, a change which implies not merely a diminution but a distortion. In other words, the ideas which are adequate in one reference and inadequate in another are not the same ideas.

The first of the 3 assertions, when taken along with its proof by means of 7 C, raises the difficulty of reconciling the existence of inadequate ideas with the exact correspondence of ideas and things.

If, as 7 C and 32 say, the *Res Cogitans* produces all ideas in such a way that they correspond exactly with their ideata and so are true, how can inadequate and false ideas come into existence? If ideas agree with their ideata and are true, they cannot be confused and inadequate. If they are confused and inadequate, they cannot agree with their ideata and be true. Or are we to say that there is confusion in the ideata, in the things themselves?

Camerer seems in one passage (p. 90) to be prepared to adopt this heroic solution: "Auch die inadaequaten und confusen Ideen . . . der vollkommen richtige Ausdruck der Vorgänge sind, welche in ihnen vorgestellt werden, und auch das, dass sie im menschlichen Geist verworren und verstümmelt vorkommen, ist der getreue Ausdruck für das, was bei den Affectionen des menschlichen Körpers mit diesem vorgeht". The *imaginationes* are confused because in the *affectiones* "die Natur des menschlichen Körpers mit der Natur äusseren Körper sich confundirt". But it is impossible to take this 'Confundirung' seriously. The external bodies act upon our body in perfectly definite ways. In an earlier passage (p. 80) Camerer himself had spoken of the confusion as being one of knowledge, not of bodies: "in den Ideen von den Affectionen des Körpers ist eine Kenntniss von äusseren Körper gemischt mit einer solchen von dem menschlichen Körper". The confusion is in our minds, not in *Extensio*. As Spinoza says in a letter to Oldenburg (Bruder II, Ep. 15 = VV 33): *Res non nisi respective ad nostram imaginationem possunt dici . . . ordinatae aut confusae.*

But if this solution will not do, we have to ask again, If there is no confusion in *Extensio,* how comes it that there is confusion in the *corresponding* ideas in *Cogitatio*? Spinoza says in 43 S that in props. 19 to 35 he has explained the causes of *falsitas,* but he did not explain how he reconciled the operation of these causes with the doctrine of the correspondence of ideas and things. I do not see how any solution of the difficulty is possible for Spinoza at all. Just as formerly the cognitive relation and the relation of correspondence were confused, so now they seem, so far as inadequate ideas are concerned, to have well nigh lost connection with each other. The *imaginationes* do not know the *imagines* at all, and they do not know in any adequate way those causal interactions between bodies of which the *imagines* are the effect.

On a Reputed Equivoque in the Philosophy of Spinoza

H. F. Hallett

AMONG THE VARIOUS AMBIGUITIES which have been invented (and I use the word equivocally) in the philosophy of Spinoza, and have been held to be fatal in respect of this or that part of it, or of the whole, none seems to have been so generally, and so undoubtingly, noted as his identification of the bodily *correlate* of the human mind with its physical *object* in *Ethics II., xiii.* And certainly no error (if it is an error) could be more fundamentally fatal to the whole speculation; an equivocal use of the term "idea" as at once the mental correlate of some neural or physiological state of the body of the percipient, and also the *essentia objectiva* of a thing extrinsic to that body—involving the simple identification of the human body with the object of the human mind that animates it —would seem to be a confusion at the source, infecting the whole system.[1]

I

Yet this very confusion was confidently attributed to Spinoza by Pollock in what was the first thoroughgoing exposition of his philosophy written in English.[2] In the *Tractatus de Intellectus Emenda-*

---

[1] Other prominent examples of imputed incoherence (I say "imputed" to guard against the supposition that I recognize it as just in either case) are his reputed atomism in physics (based on his idea of the *corpus simplicissimum*) with his monism in natural philosophy, and his implied attribution of a measure of moral freedom to a being subject to universal necessity. But the former concerns only topics incompletely expounded—indeed in part avoided (*Eth. II., xiii. Sch.*) and in part left for further study (*Ep. lxxxiii S.*) and the latter would at worst but divorce the ethical doctrine from the ontology, and leave open a final problem which (as we now see) might be attacked (if not resolved) by a Kantian approach.

[2] *Spinoza, His Life and Philosophy,* 2d ed., pp. 123–126.

tione,[3] Pollock tells us, an "idea" is "a conscious state of the knowing mind, in which the object known is represented". "If I think of Peter, the state of my consciousness is an *idea* of Peter according to Spinoza's first usage of the term"; but, he says, Spinoza also conceives an "idea" of my mind as corresponding, not with *Peter* who is other than myself, but with *my own body*: and Pollock was evidently thinking of the *Proposition* I have named, which affirms that "the object of the idea constituting the human mind is the body . . . and nothing else". He then goes on to remark, with the air of counsel hurriedly briefed to clear up a case against a taciturn prisoner in a few words of plain commonsense about the law, that "a man can easily think of his own body, but he is not always doing so, and when he does his thought will not be accurate unless he has learnt something of physiology. And even if every human being were an accomplished physiologist, the constant relation of the mind as a whole to the body as a whole would still be something different from the relation of the knowing to the known". On the evidence of such naïve and hasty lucubrations, the jury (with one or two doubting exceptions) have brought in a verdict of "Guilty" —and that in spite of the irrepressible aside of a footnote from counsel himself that "Spinoza himself once [*sic*] calls attention to the distinction: *Eth.* 2. 17, schol." [4]—for is not the prisoner thus condemned out of his own mouth?

It will be my business in what follows to show, in my "long-winded" manner,[5] that we have here no callow confusion to be thus disposed of, but the very quintessence of Spinoza's solution of the otherwise insoluble problems of human epistemology and ontology.

It might have been supposed that no one but an eminent lawyer applying his great powers beyond their scope could have been willing to make so dubious and laconic a plea with so little reflection; but evidently it is still possible for even a patient and critical mind, like that of my former teacher and honoured friend the late Henry Barker, in commenting on the case, to attempt to substantiate it in "a rather fuller statement".[6] Since, however, this more ample state-

[3] *Tract. de Intell. Emend.*, § 33.

[4] Pollock, loc. cit., p. 125 n.

[5] "I am carrying about a very solid and rather long-winded study of Spinoza's philosophy . . . called *Aeternitas*, by one Hallett" (*The Pollock-Holmes Letters*, F. Pollock, August 29, 1931).

[6] H. Barker, "Notes on the Second Part of Spinoza's Ethics (II)" (*Mind, XLVII.*, N.S., p. 295). [See p. 137 of the present volume.]

ment is based upon precisely the same fundamental assumptions, it is no matter for wonder that Barker has to conclude by agreeing with Pollock that "when Spinoza speaks of the mind as *idea sive cognitio corporis,* he is confused and is using the word *idea* in a new and strange way". What is wonderful is that Barker, who makes real progress towards a resolution of the seeming equivocation by distinguishing two sets of relations, the causal and the "instrumental", fails at the crucial point correctly to apply the results of his analysis by supposing that the two sets form a single series—whereas in obvious fact they belong to distinct perspectives: that of the percipient himself, and that of *another* percipient.

II

What, then, is this fundamental assumption which I have imputed to these writers as involving them in the judgement that Spinoza is "interpreting correspondence in two ways, epistemological and physiological, without clearly realizing that he was doing so"? I reply that it is their eccentric commonsense view of the nature of perception, derived from current post-Spinozistic empiricism, and infecting even the idealistic critics of that doctrine. It is commonly supposed that when a perceiver perceives an external object, for example, the sun, "the sun (to quote Barker) as a cause sets up light waves which travel to the earth, affect the body or eye, and so initiate a physiological process which causes a brain change, in virtue of which, as a condition, perception of the sun takes place. The series of events that starts from the sun and has its physical (or physiological) termination in the brain is in its earlier stages a causal series, but in its last stage, namely, that in which perception takes place, and in which the brain functions as the organ or instrument of the mind, we had better describe it by another adjective such as 'instrumental', for the relation of mind to body or brain is so intimate that the notion of causal action seems inappropriate".[7] On this view we have a causal physical and physiological process followed by a psycho-physical "fact" or miracle—according as mind is regarded as epiphenomenal or "substantial".

I suppose that this account of the processes and relations involved in perception strikes the commonsense empiricistic reader as a plain recital of fact, or of theory directly based on fact, and too obvious to

[7] H. Barker, loc. cit., pp. 295–296. [P. 138 of the present volume.]

be open to question—it must do so since so many otherwise astute philosophers have accepted it as the factual basis of the theory of perception—and that in spite of all the multiplex difficulties and paradoxes that have in it their *fons et origo*. Of scientists and the vulgar I need not speak, for their naiveties in this sphere can do little harm, and perhaps some good. Nevertheless, in truth, we have here not a description of perception as it is, and truly, for the perceiver, but only of the processes associated with perception as *observed* by a percipient *other than* the one whose perception is supposed to be under investigation. Nor even this, for the last and crucial stage in the process is by nature unobservable, and must be imputed. When this is taken as an account of perception *in itself* it is no wonder that we become involved in a farrago of absurdities: *perceptio a non percipiendo*! For just as in this observed process the perception alone is unobservable, and must be imputed as a "fact" or miracle, so *per contra* in perception itself, and for the perceiver, this objective process is nowhere to be found, but only the perceptual relation between the percipient mind and an object that it directly perceives: here it is the causal process that must be imputed.

Thus, of the two sets of relations distinguished by Barker, the one is experienced only by the percipient himself; the other is what is observed, not as relating the percipient and the sun in the act of perception, but as relating *another man's* mind (conceived as in his head), his body, the medium, and the sun as objects of external observation. Pollock and those who agree with him are involved in confusion because they appear to regard perception-in-act as a mere "short-circuiting" of the elaborate processes observed by another, by which the causal processes are "telescoped-in", and only the so-called "instrumental" remain in sight, by reason of the special position of the percipient viewing the causal processes as it were "end on". Spinoza, on the contrary, is involved in no confusion since for him what is prior is the direct perception of the object, and the causal processes are "telescoped-out" by projection on the eccentric axes of *another* perceiver. He does not suppose that this direct perception is incorrigible, but it is not corrigible by reference to what *another* percipient directly perceives (and imputes)—for that too is equally corrigible, so that this way lies not correction but confusion. If we are to analyse perception, it is perception-in-act that we must investigate, and not perception as it is observed and imputed by another.

III

In perception-in-act, then, there is a direct perceptual relation of the percipient and the object that he perceives: how do we come to represent the perceptual relation of *another* percipient to the thing that we suppose him to be perceiving ("suppose" because he alone perceives it, and he cannot inform us that what he perceives is the thing that we perceive) as a set of causal relations between the thing and the perceiver's central nervous system, followed by a psycho-physical "fact" or miracle? The man who perceives the sun does not at the same time perceive his own body or sense-organ with its cerebral connexions interposed between "him" and the sun. He is aware neither of a causal process with its terminal cerebral agitation, nor of any psycho-physical relation or transition "in his head". True, when he thinks that he knows by other means how the sun should appear, and notes that for his perception it appears otherwise, he is apt (in the absence of any previously unnoted external condition, such as the dark glasses on his nose) to assign the difference to the abnormality of his sense-organism. But this inference is posterior to his objective interpretation of the situation in physical, physiological and psycho-physical terms, and not the immediate deliverance of his own perception, nor based on any premiss thence derived. Indeed, if he does think of his own optical system (on the analogy of the dark glasses on his nose) as interposed between "him" and the sun, it is as a "transparency" which (by reason of commonsense assumptions) may be regarded as more or less darkened or contorted by optical defect, jaundiced by pathological condition, or overstimulated to an eccentric response. In other sense no man can be said to see his own eye-in-act among the objects that he sees. And the same is true of his whole body regarded as the objective instrument of perception as it is conceived *ab extra*.

In actual perceptual experience, of course, the situation is complicated and confused in so far as one sense-organ is instrumental in the external observation of another as an object in the world of that element of the total perception for which it is not instrumental. With the hand we can feel the eye as an object in the world mediated by touch; with the eye we can see the hand as a visual object; and so forth. And it is all too easy and seductive to complete these partial objective appearances by way of imagination to the form of a body among (and like) the observed bodies of other men which, as objects, are not subject to this strict privation. The mirror seems to bear this out, though what the mirror shows is what another would see if placed behind the mirror with the mercury removed. Thus, though we cannot see our eye-in-act we believe that it is there just as others see it, and we feel it, and see it in the mirror, and we presume that it is but an accident of position that prevents us from seeing it directly for ourselves—an accident of bodily structure similar to that which prevents us from seeing the back of our neck (which also we can see in a mirror). Yet *it is no mere accident, but the very essence of the situation;* neither the eye itself, nor anything else, is standing in the way of the eye, and shutting it off from the sight of itself. On the contrary, it is revealing itself as it is in act, and by so doing revealing its world of visual objects—as it were patterned upon its transparency. And so of all the sense-organs: their absence from the worlds of objects in relation to which (as distinct objects for other men) they appear as instrumental, is *the very ground of their instrumentality*: they are absent from *among* these objects because in some manner they are present *in them all*. We may go so far as to say that for visual perception the eye-in-act is the visual field in which the objects of vision are related and distributed —though its appearance as field reciprocates with the appearance of objects, partial or total, upon it. For the eye that sees no object sees not at all, and is no eye-in-act.[8] And so, *mutatis mutandis,* of the whole body in the complex perception of its world. The "body" which is the *real* correlate of the percipient mind is not the object of some *other* mind, is not the "body" as it is observed *ab extra* (and even in part by the mutual instrumentality of its members), but the "body" as is *in itself,* and which as affected by other bodies, is the *object* of the mind's perception. The real correlate *is* the object, but not *one* of the objects constituting the mind's world: it is the mind's world operating as its measure of the real world that transcends it; it is the body with the *affectiones* concomitant with its relation with an extrinsic complement which thus only is represented in it. The body as it is in itself is, as it were, an instrument which manifests and measures the universe, and its *affectiones* are the "pointer-readings" to its other on the "scale"

[8] Sight, like all sense-perception, is essentially a function of a finite individual with respect to its other; the "eye of God" that "sees all things", "sees" them as "conscience" within each.

of its nature, by which that nature is in determinate reciprocation
with its complement—a complement which is thus perceived *in
projection*: in the form of the spatio-temporal transparency that
is the objective appearance of the body itself in relation with its
complement, decorated and shadowed with the unintelligible *data*
which are the objective appearance of the transcendence of the
world of others in relation with the body whose complement it is.
As Berkeley suggests,[9] the form of space timelessly objectifies the
unimpeded agency of the body; and we may add that the durational
"materials of sense" objectify the modifications of the body by reason of its response to the complex impedance of the other. And thus
the world of perception is the objective appearance of the body as
"affected" by its active complement in Nature, and its objectivity
but a sign and symbol of the relative impotence of the body in
comparison with the magnipotence of its complement. For bodies
and the universe, in themselves, are not mere "things", but *agents,*
and their objective appearances but privations of mutual projection.[10]

IV

This brings me to Spinoza's own account of the human body and
its *"affectiones"*. By an *"affectio"* in general Spinoza means any state
of an entity referable to what is distinct from the entity itself.
"Affectio", *"modus"*, and *"modificatio"* are terms interchangeable

---

[9] *Principles,* § 116.

[10] The application of these principles to the different senses as these are *externally* conceived is, of course, on no unvarying plan, though as conceived as
senses-*in-act* the differences are less striking. Sight, in terms of which my exposition has, in the main, been fashioned (the world of sight having a greater
temporal totality than the world of touch) presents objects *at a distance* from
the objective eye, whereas touch is a contact-perception. Thus an account in
terms of touch would, perhaps, seem to the unconverted less speculative than
one in terms of sight, since here what lies on the near side of the common surface of contract is "body", and what lies on the far side is the tactual "other."
But yet, I suggest, even this difference is but another example of the main principle, and what seem for *another* perceiver to be the limits of the "body" may
not be its true limits for the percipient *himself*. The blind man (as Descartes
points out) *feels* the pavement with the ferule of his stick; and when I observe
Orion my *eye-in-act* (i.e., *my total optical system*) extends to the limit of my
visual percipience—it "rests upon Orion" (*vide* "On Things in Themselves",
Philosophy XIV., 1939, p. 177 n).

save by special usage in different connexions (e.g., a "mode" or "*affectio*" of Substance is an individual thing[11] which, again, may be variously "affected" by other individual things or "modes" of Substance—thus having its own "*affectiones*"; but even here the "modes" "affect" one another only because all are "*affectiones*" or "modes" of Substance).[12] Take now two interacting modes of Extension, for example, a diminutive and a bulky body in impact: they can impinge on one another only because both are modes of Extension; their "action and reaction" at impact are "equal and opposite" because, as Newton says,[13] the *vis insita* of each is an evocation of the *vis impressa* of the other (the *vis inertiae* of each measuring only the complete impotence of its isolation—for, *ex hypothesi*, it has no other to accelerate or retard, and its "inertia" is its impotence to accelerate or retard itself); but the "*affectiones*" of the two bodies are different by reason of their difference of bulk— the diminutive body being most "affected": their changes of speed being inversely proportional to their bulks. This is an elementary example of the general principle that the "*affectio*" of a thing is a function of its own nature and of the nature of the other by which it is "affected"; for though the *affectio* is a state of the thing itself, and belongs to it as a distinct entity, it is a state that is in part determined by the nature of its other. Because the mutually actualizing "action and reaction" are "equal and opposite", and the bulks are different, the "*affectiones*" (i.e., the acceleration or retardation) are different in inverse proportion to their differing bulks.[14]

Furthermore, these "*affectiones*" (as our example also illustrates) in the end *constitute* the things said to be "affected". There can be no isolated body (for the *vis inertiae* of the isolated body is total impotence—it is actualized as *vis insita* only by reaction to *vis impressa*); save as affected by another it is nothing. We thus reach the general principle that a finite thing is what it is solely by reason of its reciprocation with a complement, and has its perfect nature only by reciprocation with its exhaustive complement in Nature. It is thus that it is *constituted* by its *affectiones*, and what are commonly regarded as its *special affectiones* with respect to this or that selected

[11] *Eth. I., xxv. Cor.*

[12] "*Affectio*" is to be distinguished from "*affectus*" which is a *disposition* towards another arising from an *affectio* or *state* determined by that other.

[13] *Principia I., Def. iii.*

[14] *Eth. II., Ax. i. post Lem. iii. Cor.*

other are but differentiations of its constitutive *affectiones*. As Whitehead has expressed the same doctrine (for "there is no new thing under the sun") there are no "things" having "simple location" and standing in "external relations" with other things.

It is of first importance, however, not to fall into the error of supposing that this implies that a body is nothing but a conventional focus characterized by the *resultant* of world-forces as concentrated upon it (on the analogy of the "centre of gravity" of a body). This might be adequate enough as a description of any supposed mere point-instant on which these forces converge—for then the resultant is zero, and the point-instant nothing actual at all. Each body, on the contrary, is a part of the universe, affected, not by the whole, but by its *complement* in the whole; and in so far as it is actual it has its own nature as *reactive* to the action of that complement. Though an *isolated* body is nothing, as reactive to its complement it is actual *with* that complement. To return to our example: in impact, each of the impinging bodies has its *vis insita* evoked by the *vis impressa* from its other, and operating *by way of reaction*.[15] Thus, each body is a *reactive focalization* of its complement, and its actuality is its reagency. It is thus only that the universe of bodies is actual: for if each were but the resultant at a conventional focus of the actions of all others, similarly defined, all would be reduced to nonentity in a vicious circle of *vires inertiae*. And a world of point-instants would be doubly inert—the very acme of nonentity.[16]

Each body, then, is the reactive focalization of its world, and when two bodies are conceived as affecting each other, their *affectiones* are not in truth modifications supervenient upon their otherwise wholly independent absolute natures, but differentiations of the integral reactivity of all other bodies as focalized in them. The

---

[15] What this means is that the notion of otherwise isolated bodies impinging on one another is an abstraction: *at impact* they form a strained *totum;* as *isolated* they are but abstracted "poles" of "universal" stresses relative to themselves— and in that relation alone are actual. Thus the finite body is at once an abstraction taken alone, and an actual reactive "pole" of "universal" stress. Yet the universe as a whole suffers no stress, for it is complementary, not to any actual part of itself but, so to say, to the point-instant, which is nothing actual, and nothing distinct.

[16] Those who have supposed that Spinoza's doctrine entails the illusoriness of all finite modes in the integrity of Nature, have perhaps been influenced by some such error. I am not as yet able to say whether Whitehead himself does or does not, in whole or in part, avoid the error.

reagency of each is the evocation of the agency of all others, and the *affectiones* of each are the changes in its abstract nature reciprocating with the abstracted agency of *this or that* extrinsic body. Here we are dealing with an abstracted partial system of bodies, and in that reference an affected body suffers a change of its abstracted nature, and its modification or *"affectio"* with respect to its other registers the change suffered by its actual nature *as abstracted*—a change which, in respect of its *total* nature may be either a privation or an achievement. For its other may be either an aid or a hindrance to its perfection. It cannot but change its abstract temporal actuality, but this change may either involve concretion with Nature or further abstraction from it.

In the interaction of finite bodies, therefore, the *affectiones* partake both of the nature of the body affected and of that of its other —its own nature being, as it were, the scale on which its pointer indicates the power of its other. Just as the galvanometer measures with its needle on its disc the value of this or that selected electromagnetic field only by reason of its inductive reaction to that field, so the human body reactively focalizes its world, so that its special *affectiones* are differential pointer-readings on its scales, distributively measuring the reagency to it of all other bodies in that world to which it is capable of reacting. And the principle must be fully generalized—for all bodies whatsoever, like the galvanometer and the human body, are composed of parts similarly related in their orders to reciprocal complements, measuring them in their own ways, by the pointers of *"affectio"* on the scales of their own natures, *ad indefinitum*. The reactive essence of every finite body is a "pole" of the "universal" stress at that level in the hierarchy of Nature: an agency "equal and opposite" to the agency of its congruent complement.

In speaking of the "hierarchy of Nature" I am thinking of the doctrine of orders of corporeal individuality expounded by Spinoza in *Ethics II., Lem. vii. Sch.* An individual is actual, not by aggregation but by reciprocal action of its parts; and each part is actual only as the reactive focalization of all others. Each part in so far as it is individual is a microcosm of the whole, and thus also ultimately of the macrocosm. It reproduces its whole, and *the* whole, in the degree in which its complement can affect it, that is, in the degree of its microcosmicity; and the nature of the microcosm is contributed to the whole both as affected part and as reactive focalization of its complement in turn, in due measure, affecting that complement. But the "contribution" is not by way of *addition,* but by way of *expression* more or less eccentric according to the status of the part and its abstractedness.

I have made use of the analogy of the scale and pointer-reading, and it may be well to consider the adequacy of the analogue: measures are, of course, always relative to a unit of measurement, and the calibration of the scale of a measuring instrument is essentially conventional. Thus the value of a pointer-reading on a scale is absolute only in so far as an absolute unit can be provided. It is thus that in our mathematical formulæ for expressing the laws of nature the pointer-readings of our instruments always qualify *variables* which stand for the absolute scales which the conventional scales of our instruments are made to represent. By themselves pointer-readings are of course without significance. The footrule measures distances, the clock durations, the galvanometer electromagnetic forces, and the human body the world of things by which it is affected, only in so far as these instruments, and the calibration of their scales, can be taken to be absolute. In scientific practice the pointer-reading is significant because all that is required is a comparative measure of the variable; but for natural philosophy a more concrete attitude is desirable: the instrument is a part of the physical world short-circuiting its own nature in its scale as calibrated from a zero of abstract isolation, so that it gives only a differential measure of the abstracted other that differentially affects it. But when we come to deal with the human body, as the fundamental instrument of human observation, an instrument that is inescapable yet not itself observed in act (or capable of being calibrated in relation to an observed other), this short-circuiting ceases to be tolerable to the philosopher, and he is compelled to note, not merely its comparative pointer-readings on its native scale, but also the nature of the variable itself which constitutes that scale, and makes it humanly absolute (though not therefore universally incorrigible). At least he must do so if he is to gain true knowledge of the physical universe which integrates the body and the world that transcends the bodily instrument of observation. Not merely the magnitude of the bodily *affectiones* but their nature must be considered—all, indeed, that the short-circuiting of the instrument neglects when we merely take its pointer-reading. And, of course, even the precise instruments of the scientist require an *observer* who is no disembodied spectator of isolated observable apparatus.[17] Even a supposed *generalized* observer is one that observes by means of a generalized human body, and not *without* a body, and it is the *affectiones,* individual or generalized, of the body that must provide an absolute (though not necessarily incorrigible) scale and pointer-reading for man's knowledge of his complement under the short-circuiting of the human body—and thus (under correction) of the world that is the integration of the body and its complement. In a word, where natural science is rightly content to short-circuit (and thus exclude from Nature) the ineluctable body of the observer (individual or generalized) corrected to normality, natural philosophy must embark on a final movement of integration bringing the body of the observer within the ambit of Nature, not as one of the observables (for *in act* it is the *instrument,* and not one of the *objects,* of observation), but as the fundamental variable the variations of which alone register the nature of its complement, which is thus observed in *its* affected nature. The *affectiones* of the body are thus, as I have said, the pointer-readings that measure the nature of the body's congruent complement on the scale of its reactive nature. What the mind *ob-*

---

[17] Many philosophers (and some scientists) have realized the importance of the *observer* in the understanding of Nature, but one and all have thought of the observer as a localized and dated *mind* to be corrected for by the elimination of all supposedly mental additions to the physical objects. This is a fundamental and far-reaching error. It is the *body* of the observer that is located and dated as an *object,* and is instrumental as the ineluctable instrument of perception. And it is the *relativity* of the objects of perception and science to this unnoted medium that cries aloud for correction in a credible natural philosophy.

Perhaps I may be allowed to add, in this connexion, that it is this forgetfulness of the function of the body in perception that has led so many thinkers to embrace an idealistic philosophy. Realizing that the physical world is no isolated *datum* externally related to the percipient, they have hastily concluded that it is internally related to the percipient *mind*—an error that has, perhaps, been made more credible by the absence for perception-in-act of the percipient's own body from the observed world. And when they have brought themselves to consider the status of the percipient's body in relation to his mind, they have been content to regard it as one of the objects internally related to his mind though accidentally occulted in the act of perception. Its essential instrumentality in perception has thus been at once allowed and ignored. The primary derelativization of which the observed world stands in need is of its relation to the body-in-act, and not of relation to finite mind; and this is a process that may require the re-interpretation of the nature of physical things as agents and reagents, but can hardly require their reduction to the status of "ideal contents" ordered by mental activity.

serves is its own disc and pointer, and from these *taken together,* in the light of their presuppositions, we must gather the essential nature of the physical real.[18] Man measures what is not man by his *affectiones,* and the world of observable Nature *is* thus his bodily *affectiones* projected upon, and decoratively shading, the screen of his partial community with his other with the unintelligible *data* of its partiality. But it is not from these *data* that knowledge of Nature as integrating man and his complement must be sought. Such knowledge must come from the *emendation* of their relativity as resulting from the human predicament; and that cannot be accomplished by any generalization or integration of their relativities. Knowledge of the whole is not to be sought in the perspective of the part, but only in the emendation of the part to the fashion of the whole—a process that is only possible in so far as the part is no mere section or selection of the whole, but its microcosm, reproducing in its limited form the nature of the macrocosm, and, in its own perspective, confusedly reproducing the nature of its complement. And a true natural philosophy must proceed by rational speculation (as opposed to imaginative guesswork), within the framework thus provided, to the determination of the nature of the physical macrocosm, and even of the negation that is implicit in its determinate nature as "physical".

V

We are now in a position to understand the significance of *Ethics II., xiii.* with its elaboration and *éclaircissements* in the propositions, postulates and *lemmata* that follow. These are, of course, partly epistemological in character and partly physical, but it is with their physical significance that we are now concerned. Emphasis is repeatedly placed by Spinoza upon the "fitness of the body for doing or suffering many things" as reciprocating with the mind's

---

[18] The same principle is also applicable to the instruments of scientific practice: we must know *what* they measure—the nature of the variables in the mathematical expressions of natural process and constitution. Mere pointer-readings are without significance save as we presume the nature of their measurables. Nor (though these are often reducible to functions of the measures of more elementary variables—as "kinetic energy", e.g., is a function of "mass" and "velocity") can measures alone constitute a measurable, however simple it may be. Even "space-time" requires a foot-rule and a clock if it is to be measured—or some substitute for these.

power of understanding or perceiving many things[19] (a principle which is vitally prominent again in the ethical portions of the treatise).[20] The *Lemmata* then expound the broad principles of corporeal individuation and integration, beginning with "very simple bodies"[21] distinguished only by their "motion and rest, speed and slowness". These are determined by one another,[22] in such a manner that the determination of each is a function of its own nature and also the nature of its other.[23] Spinoza then passes to the way in which complex individuals are constituted, and the relations holding between their simpler parts, in virtue of which they are individuals. The human body is thus constituted of parts which are affected in various ways by external things;[24] it retains *"vestigia"* of these *affectiones*, and in turn reacts on these things and thus affects them.[25] Further, each *affectio* of the body is a function of its own nature and of the nature of the external thing affecting it; so that in perceiving its own body with its *affectiones* it is *eo ipso* perceiving the natures of external things as involved in the nature of its own body:[26] more or less abstractly according to the hierarchical perfection or imperfection of the body; and more or less confusedly as it has less or more in common with external things, that is, according as its *affectiones* correspond with the intrinsic natures of external things.[27]

We have thus passed from the simple affirmation of *Ethics II.*, *xiii.* that the human mind perceives only its own body, to the series of propositions and corollaries following the *Lemmata* (in which the hierarchical individuation of Nature is indicated) according to which the mind, in perceiving its own body with its *affectiones*, in the same act perceives the nature of many things[28] in terms of their community (more or less limited and confused by projection upon the reference system of the body) with the body,[29] and as present dis-

[19] *Eth. II., xiii. Sch.*
[20] *Cf. Eth. IV., xxxviii; V., xi., xiii., xxxix.*
[21] *"Corpora simplicissima".*
[22] *Eth. II., Lem. iii.*
[23] *Eth. II., Ax. i. post Lem. iii.*
[24] *Eth. II., Post. iii. post Lem. vii.*
[25] *Eth. II., Post. iii., v., vi. post Lem. vii.*
[26] *Eth. II., xvi. et Corr. i. et ii.*
[27] *Eth. II., xxxviii, xxxix.*
[28] *Eth. II., xvi. Cor. i.*
[29] *Eth. II., xvi. Cor. ii.*

tinct from the body by reason of the body's reagency to their agency;[30] and further, the mind perceives its body, and knows it to exist, only through these same *affectiones* registering in it the actions of other things as evoking the reactions of the body.[31] Though the mind perceives *only* its body, yet to perceive the body as existing *alone* would be to perceive an illusion: for the body is nothing save as reactive focalization of its complement in Nature up to the measure of their community of essence, that is, in so far as the body is "fit for doing or suffering many things". In perceiving its body as affected the mind perceives its complement as affecting it: the body and its other are at once *distinct* as *poles* of a common stress, and *identical* as poles of a *common* stress. It is thus that in so far as the *affectio* confuses the natures of self and other (through defective community) they remain one *for observation,* yet distinct as mutual *agents.* Contrariwise, in so far as the *affectio* (by reason of perfect community) is clear and distinct, *observation of* an other gives place to *love for* another.

In *mera experientia* these conditions are operant together in various measures: in part, there must always be some measure of clarity in our *affectiones,* since all interaction is based on community;[32] in part, there is always some measure of confusion in *mera experientia,* through which the other presents unintelligible content for observation—content the unintelligibility of which so darkens our awareness as to startle the commonsense consciousness into the fundamental empiricistic error of supposing that here we have "fact" *par excellence,* the reality of which, as resisting intellectual analysis, posits itself as transcendent. And beyond this, as with all human percipience, there is simple defect by reason of the stultitude of the human body. Thus there is formed the perception of a world of qualitied "things" external to, and acting upon, one another: the "common order of nature" variously compounding the elements of objective

---

[30] *Eth. II., xvii.* It ought to be noted that Spinoza is here led, by his wish to explain the bases of fictitious imagination and memory (*Eth. II., xvii. Cor., Sch., xviii. et Sch.*), to leave unemphasized the real source of our belief in the present existence of external things, viz., their reagency to the agency of the body. For we do not, in fact, merely await a new *affectio* to exclude that which has occurred in order to discover whether a thing has been removed—we *seek* a new *affectio* by experimental activity. But of course the agency and reagency of self and other are intuited as mutual.

[31] *Eth. II., xix.*

[32] *Eth. I., iii.*

datum, of relation, and of limitation—a world that is the body of the perceiver with its *affectiones,* mirrored to the mind in the speculum of the active other, of which the body is the otherwise unperceived reactive focalization.

VI

What, then, is the true "pathway to Reality"? Broadly speaking it is the accommodation of the human body to the nature of the universe. But this is evidently a process subject to strict limitation: for the human body is, after all, only a subordinate *part* of Nature, a microcosm of the macrocosm which, as such, has its proper limitations. The most that can legitimately be sought is thus their extension to their limit, and (more especially) the clarification of, its *affectiones*—the broadening of *mera experientia* and the elucidation of its confusion. In Nature as it is in itself all things enjoy perfect community as flowing from their unique and indivisible source, and their *affectiones* are individually constitutive "without confusion of persons". Confusion arises from the eccentric reference of all things to the partial self to which the part is decoyed by its own simultaneous partiality and distinctness; distinction is read as isolation with external relation, and the indivisible Nature that integrates self and complement is projected in the perspective of the part as a world of more or less unintelligible others from which the body-in-act is distributively absent (while yet forming a part of it by distributive remainder—which remainder, by illegitimate imputation, is taken as total). Thus the proper defect of the part, with its proper perfection, becomes the source of the privation and eccentric projection of the remainder in the reference system of the part: an "imagination" that can only be corrected to yield a true view of the whole by "referring all things to God", that is, by so transcending the axes of the self as that both self and complement are understood as flowing from the undivided essence of Nature: the absolute "origin" of the reference system of creation. In that creative perspective the human body is a microcosm reproducing in its measure the "fashion or make of the whole universe",[33] a reactive focalization

---

[33] *"Facies totius universi"* (Ep. lxiv.). As I have often said, the universal translation of *"facies"* as "face" in this phrase is most unfortunate, emphasizing as it does the danger of identification with the visible universe, or "common order of nature".

of its complement in Nature, with which (in so far as the body is responsive to its other) it is identical in mode and distinct in agency—forming with it, as it were, a universal stress of "action and reaction equal and opposite": a cross-section of the hierarchy of creation.[34]

[34] To this cross-sectional structure there are set two limits: Nature as a whole, and the "point-instant", neither of which is a self acted upon and reacting to a complement. The latter raises no special difficulty, for the point-instant is the zero focus of all stress in Nature—a mere ideal limit without modality, or even *distinct* place and date. The former, viz., Nature as a whole, might seem also, on the principles elaborated, to be an unreal limit in the absence of a complement awaking it to reaction. Such a supposition is based, however, on a too abstract reading of the character of the stresses of finite bodies in Nature. We think of two bodies as actualizing each other by impact, through which the *vis impressa* of each evokes the *vis insita* of the other—forgetting that two bodies can only impinge on each other if they are *in motion* relative to one another. But, indeed, just as a man who pushes a boat into the water presses the ground under his feet in the opposite direction, and the water presses backwards upon the boat, with equal force (the changes of relative motion in the system being changes in *affectio* in its parts by reason of these balanced pressures operating on bodies of unequal mass), so the reaction of bodies in impact are balanced by the assumed, but neglected, actions by which the bodies are in relative motion. Thus each body is not only a pole of external stress but also the seat of internal stress, and is concretely actualized only thereby. In imputing relative motion to the impinging bodies, we are abstracting from their concrete setting in Nature, and supposing (with Descartes) that the motion *belongs* to the bodies, and that the impact of bodies thus constituted can provide *a priori* principles for the deduction of the results of impact of complex bodies, more or less elastic, regarded as "second order" phenomena. But all bodies are complex and in some measure elastic—nor can a Cartesian simple body be intelligibly conceived.[a] Because the actuality of a finite body is the *reactive* focalization of its complement in Nature, a multipolar stress balancing the multipolar stress of its complement, Nature as a whole is the very basis of the reality of both, and no mere ideal limit.

[a] Descartes's *Rules of Motion in Impact,* taken as directly applicable to empirical bodies, seem to assume perfect elasticity where change of direction is required, and perfect inelasticity where it is not. Hence the apparent contradiction of his assertions that all motion is relative, and that the result of the impact of two bodies with a given relative motion depends on whether both are moving in the same or opposite directions, or one is at rest. But, of course, Descartes himself never supposed that his *Rules* are capable of such direct application, seeing that all bodies are, for him, embedded in the plenum (*vide Princip. Philos., II.,* Artt. 53, 56–60).

VII

Aptness of the human mind for understanding Nature thus corresponds with the aptness of the human body "for doing and suffering many things", and it will be well, in conclusion, to inquire into the degree and the limitations of this aptitude. There is nothing in Nature as veridically observed, or rightly inferred from what is so observed, that is not an *affectio* of the body of the observer, clearly and intelligibly identifying the natures of both body and its complement, or obscurely and unintelligibly combining them under unilateral reference to the axes of the body. In things as they are in themselves in the eternal stream of creation, in so far as there is community of nature in the body and its complement, they form the identity of a single stressed system the poles of which are mutually reactive. Projected upon the axes of the body, however, this mutuality is restricted and the identity destroyed so far as relates to reality, while being retained in appearance (hence the *body-in-act* and its complement *for observation* are identical), so that the bodily *affectiones* confuse the natures of body and complement, and can be rightly imputed to neither in itself. In this eccentric perspective the way to truth seems to lie in the analysis of the *affectiones* so as to reconstruct body and complement in isolation. But this process can proceed but a little way (to parody Bacon—sufficient to "convince" positivism but not to "inform" metaphysics) sufficient to exclude perceptual illusions and objective obfuscations, but not to establish reality. For the body and its other are not as such isolable, but actively distinct while remaining internally related. Each is in the end *constituted* by its *affectiones*. Truth, therefore, lies not in the mere analysis of the bodily *affectiones* but in their emendation to intelligible form by the correction of the axes of reference by relation to which they are unintelligible. In so far as there is difference of nature between the body and its other (a difference necessarily embedded in identity) the body is inapt to react to the action of the other. And this stultitude must affect the mind's cognizance of its other, in reality limiting it, and in appearance confusing its limited apprehension. Its limitation is its *ignorance,* its confusion the seat of *error* in so far as unintelligible *affectiones* are taken as verificatory norms, that is, as revealing the character either of the body itself or of its other as it is in itself, as distinct interacting physical

agents. Thus the power of the mind to understand Nature corresponds with the aptness of the body for actualizing its other by
reaction to its agency; and the impotence of the mind to render its
affectiones intelligible arises from the privation of the mutality of
body and other as agents-in-act by the unilateral projection of their
stress upon its bodily pole.

Putting aside the problem of ignorance (founded upon bodily indifference to factors in the real), and of the grounds of our awareness
of ignorance, as beyond our present scope, we may say that the intelligibility or otherwise of the objects of our cognizance measures
the aptness or otherwise of our bodies for doing and suffering many
things.[35] In fact, of course, these objects are always in part intelligible and in part unintelligible—for mere *data* are nothing but "blind
spots" on the field of mental vision. The resolution of the phenomenality of the "common order of nature" lies in the simultaneous integration of the body with its complement in Nature, and the
emendation of the body's eccentric perspective of Nature. And the
one entails the other.

Further, this simultaneous integration and emendation is possible
only because, and in so far as, the body is a microcosm of Nature,
and thus at once finite in fact and infinite in principle, that is, because, and in so far as, Nature integrates the body and its complement so that the body is a part of Nature apt to do and to suffer
many things from its complement. As the body is finite in fact its
objects are for it ineluctable (and this is the foundation of their
unintelligible givenness: we continue to see the "straight staff bent
in a pool" even after we have learnt the true cause of the appear-

---

[35] The difficulty that may here be raised is that the intelligible and unintelligible
elements of objective Nature seem to be inextricable.[a] But this is a problem
only for those who regard the axe and the shovel as the sole implements of the
philosopher. We are not bound to accept either the realism of commonsense,
the abstract realism of science, or the physical unrealism of Berkeley—for the
disjunction is based on the assumption that the percipient is a disembodied
spectator of the universe. And no such observer is to be found. Doubtless the
factors of illusion in our contemplated world do, in their degree, limit the
reality of the factors of reality, just as the latter lend reality to the former. But
this intelligible-unintelligible world is not given to disembodied mind, but is
an abstraction of the physically real complement of the observer's body as it
is actualized relative to that body, and in active contrast with it as reactive
focalization.

[a] E.g. Berkeley's refusal to separate sense-quality from extension, and to affirm
the physical reality of the latter while denying it to the former.

ance), as it is infinite In principle Its objects are recognized as phenomenal (and this is the foundation of their reality under correction: "demonstrations are the eyes of the mind"). It is the finiteness, the partiality, of the body in Nature that abstracts our grasp of Nature; it is the self-centred eccentricity of the body that is the root of unintelligibility in the "common order of nature", and of the topsy-turvydom by which the body which, in act, is no object to the mind that animates it, is apprehended as revealing an external world of reactive Nature decorated with mere *data* that are the *affectiones* of the body in its distributive reciprocity with a complement partially pulverized by abstraction from the "infinite, unique and indivisible" [36] Nature by relative isolation over against the body. The tail of the "Prince Rupert's Drop" of Nature is broken off, and the whole resolved to fragments. In the creative integrity of Nature alone lies reality; in the relativity of the observation by one part of the others, phenomenality; and truth is to be found only through the realization of the relations of all microcosms with each other and with the macrocosm, characteristic of eternal creation. "Fact" may be "observed", but "reality" can only be "loved". All things must therefore be "referred to God",[37] correcting the eccentricity of the self-isolated and self-referent microcosm; and in that "emendation of the understanding" the identity of the animated body with its reciprocating complement in Nature is known as active love for the reactive other, by which self and other are mutually constituted. For appearance, as in reality, finite self and other are one in modality, other in agency; and in its perfection this identity in otherness is but an abstractive differentiation of the "infinite love wherewith God loves himself" [38] in the creative action by which the infinite indeterminate potency is expressed in act in infinitely determinate form, as "infinite things follow in infinite ways from the necessity of the divine nature".[39] For the integrity of Nature, like the integrity of love, is the union of the self with its absolute other that is also its complement and absolute expression; and from the relation of God and the world is derived, and abstracted as its dim reflection, the relation of the self with its intelligible other—a reflection that is contorted and confused as the self deifies itself as cosmic, and is

[36] *Ep. xii.*
[37] *Eth. II., xxxii.*
[38] *Eth. V., xxxv, xxxvi.*
[39] *Eth. I., xvi.*

amply discredited by the appearance of unintelligible *data* in the transparency of its intellectual vision. So far, therefore, from such *data* constituting verificatory norms of certitude, they verify only the impotence of their recipients, and the "fall" that must follow upon their idle wish to be "as gods".

King's College, London

Some Incoherencies
in Spinozism (I)

A. E. Taylor

I HOPE that the title I have given to these pages will not be misunderstood; to obviate any such possibility, let me explain that its words mean just what they say. I am not offering a *redargutio* of *Spinoza;* like most great philosophers, he has a personality not to be confined within the bounds of any set of formulæ, and a personality is a thing which defies "redargution." What I am concerned with is *Spinozism,* a certain body of principles which Spinoza believed himself to have demonstrated, though, as I shall argue, he has in fact done no such thing, partly because the principles are mutually incompatible, and some of them false, partly because his own *moral* nature was too noble to allow him to be faithful to some of them. If I am at all on the right lines in what I am going to urge, it will be seen that a certain common conception of Spinoza's philosophy is the exact reverse of the truth. His doctrine has often been described, for example, by J. A. Froude, in his study of the *Ethics,*[1] as one to which we may feel a justified but unreasoned moral aversion, but one of which the logical structure is flawless when once its few initial postulates are conceded. I wish to argue that this notion of Spinoza as the terrible impeccable reasoner is completely false, that the iron panoply of logic in which he is imagined to be encased is riven from head to foot by gaping cracks, and that it is just his illogicality which leaves it possible to feel a deserved reverence for so much of his moral and religious teaching. In this matter I feel myself much more in accord with the judgments of Prof. A. Guzzo[2] than with those of the greater number of expositors, and since Prof. Guzzo's work seems to have been little

---

[1] *Short Studies on Great Subjects* (London: Longmans Green, 1867), I. 339–400.
[2] *Il Pensiero de Spinoza* (Firenze: Vallecchi, 1924), a work to which I never recur without illumination and refreshment.

189

read by students in our own country, I shall not hesitate to use it freely.[3]

I must explain also that I am not undertaking to refute a consistent and consequent Monism, or 'Pantheism,' if there has ever been such a thing, but Spinozism, a doctrine which may profess to be, and mean to be, Monism, but never succeeds in being what it would fain be. Spinoza, whatever he may be, is no consistent Monist or 'Pantheist', for the simple reason that he never succeeds in making his *substance,* or *God,* the one and only reality; his whole scheme of physics, psychophysics, and ethics stands or falls with the recognition that there really are such things as the plurality of bodies and minds believed in by the common man. It is true that he *says* that all of them are 'modes' of his one substance, but it is no less vital to his doctrine that these modes shall be really distinct modes with an individuality of their own which is never explained. Peter's mind and Paul's mind may be both modes in the 'infinite intellect of God', and Peter's body and Paul's body both "modes of God as extended", but it never occurs to Spinoza to deny that the "ideas" which make up Peter's mind 'belong together' in a way in which an 'idea' in Peter's mind and one in Paul's do not, or that the components of the 'complex mode of extension' which is Peter's organism form a whole in a way in which components of Peter's body and components of Paul's do not. Peter's head and Paul's trunk do not constitute a single 'complex mode of extension', as Peter's head and Peter's trunk do, nor does an 'idea A' which is part of Peter's mind contract an association with one which is part of Paul's mind. A really consequent Monism would have to regard the very distinction between one body, or one mind, and another as an illusion of "imagination"; a consequent 'Pantheism' would have to deny that there *is* anything at all besides its ἓν καὶ πᾶν.[4]

---

[3] Suspicion of Spinoza's logic ought to be at once suggested to any reader of the *Ethics* by his fondness for 'proofs' which are said to be immediately evident from a definition, and for the use of *reductio ad absurdum*. The former are no *proofs* at all, but a pretence that proof is unnecessary, and the latter method is almost always fallacious, since there is nearly always an 'omitted alternative' of which the so-called proof takes no account.

[4] It might be made the test of a real 'Pantheism' whether it can, like Schopenhauer, accept the Indian TAT TVAM ASI. Spinoza notoriously cannot. His whole scale of ethical values turns on the thought that the *natura* of A is always radically *different* from that of B, and therefore the "pleasures" of *A* and those of *B* (e.g., the sexual enjoyment of a man and of a horse) are different in kind

But this doctrine, true or false, is not Spinoza's. *Tat tvam asi* is no catchword of *his* ethics, any more than of those of a Southern European Christian priest or a Cartesian vivisector of the "dumb animals". Schopenhauer *is*, if you like, a consistent Monist, since he holds that my *natura*, your *natura*, and the *natura* of all the creatures round us really is one thing; it is the same *natura*. Spinoza is so far from believing anything of the kind that it is fundamental in his *Ethics* that my *natura* is not even the same *natura* as that of my fellow-man; as he explained to Blyenbergh, if Nero commits matricide and Spinoza does not, the reason is simply that matricide "agrees with the *natura* of Nero, but disagrees with the utterly different *natura* of Spinoza".[5] The very *crux* of his position is that he proclaims in one breath that there is a single all-embracing individual substance, and in the next that every one of us, though we have all just been declared to be mere 'modes' of this single individual reality, is so much of an individual as to be literally *sui generis*. The position seems logically quite untenable, but tenable or not, it is plainly not genuine unadulterated Monism. A really thoroughgoing Monism would have to dismiss the *facies totius universi*, which Spinoza told Tschirnhaus is an 'infinite mode mediately produced by God', as a mere illusion. In fact, it is only a very short step from this recognition of the indefinitely variegated *facies totius universi* as a reality to Pluralism. You have only to insist strongly enough on the point that, however true it is that the *facies totius universi* remains in some sense the same, it is equally true that it is perpetually changing, and "substance" will become, al-

---

(*Ethics*, III. 57, Schol.). Indeed, if the nominalism he professes, for example in his correspondence with Blyenbergh, is to be taken strictly, since the *naturæ* of any two men are radically discrepant, the pleasures which two *men* derive from gratification of the 'same appetite' should also be different in *kind*, though this has, of course, to be conveniently forgotten when he is constructing a general psychology and an ethics. The denial that a "common nature of man" is more than an empty name really removes Spinozism *further* than orthodox Christianity from the thought of ἐν καὶ πᾶν. (The same absolute reality of a plurality of different *naturæ* is equally implied as the foundation of Spinoza's political theory of *jus*.)

[5] *Ep.* XX. Quantum ad me, ea omitto, vel omittere studeo, quia expresse cum mea *singulari* natura pugnant. Thus the *natura singularis* of Nero or Orestes (who figure as illustrations in the discussion) is something really diverse from that of Spinoza, the distinction is not merely a *modal* one, in the scholastic and Cartesian sense.

most before you are aware of it, a mere collective designation for the complex of *naturæ* which constitute a "multiverse". And I cannot help believing that if Spinoza's life had not been so untimely cut short, he would have seen himself that his actual position was untenable, and that a choice would have to be made between adhering strictly to the unity of substance at the cost of making substance a wholly unknowable "thing-in-itself", and abiding by the knowability of substance at the cost of admitting a plurality of substances.

The real source of the trouble—as of most of the worst metaphysical difficulties in the system—is the fatal admission that there are such things as those which Spinoza calls the 'finite modes' of his infinite substance. We could, I think, just make shift to understand how the one substance expresses its *essentia* in a plurality of 'infinite modes'. We could, for example, understand the statement that extension has a uniform character which is disclosed to us by our study of the unlimited variety of the various geometrical figures possible in it. An Euclidean space has a distinctive character in virtue of the postulates which define it, but the only way to get an adequate insight into this distinctive character is to study the properties which belong, in virtue of these postulates, to triangles, parallelograms, circles, hyperbolas. . . . But all the 'modes' which come under our study in this way, as we extend our acquaintance with geometry, are the successive *determinants* of the *determinable* 'extension'. They are all 'universals', 'high abstractions'; none of them is genuinely a *this* and an individual, or, to put the same thing in another way, none of them has a history, and this is just why it is so easy to know them *sub quadam specie æternitatis*. The utmost degree of specification which can be reached on these lines is at best the *species specialissima*. It is quite different when we have to deal with the so-called 'finite' modes that are the 'particular things' of every-day parlance, which are all really individual, and have a real history. Peter, Paul, this horse, this crystal, are not simply further and more highly determined determinants of the determinable *man*, or *quadruped*, or *mineral*, in the way in which the two fundamental triangles of Plato's *Timæus* are merely further specifications of 'the right-angled triangle'. Each of them is, what the 'isosceles right-angled triangle', for example, is not, a τόδε τι. Now, as I say, we can perhaps understand that Spinoza's one substance should, as a consequence of its 'essential nature', and of nothing else, find expression in a vast plurality of specifications, so long as these specifications remain at the level of 'high abstractions'.[6] But when we come to the 'finite' modes Peter, Paul and the rest, we are dealing with genuine historical individuals with 'biographies', and we cannot evade the question what provides the principle of their individuation. There is nothing to account for it in the professed postulates of *Ethics* I, and Spinoza never touches on the subject. He is content simply to assume the reality of such genuine individuals as a fact of common experience, and to leave us to guess, if we can, how it is to be reconciled with his avowed principles.

For my own part, I confess that I do not see how the reconciliation is to be achieved. Substance, we must remember, is supposed to give itself its own specifications wholly from within, and the only clue we are ever given to the nature of the process is that it is illustrated by the connection of the specific properties of particular geometrical figures, such as the triangle, with the *essentia* pervasively characteristic of extension. (Thus I suppose we might see an example of a mode and its connection with the attribute of substance to which it belongs, in the proposition that it follows from Euclid's postulates that the three perpendiculars from the angular points of a triangle to the opposite sides are concurrent, or that, if two chords of a circle intersect, the rectangles contained by their segments are equal.) But truths of this kind involve no reference to true individuality at all. They might help us to understand the articulation of a geometrical system; what they leave wholly unintelligible is how *history* gets into the system. It is got in, in fact, simply by taking over the individual things and persons of our every-day thinking bodily, renaming them 'finite modes' of substance, and refusing to ask whether it is in keeping with the avowed principles

---

[6] And yet *can* we understand this after all? Take, e.g., the conception of *res extensa* as a something of three (or if you like, of *n*) dimensions. Is there anything *in the concept itself* to suggest the notion of the various figures of geometry? Spinoza might have profited by the advice given in the next century to Priestly by a bishop, to read the *Parmenides*. If you start your metaphysics with a single 'high abstraction', you will never extract anything from it except itself. No wonder that Spinoza has to admit (*Ep.* 9) to De Vries that he has really given one and the same definition of both *substance* and *attribute*. (Descartes, I think, escapes *this* difficulty. Substance is, with him as with Spinoza, *id quod in se est*, but not at the same time *id quod per se concipitur*; it is 'conceived' through an *attribute*. Thus God, for Descartes, is *the* substance *par excellence*, and is *per se*, but is conceived by us through the attribute of *cogitatio*, as *ens cogitans*.)

of the system that there should be such finite modes at all. It is true
that in the essay on the *Amendment of the Intellect* Spinoza had
expressed his belief that the method of which he was dreaming
would get rid altogether of abstractions and 'universals', replacing
them by 'singulars' which were somehow to do the required work
of disclosing necessary connection without paying the price for it
in abstraction. But even if such a method were possible at all, it
seems at least clear that Spinoza never attained to it. All through
the *Ethics* he is reasoning in terms of abstractions while he supposes
himself to be dealing with concrete individuals. He never even
realises that a general property, for example of the circle, is not
made into an individual fact by simply illustrating his reference
to it by a woodcut, like that used in *Ethics* II. 8.[7] One might, indeed, fairly suggest that the very possibility of "finite" modes is
already excluded by Spinoza's own line of reasoning in the *Short
Treatise*. It is argued there (Ch. 2, p. 21, tr. Wolf) that the infinite
substance cannot have given rise to any finite substance, because if
it had done so, "having been infinite it would have had to change
its whole essence". Now, this reasoning, if valid, does not depend on
the use of the word *substance;* it applies equally to an infinite
"mode"; if an infinite mode is to originate finite modes within itself,
it also, in doing so, must change its very character as infinite. (It
would be a mere juggling with words to offer the retort that the
difficulty does not occur in the case of modes, because a mode has
no *essentia*—*essentia* is always the *essentia* of a substance; since
Spinoza himself constantly speaks of that which does, or does not,
constitute the *essentia* of things which he professes to regard as
finite modes, such as the body, or the mind, of Peter or Paul, or
what he incorrectly takes to be a "particular" triangle. If there is
a single infinite individual, and this individual can give rise to no
others, plainly there are no finite individuals at all, and it is only
by an illegitimate resort to "imagination" that I make the separation between two complex modes involved in the statement that
one of them is the organism of Peter and the other the distinct
organism of Paul. To be consistent with my Monism, I must say
that the dividing line I commonly draw between the bodies, or the

---

[7] We may or may not be satisfied with any of the theories of the Schoolmen
about the 'principle of Individuation', but they were at least aware, as Spinoza
seems not to be, that there is a problem to be solved, and they seriously tried to
solve it.

minds, of Peter and of Paul is only drawn by an arbitrary fiction. But though Indian thinkers have apparently been willing to say this, Spinoza was not, and could not have said it without making nonsense of his whole ethical superstructure. Peter and Paul *have* to be for him just as much genuine individuals as they are for the 'man in the street', and the fact is only verbally disguised by re-naming them both 'modes'.)

However, let us waive this point and concede, for the sake of argument, that infinite substance can have *real* finite modes, each of which is really one, and really distinct from every other. Even so, we are only at the beginning of the troubles created for us by the existence of these modes. How grave these troubles are is seen by a consideration of the two fundamental propositions that (1) "substance" is their cause, but an immanent, not a transitive, cause (*Ethics* I. 18); and (2) that the attributes of this substance are, each of them, really indivisible, and taken to be divisible only by an illusion of the imagination (*Ethic* I. 15, Schol. The case is argued with special reference to the "attribute" of extension, but the reasoning is equally applicable to any other).

The difficulty about causality has been so admirably put by Guzzo that I must begin my remarks by reproducing the substance of his criticism. In ordinary life we constantly constate the connection between a change a in one thing A and a change β in a second thing B, and say that A has caused β in B. The causality here asserted is transitive, because the cause is one thing A, and the effect a state β in a different thing B. Spinoza would have us mend our speech by saying not that A causes β in B, but that *God*, as determined by the finite mode A, causes β *in God*, as determined by the second finite mode B. Now verbally, by this formula, we keep within the bounds of *immanent* causality, since God is verbally referred to as both cause and effect. But the device is, after all, only a verbal one for 'saving face'. The patent fact, of which we have to devise some account, is the connection between a, an occurrence falling within A, and β, an occurrence falling outside A, in B. What account of the fact are we to offer? Shall we say that it is the infinite substance itself, as such, which is directly responsible for this connection? If we do, we have broken completely with one of Spinoza's main tenets, that the cause of a finite mode is always 'God as determined by another antecedent finite mode' (I. 28). Or to avoid this difficulty, shall we say that the transaction is due altogether to the finite mode *A*? Then we are ascribing to the finite modes a connection which falls outside the activity of the infinite substance, and are denying another fundamental thesis of Spinozism, that whatever is at all is "in God" and can only be conceived "through God" (I. 15), since we are recognising in our finite modes a transitive activity which falls outside the purely immanent activity which is all Spinoza will allow us to attribute to "God". (It is really the same difficulty which is exposed by Martineau in a rather different terminology when he argues that the 'finite' modes "institute a *new kind of causality,* other than that by which property depends on essence, viz., that by which *thing comes from thing* . . . they institute a *new order of nature,* other than the order of rational necessity calculating from the dual attributes, viz., an order of scientific experience, spreading a network of *successional connection* through all dimensions of the world".[8]) And there is no conceivable escape from this *impasse* when once finite individuals, however cunningly 'camouflaged' as "modes," have been allowed to get a footing in the system; with them transitive causality inevitably makes its appearance, and the immanentism which was to be the central conception of the Spinozistic philosophy is ruined. There are, in fact, only two possible options; either finite individuality is real and transitive causality is real along with it; or else transitive causality is an illusion and there are no finite individuals, only at most "infinite modes", and the determinable of which they are determinants becomes itself no more really individual than "infinite Euclidean space" is individual. Spinozism is no more than a gallant but hopeless attempt to "have it both ways" which ends by having it neither way.

How hopeless the attempt is, is most readily seen from the glaring contradiction on which Martineau, in particular, has fastened. On the one hand, every detail of existence is to follow from the *essentia* of 'God' with exactly the same 'necessity' with which the properties of the triangle follow from its *essentia* as assumed to be formulated in its definition, and for that reason there is really neither contingency nor freedom (except in a Pickwickian sense) anywhere in the universe (I. 29); on the other, the *essentiæ* of the "things created by God" do not "involve existence" (I. 24), which must mean that the

---

[8] *Types of Ethical Theory*[2] (Oxford: Clarendon Press, 1886), I. 318.

existence of these things is contingent.[9] Strictly speaking, to ensure consistency, there ought to be *no* "things created by God"; there should be only the one universal substance, an infinite determinable inseparable from its no less infinite determinants, and the only *essentia* there is should be the *essentia* of this substance as constituted by its infinitely numerous disparate attributes, and this *essentia* should carry with it necessary existence; a "finite mode" should be a mere arbitrary figment of "imagination" without genuine existence and without *essentia*. But when once these modes have intruded into the system, since it is so manifest that their existence does *not* follow from the nature of substance "as the properties of the triangle follow from its definition", there is nothing for it but to make that existence in fact contingent while you are verbally proclaiming that contingency is an illusion of human ignorance.

Indeed, Spinoza's case is even worse than I have so far made it appear. It would not be true even of his "infinite" modes that they follow from the nature of substance as the properties of a geometrical figure follow from its definition. As Tschirnhaus told his master "from the definition of a figure you can never deduce more than *one* property".[10] He would have been still nearer the mark if he had said "you can deduce none". No mere manipulation of a definition of a figure will ever elicit from it any property except that which you have already assumed for the purposes of your definition. What you require as the premises from which you are to deduce the properties of a triangle are the whole body of postulates which together define the universe of discourse to which the triangle belongs, a region of space (Euclidean or otherwise, as the case may be). Even so it is with the deduction of anything from the nature of "substance". It has, we are told, infinitely numerous attributes, and each of them, in its own way, expresses the same *essentia*. Be it so, and define each of such attributes as is known to us as carefully and exactly as you please; from your definition of *extensio* or *cogitatio*, taken as a sole ultimate premiss, you will extract nothing but itself. That Spinoza should habitually write as though this had never crossed his mind until Tschirnhaus stated the difficulty, seems

[9] And yet, when we get to Pt. V., we shall be told there (Prop. 6) that mastery over our passions must involve our thinking of *all things* as necessary, i.e., as being just what according to I. 24 they are not.

[10] *Ep.* 82.

to me to show that he had not the same insight into 'geometrical method' as the philosophers who have been real mathematicians, Plato, Descartes, Leibniz.[11]

It might look at first sight to be a proper reply to the last paragraph to say that I have there myself spoken of the body of the postulates of a geometry as *defining* a space, and thus seem to be conceding that, after all, the infinitely numerous propositions of such a geometry do all follow from a definition, namely, from the definition of a space, or a region of space. But it has to be noted that one cannot define a space directly; one can only reach a quasi-definition of it by making a set of postulates not about *it*, but about specific configurations in it. The assumption, for example, which discriminates the space of Euclid from that of Lobachevsky or Bolyai has to be stated as a proposition about parallel straight lines, or about the angles of a quadrilateral. You have to say that Euclid assumes that only one straight line can be drawn through a given point in a plane parallel to a given straight line, whereas the other two geometers assume that two such parallels can always be drawn; or that Euclid assumes that straight lines in a plane which are not parallel always intersect, the others that there are straight lines which are neither intersecting nor parallel; or again that Euclid assumes that if three of the angles of a quadrilateral are right, the fourth will also be right, the other two geometers that it will be acute. However you prefer to express the critical postulate, *space* is never named in it, and your proposition could not be admitted as a definition of space, or part of such a definition, by any philosopher who, like Spinoza, regards it as self-evident that every proposition must assert a predicate of a subject. (If that position is called in question, there is no longer any reason why, if there is a supreme infinite substance and also a multiplicity of finite things, the finite

---

[11] Descartes, it will be remembered, had specified as the subject-matter of *Mathesis universalis, ordo et mensura* (*Regulæ*, IV). Now, both *ordo* and *mensura* presuppose a *real* plurality in that which is ordered or measured. Spinoza has involved himself in the awkward contradiction that though he professes to have demonstrated that there can be only *one* substance, 'God', it is, as he more than once says, *improprie* that God is called *unus* or *unicus*. And *he* can hardly escape by falling back on the scholastic distinction between the 'transcendental' and the 'numeral' senses of the word *one*, since the thesis which is indispensable for the whole of the subsequent construction is that of I. 5, that 'there cannot be *two or more* substances of the same nature or attribute', where it is precisely *numerical* unity that he is anxious to assert.

things *must* be unsubstantial adjectives of the primary substance. They may equally well be, as Christian orthodoxy teaches that they are, "created substances".)

The denial of transitive causality, then, seems to me a position which could only be consistently adhered to in a philosophy prepared, as Spinozism is not, to regard the existence of finite individuals as a mere illusion. Equally unfortunate, to my mind, is the persistent attempt to deny that extension, in particular, is really divisible, or has parts. Of course we see why Spinoza finds it necessary to insist on the paradox. We cannot deduce extension as a consequence of anything more ultimate. (It has generally been held that Leibniz's strenuous attempt to deduce it from differences in 'point of view' among his unextended monads really presupposes in its premisses the very difference of position in space it is intended to explain.) But since there is at least one other 'irreducible' with which a philosophic account of the universe has to reckon, *cogitatio*, we cannot identify extension with the all-inclusive substance; it must be an attribute of that substance. As an attribute it must express the *essentia* of substance, and, as substance, it is held, can be shown to be one, the attribute must express this unity; it must be rigidly one too. But though Spinoza asserts this consequence hardily enough in words, the facts are really too much for him. No one who is about to plunge into a psychophysical construction like that of *Ethics* II can get away from the recognition that my body and yours both have their environments, that your environment is not mine, any more than your organism is mine, that both our organisms are exceedingly complex. All through the psychophysical and ethical part of the treatise we consequently find the expressions *bodies*, in the plural, and *parts of body* recurring at every turn, as though the author had forgotten his own declaration that the *res extensa* is only supposed to have parts, or regions, by an illusion of the imagination. It is not surprising, then, to find, as Guzzo has noted, that Spinoza has no sooner made this declaration than he feels it to be an extravagance, and tries to water its meaning down until it becomes a mere common-place. He first reduces the proposition to a mere assertion that the extended is a continuum (which is all that his illustrative woodcut implies). But a continuum, of course, is so far from having no parts or being indivisible, that it is only a continuum because it has an infinity of distinguishable parts; it would not be a continuum if it could not be divided and subdivided endlessly.[12] Finally, we get a still further frittering away of the meaning of the paradox. As an example of the indivisibility of extension we are told that water, considered simply as water, is the same everywhere throughout its whole extent. This is only to say that all water has the same chemical or physical components, that any portion of it behaves like, exhibits the same characteristics as, any other part, a statement which obviously does nothing to justify the assertion that water is only supposed by mistake to have parts, or even the less drastic assertion that a body of water must be a continuum.[13]

The metaphysical framework of *Ethics* I thus requires, if it is to be retained, the admission that "finite modes" are mere illusions, while the whole edifice of doctrine elaborated in *Ethics* II–V, demands that they shall be nothing of the sort.

This is a bad omen for the consistency of what is yet to follow, and, in fact, there are equally grave inconsistencies yet to be faced. We are confronted with one of the worst of them in the very opening propositions of *Ethics* II about the nature of the mind and its relation to the body. The body, we are told, is a "complex mode of extension (a finite one) in God", and the mind is a "complex idea, or mode of thought in God" corresponding exactly to the body. We remark at once, then, that Spinoza simply identifies a man's mind with the series of his acts of cognition and volition; it is they which make up the complex mode of which he speaks. Commonly we distinguish three different things: (1) an act of thinking, (2) the man or person who thinks this thought, or, to speak more accurately, though less idiomatically, thinks this *thinking*, (3) that which the thinking thinks of; or more briefly, we distinguish (1) a *concipient*, if I may invent such a word, (2) a *conception*, (3) a *conceptum*. Spinoza simply identifies (1) and (2) without more ado. We commonly hold that there is such an entity as the man who does the thinking, and if we are to be proved wrong about this, we are at least not proved to be wrong by simply taking the unreality of the

---

[12] Unending divisibility is notoriously not a sufficient condition for continuity, though a necessary one. But it was the only condition recognised in Spinoza's day, and the appeal to it is enough for my immediate purpose.

[13] E.g., according to Descartes no body of water is really continuous; it always has 'pores' filled with something other than itself. But it would not follow from this that one sample of it will not behave like any other, since the matter in the 'pores' of both might be alike.

distinction for granted under cover of an arbitrary definition.[14]
When I say that I am engaged in a certain train of thought, I mean,
or suppose myself to mean, something more than that such a train
of thought is an actual occurrence, or even that it is connected in
an obscure way with the concomitant occurrence of a certain train
of cerebral processes; both those statements might be true, and yet
—or so, at least, all of us commonly think—*I* might be non-existent.
What I suppose myself to mean by *I* is neither the mental events
nor the bodily events but the man, or self, who owns both the mind
and the body. If this is to be shown to be a mistake, it must be
shown to be so by a more refined and careful analysis of *self-consciousness*. But Spinoza has no improved theory of self-consciousness
by which to correct the *naïveté* of our common thinking. He merely
ignores it. No doubt he is careful to tell us that just as there is an
"idea" in God of every mode of extension, so there is a second idea
of every idea, and this is apparently meant to be his account of
consciousness of self. But as Martincau rightly said, what is 'explained' by this theory of the "idea of the idea" is not what everyone means by self-consciousness: it is not the *man* who is said to be
aware of *himself,* but his *ideas* which are asserted to be conscious of
themselves. And the two things are very different. It is one thing
to say that I know the Pythagorean theorem and also know that I
know it; it is a wholly different statement to say that my *knowing*
of the Pythagorean theorem is a knowing that I am knowing it. The
first statement is just what all but the "sophisticated" believe to be
true, and is thus, at least, highly plausible; the second, so far as
it is intelligible, seems to be plainly false. Spinoza's doctrine does
not even explain how we could ever have fallen into the illusion
of supposing that *we* are self-conscious.

   And if it seems at least difficult to subscribe to the identification
of concipient and conceiving, there may perhaps be an equal difficulty in accepting the theory of the relation of conceiving and *conceptum* which Spinoza offers us as an account of what we mean
by knowing a natural fact. What happens, according to the theory,

[14] And we are certainly not proved to be wrong by a magisterial reference to
   Kant's assault on the 'paralogisms' of Rational Psychology. Kant's attempt to
   identify the thinker with the 'I think' which is a mere formal concomitant of
   thinking (or at least to argue that the identification is possible) seems to me a
   particularly glaring example of the 'fallacy of misplaced concreteness'. He offers us a 'high abstraction' as the complete analysis of a concrete historical fact.

when, in common parlance, I am said to know a fact about the
bodily world? Simply a compresence "in God" of a physical event
and a mental event which is its counterpart. But is this enough to
constitute knowledge? Manifestly not; on the theory itself there is
such a compresence, in God 'as constituting my mind', of an 'idea'
corresponding to *every* physical process, in God 'as constituting my
body', but of most of these physical processes we are profoundly
unconscious. If I am to know the simplest fact about my own body,
it is not enough that an 'ideal counterpart' of that fact shall *exist;*
the bodily fact and the ideal counterpart—or rather I who am the
owner of the ideal counterpart—must further stand in the unique
and indefinable relation *known-knower*. Otherwise you might have
the closest correspondence between the "modes" of extension and
of thought, there might be a determinate *a* in the one for every *a*
in the other, and yet there would be no *knowledge* of the bodily
world. The changes in that world would unfold themselves in their
regular causal order; concomitantly there would be a second world
of 'ideas' also unfolding themselves in *their* regular order, but there
would be no *cognisance* of terms of the one order by terms of the
other. Minds answering precisely to the Spinozistic definition might
perfectly well be what Münsterberg held the "mind" described by
the psychologist to be, beings which "know nothing by their cognitions and will nothing by their volitions". Münsterberg, of course,
meant his language to be a deliberately paradoxical way of saying
that the "mind" discoursed of by the laboratory psychologist is "not
the real thing", but a fiction consciously substituted for the reality.
But the question I should like to ask is whether any philosopher
who deliberately substitutes 'the existential *compresence* of idea
and *ideatum*' for "*knowledge* of the *ideatum* through the idea" has
not *un*consciously confused the fiction with the reality.

Now this confusion, which turns upon forgetting that an act of
knowing is not merely something that 'takes place along with' certain events in the extra-mental world, but is an *apprehension* of
those facts by a knowing subject, is, in Spinoza, not a mere casual
oversight; it is made almost inevitable by the fundamental *hypothesis* of his whole system. If the various "modes" can be really
sorted out as belonging each to an "attribute" of substance wholly
disparate from all its other "attributes", and if it is true that no
mode of one attribute can ever contribute to the causation (which
for Spinoza, means the rational explanation) of a mode of any other,

then thought and extension should go each its own way, each "corresponding", if you like, in the closest fashion to the other, but wholly unaffected by it. Since no appeal is to be made to any fact of the one order in accounting for any fact of the other, our psychology, theory of knowledge, ethics should never be allowed to make any mention of the existence of bodies; they should deal exclusively with relations between 'modes of thought', regarded simply as 'mental occurrences' without any objective reference. We ought to be able to construct an epistemology which should treat of knowing without ever introducing the reference to anything non-mental which is a known object. And in doing so we should be adhering strictly to the line of thought which led Spinoza to define an adequate idea as one which has the internal characteristics of truth, and to exclude all reference to the currently recognised external characteristic, 'agreement of the idea with its object'. We should have, what it seems to me later philosophers have never succeeded in attaining, a thoroughly coherent 'coherency' theory of truth.

In point of fact, however, it is so abundantly clear that no account can be given of knowing with the least vestige of plausibility which ignores the most patent characteristic of knowing, namely, that it is always the knowing of an object other than itself, that Spinoza himself habitually neglects to observe his own rule that the modes of each attribute are to be explained exclusively by reference to other modes of the same attribute. To account for the errors into which we are betrayed by 'imagination,' he is forced to fall back on the thesis that our 'ideas' of an external body, until they have been corrected by the teachings of philosophy, represent rather the state of our own body, as affected by the external body, than that of the external body itself (II, 17, Schol.). The states of my own body are thus openly introduced as the really significant determinants of my 'ideas'. For example, I have an hallucination of the presence of Peter's body in some situation in which Peter's body is not really there; this is explained by the usual 'associationist' theory that I imagine Peter to be present because, in consequence of 'association', certain parts of my brain are affected as they would be if Peter were actually there. We need not quarrel with the explanation, but it is flatly incompatible with the previously assumed doctrine that modes of 'thought' must be accounted for exclusively in terms of other modes of 'thought'. It has been now recognised that, after all, there are modes of 'thought'—those involved in sense-perception—

which cannot be accounted for except by reference to modes of 'extension'. And this necessary admission is what really gives rise to the formidable difficulty raised by Tschirnhaus,[15] why, if there are an infinity of 'attributes' and every 'mode' is represented in each of them, our knowledge should be confined to modes of thought itself and modes of extension. It might have been a consistent position—though it would have made knowledge of the extra-mental world impossible—to say that a mode of thought can be cognisant of nothing else but modes of the same attribute. But the moment it is admitted that a mode of thought can be the apprehension of a mode of extension, it becomes pertinent to point out that on Spinoza's principles the given mode of thought a_1 is related to the corresponding mode a_2 of extension *only* as it is also related to a_3, a_4 . . . a_n, the corresponding modes of all the "unknown attributes". The relation in each case, is simply that of compresence and correspondence (whatever correspondence may mean). No reason has been given for holding that there is any further and more intimate relation between a_1 and a_2 than between, say, a_1 and the 'unknown' a_3. In the case of a_2 the mere fact that it is compresent 'in God' with a_1 and, in some unexplained way, corresponds to a_1, was supposed to be equivalent to the fact, 'a_2 is known through a_1': by parity of reasoning, seeing that the same conditions are fulfilled for a_3, a_4 and the rest, it ought to follow that a_3, a_4 . . . are also known. Spinoza's reply (*Ep.* 66), as we know, was that they *are* known, though not by *our* minds. But this is a mere evasion of the difficulty. Since my mind admittedly can get at and apprehend what is not mental at all, as it does when it knows any fact about body, what is there to prevent it from getting at the whole range of non-mental modes? *Why* should it be able to burst the barriers which separate attribute from attribute in the one case of extension and in no other?

I own I suspect Spinoza of having fallen in his reply into a fallacy which would naturally be facilitated by his identification of the mind with the complex of 'ideas'. There *are* ideas of all the modes of all the attributes, he says, but these ideas 'constitute the minds of some other beings, not our minds'. Now it is true, of course, that the thought or perception of a mode a_3 of some unknown 'attribute'

[15] *Ep.* 65.

which 'corresponds' to a_2, a mode of extension, will not be the *same* thought as the thought of a_2. But this is no reason for saying that a_2 and a_3 may not be thought of or perceived by the same knowing *subject*. An electrical disturbance in the atmosphere is 'expressed' both by a flash of lightning and a roll of thunder, but we cannot infer that because the visual percept of the flash is a different *percept* from the audible percept of the thunder-clap, one percipient cannot be aware of both. It is not true that every man must be either blind and unable to see the flash, or deaf and unable to hear the crash. Tschirnhaus was entirely right in saying that Spinoza ought to have explained why, out of an infinity of 'modes' which, as expressive of the same fact, stand on the same level only one—the expression in the attribute of extension—is accessible to us.

There are, of course, philosophies to which it need present no difficulty to suppose that there may be creatures whose perceptions are wholly different from ours, revealing to them characters of the external world which we cannot even imagine and concealing from them all which are so familiar to us. But a philosophy which can consistently find a place for such a speculation must be one which is not dominated, like Spinoza's, by the conception of 'attributes', each made up of utterly disparate expressions of the same identical 'modes'. Such philosophies can intelligibly say that if there are precipient creatures such as we are imagining, the range of natural fact disclosed to them and that disclosed to us are simply *different;* the 'modes' they know are *not* counterparts of the 'modes' we know. For Spinoza the problem is insoluble because he assumes that the unknown $a_3, a_4 \ldots$ are really the same fact as the known a_2, and that further the knowing of a_2 by a_1 is accounted for by the consideration that a_1 is the same fact as a_2, only expressed under another 'attribute'.

(The same inadequate notion of what is meant by knowing has often reappeared in later writers who might have learned better from reflecting on the insoluble tangle into which it had led Spinoza. Huxley, for example, criticises Descartes' *cogito* by saying that all we are warranted in assuming as indubitable fact is not *cogito*, *I* am conscious, but *cogitatur,* there is consciousness going on. He should have seen that Descartes proved his greatness as a philosopher precisely by not falling into this trap. *His* immediate certainty is what it ought to be, a concrete personal fact, *ego nunc et hic cogito,*

ille homo qui est Renatus Descartes hic et nunc cogitat,[16] not a
mere 'high abstraction'. The only real criticism to which he lies
open is that he is content to be sure that *hic et nunc cogito,* where,
to exclude all abstraction, he should have said *hic et nunc cogito
hoc vel illud,* so preserving the necessary reference to the object of
awareness. The concrete fact is never 'awareness exists', but always
'this or that subject is now aware *of* this or that'.) It is this neglect
to insist on the unique character of all knowing as an apprehension
of an object by a subject which explains the standing and apparently unconscious Spinozistic equivocation by which 'the idea of
Peter' may mean either 'the mental complex which corresponds to
Peter's brain and nervous system, the mind of Peter', or 'the mental
complex which exists when Paul thinks of Peter', Paul's 'idea' of
Peter, or may mean both in the same breath, if it is convenient for
the argument that it should. In fact, the two 'correspondences' are
of a wholly disparate kind. The 'idea of Peter' which is the mind
of Peter 'corresponds' to 'the body of Peter,' in Spinoza's theory, in
the sense that it is the same identical thing, expressed first in terms
of one 'attribute' and then in terms of another. 'Paul's idea of
Peter' does not 'correspond to the body of Peter' in the same sense;
in that sense what it 'corresponds to' and 'represents', as Spinoza
himself is careful to tell us, is not Peter's body but Paul's body.
The only sense in which *this* 'idea of Peter' 'corresponds' to Peter's
body at all is that it conveys information to Paul about Peter's body,
has Peter's body as its *object,* and that when Paul thinks truly about
Peter, the information conveyed is correct.

I own that I should find it hard to acquit Spinoza of bad faith
if I were not convinced that this prolonged equivocation is quite
unconscious; and that it should have imposed on him I can only
explain by assuming that this is a consequence of his complete
blindness to the real character of awareness, the necessity for a concipient and a *conceptum* as well as for a conception. The trouble

[16] And yet this second transcription is not quite adequate. For it only expresses a
judgement which *might* be made by a bystander, and *he* might conceivably be
mistaken in thinking that 'the man who is René Descartes' is there, or is
thinking. And even if the judgement is made by René Descartes himself, he
might have 'forgotten his own identity'; he might be wrong in thinking of
himself as the person known as Descartes, exactly as a lunatic is mistaken when
he says he is Julius Caesar or the angel Gabriel. We cannot really dispense with
the *ego,* if our statement is to be an indubitable transcript of the immediately
certain.

in Spinoza's pretended account of knowledge is that the conception and the *conceptum* are confused together by using the same word *idea* indifferently for either, as occasion may serve, and that the concipient, if not disregarded altogether, figures as no more than an empty theatre in which the *ideæ* go through their evolutions. It is precisely the same vicious abstraction which infects so much of the "analysis" which has been so popular among us of late years. We are offered more or less ingenious speculations about the way in which mental operations may be analysed, while it is blindly forgotten that a real operation does not perform itself; it presupposes an operator and a "subject" to be operated on. And this is as true of mental operations as of surgical.

Even so, we have not got to the end of the illogicalities of the second part of the *Ethics*. What the whole of the psycho-physics and epistemology are meant to lead up to is an account of the method by which we may rise from 'imagination' with its inadequate ideas, which reveal rather the condition of our own body than the character of our environment, to knowledge. Spinoza himself frankly avows, as Guzzo has noted, that there is a great *lacuna* in the argument just at this critical point. For any detailed account of the transition we are referred (II. 29, Schol. I.) to an unwritten work which appears to be the *Tractatus de Intellectus Emendatione*. Since we only possess the introductory chapters of this projected work, we have to content ourselves with the rather meagre general information given in the *Ethics* itself. All that is said there, in the lemmas appended to II. 13, is that there are some characters which are common to all *res extensæ,* and others which, though not common to all, are common to our own organism and all the bodies of its immediate environment. Since in both these cases there can be no question of the adulteration of our idea of a property by the admixture of elements representative only of the state of *our* body, the 'ideas' of these characters are always adequate, and provide us with a body of 'common notions' from which we can deduce rigidly true scientific conclusions. It is these common characteristics of all bodies which are apparently meant by that 'adequate idea of God' which Spinoza ends by declaring to be always present in every man (II. 47). When he says that all men have, and have always had, an adequate idea of God, and that in this idea we have the foundation requisite to science, what he seems to mean is that we can deduce the contents of geometry and kinematics from a number of postulates which must be true without reserve, because they express the nature of the attribute *extension*. Now, granted that this were so, it is clear that the science you could deduce from these 'common notions' would never take you beyond the bounds of kinematics; you could not advance as far as a physics and a chemistry, still less would you have any foundation for what Spinoza really wants to construct, an ethic, a doctrine of moral values. And even so, there is a further awkward question rightly put by Guzzo.

According to Spinoza, it is so far from being true, in the words of Plato, that it is 'hard to discover the Father and Maker of all things, and impossible to speak of Him to the multitude', that all men whatsoever always have had the 'adequate idea' of God. How this is to be reconciled with the scornful language used elsewhere habitually by our philosopher about other men's 'idea of God' is his own concern. Presumably he would say, like Descartes, that they all have the true 'idea of God', but most of them confuse it with an irrelevant 'image' of a 'magnified non-natural man', though one would think the confusion ought to be impossible in a mind where the 'adequate idea' was already present. But in any case, the admitted fact remains that most men live at the level of 'imagination'; their 'adequate idea of God', which has always been with them, is inoperative. When a chosen few become philosophers, then, their previously inoperative 'idea of God' must suddenly become an effective force in their mental life. How is this startling "conversion" to be effected? Why, at a certain date, does my 'idea of God', which has hitherto been dormant, begin to dominate my whole thinking? Any answer Spinoza might have attempted would probably have been contained in the missing chapters of the *de Intellectus Emendatione*. But it is abundantly clear that he could not have made the process begin with a freely chosen turning of the mind from darkness to light, since he has expressly insisted on it that subjection to the illusions of 'imagination' is a strictly *necessitated* consequence of our position in the universe; we cannot break our own chains (II. 36, IV. 4). Nor again are we liberated *ab extra* by the rising on us of a spiritual sun which had previously been hidden by the cloak of night, for *all* men have *always* had the 'adequate idea' of God. It remains, then, an inexplicable mystery why not all of them are at any rate at home in geometry and kinematics. It appears then that, when all has been said, there is no sure way to which we can trust for the 'amendment' of our understanding. Perhaps a man will rise from the level of *imaginatio* to that of *ratio* or *scientia intuitiva,* perhaps he will not, and whether he does or does not is dependent on causes which, if Spinoza's rigid necessitarianism is true, he can neither foresee nor control. It is matter of predetermination, or what comes to the same thing, of pure chance. (For if all that can be said is that what will be will be, it makes not an atom of practical difference whether you call this doctrine absolute Predestination, as Spinoza likes to call it, or Absolute Chance.)

It is not sufficiently to the point to reply that there certainly is a great 'something not ourselves' on which we are dependent, whether we call it the 'divine decrees', or the 'order of nature', and that perhaps no philosophy has ever succeeded in showing how our personal freedom and initiative can be conciliated with this dependence. This may be so, and yet, may we not say? no philosophy can possibly be sound which does not at least recognise the need of the conciliation by admitting the manifest *prima facie* fact of intellectual and moral initiative. By his *a priori* assumption of universal and absolute "natural necessity" Spinoza really runs away from the problem with which the philosopher should grapple, and here he reveals the measure of his inferiority, *as a philosophical thinker,* to Descartes. Descartes' *Fourth Meditation* may fall very far short of being a solution of the difficulty, but at least it honestly tries to take into account all the *prima facie* facts; Spinoza mutilates the "appearances" which it is his business to "save", out of all recognition. It is simply not true to say that what I call acting with freedom means being conscious of my act but unaware of any cause for it (I. 36, Appendix). On the contrary, the very reason why I am so confident that my adherence to a doctrine or my adoption of a line of action has been *free* is precisely that, rightly or wrongly, I am convinced that I do know the cause of the decision, and that the cause is myself.

It is open to Spinoza to argue that this conviction is always mistaken, as it must be if his identification of the mind with its 'ideas' is sound; it is not open to him to confuse this definite conviction of personal initiative with 'ignorance', the *absence* of information. When Socrates remains seated in the Athenian prison awaiting the draught of hemlock, instead of taking the road to Megara or Thebes, as his friends want him to do, and gives as his reason that *he* judges it "best" to abide by the sentence of a legal tribunal, on the face of it there is no resemblance with the case, imagined by Spinoza (*Ep.* 58), of a stone, conscious of its falling, but unaware of any reason why it should be falling. For a real parallel to Spinoza's consciously falling stone we require to go not to the normal actions of responsible human beings but to the psychology of "deferred hypnotic suggestion". Now I gather from the literature of this subject that though persons who act on such "deferred suggestions" are quite unaware that they are carrying out a movement which has been suggested to them under hypnosis, they reveal, if questioned, that they are puzzled about the reasons for their behaviour, do not "quite know why" they make the movement they do make. But this at once discriminates such behaviour from the action which the ordinary man regards as the proof of his freedom; there he thinks himself free precisely because he believes that he *knows* so well why he does what he does, and is acting on his own personal judgement. *Prima facie,* at least, the two cases are as unlike as they could well be—a philosopher who proposes to explain away the difference between them is, no doubt, entitled to a hearing, but we are also entitled to remind him that the appearances are very much *against* him, and that if he is to prove his case he must do so by fairly dispelling the adverse appearances; he cannot prove it by simply assuming universal determinism.

I would add that he does not make his argument any stronger by merely dubbing the appearances unfavourable to him 'vulgar prejudices' and affecting the tone of a 'superior person'. Spinoza strikes that note far too often, especially in his correspondence, and though we must make all allowances for a man whose feelings had been naturally lacerated by the experiences of his early life, one may suspect that his frequent resort to it is, sometimes, due to an uneasy suspicion of the weakness of his case.

In a word, I would urge that Descartes has the merit of avoiding two grievous errors which are really fatal to Spinozism:

(1) He rightly insists on the *transcendency* of his *summum ens,* making it a source of all other *entia,* but never dreaming of treating it as a subject of which they are predicates; he sees, what I should say is perfectly true, that a philosophy which puts a *summum ens* at the head of things must be a doctrine of Creationism.

(2) Consequently, he, unlike all Spinozists, can be strictly consequent in his theory of nature as a mechanism. If nature is a machine at all, it ought to exhibit the obvious and salient characteristics of

all mechanism, that (*a*) there is always, behind the machine, intelligence, not its own, to construct and operate it; (*b*) that the machine is constructed with a view to definite work to be got out of it, and that 'mechanism' demands the reality of 'final causality', however presumptuous it may be in us, who only see part of its working, to assume that we know just what the purposes of its inventor and operator must be. Descartes' great machine is not, like Spinoza's, one which constructs and operates itself, and all to grind nothing. But Descartes' rejection of final causes from Physics does not mean that he has any doubt that there is a purpose in creation; it is a mere confession of our inability—apart from revelation—to say what the purpose may be.

(To be concluded.)

Truth and Falsity
in Spinoza*

G. H. R. Parkinson

§ 6.1. Spinoza does not offer a formal definition of 'truth'
in the *Ethics*, but instead shows in an axiom what he means by
the word. 'A true idea', states *E* i, Ax. 6, 'must agree with its *ideatum.*' (*Idea vera debet cum suo ideato convenire.*) By *ideatum* is
meant 'that of which the idea *is* the idea', as the Enunciation of
E ii. 5 shows by the phrase '*ideata*, i.e. things perceived' (*ideata, seu
res perceptas*). This seems to agree in the main with the Scholastic
definition of truth, with the exception that Spinoza uses the word
ideatum where the Scholastics write 'thing'.[1] For the Schoolmen
truth was 'the conformity or likeness of the thing and the intellect'
(*conformitas seu adaequatio rei et intellectus*).[2] The formula is
found in the logic manuals of Spinoza's day, and Robinson (*Kommentar*, p. 90) quotes examples both from Burgersdijck and from
Clauberg, a copy of whose *Logic* was in Spinoza's library.[3]

It has already been shown, however, that Spinoza disagrees with
the doctrine of 'intelligible forms' which figured in the Scholastic
theory of knowledge; it is to be expected, therefore, that he will
also understand the 'correspondence' of idea with *ideatum* differently from the Schoolmen. What he means by 'correspondence' or
'agreement' in this context can be inferred from his views about

---

* This article forms the sixth chapter of G. H. R. Parkinson's book, *Spinoza's
Theory of Knowledge* (Oxford University Press); hence the item numbers begin
with 6.1. References following the same system are to other parts of this book,
as are references to chapters.

[1] For the Scholastics an *ideatum* was something produced by God as a copy of the
idea which he himself had. See Robinson, *Kommentar*, p. 90 n, who quotes
Chauvin, *Lexicon Rationale* (1690), art. *Ideatum*: 'Idea est exemplar, ad quod
agens per intellectum respiciens producit ideatum.'

[2] Eust. a Sancto Paulo, *Sum. Phil.* iv. 64, quoted by Gilson, *Index Scolastico-
Cartésian*, s.v. 'Vérité'.

[3] No. 127 of the Catalogue in Freudenthal's *Die Lebensgeschichte Spinozas*.

the 'object' (also called *ideatum*: see § 5.5) of the mind. It was shown in § 5.5 that when Spinoza calls the body the 'object' of the human mind, he not only means that the mind knows the body, but also that the mind is correlated with, or united to, the body, so that he tends to confuse questions of mind-matter relations and questions concerning truth. An example of this occurs here. When Spinoza speaks of a true idea as 'agreeing with' its *ideatum*, he means that it *is* its *ideatum* expressed through the attribute of thought. This is presupposed in *E* ii. 24–31, but is perhaps shown most clearly in *E* ii. 32, which says that 'All ideas, in so far as they are referred to God, are true'. To prove this Spinoza argues that 'All ideas which are in God agree completely with their *ideata* (by ii. 7 Cor.), and so (by i, Ax. 6) are true'. The reference to *E* ii. 7 Cor. shows that the 'agreement' of idea with *ideatum* is really a relation of identity, for this Corollary says that whatever is in the attribute of extension is present, in the same order and with the same connexions, in the attribute of thought; and in *E* ii. 7 Sch. Spinoza explains this by saying that a mode of extension and a mode of thought are one and the same thing, comprehended under different attributes.

It seems to follow from this, however, that *every* idea 'agrees with' its *ideatum*, for each idea simply is its *ideatum*, expressed in the attribute of thought. This means, therefore, that every idea is true, which is absurd; for if the word 'true' is to have its usual sense, there must also be a use for its opposite, 'false'. There are, however, three possible ways out of this difficulty.

1. Spinoza may alter the way in which he speaks of the 'object' of an idea, and say that there is a difference between knowing a thing and being the mental correlate of that thing. But he could not accept this without a radical reconstruction of his theory of knowledge.

2. He may, in speaking of truth, drop all reference to the 'agreement' of idea with *ideatum*, and say that although every idea does agree with its object in the sense of 'agreement' described above, it is not for that reason true. Instead, the truth of an idea (say, *p*) is constituted by its coherence with other ideas, each of which is true because it coheres with the others and with *p*. Such a theory will be called here a 'consistency' theory of truth. It seems unlikely that Spinoza would accept such a theory, for (as will later be shown) he always insists that the truth of an idea is its correspondence with its *ideatum*, which the 'consistency' theory denies.

3. The 'consistency' theory is to be distinguished from the theory
of truth associated with Hegelian idealism, which is usually referred to as the 'coherence' theory. It might be objected to the system of ideas mentioned in (2) that it seems, as it were, to hang in
the air: for if one idea is granted to be true then all must be granted,
but it is not clear why any one idea *should* be granted. To this, the
coherence theorist replies that the preceding theory is wrong in
regarding each idea in the system as something which could exist
by itself: instead, the whole system is to be regarded as one idea,
and each constituent as merely a partial aspect of the whole. To
apply this to Spinoza: it is possible for him to say that although
every idea agrees with its *ideatum,* and is for that reason true, yet
there is really only one idea, the idea of the whole. This one idea
is the expression in thought of the infinite being—that is, God—
whereas the so-called ideas which human beings have are often incomplete, and in a sense unreal, and so do not deserve the name
'idea'. On this interpretation truth is still constituted by 'agreement', and yet it is possible to allow that there are false ideas, since
falsity is incompleteness.

The last interpretation is clearly the most promising of the three,
and since there is a good deal of evidence to support it, it will be
discussed in detail in the following sections.

§ 6.2. The first piece of evidence for this interpretation is derived
from Spinoza's theory of attributes and modes, as this is applied to
thought. It is necessary, therefore, to begin with an account of the
way in which the attribute of thought is subdivided into infinite
and finite modes, similar to that given of the attribute of extension
in Chapter IV. The finite modes of thought have already been mentioned; they are[4] particular ideas. Difficulty arises, however, with
the infinite modes.

The 'immediate'[5] infinite and eternal mode, corresponding to
motion and rest in extension, is said to be the 'absolutely infinite
intellect',[6] which is clearly the same as the 'infinite intellect of God'

[4] § 5.1.

[5] It will be remembered (cf. § 4.5) that the adjectives 'immediate' and 'mediate'
are not used in this context by Spinoza himself.

[6] Or 'understanding', as Wolf translates *intellectus: Ep.* 64, p. 308. See also *Short
Treatise i.* 9.

to which reference is made in the *Ethics*.[7] Spinoza's reason for calling the infinite intellect a mode is given in *E* i. 31, which says that 'the actual intellect, whether finite or infinite, must be referred to *Natura naturata*'. (By *Natura naturata* Spinoza means[8] 'all the modes of the attributes of God, in so far as they are considered as things which are in God, and which cannot be or be conceived without God'.[9] Spinoza refers the intellect to *Natura naturata* because[10] 'by "intellect" (as is self-evident) we do not understand absolute thought, but only a certain mode of thought, which differs from other modes—namely, desire, love, etc.—and so (*E* i, Def. 5) must be conceived through absolute thought'. His attempt to deduce this 'immediate' infinite mode seems made in *E* ii. 3, where he says that 'in God there is necessarily given an idea, both of his essence and of all those things which necessarily follow from his essence'. The last phrase may refer to those things which 'follow from the absolute nature of some attribute of God', that is, the 'immediate' infinite modes,[11] but it is not certain what Spinoza intends it to mean. If, however, *E* ii. 3 is meant as a deduction of the infinite intellect of God from the definition of God, it is easy to show that it fails. For the proof depends on *E* i. 16—that from the necessity of the divine nature there follow infinite things in infinite ways—which has already[12] been shown to be insecurely based.

Spinoza gives no example of a 'mediate' infinite mode of thought, and there has been considerable speculation as to what this might be. Pollock[13] suggests that it is the 'idea of God in thought' mentioned in *E* i. 21, but admits that it seems not to be distinguished there from the infinite intellect of God: and indeed it is this proposition which deals with the 'immediate', not the 'mediate', infinite modes. Joachim also[14] suggests the infinite idea of God, quoting *E* ii. 3 and 4. This 'infinite idea' he takes to be 'the thought-side of all bodies and all the modes of all attributes: it is the complete system of all the "souls", the ideal counterpart of the *facies totius Universi*'.

[7] *E* ii. 11 Cor., ii. 43 Sch. *ad fin.*, and v. 40 Sch.
[8] *E* i. 29 Sch.
[9] Cf. Joachim, *Study*, p. 120.
[10] *E* i. 31.
[11] *E* i. 21.
[12] § 4.3.
[13] *Spinoza*, 2d ed., p. 176.
[14] *Study*, pp. 94–95.

The argument has some plausibility; but there is no indication that
Spinoza thought of this idea of God as 'varying in infinite ways,
and yet remaining the same', as the 'aspect of the whole Universe' [15]
does. Further, the 'mediate' should follow from the 'immediate' infinite mode; but it is not clear that the idea of God does so follow,
or that it is intended to do so. This tells against Joachim's interpretation; moreover, reason will later be given for equating the infinite
idea of God with the infinite intellect, which seems conclusively to
disprove Joachim's view. It seems, therefore, that there is a gap in
Spinoza's system, in that he was unable to discover, or at least did
not state, a logical or psychological law which would correspond
to the law of physics which constitutes the 'aspect of the whole Universe'.

Returning to the 'immediate' infinite and eternal mode of
thought, it might be asked why Spinoza should suppose this to be
the infinite intellect, rather than, say, infinite desire, or infinite
love. The answer[16] is contained in E ii, Ax. 3: 'The modes of
thought, such as love, desire, or whatever affects of the mind are
described by name, do not exist unless in the same individual there
is the idea of a thing which is loved, desired, etc. But an idea can
exist, although there exists no other mode of thought.' Spinoza,
therefore, considers all mental activity to involve the presence of
an idea—that is, an act of judgment or apprehension. The idea is
thus prior to the other modes of thought, and the infinite intellect,
which may be taken as equivalent to all such ideas (or as the one
real idea, if the 'coherence' interpretation of Spinoza's theory of
truth is correct), is thus the 'immediate' infinite mode. It is also
similar to the infinite mode of extension, namely, motion and rest,
in that just as there is no extension without motion and rest, so
there is no mental activity without an idea.[17]

This third axiom of Book II of the *Ethics* may seem to imply
that desire, love, and ideas are all alike modes of thought, whereas
E ii. 1 speaks of ideas alone as modes, which seems to involve a contradiction. But what Spinoza means is that desire, love, &c., are
certain sorts of idea, or rather that each is a certain aspect of an
idea. For, according to Spinoza, an idea is not always a mere act of
judgement; it may also have what may roughly be called a 'dynamic'

[15] *Ep.* 64.
[16] Cf. Joachim, *Study,* pp. 93–94.
[17] On the 'infinite intellect' see also § 8.8.

function. For as the body's power of action is increased or diminished, so do its ideas differ.[18] The ideas which correspond to the former activity are 'adequate ideas', and give rise to the 'actions' of the mind;[19] the ideas corresponding to the latter are 'inadequate', and give rise to the 'passions'.[20] A fuller discussion of this would need to go beyond Spinoza's epistemology into his psychology, but perhaps enough has been said to indicate the way in which the idea is related to the other modes of thought.

Such, then, is the infinite intellect of God. It is not the same as the attribute of thought, for it does not include, for example, the passions. But wherever there is mental activity there must, according to Spinoza, be an idea; or, in other words, the infinite intellect is coextensive with the attribute of thought. The above arguments, it will be noted, also suggest that the infinite idea of God, supposed by some to be the 'mediate' infinite and eternal mode of thought, is actually equivalent to the infinite intellect of God.

It is now possible to consider the relation of the human mind to the attributes and infinite modes of thought. It might perhaps be supposed that Spinoza would say that the human mind is a part of the attribute of thought. Instead, he prefers to say that the human mind is a part of the infinite intellect of God.[21] There seems to be no good reason for this preference, except that the intellect is of great importance for Spinoza's ethical theory, and it is therefore natural that he should think of the human mind primarily as an intellect. This does not imply that the human mind is not a part of the attribute of thought: clearly it is, since the infinite mode itself belongs to the attribute: it only implies that Spinoza lays special stress on the intellect.

A difficulty arises concerning the mind's participation in the infinite intellect, in that *E* i. 17 Sch., p. 63, says that the intellect of God differs completely (*toto coelo*) from the intellect of man, 'nor can they agree in anything except in name; viz., as much as "the Dog", the heavenly constellation, agrees with "the Dog", the animal which barks'.[22] It is difficult to see, therefore, how the human

---

[18] *E* iii, Def. 3.

[19] *E* iii. 1, 3.

[20] *E* iii. 1, 3. See also 'General Definition of the Affects' at the end of *E* iii.

[21] *E* ii. 11 Cor., *E* v. 40 Sch., and *Ep*. 32, p. 212.

[22] This was a standard example of a homonym: see Robinson, *Kommentar*, p. 184, n. 2, and L. Roth, *Spinoza, Descartes and Maimonides*, p. 117, n. 3. The same example is given in *Cogitata Metaphysica* ii. 11.3.

intellect can be a part of the intellect of God, especially as Spinoza says that it is absurd to suppose that the parts of anything can have nothing in common with the whole of which they are parts.[23] But the contradiction is only apparent. *E* i. 17 Sch. sets out to show that 'If intellect and will pertain to the eternal essence of God, then something else is to be understood by each of these attributes than is currently supposed by men'. The sentence, it will be noted, is hypothetical, and says in effect that *if* intellect and will are attributes, they must differ from the intellect and will with which we are acquainted. But this condition is unfulfilled: for Spinoza, intellect (and the will, which he regards as inseparable from it: § 5.2) is an infinite mode and not an attribute. Spinoza does not say that between the infinite mode that is God's intellect and the intellect of man there is no resemblance, and thus no contradiction is involved.[24]

§ 6.3. After this lengthy introduction it is now possible to discuss the relations of Spinoza's theory of substance, attribute, and infinite mode to his theory of truth. If Spinoza holds that each mode of thought is not really distinguished from the attribute of thought, it follows that each particular idea or judgement is not really to be distinguished from God in so far as God makes judgements—that is, from the infinite intellect of God. Ultimately, therefore, there is only one idea, which[25] must agree with its *ideatum,* and must therefore be true. Joachim, who is the foremost exponent of this interpretation of Spinoza's theory of truth, argues forcefully for this conclusion.[26]

> Since every idea is a mode of Thought, no idea is capable of being *per se*: its being and its truth belong to it only in the complete context of God's infinite idea or intellect [cf. *E* ii. 7 Cor.; ii. 32 Dem.]. No partial idea can (except in that context) be true, for it comprises no content purely in itself: it is not separable as the idea of a separable *ideatum,* but has its being and its truth only in *natura naturata.* The only idea, therefore, which is ultimately true, is the *infinita idea Dei.* And that is true, because it sustains in itself all *ideae.*

[23] *E* i. 12.
[24] Cf. Robinson, *Kommentar*, pp. 181 ff.
[25] *E* ii. 32.
[26] *Study*, pp. 148–149.

It *is* its *ideatum*: it is identical with the modal Reality on its formal side. And its truth is its reality or completeness, its self-containedness.

It might be suggested that it is possible to assert the converse of the above, that is, that Spinoza does not deduce the view that there must be one truth from his views about mode and attribute, but rather deduces them from it. This would explain[27] why he thinks that particular ideas are modes of thought, but since there is no direct evidence that Spinoza did argue in this way, the suggestion must be regarded as tentative at the best. Moreover, reason will later[28] be given for supposing that Spinoza does not hold that there is only one truth, so that his assumption that there are modes of thought cannot be accounted for in this way.

The view that a true idea is a complete idea seems most evident in the *Ethics* in its negative equivalents—that an incomplete idea is false, and that all false ideas are incomplete. These can best be discussed in later sections.

§ 6.4. The assumption that an incomplete idea is untrue is the basis of *E* ii. 24–29, in which Spinoza shows that 'knowledge from the common order of Nature' (*E* ii. 29 Cor.) is 'inadequate', or false.[29] The knowledge which is here said to be inadequate is that which obtains whenever 'the mind is determined externally, namely by the chance impact (*fortuito occursu*) of things, to contemplate this or that, and not whenever it is determined internally'.[30] That this refers to sense-perception is shown clearly by *E* ii. 40, Sch. 2,[31] which equates knowledge through the senses with knowledge 'from the common order of Nature'.

Spinoza's arguments in *E* ii. 24–29 all follow a similar pattern, and *E* ii. 25 will serve as an example. To prove that 'the idea of each affection of the human body does not involve adequate knowledge of an external body', Spinoza argues as follows. We perceive an external body in so far as our own body is affected by it:[32] but this

[27] Cf. § 5.4.
[28] § 6.9.
[29] There are differences between 'adequacy' and 'truth'—see § 6.7—but these are unimportant in the present context.
[30] *E* ii. 29 Sch.
[31] Cf. § 7.1.
[32] Cf. § 5.5.

external body is something other than our own body, so that its idea is in God 'in so far as God is considered as affected by the idea of another thing' (namely, other than our own body)—that is, in so far as God's idea is something more than our own mind: and therefore our perception of the external body is inadequate. Here, then, and again in *E* ii. 24, 27, 28, and 29, Spinoza shows that he thinks that if an idea is incomplete—if it is only a part of God's infinite intellect—then that idea is false.

A coherence theory of truth must not only say that any incomplete idea is false, but also that any false idea is incomplete. And this is what Spinoza seems to maintain when he discusses the nature of falsity or error. He gives a brief summary of his views in *E* ii. 11 Cor., which later propositions explain in greater detail.

> When we say that the human mind perceives this or that, we say nothing else than that God, not in so far as he is infinite, but in so far as he is explained through the nature of the human mind (i.e., in so far as he constitutes the essence of the human mind), has this or that idea. And when we say that God has this or that idea, not only in so far as he constitutes the nature of the human mind, but in so far as he has the idea of another thing at the same time as he is the human mind (*simul cum Mente humana*), then we say that the human mind perceives a thing partly, or inadequately.

It appears, then, that 'inadequate perception', or error, consists in the possession of an idea which is incomplete, and which is only completed in the infinite intellect of God, of which[33] the human mind is a part. The same is expressed in the discussion of falsity in the *DIE*. 'Inadequate ideas arise in us solely from this, that we are part of some thinking being whose thoughts—some wholly, some in part only (*quaedam . . . ex toto, quaedam ex parte tantum*)— constitute our mind.' [34] This sentence is somewhat elliptic: it might be taken to mean that some of God's thoughts form the whole of our mind, others only a part. But it seems more likely that Spinoza means that some of God's ideas are present to us in their completeness, and these are true ideas, whilst of others we possess only a part, and these are false ideas.

[33] *E* ii. 11 Cor.
[34] *DIE,* p. 28, par. 73.

Spinoza discusses falsity at length in *E* ii. 35, in which he says that 'falsity consists in the privation of knowledge which inadequate, that is, mutilated and confused, ideas involve'. Falsity, he notes,[35] cannot be said to consist in privation alone (*in absoluta privatione*),[36] for it is only minds which are said to err or be mistaken— any privations which bodies undergo are described in other terms. Again, falsity is not the same as ignorance, for to make a mistake about something and to be ignorant of the thing are quite different. It must therefore consist in 'the privation of knowledge which inadequate . . . ideas involve'. That is, to make a mistake is to have an idea of some sort, although an inadequate one, whereas to be ignorant of something is to have no ideas about it whatsoever.

The proof of *E* ii. 35 rests upon *E* ii. 33, which itself seems to imply a view of truth as coherence, since it states that 'There is nothing positive in ideas on account of which they are called false'. The proof of this proposition makes use of the nature of God: suppose, Spinoza says, a positive mode of thought, which constitutes the 'form' (i.e., the reality: cf. § 2.3) of error or falsity. Now (*a*) this mode of thought cannot be in God, for[37] all ideas, in so far as they are referred to God, are true. But (*b*) neither can it be outside God, for[38] nothing can be outside God. Therefore there is no positive mode of thought of the kind required. This argument, then, implies that there is no place for false ideas, unless they are taken to be a part of the true idea which God has, which is the coherence theory of truth as it was defined above.[39]

§ 6.5. In *E* ii. 35 Sch., Spinoza introduces examples in order to show how the falsity of a statement consists solely in its incompleteness. *E* ii. 35 Sch. refers back to the end of *E* ii. 17 Sch., the two passages forming a continuous argument. In *E* ii. 17 Sch. ('Atque hinc . . .') Spinoza writes:

[35] *E* ii. 35 Dem.
[36] Gebhardt, following the *Nagelate Schriften,* adds the words 'of knowledge' (*van kennis*), so making the whole clause, 'falsity cannot consist in absolute lack of knowledge'. But this renders pointless the next clause, which distinguishes minds from bodies precisely because minds alone are said to lack knowledge. It seems, then, that the reading of the *Opera Posthuma* must be sustained.
[37] *E* ii. 32.
[38] *E* i. 15.
[39] § 6.1.

And here, so that I may begin to explain the nature of error,
I would have you note that the mind's imaginations considered in themselves contain no error; i.e., that the mind
does not err from the fact that it imagines, but only in so far
as it is considered to lack an idea which secludes the existence of those things which it imagines as present. For if the
mind, whilst it imagined non-existent things as present, knew
at the same time that those things really did not exist, it
would consider this power of imagination to be a virtue and
not a defect.

With this there may be compared *DIE,* p. 25, par. 66, which says
that there is no difference between a feigned and a false idea, except
that the latter presupposes assent: 'that is (as we have already noted)
that no causes are offered, whilst representations are offered to a
man, by which he can gather that they do not arise from things
outside himself, as he can in the case of supposal.'

E ii. 35 Sch. gives two examples of 'privation of knowledge':

Men are deceived because they think themselves free; this
opinion of theirs consists solely in this, that they are aware
of their actions, and unaware of the causes by which they are
determined. . . . Thus, when we look at the sun, we imagine
it to be about two hundred feet away from us: which mistake
does not consist in this imagination alone, but in the fact
that, whilst we thus imagine it, we are ignorant of its true
distance, and of the cause of this imagination. For even after
we know that it is distant from us more than six hundred
times the diameter of the earth, we nevertheless imagine it
to be near us. This is because we do not imagine the sun to
be so near because we are ignorant of its true distance, but
because the affection of our body involves the essence of the
sun, in so far as the body itself is affected by it.

It will be convenient to discuss first the latter of these two examples. *E* iv, Def. 6, shows that when Spinoza says in this context
that we 'imagine' the sun to be 200 feet away he is referring to a
fact about sense-perception, namely, that all objects beyond a certain distance (which he puts at 200 feet) appear to the observer to
be equidistant from him.[40] 'Imagination', then, is not 'supposal',

[40] Cf. Descartes, *Dioptric,* chap. 6, sec. 20, which is probably the source for the
figure of 200 feet.

but refers to the way the sun *looks*. A fuller account of the imagination is given in the next chapter; now, however, it has to be asked what Spinoza means by saying that such an imagination is not false in itself, but that falsity arises only when the person imagining lacks some item of knowledge. His reason for saying here[41] that the imagination by itself does not involve error seems to be that the imagination remains, even when, for example, the true distance is known: it is not eliminated, as a false *theory* about the distance of the sun would be eliminated. The assertion which remains (since all ideas involve assertion) is that the sun looks 200 feet away, and this involves no error in itself. Falsity only arises when a man says 'The sun looks, and is, 200 feet away', for then the mind lacks an idea which 'secludes the existence of' that which it imagines as present.[42] The same applies in the case of Spinoza's other example, men's belief that they are free. In so far as men say that they are aware of their own actions (which they may express as 'We feel ourselves to be free') they are not in error; the error only arises when they say 'We are aware of our actions, and these actions are uncaused', or 'We feel ourselves to be free, and are in fact free'. Here again they lack an idea which negates the second clause of their statement.

But does it follow from this that a statement's falsity consists in the fact that it is incomplete? Spinoza appears to suggest that an erroneous statement is left unchanged by the statement which corrects it, except that it is incorporated within a wider context. A false statement, on this view, may perhaps be compared to a piece of a puzzle, whose proper place in that puzzle is not known: the correction of the statement will then be like fitting the piece into the puzzle. But the examples given by Spinoza show that the knowledge which is needed to make a false statement true does not leave that statement unchanged, but contradicts a part of it. Thus, the sun *is not* 200 feet away: human actions *are* caused, &c. And it is surely the fact that fresh information corrects something previously held which leads people to say 'This corrects an error' rather than simply 'This is a new piece of information'.

Spinoza's discussion of error, it will have been noticed, is carried on with special reference to what he calls 'imagination', which[43] includes sense-perception. It is possible, therefore, that one reason for

[41] And in *E* ii. 49 Sch., p. 134.
[42] *E* ii. 17 Sch.
[43] See also Chapter VII.

Spinoza's view of the nature of error may have been the observation that every sense-perception may be said to be at least partly true, in so far as it relates to the look of things. Thus, although the sun is not 200 feet away, it is true (according to Spinoza) that it looks as if it is. The view, then, that sense-perception is at least partly true may have led Spinoza to suppose that the correction of error was merely the addition of fresh information, making the partly true wholly true. What he failed to note was that the fresh information also contradicted something of what had been held before—for example, that the sun not only looked, but was, 200 feet away.

Spinoza also discusses the subject of error in the *DIE*, arguing on pp. 27–28, pars. 72–73,[44] that to make a false statement 'indicates a defect of our perception'. Falsity, he says, 'consists in this alone, that something is affirmed of some object which is not contained in the concept which we have formed of the object' (*quod in ipsius, quem formavimus, conceptu non continetur*, par. 72). For example, the concept of a globe may be formed by supposing a semicircle to rotate about its diameter; but if this construction is supposed to define a semicircle, then it is false, for the concept of motion is not contained in the concept of a semicircle. Falsity arises, then, 'because we have as it were mutilated and truncated thoughts, that is, ideas. For we saw that the motion of a semicircle is false when it is bare (*nudus*) in the mind, but that it is true when joined to the concept of a sphere, or to the concept of another cause which determines such motion' (par. 73).

This example seems to differ from those in the *Ethics* in that it would naturally be taken to concern what is called in the *Ethics* 'verbal error', or rather 'the incorrect application of names to things' (*E* ii. 47 Sch.), and which is treated separately from the kind of error discussed in *E* ii. 35 Sch. In *E* ii. 47 Sch. Spinoza cites as an example a man who 'says that the lines drawn from the centre of a circle to its circumference are unequal'. Such a man 'understands by "circle" something other than what mathematicians mean by the word'. The same, it seems, could be said of a person who defines a semicircle in a way appropriate to a sphere.

It is probable, however, that Spinoza would consider the false definition of a semicircle to be analogous to the mistake of saying that the sun is only 200 feet away. The former error lies in the fact

[44] See also § 3.1 above.

that motion does not belong to the concept of a semicircle as used in geometry; the latter, in the fact that a distance of 200 feet from the earth does not belong to the concept of the sun as it is used in science—that is, that in a list of the properties of the sun which the physicist or astronomer would give, the property of being 200 feet from the earth does not appear. The important question, however, is whether Spinoza has shown that the falsity of the definition of the semicircle lies in the fact that it is incomplete. The crux of his argument is the statement, 'we saw that the motion of a semicircle is false when it is bare in the mind, but that it is true when joined to the concept of a sphere'. Here it seems that Spinoza is right in saying that the statement 'a semicircle revolves' is incomplete, but wrong in saying that its falsity consists in its incompleteness. The statement in question is incomplete in that if someone says 'A semicircle revolves', what he says can figure in many different contexts, in which it goes to make up a whole which may be either true or false; but by itself, it can hardly be called true or false at all. For before one can agree or disagree with such an assertion it must be asked: 'In what definition or what proof does this assertion appear?'

Spinoza's theory of the nature of falsity, therefore, seems to be unsatisfactory in itself. However, this discussion was begun in the course of considering the evidence for the view that Spinoza found the nature of truth to lie in coherence or completeness. And it can plausibly be argued from this evidence that Spinoza is looking for a theory of error which will be consistent with a coherence theory of truth, even if he is unable to find an account which is satisfactory.

§ 6.6. It might be objected that Spinoza's theory of falsity proves too much: for if a true idea is a complete idea, then it seems that God alone can have a true idea. Only that idea which is the reflection in thought of the whole universe is true, anything less being an inadequate idea.[45] But a man's body, which is the object of the idea which constitutes the human mind, is a mere fragment of extension, and therefore no man can have true ideas. But this would be an obvious absurdity, for the consequence that we can know nothing is derived from an elaborate theory concerning substance and its attributes which is itself claimed to be true by Spinoza. And

[45] *E* ii. 24–29, discussed in § 6.4.

it would be strange if Spinoza, regarded by many as the archetype
of a dogmatic philosopher, should turn out to be one of those scep-
tics whom he attacks.[46] But the 'sceptical' propositions *E* ii. 24–29
relate[47] to the senses, or to knowledge 'from the common order of
Nature', and not to knowledge as a whole. Spinoza's grounds for
his scepticism must be considered later; for the present it must be
asked how he is able to show that any knowledge is possible.

Spinoza believes that a man has knowledge when 'God, not in so
far as he is infinite, but in so far as he is explained through the nature of the human mind (i.e., in so far as he constitutes the essence
of the human mind) has this or that idea'.[48] It follows from this,
and from Spinoza's definition of 'essence',[49] that in so far as a man
knows something he *is* God. But how can this be, since man is only
a finite mode? Spinoza answers by saying that there are certain respects in which man's finite nature does not put him at a disadvan-
tage. For suppose[50] that there is something which is common to all
things, and which is present equally in the part and in the whole,
then the idea which the human mind has of this will be the same
as that which God has, for this 'something' will be equally the object of the divine mind and of the human mind. Such a thing,
therefore, must be understood, and must moreover be understood
by all men,[51] since all men must possess it.

The ideas which correspond to those things which are 'common
to all' (*communia omnibus*) are called by Spinoza 'common notions',
and are said by him to be the basis of all reasoning.[52] These have
already been mentioned in § 3.1, and will be discussed again in
Chapter VIII, where it will be shown that, as might be expected,
they are the first principles of Spinoza's deductive system. Such,
then, are the true ideas which man has; further,[53] all ideas which
follow from these are also true. Spinoza's proof seems unnecessarily
elaborate: 'When we say that an idea in the human mind follows
from ideas which are adequate in it, we say nothing else than that

---

[46] *DIE,* p. 18, par. 47.
[47] Cf. § 6.4.
[48] *E* ii. 11 Cor. For a similar formula cf. *E* v. 36.
[49] See § 3.4.
[50] *E* ii. 38.
[51] *E* ii. 38 Cor.
[52] *E* ii. 40, Sch. 1.
[53] *E* ii. 40.

(by *F* ii. 11 Cor.) in the divine intellect itself there is an idea of which God is the cause, not in so far as he is infinite, nor in so far as he is affected by the ideas of very many single things, but in so far as he constitutes the essence of the human mind alone.' This seems to amount to no more than the statement that an idea is true if deduced from true ideas—that is, that deduction is a valid method of proof. The physical correlate of deduction is left obscure: perhaps it is the same as that of the common notions, if (as in Descartes: see § 3.1) they include the principles of inference.

In this way, then, Spinoza is able to escape some of the difficulties into which his theory of the relation between idea and object leads him.

§ 6.7. So far the evidence seems to point to the fact that Spinoza's theory of truth is a modified form of the coherence theory held by idealists. It differs from that theory in that Spinoza does not hold that nothing exists but mind, but agrees with it in that the relations between thought and extension are such that only one idea can 'correspond to' its object, and so only one idea—the one complete idea—can be true. Before it is asked whether this evidence may not, after all, be misleading, something must be said of a further aspect of Spinoza's theory of truth, which may lead to the impression that Spinoza was tending towards a fully developed coherence theory of truth of the idealist type. This view is advanced by Joachim, *Spinoza's Tractatus*, p. 99, who says of Spinoza that it is 'difficult to see exactly *what* he is maintaining to be adequate to, or commensurate with, *what.* . . . One is tempted . . . to find in Spinoza, at least in its rudiments or germ, the view that Reality (*Deus sive Natura*), whether as "idea" or as *ideatum* . . . is a Dialectic—a *self*-analysis and *self*-synthesis, a Whole which *is* in, and by, and as, the development of itself.' The chief evidence for such a view is derived from what Spinoza says about 'adequate' ideas.

An 'adequate' idea is defined in *E* ii, Def. 4, as 'an idea which, in so far as it is considered in itself without relation to its object, has all the properties or intrinsic denominations of a true idea'. Spinoza adds, 'I say "intrinsic", so that I may exclude that which is extrinsic, namely, the agreement of the idea with its *ideatum*.' With this there may be compared *DIE*, p. 26, par. 69: 'A true idea is distinguished from a false one not only by an extrinsic denomination, but in particular by an intrinsic one.' *Ep.* 60, p. 300, offers a definition of an

adequate idea which is similar to the one given above, but without
the use of the Scholastic term 'denomination'.[54] 'I recognize no other
difference between a true and an adequate idea than that the word
"true" refers only to the agreement of the idea with its *ideatum,*
while the word "adequate" refers to the nature of the idea in itself;
so that there is really no difference between a true and an adequate
idea except this extrinsic relation.'

Of the nature of this 'intrinsic denomination' which characterizes
a true idea Spinoza gives no explicit account in the *Ethics*; however, in *DIE,* p. 26, par. 69, he offers two examples. He begins, 'If
a workman has formed a proper conception of (*ordine concepit*) a
machine,[55] then, even though such a machine has never existed, nor
indeed ever will exist, the thought of it is none the less true; and
the thought is the same, whether the machine exists or not.' [56] Here
the property or intrinsic denomination of the workman's thought,
which is held to make it true, seems to be the fact that he has
formed a 'proper conception' of his machine, that is, that his plans
are mathematically 'right'. The phrase *ordine concepit* refers to the
view put forward in the *DIE* that one's thoughts must be arranged
in their 'proper order'—that is, in a deductive order.

But this does not prove anything against a correspondence theory
of truth of the sort which Spinoza has been suggested to hold. What
Spinoza has argued is:[57] 'Since neither the making nor the existence
of the machine have *altered* the artificer's thought, its truth cannot
be constituted or increased by the correspondence which has now
been brought about.' But when Spinoza said that an idea must
'agree with' or 'correspond to' its *ideatum,* he meant[58] that the idea
is its *ideatum,* expressed under a different attribute. Here, however,
the 'correspondence' is that which holds between a mental plan of
a machine and the actual machine of which the plan is made. Spinoza is saying that the rightness of such a plan need not be verified
by actual tests; for, according to him, it can be seen from the plans
alone (which are here supposed to be 'in the head', and not on pa-

---

[54] On which see Gilson, *Index Scolastico-Cartésien,* s.v. 'Dénomination'.

[55] So Joachim, *Spinoza's Tractatus,* p. 94, translates *fabrica,* referring to Descartes's example in *Reply to First Objections,* H & R, vol. ii, p. 10. This seems
preferable to 'building', the translation given by Elwes and Boyle.

[56] For a similar example see also *DIE,* p. 27, par. 71.

[57] Joachim, *Spinoza's Tractatus,* p. 94.

[58] Cf. § 6.1.

per) that the machine would go if constructed. But this does not show that nothing corresponds to the workman's thought in the sense given to 'correspondence' in the *Ethics*. On the contrary, Spinoza's theory of the relations between mind and matter implies that there must be some physical events which correspond to the workman's mental activity. This will no doubt consist of those things which are 'common to all',[59] since the man's thought is said to be true, and therefore must consist of common notions and what are deduced from them. All that this example has shown is, not that there are no physical processes which 'correspond to' [60] or 'are the object of' thought, but rather that, in an *a priori* physics or mechanics, there is no need of experimental verification. This is typical of Spinoza, but not of the idealist position which this passage may be thought to indicate.

The second example given in *DIE*, p. 26, par. 69, of what is meant by an 'adequate idea' runs as follows: 'If anyone says that Peter (e.g.) exists, but does not *know* that Peter exists, then that thought is false—or, if you prefer, is not true—for him (*respectu illius*), even though Peter does in fact exist.' Here, then, is an instance in which an idea does in a sense 'correspond to' its *ideatum*, and yet is not said to be true, thus indicating that such 'correspondence' does not constitute the nature of truth. Spinoza is implying that, if a statement '*p*' is to be called true, it must be possible to say of the man who makes that statement that he knows that *p*. Thus, to be able to say '*S*'s assertion, "Peter exists", is true', it must also be possible to say '*S* knows that Peter exists'. As Spinoza himself says (par. 69), 'This statement, "Peter exists", is only true with respect to the man who knows certainly that Peter exists.'

This further intrinsic denomination of a true idea is therefore the fact that a true idea or statement is not simply a random idea or statement which happens to be right. But it must again be pointed out that this does not seem to tell against a correspondence theory of truth of the sort maintained in the *Ethics*. For the 'correspondence' which is discussed there is meant to cover ideas which are true in the strict sense, and not those ideas which merely happen to be right. Spinoza would say of the latter that they are inadequate ideas, and so do not correspond to their objects; or rather he would

[59] Cf. § 6.6.
[60] § 5.5.

say of a person who has such an idea that God does not constitute the essence of his mind.[61] The present passage, therefore, does not tell in favour of the idealist interpretation of Spinoza's theory of truth.

To sum up: two of the intrinsic denominations of a true idea, which constitute the 'adequacy' of such an idea, are shown by the *DIE* to be:

(i) The fact that such an idea is internally coherent—that, for example, it exhibits mathematical 'rightness'.

(ii) The fact that such an idea is an instance of *knowledge,* and is therefore to be distinguished from a random statement which happens to be true.

But it has also been shown that in neither case does Spinoza suggest that an idea's truth consists in these properties alone, and that the 'correspondence' he attacks is not that which is described in the *Ethics.* There is therefore no reason to modify his view, stated clearly in the *Ethics,* that truth and adequacy are not the same; that a true idea is not only adequate in itself, but also corresponds to its *ideatum.*

§ 6.8. 'Clearness and distinctness' seems to be a further intrinsic denomination of a true idea. Though Spinoza often speaks of 'clear and distinct ideas',[62] he nowhere defines the term. Evidently he assumed that his readers would know that Descartes had used 'clear and distinct' to mean 'true',[63] and therefore a formal definition seemed unnecessary. But it must be asked whether he understands the phrase in exactly the same way as Descartes had understood it.

Descartes distinguishes between 'clearness' and 'distinctness', as *Principles,* i. 45–46, show. By calling an idea 'clear' Descartes refers to his view that a true idea is perceived 'intuitively', by a mental act analogous to sight. Thus he says, 'I term that "clear", which is present and apparent to an attentive mind, in the same way that we assert that we see objects clearly when, being present to the regarding eye, they operate upon it with sufficient strength.'[64] But a 'percep-

---

[61] *E* ii. 11 Cor.

[62] E.g., *DIE,* pp. 24–25, pars. 62–64; p. 26, par. 68; p. 30, pars. 79–80; p. 34, par. 91; p. 36, par. 98; p. 39, par. 108; *E* i. 8, Sch. 2; *E* ii. 28; *E* ii. 29 Sch; *E* ii. 36; *E* ii. 38 Cor.; *E* iii. 9; *E* v. 3, 4, 10, 15; *Ep.* 4.

[63] See, e.g., *E* i. 8, Sch. 2: 'a clear and distinct, that is, a true idea.'

[64] *Princ.* i. 45.

tion' (i.e., an idea) may be clear without being distinct, though it cannot be distinct unless it is clear.[65] Descartes means that it is sometimes difficult to see exactly what proposition is intuited, and therefore true. 'When, for instance, a severe pain is felt, the perception of this pain may be very clear, and yet for all that not distinct, because it is usually confused by the sufferers with the obscure judgement that they form upon its nature, assuming as they do that something exists in the part affected, similar to the sensation of pain of which they are alone clearly conscious.' [66] In other words: a statement such as 'There is a pain in my leg' is a judgement *about* the pain, and is false; the correct statement[67] is 'I feel a pain in my leg', which is 'clear', and has also been distinguished from the judgement formed about it, to the effect that the pain is actually *in* the leg. The latter Descartes declares to be false because people with amputated legs sometimes seem to feel pain in the part which has been amputated.[68] Such people *feel* a pain, but the pain cannot be where they think it is.

It must now be asked whether Spinoza distinguished between 'clearness' and 'distinctness' in this way. The *Ethics* gives no indication that he did, but *DIE,* p. 36, par. 98, offers a hint that, at any rate in his early work, he did so. This says that 'the more special an idea is, the more distinct, and therefore (*ac proinde*) the more clear it is'. This is correct Cartesian usage, for it has been seen that a distinct idea must also be clear, but it cannot be considered certain that Spinoza has this in mind in the present passage. But there seems to be other evidence to this effect from the *DIE,* for what Descartes says in *Principles,* i. 46, about the need to separate a clear idea from the obscure judgements formed about it is echoed in *DIE,* p. 27, pars. 72–73,[69] in which falsity is said to consist in affirming something of an object which is not contained in the concept of that object.

It seems then that, at least in the *DIE,* Spinoza understands by the 'clearness and distinctness' of an idea what Descartes had understood. But are the characteristics of clearness and distinctness intrinsic denominations of a true idea? It is evident that 'clearness' is,

[65] *Princ.* i. 46.
[66] Loc. cit.
[67] Cf. *Princ.* i. 68.
[68] *Princ.* iv. 196; *Meditation VI,* H & R, vol. i, p. 189.
[69] Cf. §§ 3.1 and 6.5 above.

referring as it does to the fact that a true idea is 'self-evident'.[70] But the 'distinctness' of an idea is a more ambiguous notion. It may mean (1) that it is necessary to be sure *what* one's intuitions, or self-evident truths, are, and not confuse them with propositions which look similar but in fact are not. This can hardly be called a property of the true idea itself, but is rather an instruction to a person who wants to have true ideas. Spinoza may also mean (2) that a 'distinct' idea is 'either a very simple idea or is composed of them':[71] if this is so, he is referring again to the fact that truths constitute a deductive system. Finally, he may mean (3) that a true idea is not 'confused' in the way described in *E* ii. 24–29:[72] that is, that a true idea must correspond to its *ideatum,* and is not a mere fragment of God's infinite intellect. This, however, would be an *extrinsic* denomination, since it refers to the relation between an idea and its object, and so cannot be included amongst the intrinsic denominations which make an idea 'adequate'.

§ 6.9. After this discussion of 'adequate' ideas it is now possible to return to Spinoza's theory of truth proper, and to ask whether the 'coherence' interpretation which has been expounded in preceding sections is in fact correct. The evidence for it may seem decisive; and yet some qualifications must be added.

First, if Spinoza thinks that there is one idea only, and that only this one idea is true, it is remarkable that he never says so, but repeatedly says that *ideas* are true.[73] It can be replied, however, that although he does say this, in consistency he should not. His confusion may be traced to the way in which he speaks of 'ideas'. He thinks that there is in a sense only one idea—the infinite idea of God, or the infinite intellect of God—and that this is a complex idea,[74] just as the idea which constitutes the human mind is complex.[75] But Spinoza speaks of these complex ideas as themselves composed of ideas,[76] whereas in consistency he should have said that these components of a single idea were mere fragments of that idea. Conse-

---

[70] Cf. §§ 3.2 and 3.3.
[71] *DIE* p. 26, par. 68.
[72] Cf. § 6.3.
[73] E.g., *DIE,* p. 34, par. 91; *E* ii. 32.
[74] *E* v. 40. Sch.
[75] *E* ii. 15.
[76] *E* ii. 15, *E* v. 40 Sch.

quently, Spinoza allowed himself to say that 'ideas' are true, whereas he should have said that fragments of 'the idea' are fragments of 'the truth'. Perhaps this is so; but at any rate, it is now clear that the 'coherence' interpretation of Spinoza's theory of truth has ceased to be an account of what he did think, and has become an account of what he should have thought.

But is it even the case that Spinoza should hold a coherence theory of truth? Such a view seems to pay too much attention to the account of knowledge 'from the common order of Nature'.[77] Spinoza's account of this seemed to suggest that there could only be one true idea, that which God has, and that all other ideas are fragmentary and false. But it is a mistake to treat this as the most important feature of Spinoza's theory of truth, for it was shown[78] that at this level *no* truth can be attained by man. It is the theory of common notions which shows how the human mind can have true ideas, in so far as that which is its object is something which is common to the whole of Nature. And Spinoza indicates, by speaking in the plural of 'common notions' and 'those things which are common to all', that there are several of these true ideas, since the body, the object of the human mind, agrees with Nature as a whole in several respects. Spinoza holds, then, that an idea can be a fragment of God's idea and can yet be true, so the view that there is in a sense only one idea does not imply that there is only one truth.

Nor, again, does Spinoza's view that falsity is the 'privation of knowledge' lead necessarily to a coherence theory of truth, though it has been admitted [79] that it may imply such a theory. For although Spinoza says that error consists in a privation of knowledge, it has been shown[80] that he does not imply that all privation of knowledge is error, but only the privation of knowledge of some fact which contradicts what has been previously held to be true. Thus, to say that the sun is 200 feet from the earth involves a lack of the knowledge which would contradict that assertion, and is false: but there is no indication that Spinoza thinks that the statement 'The mean distance of the sun from the earth is approximately 92,900,000 miles' is false, even though it is made by people who do not know every fact about Nature. It is true that the knowledge of

[77] See §§ 6.4, 6.6 above.
[78] § 6.6: cf. *E* ii. 29 Cor.
[79] § 6.5 *ad fin*.
[80] § 6.5.

the sun's distance involves knowledge of many other astronomical facts, but it will later be argued that this is not the same as the coherence theory of truth as it has been defined.

Moreover, such a theory could not be entertained by Spinoza without radical changes in his methodology. Theories which say that there is only one truth, and that knowledge demands completeness, are compelled to place the acquisition of this truth in the future, and to view human knowledge as a progress towards it. But such a view, which is characteristic of Hegelian idealism, could not have been held by Spinoza. For him, as has been shown in earlier chapters, the method must start from a true idea, or set of ideas, and must deduce other truths from these. Spinoza, of course, does not say that no truths remain to be discovered—were this so, there would be no need of a method—but it is clear that he thinks that his basic principles, his definitions and axioms, will not require modification. Such certainty, however, is not possible for the idealist: for him, the next stages in the progress towards knowledge are necessarily obscure, and they are certainly not viewed as deductions from what is already known.

But, it may be asked, what after all *is* Spinoza's theory of truth? And if it is not a coherence theory, why has it all the appearance of being one? Why, in particular, does Spinoza say that sense-experience (knowledge 'from the common order of Nature') is false because incomplete? The answer can easily be provided by a further reference to Spinoza's methodology. It has been shown that Spinoza considers knowledge to be a deductive system; consequently, what looks like a coherence theory of truth, according to which there is only one truth, in fact says that all truths are interrelated as members of a deductive system. The objection to sense-experience as a means of knowledge seems therefore likely to be its unsystematic character—the fact that one falls into contradictions if one accepts as true all the information that the senses provide, supposing that square towers are round, that there are pains in non-existent limbs, and so on. Spinoza's theory of truth, then, does not seem to be a coherence theory as this has been defined. Though Spinoza insists on the importance of system, he does not say that it is necessary to complete this system before anything can be known, but only that it is necessary to know the definitions and axioms on which the whole system is based.

The 'coherence' interpretation, however, is not yet disposed of.

For it can be answered that what has been said above, though it may be true as far as it goes, has been restricted to deductive knowledge. This, however, is not the only sort of knowledge which Spinoza recognizes, but is in fact only the second of three kinds; and it is of the third of these, 'intuitive knowledge', that the 'coherence' interpretation is true. To answer this, it is necessary to discuss what Spinoza says of these three kinds of knowledge. The doctrine of the three kinds of knowledge merely complements the account which has so far been given of Spinoza's theory of knowledge, and does not contradict it in any respect.[81]

[81] For a discussion of Spinoza's three kinds of knowledge, see chap. 9 of Parkinson's *Spinoza's Theory of Knowledge.* [Ed.]

Spinoza and Language[1]

David Savan

I

PHILOSOPHICAL ANALYSTS have made a number of moves toward a reassessment of the history of philosophy. It might be expected that such historical studies would consider how the views which philosophers have held on language, mathematics, and logic have affected their thought and its formulation. Any such expectations have so far been largely disappointed.

In his recent and lucid exposition of Spinoza, Mr. Stuart Hampshire points out that Spinoza hoped to emulate the example of the geometers in freeing language of its intimate connection with the imagination so that it might be employed to express clearly and distinctly the ideas of a true philosophy.[2] Spinoza's interest in language and in the bearing of language upon philosophy is, however, considerably more important in the shaping of his thought and writings than Hampshire indicates. It is not just that Spinoza wrote a treatise on a natural language, or that nearly every one of his writings attempts some analysis of language and mathematics. Nor is it just that he experimented with a variety of literary forms in the exposition of his thought, using dialogue, autobiography, aphorism, historical and Biblical criticism, as well as the method of geometrical demonstration. Nor again is it just that he occasionally formulates philosophical theses in syntactical terms. It is also that Spinoza holds that both language and mathematics are fundamentally inadequate to the formulation or direct expression of philosophical truths. Hampshire's view, widely shared—that Spinoza thought words could divorce the imagination in order to

[1] A version of this paper was read to the meeting of the American Philosophical Association, Eastern Division, held at Boston University, December 27–29, 1955.
[2] *Spinoza* (London, 1951), pp. 18–20, 23–24, 93.

marry true philosophy—is, I believe, wrong. I shall argue that Spinoza's views on words and language make it impossible for him to hold that his writings (or anyone else's) can be a direct or literal exposition of philosophical truth. I shall conclude with a suggestion as to what Spinoza intended his writings to accomplish and how he thought they could do it.

II

Spinoza states clearly enough that imagination or opinion, knowledge of the first and lowest kind, is of two species: (1) "vague experience," or images proper, and (2) "signs" or "hearsay," as "when we hear or read certain words." [3] His theory of words is in its outlines a familiar one. Words are nothing more than bodily motions. These motions are the responses of the human body to the action upon it of external bodies. The idea of such motion will be mutilated, confused, and inadequate, since it can be properly understood only in conjunction with the ideas of the external motions which induced it. Since we do not know its cause we will either suppose it to be uncaused or to be induced by some final cause. Bodily motions which have once occurred together will tend to recur together, in company with their attendant circumstances. These attendant circumstances include our purposes, desires, and interests. In this way words arise from experience and refer to experience. They express the constitution of our own body rather than the nature of external bodies. The soldier may connect with the word "horse" the image of a war horse, armored, and in battle, while the farmer will call up the image of a slow and heavy animal plowing the fields.

Further, the limitations of the human body ensure that as a word is associated with a growing number of images the differences among the images will increasingly be overlooked. The number and significance of the differences thus canceled out will vary directly with the number of images with which a word is associated. Such transcendental terms as *being*, *thing*, and *something* are asso-

[3] *Ethics*, II, XL, S. 2. The following account of words is based primarily on Book II of the *Ethics*, but substantially the same views are to be found in the *Improvement of the Understanding*. In later citations the following abbreviations will be used for Spinoza's titles: *Ethics, E.; Improvement of the Understanding, TdIE; Tractatus theologico-politicus, Tr. Theol.-pol.; Cogitata metaphysica, C. m.;* Letters, Ep.

ciated with every image without exception. Hence, in these cases, all differences will be canceled, all images will be conflated, and the terms will be utterly confused. A lesser degree of the same confusion is illustrated by universal terms like *man, horse, dog,* and so forth. In the case of universals the selection of differences to be overlooked and resemblances taken into account will vary from individual to individual, according to the desires and interests which each person imagines. So some will imagine man as a featherless biped, some as an animal capable of laughter, and some as a rational animal. Such definitions are not so much true or false as well- or ill-adapted to the purposes of those who frame them.

The imaginative, general, and confused character of words is, in Spinoza's view, not contingent or accidental. It is not the result of ignorance and cannot be eliminated by knowledge. It is rather the necessary consequence of the action of external bodies upon our body. In the same way we necessarily continue to imagine the sun as near even after we know its true distance. No purgative can eliminate the imaginative and confused generality of words.

Hovering in the wings, only just off stage, when Spinoza speaks of words, is the image of sleeping and dreaming. While words are joined through syntax, the material flow of language in speech is conceived by him as a kind of dreaming. Speech, fiction, error, and madness are ranges—perhaps there are others—of a dream continuum. In the lower ranges of this continuum—in madness and dreams proper—we are almost entirely unaware of the external motions which stimulate our own bodily motions and their images. In the upper ranges—in error, fiction, and speech—we are aware of the external motions in a confused way but wrongly attribute our own images to them. It is easiest to fall into the error of supposing our motions and images to be true of the external world when we speak a language which, like Hebrew, tends to treat adjectives as nouns. All languages, however, exhibit this same tendency to some extent, and it is the task of the philosopher to reverse the process as far as possible. To do this properly he must have some knowledge of the factors determining memory and recollection, upon which speech in part depends. Without this knowledge he is like an amanuensis who reproduces a book written in a script and language which he does not understand.[4]

4 Ep. 40.

In nearly every important respect, Spinoza opposes true ideas to words. An idea is not an image and does not consist of words. A true idea can neither arise from experience of words and images nor can it be verified through such experience, for experience can give no knowledge of essences.[5] Whereas ideas and their *ideata* are singular and unique,[6] words are inherently general and applicable to an indefinite multitude. Whereas an idea is certain, words are uncertain. Whereas "that true Word of God which is in the mind . . . can never be depraved or corrupted," [7] words are corruptible. And whereas it is of the nature of reason to consider things as necessary and under a certain form of eternity, words are connected with contingency and time.

So sharply does Spinoza separate words from adequate ideas that it is difficult to make out for language any useful philosophical function at all. It is no more possible for us to discover and express true knowledge through language than it is for a somnambulist to communicate intelligently with the waking world. Spinoza explicitly rejects the semantic theory of truth. If Peter exists and without *knowing* this I happen to assert, "Peter exists," my assertion is not true.[8] Now suppose that Peter exists, that I know that he exists, and that while I am sound asleep I either say, "Peter exists" or dream that I say, "Peter exists." It is clear that on Spinoza's view the sentence "Peter exists" is in these circumstances not true. Now, in this example, substitute "God" for "Peter." This is the situation to which the writings of the philosopher are condemned by the imaginative and dreamlike character which, on Spinoza's view, is necessary to language. It is one thing to know that God exists and quite another to dream that I know, to imagine that I know, or to say that I know that God exists. How then can language represent, express, or formulate the clear and distinct ideas of the true philosophy? After separating the two so radically Spinoza appears to show no interest in explaining how they may be brought together. If he was aware of this situation, then he cannot have intended that the

---

[5] Ep. 10 and *TdIE*, par. 25; cf. also Ep. 37; *E.*, II, XLIII, S; *E.*, V, XXVIII.
[6] Although common motions, common notions, and properties are in a sense general, they are nevertheless either singular modes, whether finite or infinite, or real properties of such modes.
[7] Ep. 76; cf. also *Tr. Theol.-pol.*, ch. xv.
[8] *TdIE*, par. 69. Cf. Ep. 40.

Ethics should be a simple and straightforward exposition of his philosophy.[9]

III

Was Spinoza aware that his views made it difficult to accept any verbal account as a direct exposition of the true philosophy? It would be strange if he were not, in view of the evidence of his writings. It should be noted first, however, that this difficulty is hardly a novel one. Its lineage can be traced at least to the *Parmenides* of Plato. The radical inadequacy of words is something which Spinoza points out emphatically and repeatedly in most of his writings.

The most telling evidence that Spinoza was aware of this difficulty is to be found in the contradictions which abound in his *Ethics,* as well as in his other writings. If Spinoza were trying to catch the clear, distinct, and unique ideas of a true philosophy in the net of a language which is inherently vague and general, he would expect contradictory statements to appear in his exposition. Many such statements do occur in the *Ethics,* often in such close proximity to one another that it is hardly believable that so careful a writer as Spinoza was not aware of them. Since he allows the contradictions to stand it is to be presumed that he did not intend the *Ethics* to be a simple exposition of truth.

The contradictions to which I refer may be classified as follows: (a) those arising from the attempt to define in words the nature of the unique entity, substance; (b) those arising from the attempt to define or describe the unique properties of substance; and (c) those arising from attempts to define or describe modes or modal essences.

(a) Are the definitions of substance and God [10] intended by Spinoza as adequate formulations of our knowledge? Yet he disowns the terms used in these definitions. Substance "is in itself and conceived through itself." The term *being,* however, together with the other transcendentals, is called by Spinoza, "in the highest degree confused." [11] The term *conceive* is a universal term only

---

[9] The inadequacy of Spinoza's theory of language will be obvious to the reader today, and of course the particular difficulty with which I am concerned will not arise in a more adequate theory of language.

[10] *E.,* I, def. 3, 6.

[11] *E.,* II, XL, S. 1.

somewhat less general and confused than *being*. For by *conceive* he wishes "to express the action of the mind," that is to say, understanding.[12] But, he writes, "In the mind there exists no absolute faculty of understanding, desiring, loving, etc. These and the like faculties, therefore, are either altogether fictitious, or else are nothing but metaphysical or universal entities, which we are in the habit of forming from individual cases." [13] As to being conceived *through itself,* the purity of this notion is at least compromised by Spinoza's repeated attempts to conceive the activity of substance through something else—namely, through geometry.

God is defined as "being absolutely infinite." It has already been pointed out that Spinoza rejects the term *being*. By "infinite," the other important word in this definition, is meant "absolute affirmation of existence of some kind." [14] But he equates existence with the transcendental, *being*. Like *being,* existence is general, abstract, and confused.[15]

It is obvious that Spinoza wishes to refer his readers to a being and an existence which is concrete, singular, and unique. It is clear also, however, that he is willing to use language which he regards as radically inadequate. When he writes that "the reason why we do not possess a knowledge of God as distinct as that which we have of common notions is . . . [that] we have attached the name God to the images of things which we are in the habit of seeing, an error we can hardly avoid," [16] he is speaking of philosophical as well as of popular uses of the word "God."

(b) A second and more obvious set of contradictions occurs in the discussion of the properties of substance or God. In the *Ethics* unity, love, joy, will, intellect, and perfection, are all both explicitly affirmed and explicitly denied of substance.

The demonstration that God is one—both single and simple—is listed by Spinoza in the Appendix to Book I of the *Ethics* as a major conclusion. Nevertheless, in Book I he also writes that "a definition does not involve or express any certain number of individuals." [17] What this means in regard to substance or God is stated

---

[12] *E.,* II, def. iii, and *E.,* IV, xxiii ff.
[13] *E.,* II, xlviii, S.
[14] *E.,* I, viii, S. 1.
[15] *TdIE,* par 55; cf. *E.,* II, xlv, S.
[16] *E.,* II, xlvii, S.
[17] *E.,* I, viii, S. 2.

more explicitly in the early *Cogitata metaphysica* as well as in a letter written late in Spinoza's life. "It is certain that he who calls God one or single has no true idea of God, or is speaking of him inappropriately."[18]

Again, he writes that "properly speaking, God loves no one."[19] Yet, a few propositions later, he attempts to demonstrate that "God loves himself," and that "God . . . loves men."[20] Since he has defined love as involving pleasure, he attempts to demonstrate that God "cannot be affected with any affect of joy or sorrow." But he goes on to contradict himself by writing that "the nature of God delights in infinite perfection" and that God's love "is joy [granting that it is allowable to use this word], accompanied with the idea of Himself."[21]

With respect to will and intellect, we are offered a demonstration that they can no more be ascribed to God than flesh and blood can be ascribed to the constellation of the Dog. Nevertheless, he continues, and in the same book of the *Ethics,* to speak of God's intellect and will.[22]

Although Spinoza follows tradition in calling God perfect, when he discusses the origin and meaning of the word in the Preface to Book IV of the *Ethics,* he identifies it as only a mode of thought, an *ens rationis* formed through the comparison of particular things and sharing the generality and confusion previously ascribed to "being." Other properties of God, such as freedom and eternity, are explained through the notion of existence, already discussed above.

(c) In discussing modes and *natura naturata* Spinoza's theory of words leads him into two kinds of difficulties. First, he ascribes to some modes properties previously defined by him as applicable only to *natura naturans.* So he speaks of man as free and man's mind as an "eternal mode of thought." He speaks also of necessary, infinite, and eternal modes which exist under every attribute of God.[23] Nevertheless, it is evident from the definitions of the words "free," "eternal," "infinite," and "necessary," given at the beginning of the *Ethics,* that these words can apply only to God as *natura naturans.* He demonstrates, indeed, that "God alone is a free cause"

[18] Ep. 50, and *C. m.,* I, 6.
[19] *E.,* V, xvii, C.
[20] *E.,* V, xxxv and xxxvi, C.
[21] *E.,* V, xvii, xxxv, and xxxvi, S.
[22] *E.,* I, xvii, S.; *E.,* I, xxxiii, S. 2.
[23] *E.,* IV, lxvi ff.; *E.,* V, xl, S.; *E.,* I, xxi—xxiii.

and that he differs radically in essence and existence from every
mode.[24] To apply to a mode a term which applies to *natura naturans*
is like expecting the constellation of the Dog to bark.

Second, when Spinoza applies to modes terms which are proper
to *natura naturata* he again contradicts himself. Desire, he states,
is the essence of man, and desire which springs from reason is the
essence of the human mind insofar as it acts. This in turn is nothing
other than the effort to understand.[25] But we have pointed out
above that Spinoza regards desire, understanding, and will as either
altogether fictitious or else as metaphysical or universal entities.
Furthermore, insofar as they designate characteristics which are common to a number of modes, they cannot form the essence of any
individual mode.[26]

Consider next the word "good." Spinoza speaks of knowledge of
good (and of evil) which is true, adequate, and certain.[27] Nevertheless, he writes also that the notion *good* is an "entity of the imagination," "indicates nothing positive in things considered in them
selves," and is general or universal.[28] In fact, "if men were born
free [and were led by reason alone], they would form no conception
of good and evil." [29]

A similar difficulty arises in Spinoza's discussion of the passions.
Although these are inadequate and confused ideas, we can nonetheless form some clear and distinct conception of them. They follow with the same natural necessity as do other modes, they may
be understood through their causes and properties, and the method
pursued in the discussion of God and the mind is to be applied to
them. It would appear, then, that the discussion of the passions
in Book III of the *Ethics* is a direct statement of our knowledge of
the passions. Spinoza writes, however, that "there are as many kinds
of each affect as there are kinds of objects by which we are affected;
. . . men are affected in different ways by one and the same object . . . ; and, finally . . . one and the same man is affected in
different ways towards the same object." [30] His analyses and definitions must, therefore, overlook and confuse together the specific

[24] *E.*, I, XVII.
[25] *E.*, III, IX, S., and Appendix, def. 1; *E.*, IV, LIX, LXI; *E.*, IV, XXIII, XXVI.
[26] *E.*, II, XXXVII.
[27] *E.*, IV, XIV ff.; *E.*, IV, XXVII ff.
[28] *E.*, I, App.; *E.*, IV, Pref.; *E.*, IV, LXII, S.
[29] *E.*, IV, LXVIII; cf. *E.*, IV, LXIV.
[30] *E.*, IV, XXXIII; cf. *E.*, III, LI, LVI, LVII.

differences among the actual affects. That is to say, Spinoza's discussion is in terms of words which are abstract, general, and confused.

Finally, it is to be noted that Spinoza admits that even in his discussion of the third and highest kind of knowledge he must speak in terms of time and change—that is to say, in terms of the imagination—"in order that what we wish to prove may be more easily explained and better understood." [31] Yet only three propositions earlier Spinoza had written that "ideas which are clear and distinct in us . . . cannot follow from mutilated and confused ideas, which are related to the first kind of knowledge."

In sum, then, in Spinoza's discussions of substance, its properties, and its modes, contradictions and difficulties occur so frequently and so clearly that it is probable that Spinoza was aware of them. He allowed them to stand, I suggest, because his theory of language led him to believe that no simple, direct, precise, and consistent verbal account of the true philosophy was possible.

IV

How is the *Ethics* to be understood? Spinoza's theory of language is inadequate. He is so concerned to associate words and language with imagination that he offers no theoretical account of how words can convey ideas (in his sense of "idea") or of the proper function of language in the communicaion of philosophical truth. The fact that Spinoza makes no attempt to deal with this question in the *Ethics* is, perhaps, the strongest argument against the thesis of the first part of this paper, that Spinoza was aware of the difficulties in which he was involved through his theory of language.

Be that as it may, I wish to point out briefly that Spinoza does explicitly hold a general theory of *entities of reason* and that it is this theory of *entia rationis* which underlies his method in the *Ethics*.[32]

An entity of reason is "a mode of thought which serves to make what has been understood the more easily retained, explained, and imagined." [33] Such an entity has no existence outside the intellect.

---

[31] *E.*, V, XXXI. S.
[32] The following account of *entia rationis* is based upon the *Cogitata metaphysica*, Epp. 12, 19, 50, 83 and *E.*, I, App.; *E.*, IV, Pref.
[33] *C. m.*, I, 1.

Since it has no extramental object which could be clearly and distinctly conceived, Spinoza denies that it is an idea or that it can be called true or false. It is a characteristic error that philosophers, misled by the words associated with entities of reason, hypostatize them and ascribe to them some reality outside of the mind. They are of use to us only if they function as tools or mental aids and are not treated as if they had some independent status.[34]

Entities of reason originate because it is easier for our minds to imagine things abstractly than to conceive things as they are, in their specific connection with substance. So we find it easier to remember things if we can group them together in such classifications as genus and species. So too we imagine extension abstractly—that is, apart from the substance of which it is an attribute—and then try to explain this abstract extension by comparing one part of it with another through the aid of measure and geometrical figures. Or again we may abstract finite modes from the substance, attributes, and infinite modes upon which they depend and then try to explain the resultant images by using factitious instruments like time and numbers to assist us in comparing the images. When these aids are clearly understood to be abstractions, existing only in the intellect —as they are by all good mathematicians—they can assist us to discover and formulate such truth as is proper to the imagination. I shall return to this point in a moment, for it is the clue to the correct understanding of the *Ethics,* as well as of Spinoza's writings on natural science, Hebrew grammar, and Biblical criticism.

Since entities of reason are, like words, functions of the imagination, words have a proper role to play in their formulation. In particular, philosophical entities of reason such as the distinction of God's essence from God's existence, power, and other properties, genus and species, the transcendentals, the modalities, the notions of nonbeing, opposition, order, relation, conjunction, accident, perfection, good, and evil—all these arise through *verbal* comparisons of modes given to us through the imagination. Philosophers have been particularly prone, therefore, to two kinds of error: (a) they have often given unsuitable or misleading verbal descriptions of their entities of reason; (b) even worse, through not distinguishing the imagination from the intellect clearly enough, they have supposed that the words they used were names of entities existing out-

[34] Hence *entia rationis* cannot be assimilated to *ratio,* or knowledge of the second kind.

side the intellect. When he encounters this latter confusion, Spinoza
prefers to speak of "entities of the imagination" rather than of "entities of reason." Properly defined and properly understood as abstractions, however, the entities of reason may serve the philosopher
(as they do the mathematician) as eyes, as it were, through which
the intellect may see more clearly what is presented confusedly in
the imagination.

Correctly employed, then, entities of reason may assist the philosopher in at least three ways. (1) When one image is compared
with another they may enable the intellect to discover that truth
which is resident in imagination. (2) By constructing certain general
models or exemplars we may see how a collection of things whose
detailed natures we do not understand may nevertheless in general
exemplify our adequate ideas of infinite modes and attributes of
substance. (3) By recognizing the abstract character of such negative
entities of reason as *nonbeing, limit,* and *falsehood* we may hold
more firmly to the positive content of the clear ideas which are
native to the intellect. We will not then confuse them with the
verbal entities and verbal distinctions of the traditional philosophers.

(1) By comparing our experiences, and with the assistance of
mathematical and philosophical entities of reason, scientists have
discovered the true size and distance of the sun. We are thereby
enabled to see that our image of the sun as small and near is our
response to external motions and thus a sign of our native strength
and power. So too in his discussion of the passions Spinoza compares a variety of experiences in order to show the limitations and
the positive strength of the passions. Spinoza's resort to a posteriori
argument is not an inconsistency but an integral part of his method.

(2) In the Preface to Book IV of the *Ethics* Spinoza states that
he wishes to form an idea of man which can serve as a model or
exemplar of human nature. In other places in the *Ethics* Spinoza
speaks of this idea of man as universal and of the proofs concerning it as general.[35] In a letter of 1665 he points out that the abstract
and general definition of man by which all who have a similar external appearance are classed together is an entity of reason.[36] To
construct this universal idea of man he has used such entities of
reason as *good* and *evil* and such "metaphysical" entities (i.e., enti-

[35] *E.,* III, LV, S., and *E.,* V, XXXVI, S.
[36] Ep. 19.

ties of reason) as *understanding, desire,* and *will*.[37] The value of
this method, which occupies a major part of the *Ethics,* is that these
entities of reason, corresponding to nothing outside the intellect,
enable us to use words correctly in comparing the experiences which
our imagination provides us. They enable us to see how our adequate ideas of substance, thought, extension, motion and rest, and
so on, ideas which are native to the intellect, operate within our
experience. This, I would suggest, is what Spinoza means when he
writes that "demonstrations are the eyes of the mind by which it
sees and observes things." [38] In a letter of 1664 he puts it thus: "We
see that the imagination is also determined to a great extent by
the constitution of the soul; for, as we know from experience, in all
things it follows the traces of the intellect and concatenates its
images and words in a certain order, and interconnects them, just as
the intellect does with its demonstrations." [39]

In the Preface to Book IV of the *Ethics* Spinoza also gives a detailed account of the genesis and growth of another entity of reason,
perfection. He seeks to show how, through the comparison of our
experiences and with the mediation of words, we confuse perfection
with the final cause of a thing. When we come to see, however, that
perfection is an entity of reason, existing nowhere outside the
mind, we recognize it as an aid to the consideration of the specific
reality, essence, and action of every mode which we experience.
Every individual thing, considered in terms of its own essence and
activity, is perfect.[40]

(3) Finally, there is a third way in which entities of reason can
assist the philosopher. Negation, limitation, determination, and
falsehood cannot be ascribed to God, for they are only entities of
reason. Without introducing negation or determination in some
form, however, we cannot distinguish one substance from another,
essence from existence, power from action, or necessity from freedom. Hence God is unique, and in God essence, existence, power,
necessity, and freedom are one and the same. They can be distinguished only verbally. As Spinoza puts it, to distinguish God's
essence from his existence is to confuse truth with falsehood.[41]

[37] *E.,* II, XLVIII, S.
[38] *E.,* V, XXIII, S.
[39] Ep. 17.
[40] Ep. 19; cf. also Epp. 21 and 23, and *E.,* I, XXXIII, S. 2.
[41] *E.,* I, VIII, S. 2.

Philosophers and theologians have been confused by words into supposing these distinctions in God's nature to be real. A large part of the task of the *Ethics* is to show the philosophers how many of their errors originate in the confusion of entities of reason with entities existing outside the intellect, that is, in confusing the intellect with the imagination. The positive task of the *Ethics* is to show that once the limitations of language are recognized we can conceive of substance and its modes through their own living ideas. Language may indeed express philosophic truth, just as one may dream of gray elephants as well as of pink elephants. But in order to know what is true and what is false in one's dreams one must first wake and understand that dreams have their own laws. They cannot be read as simple, straightforward prose narratives.

The several arguments in demonstration of a single proposition are different ways of deploying the entities of reason. The definitions of *substance* and *mode* do not involve reference to any positive ideas. A comparison of the rules for defining created and uncreated things (given in the *Improvement of the Understanding*) with the definitions of the *Ethics* will show that the latter simply translate the formal rules into the material mode.

It is Spinoza's view, then, that "a thing is understood when it is perceived simply by the mind without words and images." [42] So far is he from supposing that words can be disengaged from the imagination in order to represent true ideas. Spinoza concludes the *Ethics* with the warning that he has shown us a road which is difficult to travel. If, however, anyone "had acquired new ideas in the proper order, according to the standard of the original true idea, he would never have doubted of the truth of his knowledge, inasmuch as truth, as we have shown, makes itself manifest, and all things would flow, as it were, spontaneously toward him." [43]

[42] *Tr. Theol.-pol.*, ch. iv.
[43] *TdIE*, par. 44.

Spinoza's Theory of Knowledge Applied to the *Ethics*

Guttorm Fløistad

This paper is a discussion of which kinds of knowledge Spinoza himself employs in developing the system of the *Ethics*. The problem is raised by Professor D. Savan and further discussed by G. H. R. Parkinson. The thesis is (1) that no occurrence of the first kind of knowledge is to be found in the *Ethics* (against Parkinson), (2) that the main part of the analysis in the *Ethics* is conducted on the level of the second kind of knowledge (in agreement with Parkinson), and (3) that the third kind of knowledge occurs frequently and plays a most important role in the *Ethics* (in part against Parkinson). The relation between knowledge and language, the distinction between two types of imagination, or two ways of imagining things, the translation of knowledge of modes of extension into knowledge of the mind, and the relation between the second and third kind of knowledge are main parts of the argument. The third kind of knowledge derives its significance in the *Ethics* from the definitions and axioms, particularly in Part 1. These definitions and axioms form the basis of the whole system of the *Ethics,* and at least some of them, it is suggested, belong to the third kind of knowledge.

SPINOZA CLAIMS in the *Ethics* to have shown that there are altogether three ways of knowing or forming ideas of things, that is, three kinds of knowledge, knowledge by imagination (first kind), by reason (second kind), and by intuition (third kind) (cf. 2P40-Sch2).[1] It follows that Spinoza must himself be using one or two

---

[1] This is an abbreviation for: Part 2, Proposition 40, Scholium (note) 2. Other abbreviations are: Dem—demonstration (proof), D—definition, A—axiom, Cor—corollary. Aff—affectus (emotion), Ep.—epistola. TIE is an abbreviation for *Tractatus de Intellectus Emendatione.*

or all three kinds in developing his own system in the *Ethics,* including the propositions in which he is talking *about* the kinds of knowledge themselves. The question is, which? This essay is devoted to a discussion of this problem.

The problem is raised by Professor D. Savan in connection with his discussion of Spinoza's view on words and language,[2] and discussed further by G. H. R. Parkinson in his reply to Savan in the present issue of *Inquiry*.[3] According to Savan, Spinoza's view on words and language is such that his writings cannot be, nor were intended by Spinoza to be, 'a direct or literal exposition of philosophical truth' (p. 237). Since in an important sense we have access to the propositions (or knowledge) of the *Ethics* only via its 'words and language', this presumably means that our problem is extremely difficult, if at all possible, to solve. At any rate Savan provides no solution to it.

Parkinson argues that Savan's interpretation of Spinoza's view on words and language is 'radically misconceived' (p. 15); Spinoza's view does not have the logical implications stated by Savan. In particular, there is nothing in Spinoza's view from which it follows that language is in principle unsuitable for expressing true knowledge. From this, Parkinson then goes on to discuss the problem of which kinds of knowledge are to be found in the *Ethics*. The bulk of the propositions, he thinks, belong to knowledge of reason, or the second kind. However, instances of knowledge of imagination, or the first kind, and of intuition, or the third kind, do occur. Difficulties may arise as to the correct interpretation of the passages exemplifying the various kinds of knowledge. The point, however, is that we may safely assume that Spinoza would have claimed to have stated adequately, in words, the examples he gives of the three kinds of knowledge (cf. pp. 33–39).

In the following I shall argue in part against, in part in agreement with Parkinson. I wish to hold (1) that no instances of knowledge of the first kind occur in the *Ethics,* nor are allowed to enter into its system, (2) that the major part of the propositions of the *Ethics,* with some qualifications, belong to the second kind of knowledge, and (3) that knowledge of the third kind occurs much more

[2] D. Savan, 'Spinoza and Language', *Philosophical Review,* Vol. 67 (1958) pp. 212 ff. (See p. 236 ff. of this volume.)

[3] See G. H. R. Parkinson, "Language and Knowledge in Spinoza," *Inquiry* (1969), pp. 15–40. All page references to Parkinson are to this issue of *Inquiry*.

frequently and plays a more significant role in the *Ethics* than Parkinson seems to maintain. I shall enter only briefly into the controversy between Savan and Parkinson as to whether or not true knowledge may be adequately expressed in language. This is not to say that I regard this problem as irrelevant to the present case, nor as being in any way exhaustively discussed by the two participants; rather a discussion of which kinds of knowledge Spinoza himself uses in the *Ethics* presupposes a solution of the 'expression-problem', to the effect that knowledge may somehow be adequately expressed in language. This seems to be Parkinson's position, too, and Savan would presumably agree. 'Language may indeed express philosophical truth,' he says (p. 248). He merely differs from Parkinson in his explanation of how this is achieved. Given, then, *that* true knowledge may somehow be expressed adequately in words, the problem as to which kinds of ideas or knowledge do occur in the *Ethics* may, as I shall try to show, be argued, at least to a large extent, independently of any explanation of how such knowledge can be expressed.

I

1. Does the *Ethics* contain instances of inadequate ideas? A few premisses may yield a preliminary answer: Knowledge or ideas of imagination are inadequate and false, whereas knowledge or ideas of reason and of intuition are adequate and true. And, adequate and true ideas cannot follow from inadequate and false ones, nor themselves give rise to other than adequate and true ideas (cf. 2P40, 5P28Dem). As the *Ethics* presumably must be said to contain some true propositions, and if, furthermore, it is regarded as a structured whole, that is, as a system of coherent propositions, it would seem to follow that no inadequate or false idea can occur in the *Ethics*. Spinoza's treatment of inadequate ideas, including the so-called passive emotions (cf. 3AffGenD) present no difficulty here: hate of someone, for instance, is based upon and involves an inadequate and false idea; an idea or, as one may also say, a description of one person hating another may itself perfectly well be adequate and true. Or in general, ideas or descriptions of inadequate and false ideas may be adequate and true. Since a true idea is the 'standard of itself and falsity' (2P43Sch) we may even say that ideas of other ideas being false, are necessarily true. It is logically impossible to

know something to be false unless this knowledge itself is adequate and true (cf. 2P42, Dem).

The weak premiss in this argument is of course the assumption that the *Ethics* is a coherent system of propositions. Many or even most writers on the subject are inclined to see a number of incoherences in the *Ethics*. Savan is one of them. To decide exactly where incoherences in fact lie is notoriously difficult. Hardly any two writers are in complete agreement. Thus Parkinson rejects most of the incoherences detected by Savan. I shall, in the course of this paper, suggest some possible incoherences, and, indirectly also suggest why it is so notoriously difficult to decide what is and what is not incoherent. At present it suffices to say that if but one incoherence is admitted the above argument is likely to be worthless.

Parkinson points to a similar general argument against the occurrence of ideas of imagination in the *Ethics*. Spinoza, he rightly says, is 'concerned in the *Ethics* to establish necessary truths'. This means, for example, that 'he is not . . . interested in establishing such propositions as "Hatred is seldom good"; rather, he wants to prove that hatred *can never* be good' (p. 35). Imagination, which Parkinson takes to involve sense-experience and induction, 'do not provide us with necessary truths, and this, it might seem, debars the imagination from playing any part in the *Ethics*'. He adds, however, that despite this, 'imagination has a part to play in the argument of the *Ethics*; not a major part, certainly, but at any rate a supporting role' (ibid.).

Parkinson then proceeds to point out various 'supporting roles' for experience. He mentions 2P17Sch, where Spinoza talks about all the (true) postulates which contain hardly anything 'that does not agree with experience' (*quod non constet experientia*). A second 'more common use of the testimony of the experience in the *Ethics* is to support conclusions that have been established deductively' (p. 36). Thus Spinoza says in 3P2Sch that he wants to prove these conclusions 'by experience' (*experientia comprobavero*). Incidentally, in the same scholium, and in many other places, he also uses the phrase 'experience teaches (us)' (*experientia docet*).

There is no need here to go into further details. The problem is clear enough: Do these (and similar) occurrences of the term 'experience' in the *Ethics* justify the conclusion that experience, that is, imagination in the sense of inadequate ideas, plays a 'supporting role' in the *Ethics*?

Parkinson's affirmative answer is difficult to accept. The trouble lies with the meaning of 'supporting role', that is, according to the instances quoted above, with the meaning of 'agreeing with', 'prove by' and 'teach'. The affirmative answer says that adequate ideas may be supported by, that is, agree with, or be proved by, or taught to us by inadequate ideas. On a very plausible interpretation this means that adequate ideas (postulates, deductively proved propositions) may somehow follow from inadequate ones. And this contradicts the statement that adequate ideas cannot follow from inadequate ideas.

However, a closer look indicates that the interpretation of the various expressions (agreeing with, etc.) for the 'following from' is incorrect or at least imprecise. If we were to describe what happens when experience is taken to support, in various ways, an adequate idea, we should have to say something like this: The ideas of experience are not inadequate ideas in the usual sense. They do not, strictly speaking, occur in a sequence of inadequate ideas, but rather, somehow, in a sequence of adequate ideas. The starting-point is not experience itself alone, but the adequate idea, which experience is taken to support. Experience is hence regarded from the viewpoint of, or within the frame of, the adequate idea. That this is so may even be taken as a condition for grasping the supporting role of experience. Thus experience in no way stands on its own feet. It enters into a sequence of adequate ideas by way of its supporting role, that is, because of the preceding adequate idea to be supported. Or, more precisely, experience enters into a sequence of adequate ideas because of the (presumably adequate) idea that an adequate idea (a postulate, a deductively proved proposition) may be supported by (seen to agree with, or proved by) experience.

For this reason it is incorrect or imprecise to say that it is a matter of an adequate idea following from an inadequate idea of experience. Primarily, we may say that the idea formed on the basis of experience or imagination *follows from* the adequate idea in question, together with the idea of experience supporting this adequate idea. It is only on the basis of such a preceding 'following from' that we may turn round, as it were, and say that the adequate idea follows from or is supported by, or agrees with, or is proved by experience.

2. It is admittedly difficult to grasp exactly how our knowledge or understanding operates in the 'supporting-relation' between an adequate idea and experience. The above description, no doubt in-

complete, may therefore perhaps be made more intelligible by way of an example. Let us take the deductively established proposition that 'every individual thing, or whatever thing that is finite and has a determined existence, cannot exist or be determined for action unless it is determined for action and existence by another cause which is also finite and has a determined existence' (1P28). Or in short, roughly, every individual thing (bodies, ideas, actions) has a cause. This is a 'common property' on account of which 'we can have only a very inadequate knowledge (that is, by imagination or experience) of individual things which are outside us' (2P31, Dem).

Ideas of common properties are ideas of reason (cf. 2P40Sch2, 2P39Dem). In 1P28 we therefore have an instance of the second kind of knowledge. Spinoza does not directly set out to prove this deductively established proposition by experience. In a sense he rather uses experience as counting against the proposition. In 3P2Sch, where he proceeds to give a number of proofs by experience in favour of 3P2, he says: '. . . experience teaches as clearly as reason that men think themselves free on account of this alone, that they are conscious of their actions and ignorant of the causes of them.' This is in many ways an interesting statement with regard to our problem. Strictly speaking, experience is not said here to count against the truth of the idea of the common property; experience is merely said to show the failure of man to recognize the common property. However, it is just this use of 'experience', I think, that can illuminate what Spinoza has in mind when, in various ways, he talks about the 'supporting role' of experience. 'Experience' in the quotation clearly does not denote the experience or imagination characteristic of the person who inadequately thinks himself free because he knows no cause of his actions. Such a person would not possibly admit nor understand that 'experience teaches as clearly as reason . . .' etc. What Spinoza has in mind is rather the experience of the philosopher who *beforehand* knows the truth of the principles that every individual (his actions, etc.) has a cause. This knowledge is, so far as I can see, simply to be regarded as a necessary condition for saying, that is, stating in words, that 'experience teaches as clearly as reason that men think themselves free on account of this alone, that they are conscious of their actions and ignorant of the causes of them'. Particularly the use of the phrase 'ignorant of the causes' shows clearly that the case is viewed from the point of view of some 'deeper', adequate insight. The person who thinks himself free is unlikely to admit any ignorance lying behind his 'freedom'. In view of this the beginning of the quotation ('. . . experience teaches as clearly as reason . . .') becomes understandable. Experience is clear and it is as clear as reason. Spinoza could not have said this unless experience had to do with clear and distinct, that is, adequate ideas.

We may ask whether experience and reason, or, more precisely, whether the adequate idea of experience and reason, are in this case one and the same or different. The question is difficult to decide. The fact that they teach us 'clearly' the same state of affairs suggests that both cases concern one and the same adequate idea (the idea, namely, that men think themselves free . . . etc.). This adequate idea, it may be said, results as an application of the adequate idea of the common property expressed in 1P28 to how men commonly think about their freedom. In this application, then, experience and reason apparently count as equal. However, they can hardly be said to be the same. The idea of the common property in 1P28 applied to 'men' is undoubtedly an idea not of experience, but of reason. What experience may be said to do then is to confront this idea of reason with 'actual life', that is, with particular individuals in general. But this experience, or imagination, does not descend, as it were, to the level of inadequate ideas characteristic of men who unjustifiably think themselves free. Experience must all along have regard for the common property in its concern with particular instances in general. This regard for the common property is presumably the reason why Spinoza is able to align experience with reason, and moreover, to say that experience may in various ways support propositions deductively established by reason.

3. Whatever the right interpretation of the supporting role of experience may be, it is fairly clear that experience, or imagination, may involve adequate ideas and hence that ideas of reason may agree with or be proved by or in a sense follow from experience. The *Ethics* contains some evidence of the adequacy of experience or imagination. Thus a statement in 2P47Sch runs: 'But that men have knowledge not so clear of God as they have of common notions arises from the fact that they cannot imagine God as they do bodies.' Spinoza seems here to be saying that men owe at least some of the clarity of their knowledge of common notions (to which belongs knowledge of common properties, cf. 2P39 and 2P40Sch1) to the fact that they can imagine bodies. The question arises as to whether

'imagine bodies' here means 'imagine bodies as particulars' or 'imagine the common properties of bodies'. Since the clarity has reference to common notions or properties, it presumably means the latter. This answer is suggested in 5P7Dem, where Spinoza talks about 'common properties of things, which we always regard as present and which we always imagine in the same manner'. These common properties are presumably what Spinoza has in mind when now and then he talks about things which we may imagine clearly and distinctly (e.g., 3P53, 5P6Sch) and also when suggesting the possibility of imagining things 'to be necessary' (4P11Dem).

It follows from these considerations that we shall have to distinguish between two kinds of imagination, or for that matter, of experience, in the *Ethics*. On the one hand, imagination designates a kind of knowledge, namely the first kind, which is throughout inadequate and false. On the other hand, it refers to what may be called an adequate use of a certain faculty of mind. In the latter case imagination agrees 'with the laws of human reason' (4P18Sch), or as Spinoza also puts it, it is 'united to true thoughts' (5P4CorSch).[4] As such, imagination or experience may consistently be said to support deductively established propositions.[5]

Parkinson, consequently, is right in saying that experience has a supporting role in the *Ethics*. He is wrong, however, in thinking that the experience in question involves inadequate ideas or knowledge of the first kind. And since these are the only instances of inadequate ideas he is able to point to, the conclusion seems to be that no instance of such ideas actually occurs in, nor for that matter, is allowed to enter into the system of the *Ethics*. In other words, Spinoza in the *Ethics* is at most employing knowledge of reason and intuition only.

[4] Strictly speaking, Spinoza is here talking about emotions which agree with 'the laws of human reason' and an emotion which is 'united to true thoughts'. However, that 'imagination' here may be substituted for 'emotion' is clear from 3AffGenD. Cf. also 4PDem. Concerning the distinction between an emotion and an idea (e.g., of imagination) cf. 4P8Dem, 5P3Dem.

[5] Parkinson distinguishes also between 'two types of imagination, corresponding to (though not exactly the same as) Kant's distinction between the transcendental imagination which is concerned with the *a priori* or necessary, and the empirical imagination whose laws are discovered inductively.' I don't feel at all certain as to the validity of drawing this distinction within Spinoza's view on imagination. I would rather prefer to classify his use of imagination in all cases as empirical. However, there is no need to decide this question for the point I want to make. Parkinson is clearly discussing the supporting role of the empirical type of imagination (in his sense of 'empirical').

This appears to be Spinoza's own view as well when he says that true ideas only are allowed to occur in philosophical speculation (cf., e.g., Ep. LVI).

II

1. Knowledge by reason consists in having and forming 'common notions and adequate ideas of the properties of things' (cf. 2P40Sch2). As common notions Spinoza mentions the notions of the attribute of extension and of motion and rest (cf. 2P38Cor, Lemma 2 after 2P13). Properties are that which is common to the human body and certain external bodies by which the human body 'is used to be affected' (2P39). Ideas of such properties are hence also common, though in a restricted sense, and are in fact sometimes so called by Spinoza himself (cf., e.g., 2P40Sch1). To adequate ideas of reason belongs, furthermore, 'what we may deduce' from the ideas of the common properties (cf., e.g., 5P12Dem). Hence reason is or involves deductive knowledge. A further characteristic of ideas of reason is to be found in 2P40Sch2 and 5P36Sch: they are universal.

What does this mean? Parkinson suggests as instances of common properties the basic truths and concepts of science such as physiology (p. 34). To knowledge by reason belongs also knowledge derived from such basic truths and concepts. The universal character of this kind of knowledge may be explained, according to Parkinson, by saying that 'the science of physics, for example, is concerned with a falling body simply as a falling body, and not as *this* falling body'. And the science of physiology is universal in the sense that it 'is concerned with a human heart simply as a human heart, and not as the heart of this particular person' (ibid.).

This account may very well be true. However, the question at present is whether or to what extent Spinoza's views on the second kind of knowledge apply to his own procedure in the *Ethics*. The question is, in other words, whether or to what extent the *Ethics* itself is an expression, in verbal form, of the second kind of knowledge.

Parkinson feels tempted to suppose, according to his interpretation of Spinoza's view on reason, that with a few exceptions 'the whole of the *Ethics* is an expression in verbal form of the knowledge of the second kind' (p. 35). The exceptions are instances of imagination and of intuition. According to the above argument against the occurrence of the first kind of knowledge in the *Ethics,* the exceptions should be even fewer.

There are good arguments for this position. It is clear that the *Ethics* has throughout a kind of deductive form. The propositions are derived from basic definitions, axioms and postulates. This applies to Spinoza's treatment of ontology in Part I, as well as to his short treatment of bodies after 2P13, and to what is his main concern in the *Ethics*: the explanation of the human mind. The deductive procedure is perhaps most obvious in the theory of emotions: desire (*cupiditas, conatus*), pleasure (*laetitia*) and pain (*tristitia*) are the three basic emotions, from which all others are derived. Most propositions of the *Ethics* clearly also fulfil the requirement of universality: they are, for instance, about finite entities, about the mind and body and about desire, pleasure and pain, etc., *in general.*

The position, however, is not as straightforward as this account may suggest. In fact it is complicated by at least three factors: (i) by Spinoza's view on language, (ii) by his account of the second kind of knowledge itself, and (iii) by his account of the third kind of knowledge. Parkinson discusses (i) fairly extensively in his reply to Savan: he seems to encounter little or no difficulty concerning (ii), and leaves (iii), that is, possible consequences of occurrences of the third kind of knowledge for occurrences of the second kind, entirely out of consideration. I shall comment on (i) and (ii) in turn, and then say a few things about (iii) in connection with a discussion of the role played by the third kind of knowledge in the *Ethics.*

2. The main difficulty in Spinoza's theory of language with respect to the present problem arises from his view on the so-called transcendental terms (such as 'being', 'thing', 'something') and on universal or general terms and notions (such as 'man', 'dog', 'horse'). According to Spinoza these terms and notions belong to imagination or the first kind of knowledge and are consequently inadequate for the expression of true knowledge. Savan then makes the valid observation that these terms and notions do, nevertheless, frequently occur in the *Ethics,* the effect in his view being that the *Ethics* abounds in contradictions. This, then, becomes a major premiss in his conclusions that language, as viewed by Spinoza, cannot be, nor can have been intended by Spinoza to be, a direct or literal exposition of philosophical truth.

Parkinson attempts to solve the problem by arguing for the view that even if Spinoza thought some uses of the objectionable terms and notions to be inadequate, it does not follow from this that he thought all uses of these terms and notions objectionable. Most of Spinoza's own statements on transcendental and universal terms may in fact be so interpreted as to accord with reason. God and also any finite thing as a part of God, Parkinson says, may very well, according to Spinoza, be called a thing. In this case 'thing', therefore, stands for a common notion. And similarly, 'to conceive', or rather 'conceiving', as a universal or general term may be predicated both of God and of a finite mode of thought. Hence 'the concept of conceiving is . . . a common notion, and words like "conceiving" and "conceive" are justified, to the extent that they stand for this common notion' (p. 24).

Parkinson's conclusion with respect to the use of transcendental terms and terms for universal notions, and also with respect to the use of language in general, is, I think, true: language may adequately express true knowledge. To show this is his chief concern in refuting Savan's view. It is interesting, however, to notice another significant conclusion which is clearly contained in his way of arguing. This is the conclusion that the question of whether or not a certain term may adequately express a true idea does not depend on the term itself, but on the idea (or knowledge) to be expressed by the term. Thus the first step in his argument is throughout to point to some adequate idea, particularly common notions, and he then goes on to say, for instance, that words like 'thing' and 'conceiving' are justified *in so far as (or to the extent that)* they stand for such notions. He knows well, in other words, that terms such as 'thing' and 'conceiving' may stand for or express intuitive knowledge, for instance when used to denote the 'essence of things' (cf. 2P40Sch2 and Sect. III below). In Parkinson's account of the supporting role of experience or imagination, the terms 'thing' and 'conceiving', as actually used in the *Ethics,* may occasionally stand for inadequate ideas ('thing') involving an inadequate or partial thinking activity ('conceiving', cf. 3D1 and 3D2). (Since 'conceiving' is used in the *Ethics* to cover the activity of thinking in general, including imagining or imagination, it is conceivable, in Parkinson's view that Spinoza occasionally uses 'conceiving' to signify a way of thinking in which he only partially or inadequately knows what he is saying.)

With respect to this dependence-relation between language and knowledge, Parkinson's view (indirectly expressed) is in agreement with that of Savan (cf. Sect. I above). This view I take to represent

Spinoza's main contribution to a theory of language. The theory concerns the non-linguistic, epistemological conditions both for expressing true (and for that matter, also false) knowledge adequately in language, and for language being able to express and thus communicate true (and false) knowledge adequately to some hearer or reader. His thesis, generally formulated, would run something like this: Whether or not language may adequately express knowledge by imagination, reason, and intuition depends not only on language, that is, the right application of words (cf. 2P47Sch), but also on the kind of knowledge or way of knowing things which one is exercising or is able to exercise.

The thesis has a number of implications, particularly in the field of communication. To work them out in any detail is a major task in itself and one which exceeds the scope of this essay. I shall therefore merely indicate some of those which are important for the present communication problem: to decide from a reading of the *Ethics* which kinds of knowledge are expressed in the language of the *Ethics* itself.

First, the thesis makes it conceivable that one and the same term or formula may be used to express each of the different kinds of knowledge. Thus the term 'God' as used in the *Ethics* may apparently stand for an adequate idea of both the second and third kinds (cf. Sect. III below), and also for some inadequate idea when used by people labouring under a misconception of God (cf., e.g., 1P15Sch). Secondly, it is conceivable that a certain term or formula used to express a certain kind of knowledge may be taken by some reader or hearer to express a different kind of knowledge, depending upon the kind of knowledge or way of knowing things he is able to exercise in connection with the term or formula in question. Thus the term 'God' or 'substance', when used by Spinoza to stand for an idea of intuition, may be taken to stand for an idea of reason or of imagination.

Thirdly, it is conceivable—and this is a concession to the significance of the right application of language—that certain terms or formulae, or set of terms or formulae, are more suitable for expressing one kind of knowledge than for expressing another. The term 'God' again provides an example, likewise expressions for characterizations of God, such as 'God is the cause of himself'. However, the third implication is presumably subject to qualification, particularly in terms of the second implication above. For even if certain terms or formulae, or set of such, are more suitable for expressing one kind of knowledge than for expressing another, one has still somehow to understand these terms or formulae, that is, the idea expressed by them, in order to see that this is so. Since every idea, on Spinoza's account, is of necessity causally connected with other ideas, this means that the decision concerning the third implication (and hence also the second implication) requires consideration of context.

These implications pose an important problem for our discussion: Does the recognition of the occurrence of a certain kind of knowledge or way of knowing things as expressed in the language of the *Ethics* require that one actually be in possession of that kind of knowledge oneself? This question is difficult to answer. If one were to classify all ideas in the *Ethics,* the answer would presumably have to be yes, particularly due to the first and second implication above. This, however, is evidently tantamount to saying that one would have to share Spinoza's total world view. And a modern interpreter, or at any rate most of them, would obviously find themselves in a difficult position.

The task at present, however, is the more general and therefore more modest one of deciding upon the kind or kinds of knowledge employed by Spinoza in the *Ethics.* And this task, on account of the third implication in particular, can presumably be undertaken without committing oneself (at least not entirely) to the ideas taken into account. The fact, however, that the third implication is subject to qualification in terms of the second implication above, inevitably yields for the analysis an element of uncertainty.

3. In accounting for knowledge by reason Spinoza, so far as I can see, mentions as objects of this kind of knowledge the attribute and (finite and infinite) modes of extension only. It is of these objects that reason is said to form 'notions which are called common and which are the fundamental principles of our ratiocination' (2P40 Sch1). Applied to the *Ethics* this account of reason encounters two difficulties. The first arises from the fact that Spinoza's chief (or rather sole) purpose in the *Ethics* is to explain the human mind, and not objects of extension (cf., e.g., 3P3Sch), and the second arises in view of the principles, that is, the definitions and axioms, actually forming the basis of his own 'reasoning' in the *Ethics.* It is in no way self-evident that these principles belong to the second kind of knowledge. I shall remark on the two difficulties in turn.

The discrepancy between the account of the objects of reason and the subject actually dealt with in the *Ethics* could in general be taken to suggest that Spinoza does not, at least not explicitly, have his own propositions of the *Ethics* in mind when dealing with knowledge by reason. He is rather thinking of sciences such as physiology and physics (as suggested by Parkinson), which, presumably, are to be developed on the basis of his account of knowledge by reason and presumably also within the frame of his short treatment of bodies inserted after 2P13. However, even if this is so, it does not follow that his account of reason is not applicable to the *Ethics* itself, that is, to the analysis of the human mind. There is in fact ample evidence that it is, so ample indeed that Parkinson apparently finds it superfluous to adduce it. He merely assumes 'conceiving' to be a possible common notion, characteristic of knowledge by reason. In the context of the present discussion the evidence may nonetheless be worth considering, even if it should merely confirm Parkinson's procedure.

4. The problem may in general be conceived as one of translating ideas of extended or physical objects into ideas of the mind. I shall first consider the necessity of such a translation in Spinoza's theory of the mind, and then secondly its possibility.

The necessary character of the translation is stated in 2P19, 2P23, and 2P26. It follows from these propositions that the mind can have no knowledge of itself unless it perceives (conceives, forms ideas of) modes of extension, more precisely, the modification of its body as affected by external bodies. I shall leave aside the problem of what 'modification' or 'affection' means here. The important thing at present is the view that the mind's knowledge of modes of extension is a necessary condition for a theory of the mind. It would seem then that Spinoza, in dealing with knowledge by reason in 2P40Sch2, according to himself at any rate, is doing the right thing.

As to the possibility of the translation there seems to be but one answer: Every idea of a physical object is translated already into the mind's knowledge of itself. The meaning of this somewhat peculiar saying may perhaps be brought out in the following way. An idea of a physical object (i.e., a modification of the body by some other body or bodies) is primarily an idea of *the object*. But it is evidently also an *idea* of the object. One cannot have the one without the other. Or, an object can only be an object to us in so far as it modifies or affects us, that is, in so far as we have conceived or formed an idea of it. In still other words, we have no access to an object except by having formed an idea of it (cf. 2P26). However, that an idea of an object is an *idea* of the object is not brought out in the idea of *the object*. A higher-order reflection is called for in the sense that one has to form an idea of *the idea* of the physical object. In this way the mind comes to know itself explicitly, that is, its ideas of objects, a self-knowledge which is present in an implicit manner in the idea of an object.[6]

If we ask how the mind's self-knowledge or its higher-order reflection is brought about, Spinoza has little to say. To him (as, incidentally, to many other philosophers) it is a given capacity of the mind, a capacity which notably is always exercised in one way or another. That is to say, in having an idea of some physical object, the mind also has an idea of this idea and thus of itself (cf., e.g., 2P17Sch). However, problems connected with the transformation of the mind's knowledge of physical objects into its self-knowledge need not detain us here. What matters is *that* knowledge of physical objects necessarily is or involves the mind's knowledge of itself, and that this is made possible in virtue of two facts, (1) that an idea of an *object* is an *idea* of an object, and (2) that this is brought out by the given capacity of the mind to reflect upon its knowledge of physical objects, that is, to form an idea of its ideas of such objects.

The Self to be known by the mind, then, consists of ideas of modes of extension (i.e., of modification of the body by some other mode of extension) (cf. 2P13 and 2P15). They may be termed first-order ideas. And knowledge of this Self consists in ideas of such ideas. They are second-order ideas. This state of affairs explains and justifies a significant trend of Spinoza's theory of man. Although primarily (or solely) meant to be a theory of the human mind, Spinoza, as mentioned above, finds it necessary to give at least a brief account of modes of extension in general and of the human body in particular. Of equal significance is the fact that most propositions in the *Ethics* are about, or contain a reference to, the human body and thereby indirectly (on account of 2P19) to modes of extension in general. In other words, most propositions in the *Ethics* are, or contain, first-order ideas. On the other hand, most propositions are also about the human mind, that is, they consist of second-order ideas. Thus in Spinoza's theory of the human mind ideas of the two orders fre-

[6] For a further discussion of this problem cf. G. Fløistad, *The Problem of Understanding in Spinoza's Ethics,* doctoral dissertation (mimeo.) (University of London, 1967, to be published).

quently occur side by side. Or, more precisely, in arguing his case
Spinoza frequently switches from ideas of the first order to those of
the second, and vice versa. Spinoza's view of the genesis of the mind's
self-knowledge, and hence also of the theory of the mind, may be
taken to explain the significance of, and to justify, this procedure.

If we asked for further explanation of, and justification for, this
procedure, Spinoza would undoubtedly refer us to what may be
called the thesis of identity of thought and extension. This thesis
may in fact be identified as one of the major premises for the proposition concerning the genesis of the mind's knowledge of itself
(2P23). The thesis says, as is well known, that thought and extension
are one and the same thing, but expressed in two manners. The
thesis applies to the attributes as well as to the modes: the attributes
of thought and extension (or thinking and extended substance) 'are
one and the same substance which is now comprehended through
this and now through that attribute'. And similarly, 'a mode of extension and the idea of that mode are one and the same thing but
expressed in two manners' (cf. 2P7Sch). Since the human mind consists of ideas of which the body, or its modifications by other modes
of extension, are the objects, the same holds good for the mind and
body (cf. 2P21Sch). Spinoza here apparently has only finite modes
in mind, but he is certainly committed to holding the same view as
to the infinite modes.

In short, we may say that whatever goes for the attribute and
modes of extension goes, respectively, for the attribute and modes
of thought. It is this thesis that forms, if not a sufficient, at least a
necessary condition for the possibility of transforming knowledge
of the body and physical objects in general into knowledge of the
mind. The thesis may now assist us in deciding the role played by
the second kind of knowledge in the *Ethics*.

5. The common notions said to be granted common to all men
(i.e., the notion of the attribute of extension and of motion and rest)
(cf. 2P38Cor) present no problem. On account of the identity thesis
they are readily translated into the corresponding common notions
of thought, the notion of the attribute of thought, and the notion of
absolutely infinite understanding. Both pairs of notions may perfectly well be said to belong to the fundamental principles of our
ratiocination (2P40Sch1) or, more precisely, to be *the* basis of reason
(cf. 2P44Cor2Dem). The former pair, being first-order notions, are
the basis, we shall have to say, of our reasoning about modes of ex-

tension, whereas the latter, being second-order notions, are the basis of our reasoning in matters of thought, for example, about the mind and its ideas.

In what sense, then, can these notions possibly be said to be the basis for the propositions of the *Ethics* and thus help to decide the kind of knowledge expressed in these propositions? In trying to provide an answer to this question I shall follow Spinoza's own procedure and focus on the role played by the attributes, leaving the infinite modes out of consideration.

The *Ethics* itself allows of various interpretations. A minimum interpretation, as one may call it, is suggested in 2P45: Every idea of every body or individual thing actually existing involves the eternal and infinite essence of God, that is, the conception of the attribute of extension (cf. 2P45Dem). In other words, whenever Spinoza is presenting ideas of modes of extension, these ideas involve and express (cf. 1P25Cor) the conception of the attribute of extension. The same ideas, however, being finite modes of thought, necessarily involve and express the conception of the attribute of thought. This is, or rather may be, made explicit in second-order ideas (which of course themselves involve and express the attribute of thought).

I shall not enter into a discussion here of difficulties connected with a first-order idea being an expression of the attributes of extension and thought alike, nor of those connected with the possibility of a second-order idea being an expression of the attribute of thought only (cf. 2P17Sch). The question at present is whether the interpretation of common notions as the basis of reason in terms of involvement or expression may help to decide our initial problem. The answer, I think, must be no. One cannot on this interpretation decide whether propositions about modes of extension, or about ideas of such modes, belong to the second kind of knowledge. For one thing, one cannot, for instance, on the basis of Spinoza's use of the term 'body' or 'idea' or 'mind' in certain propositions, decide whether these propositions involve and express and are thus based on the notion of the attribute of extension and thought as common notions characteristic of reason. The use of certain *terms* is here in principle insufficient. It is perfectly conceivable that propositions concerning modes of extension and thought express knowledge of the third kind (cf. Sect. II, 2 above). Presumably one is entitled at most to say that an (implicit or explicit) use of the *distinction* between modes of extension and thought (e.g., between the mind and body or between an idea and its object) is a necessary condition for a proposition expressing knowledge of reason. This is suggested by the account of knowledge of reason itself, and also, though indirectly, in Spinoza's account of intuitive knowledge (cf. Sect. III below).

Other interpretations of the common notions as the basis of reason appear to be more promising. In the statement that 'the bases of reason are the notions which explain these things which are common to all . . .' (2P44Cor2Dem), 'explain' may be taken to refer to propositions concerning the attributes. Thus an attribute is said, for instance, to be 'that which the intellect perceives as constituting the essence of a substance' (1D4) and (therefore) to be in itself conceived through itself, to be eternal and exist of necessity, and to be the cause of the modes, i.e. its modifications (cf. 1P7, 1P10, 1P11, and 1P16).

Does this mean that all propositions in the *Ethics* which are deduced from, or proved by, these propositions explaining common notions belong to the second kind of knowledge? If there were propositions exclusively proved by such propositions explaining the common notions it would be tempting to answer in the affirmative. The trouble is that Spinoza's actual procedure in the *Ethics* makes it extremely difficult to decide whether there are any such propositions. A closer examination shows in fact that propositions concerning God or Substance somehow enter into the premises of almost every proposition, and certainly into the premises of those propositions explaining the common notions themselves. And although God, or Substance, may in a sense be the object of reason (namely in so far as he is conceived in terms of an attribute), he is no doubt, on Spinoza's account, primarily the object of intuition (cf. Sect. III below).

This is of course not to say that knowledge by reason is not employed by Spinoza in the *Ethics*. It merely suggests (i) that it is difficult to decide whether a proposition belongs to knowledge by reason by considering the common notions forming the basis of this kind of knowledge, and (ii) that possible occurrences of knowledge by reason in the end depend on knowledge by intuition.

6. In order to decide whether the 'bulk of the propositions' in the *Ethics* belong to the second kind of knowledge, another, more adequate, criterion is called for. The only one offered by Spinoza, as mentioned earlier, is found in 2P39Dem in the idea of properties

common to 'the human body and certain external bodies by which the human body is used to be affected' (cf. Sect. II, 1, above). This idea is apparently not basic to reason in the same sense as, say, the notion of the attributes; it belongs, however, together with the basic common notions, to the fundamental principles of our ratiocination. It is this criterion or idea of common properties that underlies Parkinson's conclusion concerning the occurrence of the second kind of knowledge in the *Ethics*.

There is much to be discussed here. First of all there is the problem of translating (first-order) ideas of common properties into the corresponding (second-order) ideas of common ideas or notions, and then, secondly, the problem of applying this part of Spinoza's account of the second kind of knowledge to his own procedure in the *Ethics*. The latter problem is a twofold one, due to the distinction between mind and body. However, any satisfactory treatment of these problems would take us too far for present purposes. I shall have to confine myself instead to pointing out briefly certain difficulties connected with the translation and application of the account of reason in question, in particular certain difficulties which indicate the need to take account of intuitive knowledge.

7. The solution of the translation problem is in principle suggested in 4 above. Spinoza in fact performs the translation himself when he calls ideas of common properties 'common' (cf. 2P40Sch1). We should note, of course, that in the present case we are concerned with ideas of properties common to a (more or less, cf. 2P39Cor) limited range of individuals, and that a first-order idea of such a common property is to be regarded as an expression of this common property as well as of the attribute of extension (being common to *all* modes of extension), and (indirectly) also of the attribute of thought (being common to all ideas or modes of thought).

The more immediately relevant problems arise, however, when we attempt to apply the idea of common properties, and its translation into common notions, to the propositions of the *Ethics*. An example may be helpful, and the most natural choice is 2P39 itself, where Spinoza presents his view on common notions: 'That which is common to and a property of the human body, and certain external bodies by which the human body is used to be affected, and which is equally in the part and whole of these, has an adequate idea in the mind.'

To Parkinson this proposition, presumably, is a common notion and belongs as such to knowledge by reason. In one sense the proposition undoubtedly is or represents a common notion: it explains what commonly has an adequate idea in the mind. Our question, however, is whether the proposition is common in the sense which it itself prescribes. In other words, can 2P39 be interpreted as concerning itself?

The case may presumably be argued in various ways. One way is this. The proposition clearly opens with a first-order idea ('That which is common to . . .'), and it says about the object of this idea that the idea of it is adequate. Thus the proposition ends up with saying something about an idea, that is, it ends up by itself being a second-order idea. It is not an idea of an idea of a *certain* common property. It is rather a second-order idea of *the adequacy* of such ideas and their objects *in general*. In other words, 2P39 is a generalization concerning the adequate character of certain notions. And the concept of being such a generalization is certainly different from the concept of being common, applying to the object of the generalizing propositions. It would seem, then, that 2P39 is not, at least not immediately, applicable to itself.

Despite this, 2P39 may still in a sense be regarded as a common proposition or notion. Its common character concerns the adequacy of a certain type of ideas. The point is merely that this common character is not accounted for in 2P39 itself. And it is even hard to see how it can be accounted for in a way similar to the account given of a common notion in 2P39. The concept of adequacy of ideas seems, for instance, to have no reference to modes of extension as have ordinary common notions. Adequacy of ideas seems to be a purely mental phenomenon, which cannot be arrived at by any translation of common properties of modes of extension into common notions. The theory of knowledge of reason presented in 2P39 will therefore have to be supplemented if this theory is itself to belong to knowledge by reason. The way to supplement the theory is already suggested in the above argument. One has merely to postulate the capacity of the mind to reflect upon and form common notions of its ideas of common properties of things. To Spinoza such a postulate appears to be a matter of course (cf., e.g., 2P21Sch, TIE § § 30 ff). And it is this capacity which is tacitly exercised in 2P39 as well as in most other propositions of the *Ethics*, including those, for instance, in which 'conceiving' explicitly occurs as a common notion.

In view of this the above interpretation of 2P23 concerning the genesis of the mind's self-knowledge, if it does not break down, at least will have to be modified. The mind may perfectly well have no knowledge of itself save in so far as it perceives the ideas of the modifications of the body. But this self-knowledge, we shall have to say, is not restricted to second-order ideas merely corresponding to particular first-order ideas. It also comprises second-order ideas whose objects are first-order ideas in general. If this is correct the mind seems to occupy a position superior to that of the body within the system of the *Ethics*. And the thesis of identity of the mind and body consequently does not hold good in general.

8. Other propositions in the *Ethics* present difficulties of a different kind. Take for instance 2P41: 'Knowledge of the first kind is the only cause of falsity; knowledge of the second and third kind is necessarily true'.

This proposition, in which Spinoza offers a general characterization of the three kinds of knowledge, may also perfectly well be conceived of as a (complex) common notion. It states, for instance, that it is a common character of the first kind of knowledge to be the only cause of falsity. Again it is hard to see how this common (or general) character is taken care of in the account of reason in 2P39. This, however, is not our present concern. Granted that the proposition belongs to knowledge by reason, we are faced with the problem of how an idea of reason can have all three kinds of knowledge as its objects.

That we may have a common and adequate idea of the concept of the first kind of knowledge is perhaps not so peculiar. The concept of the first kind of knowledge being false is itself an adequate idea, at least of the second kind. This follows from the statement that 'knowledge of the second and third kinds and not of the first kind teaches us to distinguish the true from the false' (2P42). In other words, in 2P41 the reasoning activity of the mind is, as far as the first kind of knowledge is concerned, simply reflecting upon an idea produced by itself. The occurrence of the concept of the second kind of knowledge is even less peculiar. Here reason is simply reflecting upon, or forming, an idea of itself in general (the idea namely that the common notions produced by it are necessarily true).

What is not a matter of course, to the reader at least, is how the concept of the third kind of knowledge may occur as an object of reason. This means that reason in 2P41 is said to reflect upon intuition, not upon any particular intuitive idea, but upon intuitive ideas or the intuitive way of knowing things in general. And why is this a difficulty? Above all because of the thesis of identity between an idea and its object, here applied to the relation between first and second-order ideas (cf. 2P21Sch). The object is the idea of intuitive knowledge being true. If 2P41 is regarded as an idea of reason, this means, in view of the identity thesis, that an idea of (i.e., about) intuitive knowledge may be translated into, and is the same as, an idea of reason. In the case of the concepts of the first and the second kind of knowledge occurring in 2P41 this difficulty does not arise. The concepts of both kinds of knowledge belong to, or may belong to, knowledge of reason and are consequently translatable into a higher order idea of reason. In view of the occurrence of the concept of intuitive knowledge, the possibility of such a translation, advocated by the identity-thesis, seems to break down.

To this problem there seem to be two possible solutions. It is first of all tempting to apply the distinction between 'use' and 'mention' to 2P41 and to say that in this proposition Spinoza is not actually using but merely mentioning the third kind of knowledge. He is saying something *about* it. And this is surely possible without exercising intuition. In this case the difficulty just mentioned appears to be wholly fictitious. The idea about the third kind of knowledge in 2P41 is an idea *of* a property common to all intuitive ideas and hence (possibly) an idea of reason.

However, I do not feel at all sure as to whether the use-mention distinction *necessarily* applies to 2P41 (or, for that matter, to a number of similar propositions) as *used* by Spinoza. Is it in principle impossible for an idea about a certain kind of knowledge to belong to that kind of knowledge itself? It is certainly possible in the case where the object of the idea is the concept of the first and the second kind of knowledge. And why should not an idea about intuition itself be or at least involve an intuitive idea?

One reason for holding this view I find in the fact that Spinoza could not possibly have used the concept of the third kind of knowledge in 2P41 unless he had previously exercised the intuitive way of knowing things. It may even be said that the concept of the second kind of knowledge in the context of the *Ethics* presupposes the concept of the third kind. The second kind of knowledge is second in the *Ethics* not only in relation to the first kind but also

to the third. And in view of the great importance attached to intuitive knowledge, particularly in Part V of the *Ethics,* it is hard to
see how Spinoza (presumably unlike his readers or hearers), while
using the concept of intuition could wholly have dispensed with
that kind of knowledge itself.

Granted, then, in view of these in no way conclusive reasons, that
the idea about intuitive knowledge as used in 2P41 may itself possibly be, or involve, an intuitive idea, the difficulty we are concerned with is a genuine one. And in view of the identity thesis concerning an idea and its object, there appears to be only one way
of solving the problem: we shall have to question the assumption
that 2P41 (and similar propositions) is an expression of the second
kind of knowledge only. For it may, at least in part, be an expression
of intuitive knowledge.

It is time to consider, briefly, the third kind of knowledge and
its relation to the second kind.

III

1. Intuitive knowledge is said to proceed 'from an adequate idea
of the formal essence of certain attributes of God to the adequate
knowledge of the essence of things' (?P40Sch2). I shall first explain
some aspects of this account of intuition and then try to show its
relevance to our problem.

We may begin by considering the meaning of 'proceeds'. Now a
most reasonable interpretation seems to be in terms of a process of
increasing knowledge. That is to say, 'proceeds' signifies that the
mind comes to know more and more by intuition. Intuitive knowledge of the essence of things is thus more advanced than intuitive
knowledge of the formal essence of certain attributes of God. How,
then, is this possible? How can knowledge of the essence of finite
modes rank higher than knowledge of the attributes? A natural
answer to this question is suggested by asking: What is there to be
known over and above the formal essence of the attributes, that is,
the essence of each attribute considered separately (this is what
'formal' means)? The natural answer is: the attributes in their relation to one another, more precisely, in their unity. And knowledge
of the unity of the attribute in God is undoubtedly a far more genuine knowledge of God than knowledge of him in terms of one of
the attributes alone.

That knowledge of the essence of things is knowledge of God is clear from a number of propositions in Part 5 (e.g., 5P24, 5P25Dem). That this knowledge is of God as a unity of thought and extension (of mind and body, of an idea and its object) is not explicitly stated in these propositions themselves. Here Spinoza makes rather frequent use of the mind–body distinction. This may be interpreted in two ways. He is either, for the most part, discussing the initial stages of intuitive knowledge only, or, in addition to this, he is also accounting, in an indirect manner, for the more advanced 'unity-directed' stages of intuitive knowledge. 'Indirect' here refers to the fact that the unity of thought and extension, on Spinoza's account, is a phenomenon of thought. This follows, for example, from the statement that a (second-order) idea of the mind (of its first-order ideas) is united to the mind in the same manner as the mind (or its first-order ideas) is united to the body (or the extended or physical objects of the first-order ideas). It follows that whenever Spinoza uses the concept of the mind (or an idea) in Part 5 (and for that matter in all previous parts) he *may have* the unity of thought and extension 'in mind'.

The above interpretation of 'proceeds' in terms of a process of knowing in which the mind finally comes to know ('intuit') the unity of thought and extension, may thus still hold good. Apart from that, however, a similar interpretation of the account of intuitive knowledge in 2P40Sch2 is called for if this account is to cover a number of basic statements in the *Ethics*. What I have in mind are, first of all, statements concerning God in Part 1, such as that he 'is one alone' (1P14Dem, Cor) and that he is 'a being absolutely infinite, that is, a substance consisting of infinite attributes . . .' (1D6). The point is that statements such as these are an expression of a kind of knowledge that clearly goes beyond any knowledge of attributes, be it of the second or the third kind.[7]

The presumed intuitive knowledge expressed in such statements may, I think, be detected in one way or another in a large number of cases. Most definitions, as well as some of the axioms and quite a few propositions of Part 1, in fact make explicit use of the concept of God as being something, or someone over and above an attribute and its modifications. This applies to the very definition of an attribute itself (1D4). The implicit occurrences are even more fre-

---

[7] The problem is discussed in detail in Fløistad, op. cit.

quent. In using expressions such as 'being the cause of itself' (1D1), 'being in itself' and 'being conceived through itself' (1D3, 1A1, 1A2) Spinoza no doubt has God as an absolutely infinite being primarily in mind (and not the attributes to which the expressions also apply). As premises of propositions, the same 'highest level' notion of God occurs throughout the *Ethics*—as suggested above, because in the proof of most propositions Spinoza makes use of premises which in the end go back to definitions, axioms and propositions explaining this notion of God. It is presumably for this reason that nothing, and in the present context that means no proposition of the *Ethics*, can exist or be conceived without God (cf. 1P15).

2. This yields a unique position to the intuitive knowledge in the *Ethics*. And we may ask whether this position invalidates the view that most propositions in the *Ethics* belong to knowledge by reason. Not necessarily, but it certainly calls for a qualification of this view, particularly in terms of an account of the relation between the second and third kinds of knowledge. I shall here suggest but one step in direction of such a qualification.

Consider the structure of the *Ethics*. In Part 1 it offers an account of God and of what follows 'from his essence'. This account, apparently, has no purpose in itself. It merely provides a basis for Spinoza's main concern in the *Ethics*, to explain the human mind. The explanation is centred around the idea of the liberation of the mind towards its 'consummate blessedness' (cf. 2 Preface). This is a matter of knowledge, that is, of the way of knowing or understanding things. The more the mind is able to know things by the second and third kinds of knowledge, the more liberated it becomes, and the more lasting is the satisfaction it enjoys (cf., e.g., 5P20Sch). Intuitive knowledge is here far more advanced and powerful than the second kind (cf. 5P36Sch). From the third kind of knowledge 'the greatest possible mental satisfaction arises' (5P27).

In the context of this idea of liberation Spinoza now says that 'the endeavour or desire of knowing things according to the third class of knowledge [can] arise from . . . the second class of knowledge' (cf. 5P28). In other words, the thinking activity characteristic of intuition may arise from the thinking activity involved in ideas of reason. Or, ideas of reason may give rise to ideas of intuition.

To explain exactly how this transition actually takes place is a difficult task. But the account given in 2P40Sch2 of reason and intuition makes it perfectly conceivable. As it appears from this account, both reason and intuition (in its initial stage) have as their object the attribute of extension. The difference is that to reason the attribute is a common notion, whereas intuition is able to form an idea of its formal essence. The transition may hence be conceived of as a transition from a common notion of the attribute of extension to a notion of the formal essence of the same attribute. Due to their 'common' object, the two notions, the one being the 'end' of reason, the other the beginning of intuition, are obviously closely related.

However, the point I want to make at present does not so much concern the possible and exact character of the transition as the mere saying itself that the ideas of intuition may arise or follow from ideas of reason. To say this obviously presupposes the concept of intuition. It presupposes that one knows what intuition is about. The position of the author of 5P28 concerning the transition is hence different from the position of the mind talked about. The latter is presumably able to exercise reason only, and the proposition says about him that he, on the basis of this ability, may come to know things intuitively.

If we ask for the source of this knowledge expressed in 5P28, we shall, I think, have to go back to the procedure in Part 1 to find an answer. Here Spinoza appears to go exactly the opposite way to that prescribed to the mind in 5P28 (and in other propositions in Part 5). He begins with an intuitive knowledge of God as an absolutely infinite being and opens the way to the lower-level knowledge by intuition, and also to knowledge by reason by defining an attribute and its modes. The relation to God as an absolutely infinite being is all along taken care of, particularly in the definition of an attribute. Knowledge by reason expressed in later propositions thus appears to be derived from knowledge by intuition. For this reason, presumably, Spinoza is able to say in Part 5 that knowledge by reason may give rise to the intuitive way of knowing things.

Where does this take us? Not very far, I am afraid. The account merely suggests that the highest-level knowledge of intuition is the basic knowledge expressed in the *Ethics,* and that this knowledge, to Spinoza at any rate, is somehow present and thus expressed in every proposition of the *Ethics,* including those classified as knowledge by reason. How this is possible would require an extensive discussion of the relation between the third and the second kind of knowledge. The clue to a proper understanding of this relation is not, I think, to be found primarily in the theory of knowledge summarized in 2P40Sch2, nor in the account of the liberation of the mind in Part 5, but in Spinoza's own deductive procedure in Part 1.

At present we may rest content by stressing once more the unique position of intuitive knowledge in the *Ethics*. Its significance is perhaps best brought out by saying that the ability to exercise intuition is a necessary condition for framing the ontology as well as the epistemology, psychology and moral and social philosophy characteristic of the *Ethics*. In other words, without possessing the intuitive way of knowing things, Spinoza could not possibly have written the *Ethics*.

Spinoza's Doctrine
of Privation

Raphael Demos

According to Spinoza, the categories of good and bad—in fact, all categories of value—are relative. The only valid category is that of substance; value as distinct from reality has no genuine meaning. Spinoza's attack on valuation is based on two sets of arguments, one rationalistic and scientific, the other religious and theological. We will consider each in turn.

(A) The world is governed by law; whatever happens, does so by necessity. Now, we easily believe this of external nature, but we balk when we come to human nature; we say man is free to do what he likes. Yet man is not a kingdom within a kingdom; he is part of nature, subject to the same general processes. Human emotions such as hatred, anger, envy, follow from the same necessity as other things, and can no more be reviled or criticized than the cold dampness of the rain or the screeching of the wind. So, Spinoza proceeds to say, "I will consider human actions and appetites just as if I were considering lines, planes, or bodies."

What are the forces which control human conduct? They are both internal and external. (a) We are determined by our own respective characters. "The infant believes that it is by free will that it seeks the breast; the angry boy believes that by free will he wishes vengeance; the timid man thinks it is with free will he seeks flight; the drunkard believes that by a free command of his mind he speaks the things which when sober he wishes he had left unsaid. Thus the madman, the chatterer, the boy, and others of the same kind, all believe that they speak by a free command of the mind, whilst in truth they have no power to restrain the impulse which they have to speak; so that experience itself, no less than reason, clearly teaches that men believe themselves to be free simply because they are conscious of their actions, and ignorant of the causes by which they are determined" (*Ethics,* Bk. II, Prop. II, Scholium). The rose is fragrant by the necessity of its own nature, and a thorn pricks; similarly a man with a bad character behaves badly, and should no more be blamed for that than the thorn for pricking. All things, all bodies and all minds, have a determinate nature; as we know to-day, water is a determinate ratio of oxygen and hydrogen, coal is a ratio of other elements, and out of this determinate nature inevitably flow the various properties and behaviour of things.

(*b*) Causation is, moreover, external. We are determined by our characters, and our characters come from heredity and from the environment. The individual is an inseparable part of the universal scheme of things. We are a particular confluence of the forces of nature, or, as Spinoza would express it, we are modes of the Infinite Substance. Our actions and our desires and our make-up are a necessary outcome of the nature of things. We are what we are because the Universe is what it is. In such a scheme, obviously there is no place for freedom, and therefore no place for moral judgment. We come at the conclusion of a long process of development: we issue from the dark womb of Being. We are aware only of the last stages of this continuous process, and are unaware of its deep sources; therefore we have the delusion that we are independent individuals controlling our destinies. Imagine, suggests Spinoza, a stone, hurled high by a man; imagine further that the stone, as it reaches the peak of its curve, comes to consciousness. The stone then would naturally think itself as free because it is ignorant of the forces that launched it; and the stone would then congratulate itself on its success on rising so high. So are we, human beings, missiles flung into the air of life by the hand of Nature, and we delude ourselves with the thought that the course of our lives is traced by our will.

From all this, the denial of the categories of good and evil, of praise and blame, follows as a matter of course. Praise and blame of action presuppose that the act might have been other than it actually was. You blame me for going to the show instead of staying at home and working, you praise me for rushing into the water and saving the drowning man instead of staying on the bank, because, presumably, the other alternative was equally open to me. Otherwise your praise or your blame are as ridiculous as Xerxes' chastising of the waters of the Hellespont because they wrecked his ships. In other words, in order that the ethical attitude be significant, possibilities must be real. But, as Spinoza says, possibility is a confused idea. What is, must be; what is not, is determined not to be by a cause. There is no middle ground of possibility, and everything happens, or fails to happen, of necessity. We conclude, therefore, that the ethical attitude of valuation belongs to a primitive stage of thought, and must retire as soon as the rational, scientific view of things comes on the scene.

The "ought" then has no objective meaning. It is futile to say to ourselves: I ought to do this or that, for I will do what I will do. Similarly, striving, aspiration, the ideal of self-improvement, are attitudes which arise from a confused idea. You do something because you are compelled to do it by your nature; you will do it anyway; and effort of will adds nothing to the result. In fact, Spinoza maintains that the doctrine of self-improvement is vicious; it means altering your nature, in other words, destroying yourself. By changing yourself, you have become somebody else; you are not yourself any more, therefore you have not even improved yourself. But of course such a thing is impossible, because it entails a contradiction. You cannot make yourself other than you are; you and your acts are a manifestation of your nature, and the two are logically inseparable.

(B) The ethical standpoint sins not only against science but religion as well. Theology, as well as reason, is an opponent of our moral ideas. How so? God is infinite; nothing limits Him, nothing is outside Him. God encompasses everything; He is in the world, and the world is in Him. If so, we cannot describe anything in the world as evil since the world is an expression of God. The whole antithesis of good and bad loses its meaning; everything is good, or rather everything is an expression of divine perfection. God is above good and evil. A thing is good or bad purely in relation to ourselves; what suits us we term good, what thwarts us we call bad. We isolate ourselves from the totality of things, and setting up our little selves as standards, judge the universe. In short, the moral attitude is an expression of our conceit and our provincialism. As we rise to "the intellectual love of God" and see things *sub specie aeternitatis,* we correspondingly abandon our miserable moral distinctions, and view all modes as part of the divine perfection. But, the reader might ask, what about sickness, what about earthquakes, what about the ferocious tiger and the malarial mosquito—are not these evil in themselves? Not at all, Spinoza would answer. Take sickness, for example: it seems bad because I see only its immediate effects, in relation to myself now; but if I had a universal vision extending throughout all time, if I saw my sickness as a link in a chain of events stretching infinitely behind me, and infinitely ahead of me, and infinitely around me, I would perceive it as fitting into a general pattern. As for the tigers and mosquitoes which eat us, that is bad from our point of view, but quite all right from theirs; we are food for one another, and, in so far forth, exhibit the universal interdependence of things. We eat lambs and fowl, and yet do not think ourselves ferocious for that; yet imagine the picture of human character in a history that might be written by these animals.

Spinoza considers other examples. This man is blind; surely, that is an imperfection? Now, Spinoza emphatically denies this. This man is *without* eyes; but that is not the same as saying that he is *deprived* of eyes. Negation must not be confused with privation. A stone has no eyes, yet we do not say it is deprived of eyes, nor do we bewail its fate. Privation means denying of a thing something which pertains to its nature; but if a man is blind, then it is his nature not to have eyes, and he is not deprived of anything, any more than the sightless stone or tree. It was in the infinite decree of God and according to the nature of things that this man should not have eyes, therefore the blind man is adequately fulfilling his nature in being blind. But you may say, suppose this man was born with good eyesight and then lost it by sickness or accident? Then, Spinoza answers, it was his nature to have eyesight for a certain number of years, and after that not to have it. The accident or the sickness happened necessarily from the nature of things, and therefore the blindness ensued as an expression of the man's nature.

In short, a thing's nature is what it actually is; if a thing is without something, then it is not in its nature to possess it. A square is not a circle, but that is no ground for complaint by the square; a square cannot be anything but a square. But, the reader might protest, other people have eyes, whereas this man has not. Precisely, answers Spinoza; why should this man be like other people? Why expect Peter to be like Paul? Each man possesses his own individual nature which is different and unique; each has his own peculiar way of manifesting the divine character. Let us take an example of our own. My friend has one leg only, and I call him a cripple. I have two legs; some other being in another planet may have three legs; am I therefore deprived of a third leg? I have no wings; angels presumably have; am I therefore to be condoled with as lacking wings? I have no automobile, and I say to myself that I am deprived of one, so I procure myself a Ford. But a Buick is better than a Ford, and I have no Buick, so I get myself one. But when is this process going to stop? There is a better car still, the Cadillac, then there is the Rolls-Royce, then perhaps aeroplanes, and so on *ad infinitum*. This idea that I am deprived of a good thing because I do not have it launches me into a feverish career of acquisitiveness, in which there is no genuine satisfaction, because there is no point of rest. And it is true that a good deal of present-day unhappiness arises from just this conception of privation with its consequent overweening ambition.

Let us get back to our blind man. The opponent might put forth the following argument: it is in the nature of man *in general* to have two eyes, and any individual who lacks two eyes is thwarted in his nature. Spinoza's answer is that man in general is a fiction; what we have is Peter, Paul, John, and so on. The root of the whole trouble arises, according to Spinoza, in the false Platonic doctrine of universals, which holds that there are general essences apart from individuals. Spinoza maintains that there is no such thing as a universal; each individual is distinct and different, and the word "man" is merely a word. We construct from our own minds a universal pattern of man to which we expect every individual to conform. In fact, Peter, Paul, and John should express or rather can express only their individual natures: Peter as sightless, Paul as one-eyed, John as possessed of two eyes. A Platonic universal is a confused idea; instead of considering each individual in himself, we lump them together for the sake of convenience, and construct an average man; thereupon we judge the individual by reference to this average man. But the latter is nobody and nothing; the only reality is the mode and the Universal Substance which is God.

In such a scheme there is no place for the conception of an ideal, and for striving to achieve ideals. The ideal is already realized, since God is one with the world; everything expresses perfectly its own limited nature. A criminal is perfect of his own kind. An ideal, as usually conceived of, is something from the outside, controlling the actual. But activity is from within out, like the blossoming of a flower, like the artist's self-expression; it is self-determining, whereas a conscious moral end is something that constrains man.

Supposing we agree with Spinoza's dictum that negation is not privation, we might still ask him, why negation at all? Why does not a thing possess all possible qualities? Why should it be without this or that property? The answer is that, to be is to be determinate, finite, limited. A thing (in the created world) is what it is by virtue of what it excludes. Affirmation, among modes, is correlative with negation. Thus it is in the very character of ourselves as concrete existences that we should be without certain qualities. If we were everything, then we should be nothing. (This, however, does not apply to God.)

Yet there are certain difficulties which Spinoza has to consider. Are we to place on the same level, the intelligent man with the fool, the pious with the ungodly, the honest man with the thief? Do the wicked serve God as much as do the good, since they do what they can in accordance with the decree of God? Surely there is a difference. Spinoza answers this point as follows: In the first place, God is not a tyrant who gets angry with the wicked for their acts, nor even is He a judge apportioning blame or praise. From that point of view, He does not differentiate between the pious and the ungodly. But though all individuals express their respective natures adequately, that does not put them on the same level. Some natures have more of substance, express more of God, or rather express God in a deeper, more integrated manner than others. All modes are created and operate in accordance with the decree of God, but each mode exhibits the Divine Substance in a different manner. There are degrees of perfection. To quote: "It is, indeed, true that the ungodly express the will of God according to their measure, but they are not therefore in any way to be compared to the pious. For the more perfection anything has, the more does it participate also in Deity, and the more does it express the perfection of God. There- fore, since the pious have incalculably more perfection than the ungodly, their virtue cannot be compared with that of the ungodly because the ungodly lack the love of God which springs from the knowledge of Him" (Letter XIX). And elsewhere: "For although a mouse is as dependent on God as an angel is, and sadness as much as joy, yet a mouse cannot therefore be a kind of angel, or sadness a kind of joy" (Letter XXIII).

How should one be able to speak even of degrees of perfection, if categories of value are abolished? In fact, degrees of perfection are degrees of reality; a thing is less or more perfect only in the sense that it has a lesser or greater depth of reality, in the sense that it expresses God's nature less or more adequately. One man is better than another in the sense that there is more stuff to him. And of course there is no return to the "ought," to aspiration, or to trying to pass from one degree of perfection to a higher one. If I am determined by God to have so much perfection and no more, then I should accept my nature and not aspire to change it. A correspondent asked Spinoza: Supposing it accorded better with the nature of someone that he should hang himself, would there be any reasons why he should not hang himself? In a remarkable passage, Spinoza answers that if someone sees that he can live better on the gallows than at his own table, he would act most foolishly if he did not go and hang himself. "And he who saw clearly that he would in fact enjoy a more perfect or better life or essence by pursuing crimes rather than by following virtue, would also be a fool if he did not pursue them. For in relation to such a perverted human nature crimes would be virtuous" (Letter XXIII). However, Spinoza insists that the situation entailed in the question is an impossible one; it cannot accord with the nature of anyone that he should destroy or pervert himself, because that is a contradiction.

At the same time, though the wicked cannot be blamed for their condition, it does not follow that they will be as happy as the godly. God awards neither rewards nor punishments; nevertheless virtue provides its own intrinsic reward, and evil its own punishment. The same principle of universal necessity which makes it nonsense to judge human acts also requires that consequences inevitably follow the act. "He who goes mad from the bite of a dog is, indeed, to be excused, and yet is rightly suffocated; he who is unable to control his desires, although he must be excused for his weakness, is nevertheless unable to enjoy peace of mind" (Letter LXXVIII).

There is something extraordinary in the manner in which Spinoza defends his position. Traditionally, the idea of God has been used to bolster up our moral nature; God has been represented as a guarantee that ideals and moral effort are valid. The voice of conscience has been regarded as authoritative, because it is the voice of God. With Spinoza, the function of the idea of God is just the reverse. Its effect is to destroy the significance of ethics; far from serving as a support of conscience, God is described as being above good and evil. The more divine we become, the more we remove ourselves from ethical conceptions. Spinoza asserts that the statement in the third chapter of Genesis is correct: the fall of man came about through the knowledge of good and evil. The contrast with the Kantian philosophy is evident. For Kant, God is a postulate of the moral consciousness, whereas for Spinoza, the idea of God negates the distinction of good and bad. What we have here is really two forms of the religious sense: the former is a religion of which the central core is ethical, practical, an incitement to duty; the latter is a religion essentially mystical in character, for which the highest manifestation of life is contemplation of God and union with Him.

Spinoza's relentless logic carries him to certain curious, even tragic paradoxes. His self-confessed aim in launching into philosophy is to discover man's highest good, the ideal of life; yet the result of his philosophy is to teach him that the conception of an ideal, of values, is a confused and inadequate idea. So strong is the moral motive in him that to his great metaphysical opus he gives the name 'Ethics'; yet the conclusion of his book on Ethics is that, logically speaking, there is no ethical standpoint. However, Spinoza does not maintain that we human beings, situated as we are in time and circumstance, should abandon the moral attitude of aspiration after ideals. It is true that from the standpoint of God there is neither good nor evil, but we are not the Deity. We are modes—limited, circumscribed in our nature, and through the fact of our limitation condemned to inadequate ideas. We are human, all too human, therefore provincial in outlook; consequently, we are obliged to govern our lives by conceptions which are confused: we set up ideals, we conceive of a possible pattern of life which we pursue. Not only do we do so, but we are constrained to do so; limitation is in our nature, and we cannot help expressing our nature and therefore proceeding according to the inadequate ideas of the moral sense. A striking conclusion indeed. The doctrine of necessity gives birth to two children which fight one another: it implies that since man is not free, praise and blame have no objective significance, and it also implies that since man is not free, he is constrained to act according to his limited nature, and so use the confused ideas of praise and blame. But there is a further side to this paradox. Spinoza accepts the limitations of human nature, and sets about discovering the good which man should pursue; this, in fact, is the quest of the *Ethics*. And the result of the quest is to discover in the fifth book that there is, in the ultimate sense, no valid significance to the life which consists in the pursuit of a good, and that men should accept reality, which is God. In other words, we have a double process of reasoning; and in each case the premise leads to a conclusion which is inconsistent (if not logically, at least practically) with it. The idea of necessity entails a form of life which denies necessity; and this form of life, in its turn, leads in the end to an assertion of the doctrine of necessity, and to an attitude in conformity with this doctrine. May not this succession of paradoxes mean that the theory itself is wrong, or inadequate? This gives us the clue for a consideration of the grounds of the Spinozistic attack on the moral consciousness.

We are here confronted with the conflict between the rationalistic and the ethical viewpoints. The former demands necessity, the latter requires possibility; the former asserts what is, the latter what ought to be; and if we follow out the implications of necessity, the category of the "ought" is seen to be invalid. Granting that there is a conflict between the two, what right has Spinoza to assume the rational standpoint and then test and criticize the ethical standpoint by reference to it? Why assume that the rational standpoint is prior and ultimate? That a person can take the opposite position is shown in the philosophy of Kant. For Kant, the categories of the intellect are limited in their application to the phenomenal world; they are relative to the subject, they do not reveal the nature of the object. On the other hand, the moral categories are metaphysically absolute. Perhaps, neither the position of Kant, nor that of Spinoza, is justified; it is more probable that the rational and moral categories are co-ordinate; the type of argument which proves—with Spinoza— that the moral categories are subjective, can easily be applied to show—as with Kant—that the categories of the intellect are subjective. But this invalidates neither the rational nor the ethical standpoint; all human attitudes are characterized by limitation; they are an approach to the real from a certain selected focus; they involve an aspect of subjectivity. That is why philosophy is necessary, in the sense that philosophy is the attempt to overcome the provincialism of the various special attitudes. But it overcomes this by synthesizing, not by abandoning them; each one is a perspective of the universe, and to that extent each one is a type of insight. What philosophy does is to correct them by a process of inter-comparison. Thus, while it takes over from science the conception of necessity, of law, of an order of nature, it also takes over from ethics the conception of a moral order and the distinction of good and bad.

To come back to Spinoza. Though he is critical toward the moral attitude, and demands that it prove itself, he never questions the validity of reason. He simply assumes that the categories of reason are objective; he does say that intuition supersedes the intellect, but all along he is certain about the category of necessity, of law, of the proposition that things completely determine one another. Thus Spinoza, while he is self-conscious about the moral sense, is not self-conscious about the intellectual categories. He grants them. Why? One might answer: because he cannot help it; they are involved in our very nature. But so are the ethical categories, as he himself admits. Then why put the second on a lower level than the first? An ordinary man may make assumptions uncritically, but that is not permissible to a philosopher. Granting the limitations to which all human attitudes are subject, we suggest that ethics is cognitive, a form of insight, that its categories are objective; and therefore that any metaphysical interpretation of the universe is bound to take account of ethical concepts. There is then the naïve, a priori argument in favour of ethics being epistemically valid. There is, also, the point that Spinoza's position, even though it be irrefutable, is incredible; it is not one which a person can illustrate in his practical life. One cannot act by it. Bettering one's condition is a law of life; criticism is part of reason and of human nature; if so, the idea of privation must somehow be valid. In the end, the separation between reason and the "ought" breaks down, because reason itself is an activity that pursues an end. Truth is an ideal; it is what one ought to believe. In this sense, cognition is a branch of ethics. One destroys the conception of the "ought" in ethics, only to rediscover it as a practice of reason. Thus, to deny the validity of the "ought" on the basis of rational considerations is ultimately to deny the validity of these considerations themselves.

This is of course a dialectical argument. The argument which has genuine persuasive force is the one expounded still earlier, and is no argument at all; it is an appeal to human nature in its simplicity and naïveté, it is the assertion that, in so far as we are unbiassed, we find the moral consciousness to be an integral aspect of the human mind in the same sense as the intellect. And if we accept ethics, we must accept its implications. We must accept teleology in some form, some sort of a doctrine of Platonic kinds, and the conception of genuine possibility. The denial of possibility is at the root of Spinoza's other negations in this connection. All is necessary, therefore "may be" has no genuine meaning. It follows, for Spinoza, that hope and fear are foolish emotions, because they are based on the idea of what might be or might have been. Imagination, in the sense of play of fantasy, is excluded, since there are no possibilities, no fictions, to be contemplated aesthetically; there are only truths to be asserted, affirmed, or denied. There is no teleology; what will be, will be; I shall do what I shall do, whereas purpose implies the possibility of deciding in favour of another alternative. Thus the crucial issue between the rational and the ethical viewpoints is whether genuine possibilities exist; and if the ethical standpoint is valid, then they must exist.

Let us now consider the presuppositions of ethics on the religious side—presuppositions in the sense of the sort of world without which moral action would lose its basis. Now, a great deal of ink has been spilled in order to prove that the idea of God is necessary for the validation of ethical conceptions. Kant is a familiar case in point. If by God we mean an actuality in which values are preserved, a ground by which moral achievement is recognized and made durable, then it may be argued that without such a God moral effort is meaningless. Achievement must endure in order to be worth while, in fact it must be eternal—if not in itself, at least through its consequences. A teacher who knew that his teachings were forgotten by the students as soon as they were learned would be foolish to continue teaching. If the results of human achievement are not preserved, then our efforts are not different from those of the child which builds ditches and walls in the sand by the seashore only to have them washed away by the next wave. Thus eternality is the groundwork of the significance of moral effort.

But we are not concerned with defending this position just now, only in showing that it is a relevant position. It may be that the hypothesis of God is necessary to the justification of ethical action; but our study of Spinoza has shown that it is possible to have too much God for the good of ethics; we need so much but no more of God, in order to make the world safe for ethics. For if we define God as Infinite Substance, then He is one with the world (since He includes everything), and it becomes impossible to apply critical judgments to the world. Everything is good, therefore the conception of good is meaningless. The rationality of ethics requires a divorce of the ideal from actuality, in other words, a separation of God from the world. With Spinoza, there is no distinction between standards and objects; the actual is the ideal; yet criticism involves the conception of a standard distinct from the actual situation and brought to bear upon it. There must be something which transcends

the actual, and to which the actual is compared, in order that valuation may be possible. Morality is criticism, it is also action. Now
moral action, too, moves in a world in which there is a distinction
between the ideal and the actual; for moral action is the effort to
approximate the actual to the ideal. Moral action, in so far as it is
significant, requires two things: the distinction between the ideal
and actuality, and the possibility of joining the two together.

The idea of God, as we find it in the Christian religion, is analys-
able into elements, all of them necessary components, yet fighting
each other. There is the infinity of God, and there is the moral
nature of God; both attributes are indispensable to the nature of
God, and yet, apparently, they are inconsistent with one another.
Spinoza starts with the conception of God as infinite, and then
denies His moral nature; for if God is infinite, then He includes the
world with all its attendant evil. Then either God is non-moral, or
else moral categories have no objectivity. Spinoza chooses the latter
alternative; Aristotle may be said to choose the former. The exclusive emphasis on the infinity of God leads to the type of religion
which is mystical. But if a person's nature is practical and active, he
is led to favour the moral categories; the world must be such that
something needs to be done about it. Bad is bad, and if the world
includes evil, God is out of it. God is distinct from the world. God
is limited by the world, in short, God is not infinite. The task of the
philosophy of religion has been to devise an intellectual framework
by which both the infinity and the moral nature of God might be
saved.

To sum up, Spinoza uses the weapons both of reason and of mystical religion in order to batter down the ethical categories. It is really
a fight between the giant and the pygmy, between Goliath and
David. On the one hand, we have the sublimities: the ideas of
necessity, eternity, universal law, infinite substance; but the world
of ethics is a lowly, somewhat vulgar world; the medium of action
is time and space and matter. Action deals with particular, finite
situations; action discovers imperfection and battles it with concrete
physical weapons; action presupposes an agent who is free, who can
be blamed or praised, in other words an agent whose choices are
not fully determined. In the world of action there is a measure of
contingency, even anarchy. Contingency, temporal change, bad and
good, physical agencies, the particular: contrast these with the basic
notions of reason and religion—with eternity and essence, with all-

encompassing perfection and with the idea of law; surely, there is something very low-brow and plebeian about the moral realm. Yet perhaps this is the contribution of moral insight to philosophy: that it introduces the halt, the maimed, and the blind into the banquet to which all real things are invited.

There are still two questions which demand an answer, and which will be briefly disposed of in the ensuing paragraph. (*a*) We have argued against Spinoza, and in favour of the moral sense, taking our stand on the ground of common sense. But there is a deeper insight in man, which must also be respected. Man is engaged in action, and in distinguishing between good and bad, but even while so engaged he has the sense that these distinctions are finite, human, limited, that, from any absolute point of view, they must vanish. The truth of this insight cannot be appreciated, however, unless it be understood properly. Its meaning is that the ethical outlook, being one of the many outlooks, cannot be taken into any synoptic philosophical outlook, as it stands. It is the insight that the ethical viewpoint must be corrected by the other special viewpoints. Now such a correction is necessary not only for the moral standpoint, but for any other of the attitudes of the mind—aesthetic, religious, or scientific. Every special discipline is limited, and it abstracts from reality. So is the ethical outlook an abstraction; its limited aspect is therefore not a reason for its abandonment, but only a reason for its criticism by reference to a wider ground. (*b*) It is not enough to say, as we have said in this paper, that the moral categories must be allowed a co-ordinate rank with the categories of the intellect. We are faced with the problem that the two entail contradictory consequences. Some further scheme must be devised in which the two are reconciled by having modifications imposed upon them. That is a genuine problem, but its solution is beyond the scope of the present paper.

Some Incoherencies
in Spinozism (II)

A. E. Taylor

HITHERTO I HAVE in effect been arguing that Spinozism can produce no intelligible theory of natural knowledge, because by ignoring the *concipient,* it has made its "mind" into one which may be called a theatre of "psychical occurrences," but really *knows* nothing. I want now to contend that the system, if consistent, is precluded from having any genuinely ethical doctrine at all by its proposed exclusion of the notion of moral value. The exclusion is explicitly accomplished in the famous *Preface* to *Pt.* III., where Spinoza compliments himself on his superiority to the common run of moralists, who are accustomed to praise or condemn human "affects" and human actions, and announces his intention to consider the subject-matter as indifferently as though it were that of geometry, "lines, planes, solids". The words might be harmless if their purpose were merely to censure the pulpit-eloquence into which the treatment of ethics may degenerate in the hands of third-rate writers. But Spinoza means a great deal more than this. The "prejudice" from which he proposes to show himself free is, as he candidly admits, that of believing in any objectively valid standard of values at all (III. 39 schol.), and the "geometrical" treatment of human passions and the acts to which they prompt is intended to mean a merely naturalistic psychological account of the way in which the various "passions" are generated and the kind of acts to which they lead. The declaration of the *Preface* prepares us for the subsequent enunciation of the proposition that "we do not desire a thing because it is good; it is good because we desire it," that is, *good* is only a name for whatever is in fact desired by the person using the word.

It ought to be obvious that on such an assumption neither a moral code nor a philosophy of morals is possible. Both are possible only on the presupposition that it is possible to pronounce on the *worth*

289

of different human passions and desires by reference to a standard
independent of the passions and desires to which it is applied, just
as Mill's insistence on a difference of *worth* among pleasures was
only possible to Mill because in his heart he did not believe, as his
exaggerated reverence for Bentham and his own father led him to
imagine he believed, that pleasurableness and goodness are the
same thing. I am not here denying that the great Greek tradition,
according to which all of us, at the bottom of our hearts, have an
inextinguishable desire for the 'true good', is sound; in fact I am
prepared to maintain the view myself, with the necessary explanations. But if we are to hold such a view, we must also be prepared
to say that most men do not know what it is that they are really desiring, that the things they spend their lives in pursuing prove to be
really *not* what they desired. For what they pursue is, to speak with
Aristotle, the 'apparent good', and the 'apparent good' and the good
are commonly different things. Hence it would be in principle impossible to Plato or Aristotle, as much as it would be to a 'deontolo-
gist' like Kant, to grant that the good is not pursued because it is
good, but is good because it is desired, or that 'this is good' *means*
that this is being actually pursued. And the much admired proposal
to treat moral actions exactly as though they were geometrical figures is really ridiculous. It is to ignore their specific character as
moral. To construct a morality from which the distinctions of the
objectively good and evil, right and wrong, are absent, is like proposing to construct a geometry superior to the 'vulgar prejudice'
that there is a distinction between straight and curved.

This is really the central point at issue in Spinoza's correspondence with William Blyenbergh, and it is not to the credit of the
exponents of Spinozism that it should have been left to Prof. Guzzo
to point out that, though the worthy merchant was, as he said, a
tyro in metaphysics, his main ethical contention is absolutely sound.
When we divest the debate between the correspondents of terminology borrowed from a now obsolete Calvinistic theology, the question is simply this. Spinoza himself, let us say, is what we commonly
call a morally good man, Nero or Cesare Borgia a very bad one. But
is there any real distinction between these men which corresponds
to the verbal distinction we have just drawn? Clearly not, if we are
to stand by the principles laid down in the *Preface* to *Pt.* III.
Spinoza, Nero, Borgia, each has his characteristic individual *natura*,
and can have no other, and the life of each of them is a *conatus* to

preserve this *natura* and assert it against opposition. Their *naturae* are different, no doubt, but only as the curvature of one circle is different from that of another circle of different radius; or perhaps, in view of the inconsistencies of human action, it would be better to say, as the curvatures of one ellipse are from those of another of different eccentricity. In this there is no more ground for asserting the *moral* superiority of one of the three men to another than there would be for discriminating between the moral worth of one circle or ellipse and that of another. It is true, no doubt, that *I* might find the existence of Spinoza in the circle of my associates of high advantage to me, and that of Nero or Borgia a menace or a nuisance. But this is a purely extrinsic denomination, and, in point of fact, if Nero is a nuisance to me, to another man he might be a convenience, and Spinoza the nuisance.[1] The accidental circumstance that I find Nero or Borgia the nuisance is assuredly not what I mean, truly or falsely, to assert when I call them bad men.

Yet it is all the difference Spinoza can allow to be real, and for that reason he has to explain in so many words that he regards the distinctively ethical notions of *merit* and *demerit* as baseless, and elsewhere to justify the punishment of criminals as being exactly on a par with the shooting of a rabid dog or the killing of a venomous snake. In the matter of the administration of criminal justice *his* morality will literally 'treat a man like a dog', a procedure which has always been held to be morally particularly objectionable. May we not retort on this that no one who does not understand that even a murderer is a man to whom we have obligations, and not a dangerous animal, should pretend to have a *moral* theory? [2]

[1] Nero was an advantage to Poppaea; she would probably have found the company of Spinoza a nuisance.

[2] In the correspondence with Blyenbergh Spinoza ends by fairly involving himself in a formal contradiction. In *Ep.* 19 he had laid it down that, though the *improbi* are fulfilling the 'will of God' by their misdeeds no less than the *probi* by right action, the difference remains that the *improbi* are the less "perfect". I.e., the world is really and objectively a *hierarchized* world. In 21 he goes on to explain the statement by saying that the proper method of estimation in every case is to judge by the *quality of the deed alone* (*ex operis qualitate, non vero ex potentia operatoris*). That is, an *act* of justice, as such, has a higher "perfection" than a theft, and *therefore* we pronounce the honest man "more perfect", and so better than the thief. But in the very next letter (*Ep.* 22) this position is reversed, and we are told that if we regard only their *opera*, a just man and a thief are *equally* "perfect". I do not know a better example of the 'circle' which Kant says is unavoidable in a "perfectionist" doctrine of morals. The thief is

The point comes out with particular distinctness in the final exchanges between the disputants. Blyenbergh had asked, 'why, on your principles, should you not commit the actions of a Nero'? and had received the answer (*Ep.*, 21) 'because they do not agree with my particular nature, exactly as I abstain from certain dishes because they do not agree with my digestion'. To which he replies (*Ep.*, 23) 'a man who *only* abstains from crimes because they disagree with his particular nature cannot plume himself on his virtue'. And the reply is really fully justified. A man who refused an unwholesome dish merely because its flavour had no attraction for him could not, of course, claim to be showing himself properly attentive to dietetics, for, if his *only* reason for abstinence were the one he gives, it follows that if he had happened to like the flavour, he would have eaten the unwholesome thing for all its unwholesomeness. It is equally true that no man shows himself to be particularly virtuous by not committing sins which have no attraction for him; where I *prove* my virtue is in resisting the temptations which *do* appeal to me. A decent man does not want to commit acts of license, for example, but even if he did feel a keen desire to commit them, he would refuse to do so; his reason for avoiding vice is not merely that he in particular has no taste for it, but that it is doing what is *evil* or wrong. There can be no moral philosophy at all if the distinction between right and wrong can be reduced to one between what does in fact attract a certain man, or type of man, and what repels him. From premises which state mere non-moral 'matters of fact and relations between them', you cannot deduce ethical conclusions. On this point Blyenbergh, crudely as he puts the matter, and influenced as he probably was by the anxiety to provide a hell after death for sinners, was simply right.

In fact, Blyenbergh is really putting in a crude way the very objection which Kant was afterwards to urge against 'Perfectionism'. Presumably it is Leibniz rather than Spinoza, whom he seems never to have read, whom Kant actually has in mind here, but his criticism is really more directly effectual against Spinoza. He urges that if Per-

---

first declared to be the worse man because his act is the less perfect; then we are told that the thief's act is only to be called "less perfect" because the agent is a worse man.

The argument about the rabid creature (I think it means really rather a *man* suffering from the bite of a rabid dog than the dog itself) will be found in *Ep.* 78 (to Oldenburg).

lectionism is to work, it will have to presuppose the very principle (that of the distinction between right and wrong) which it pretends to explain, and is thus committed to reasoning in a circle.

This is exactly true of Spinoza. He professes to explain our moral distinction between the good act or man and the bad one by reducing it to a difference in degree of *realitas* or *entitas*. (It is not clear to me how such degrees are supposed to be measured, but I presume he, like Descartes, would have said that *A* has more *realitas* than *B* if the number of positive predicates which can be ascribed to *A* is greater than that assignable to *B*.) But how does he know that a morally good man *has* more *realitas* than a morally bad one? In what respect is the 'finite mode' of God which we call the Apostle Paul more *real* than that other 'finite mode' which we call the Emperor Nero? *Plato* might have replied that the one is 'more *like* God' than the other, but to say this would be to fall into the anthropomorphism Spinoza is most anxious to avoid. There can be no likeness, near or remote, between the mode and the infinite substance. If you equivocate on the word *perfect*, and argue that the good man is 'morally more perfect' than the bad, and *therefore* has more *realitas*, you are, as Kant said, presupposing as an independent given the very moral distinction you are pretending to explain.[3]

The best defence of Spinozism in this matter that occurs to me is to say that Spinoza's ideally virtuous man is supposed, as we see from *Pt. V.*, to have a wider range of insight than other men into the universal order and concatenation of things, and that thus we might say his *intellectus* is at any rate more like the *infinitus intellectus Dei* than that of any one else.[4] But it seems to me a highly dubitable assumption that a man with an intellect thus capacious might not be morally one of the worst of mankind. I do not see why

---

[3] Or it would be pertinent to say that Spinoza's reasoning entirely overlooks that ambiguity of the words *nature, natural* rightly insisted on by Butler. No doubt, since Spinoza does not, like Nero or Orestes, commit matricide, there is *something* in the 'particular nature' of Spinoza to which matricide is distasteful. But for the moralist the all-important question is what this something is. Is it a mere 'idiosyncrasy', like a disrelish for tobacco or port wine, or is it 'conscience' with its universality and its 'manifest authority'? Is matricide to be avoided because *A B* has no taste for it, or because it is 'contrary to the nature of *man* as a *system*'? Unhappily Spinoza's nominalism—a relic of the decadence of scholasticism—requires him to deny that there *is* any 'nature of man'.

[4] Though this is a poor 'best', since the *infinitus intellectus* is really only a collective name for all the finite intellects there may happen to be (V. 40 Schol.).

a great man of science, profoundly alive to the concatenation of
cause and effect throughout nature, might not be morally a very
bad man indeed, and it is quite certain that a man who has never
accustomed himself to think of the 'unity of all nature' and the
universal *commercium* between all the constituents of nature, may
be morally exceptionally virtuous. It seems to me, therefore, that
Spinoza never succeeds in showing any connection between *perfectio*
(in the only sense in which he professes to use the word) and *moral*
perfection, and that if he had attempted to show the connection (as
it is vital to his way of treating moral questions that he should) he
would have had to fall into the very fallacy which Kant was expos-
ing. All that really follows from his professed principles is that bad
men are psychologically *different* from good men, and that the exceptionally bad man must be, judging from the standpoint of the
average human being, what one of Charles Lamb's friends used to
call atrocious murderers, 'highly eccentric'. But the *moral* difference
between the two types is just the one difference Spinoza (correctly
on the principles of his *Preface*) refuses to allow, a difference in
desert. It is in keeping with this that the very word *duty* or *obligation* hardly occurs anywhere in the *Ethics,* and that, though Spinoza
had fine things to say about the virtue of benevolence, he is curi-
ously silent about the great virtue in which the concept of a *debitum*
is most markedly prominent, the virtue of *justice*. But I should say
that there must clearly be something wrong with the very foundations of a moral theory which can be worked out without reference
to justice and obligation.

Even if these criticisms can be completely met, there remains what
seems to be an insuperable practical difficulty. How, on Spinoza's
theory, does the transition from servitude to passion into the
'freedom' of action at the dictate of reason come about? This is
really, at bottom, the same problem we met before when we were
considering the transition from *imaginatio* to *ratio*. Antecedently
we could suppose the process to take place in either of two ways.
A man might undergo an intellectual enlightenment, he might
experience a 'day of Damascus', when he beheld for the first time
with unclouded eyes the vision of the true good, and this clarification of the intellect might effect a liberation from the passions connected with illusion and inadequate thinking. The man might cease
to care for his old false gods, because, in the light of the vision, he

had seen them to be false. Or conceivably the change might be wrought from the other side. A man might pass through an emotional crisis, he might awaken to noble emotions to which he had been a stranger, and the purification of emotion might be supposed to have a clarification of the intellect as its effect. It was, as we know, in the first of these ways that Plato and his followers supposed 'conversion' to be effected; the 'eye of the soul' was to be turned in the direction of the good. The memorable 'conversions' in the history of Christianity have been largely of the second kind. My trouble with Spinoza is that he seems to block both routes. For he lays it down expressly that we are of necessity under the dominion of the passions so long as our ideas remain inadequate. We should expect him, then, to teach a doctrine of intellectual conversion, making escape from the passions consequent on the attainment of adequate ideas. But if he is to take that line consistently, he must be prepared to hold that truth, at least truth about the good, as truth, has an inherent attractive power which can master the emotions. Reason must be able to encounter and defeat the passions in its own strength. But (and here again the difficulty seems to have escaped most, if not all, the expositors except Guzzo) it is Spinoza himself who also says that a true and adequate idea has in itself no more hold over our 'passional nature' than a false and inadequate one; it can only prevail if it happens to be associated with a more powerful 'affect' (IV. 7, IV. 14). Thus it seems in the end to be an accident, dependent on those circumstances of our environment which Spinoza tells us are, taken together, so much more powerful than ourselves, whether we ever escape out of our bondage or not, though the object of the whole *Ethics* has been to show us how we may compass our own deliverance.

Its promises, like the unerring prophecies of Tiresias, end in *quidquid dicam aut erit aut non*. If they really inspire hope in the reader, it is because he silently presupposes all the time that truth seen to be true has a compelling power due to its truth; he fancies that illusions, once known for what they are, will lose their grasp on him just because "killing *Truth*" has "glared on them". But this is just what his author maintains will not happen.

Thus the old question "what must I do to be saved?" receives no answer. Or at least it only gets the unsatisfactory answer offered by Leibniz to readers frightened by *his* Predestinationism into asking

whether they may not be among the predestined to damnation, 'As
you don't know, you may as well make the more agreeable guess that
you are among the elect.'

When we turn, however, to the detailed teaching of *Pt.* V. about
the road which leads to 'freedom' and life, Spinoza might almost
seem to have forgotten the emphatic declarations in *Pt.* IV. upon
which we have been remarking. For what are the practical recommendations he sets before us? They are, in effect, that we should
use our cool hours in meditating on the inevitable necessity of the
law of cause and effect, and the enormous complication of the cause
of every event, in virtue of which the contribution of any one particular man or thing to our happiness or misery may be considered
infinitesimal. We are, in fact, to remember two maxims, that nothing can possibly occur except precisely as it does occur, and that it
takes the whole of the universe to cause any particular effect. Such
meditation will, in the end, liberate us from unreasonable passions.
For such passions are due to two concurrent delusions. We fancy
that the favours or the blows of fortune are dealt out with conscious
purpose, that there is 'some one' who is at work to convenience or
to spite us in all that befalls us. And also, we wrongly single out
some one thing or person which, or who, has been merely contribu-
tory, along with all other things or persons, to our ill or good fortune, and make it or him the exclusive object of our gratitude or
resentment. The dissipation of these errors may be expected to
moderate our transports whether of love or of hate, and to leave us
with an equal mind, *in utramque sortem paratos.*

Now all this seems to take it for granted that the thoughts of universal necessity and the thorough-going complication of causes have,
after all, only to be steadily entertained as truths, and their very
truth will make them victorious over the most violent 'affects',
though we had been told in *Pt.* IV. that truth can only win the
day when it has a *'stronger* affect' for its ally. I do not see how we
can escape recognising a contradiction here, for, on Spinoza's own
showing, 'an affect towards an effect which we regard as necessary
is *ceteris paribus* not so strong as though the effect were supposed
free' (III. 49). At least, then, though the emotional moods evoked
by the meditations recommended may, by habitual practice, be made
more *usual* with us than the violent passions they are to subdue,
they will not be made 'stronger', and it was 'stronger affects' which
had been declared in *Pt.* IV. to be necessary if the "passions" are to

be mastered. We may fairly say, I think, that if we accept Spinoza's own reasoning, the effect of habitual meditation on the lines recommended should not be to generate "stronger" rivals to the 'passions' which he desires to control, but rather to bring about a general deadening and flattening of the emotional life. Perpetual preoccupation with the thought, 'what has happened to me could not have been other than as it is, and no one and nothing in particular has had very much to do with it' is less likely to give rise to a *summa mentis acquiescentia* which can colourably be called a 'love of God' than to that dull and hopeless indifferent listlessness which the Middle Ages knew as *acedia* and recognised as a peculiarly 'deadly' sin. And the literary records of humanity seem to show that where the original 'passive affects' were really strong, or where they are reinforced by grievous external circumstances, meditation on the inevitable necessity of all that happens cannot be counted on to beget even indifference; it may arouse angry revolt against the whole scheme of things. The author of the *Shropshire Lad* gives every sign of being as convinced as Spinoza of the interconnection and iron necessity of all events, but the thought does not temper his resentful animosity against 'whatever brute or blackguard made the world'. Hardy, in *Tess of the Durbervilles,* constructs a train of events which is inevitably to lead his heroine to the gallows, but the inevitability does not prevent him from shaking his fist in the face of the 'President of the Immortals'; he is so transported by his 'affect' that he comically enough forgets that it was not God but Thomas Hardy who "made" Tess, and made her expressly for the purpose of getting her hanged.

It is true that Christians *have* been enabled to take the worst as well as the best the world has to bestow with *summa mentis acquiescentia,* but they have been able to do so precisely because of their belief, which Spinoza does not share, that if the course of all things has been predetermined, it has been predetermined for a good, though hidden, purpose by a Creator who is both wise and loving, and therefore there is ground for *gratitude* in all that befalls them. If they overcome the world, it is not in virtue of the mere belief in complete preordination which some of them have in common with Spinoza, but in virtue of what they add to this conviction, their belief that the preordination is purposeful, and that the purpose, when disclosed, will be seen to be good.

No one, I take it, doubts that Spinoza's own contemplation of the order of the universe brought him the serene and solemn joy which he describes; if he had not felt it in himself, he could not write of it as he does. But that the contemplation brought him that joy is only explicable if it included features which are not represented in his professed account of its object, *natura sive Deus,* and never justified in his metaphysic. Like most of the rest of us, he had a religion which could not be decanted, without spilling, into any set of metaphysical formulæ. If you doubt this, imagine a perfectly possible situation, which has often enough been the actual situation of a British subject. 'Here am I, in prison, aching from the rack, and to-morrow I am to be taken out to be hanged, drawn, and quartered. What I have done to bring this on me, I do not know, but there is the fact; it cannot be altered, and nothing that I, or any one else could ever have done, could have made any difference to it. *Che sarà, sarà'.* What is there here to breed *acquiescentia mentis* in any child of man?

Also, it ought not to be forgotten that, be they good or bad, the directions given us in the *Ethics* for the conduct of our meditations presuppose that very kind of freedom which Spinoza has repeatedly declared to be an illusion of ignorance. It is taken for granted that we can *at will* determine for ourselves what we will meditate upon, in what light we will consider the course of things,—or at least, that we can do so 'in a cool hour'. (In fact the same assumption had been made less obviously in *Pt.* II. in using the very word *dictamen,* with its suggestions of command and self-direction, to describe the deliverances of 'reason'.) But according to the teaching of the earlier parts of the *Ethics* a man has no power over the direction of his thoughts, in any hour, however 'cool'. My present thinking is a 'mode' of God necessarily determined to be there, and to be what it is, by another earlier mode, itself similarly determined by a yet earlier mode, and so on *in indefinitum.* Nowhere in this chain of successive 'ideas' do *I* appear as a being with any power whatever to deflect the succession from its predetermined course. Recommendations to practise meditation, such as Spinoza gives, would have been consistent enough in Descartes, because Descartes believed in a man's power of self-determination; they are out of place in Spinozism, which allows of no such power. The only liberty Spinoza can consistently recognise is a mere matter of fact, the fact that some men are, though most men are not, superior to the 'passions'. But liberty as something which we as yet do not *possess* but may set ourselves to *acquire* by following certain precepts, is a matter not of fact, but of *right* (*ius*); whether it will be translated into actual fact or not depends on our observation or neglect of the precepts, and hence, unless the right is merely illusory, the very giving of the precepts presupposes that a potentiality not yet realised is not a mere nothing, and that the actualisation of *this* possibility of life free from the tyranny of the passions depends on the *liberum arbitrum* of each of us. We can "make a right use of our presentations", as the Stoic formula puts it, if we will.

It is, indeed, so manifest that 'free will' is the *causa essendi* of the moral life and the moral law that no one, in all probability, would ever have disputed the fact but for the unlucky confusion of free will with a supposed 'motiveless choice between motives'. When I choose to do an act simply because I judge it right that it should be done and wrong that it should be left undone, I am not making a *motiveless* choice; it is the rightness of the act (or, if you prefer to say so, the wrongness of leaving it undone) that is the motive influencing my decision. Unfortunately Spinozism, like all 'naturalistic' doctrines of morals, cannot consistently admit determination by such a motive. The only determination it can admit is determination of a particular natural fact, or event, by others, which are in turn determined by yet others, and so on *in indefinitum*. And the rightness or wrongness of an act is not such a natural event, either in the series of modes of extension or in that of those of "thought". In a world which is simply a complicated chain of events, or a number of such chains, and nothing more, there is no room for right and wrong themselves, and therefore, of course, no room for a choice of right simply as right.

That Spinoza himself was alive to this seems to be proved by his assertion that the true antithesis is not between *free* and *necessitated,* but between *free* and *fortuitous* (*Ep.* 56, cf. *Ep.* 58). His purpose is, of course, to make free action one special case of necessitated action, the case in which the necessitation arises not from without, but from the internal constitution of the agent. But the result of drawing the distinction in these terms is that one would have to class together as equally 'free' acts which are done to gratify an over-mastering passion (the very kind of acts from which the precepts of the *Ethics* are meant to deliver us) and acts which are done for the sake of their goodness or rightness. When a man has to say to himself, as the sole justification of his acts, *sit pro ratione voluntas,* he is exhibiting an example of the very thing which Spinoza himself calls *servitus humana*; when he acts 'from the dictate of reason' he is exemplifying *libertas*, but equally in both cases he acts *nullo cogente*. Yet morally the two actions are as far asunder as the poles, and this is why I believe that the mere description of man as an *automaton spirituale* will never satisfy any thinker who, like Kant, takes the moral law seriously. Any account of moral freedom which is to be acceptable to any one who is at once clear-headed and in earnest about morality must somehow involve the recognition of *indetermination; so far*, it seems to me, Descartes was manifestly in the right.

Where the indeterminist moralist is in danger of going wrong, I should say, is not in frankly treating indetermination as a fact, but in an elementary mistake about the nature of the fact. What is indispensable to ethics is that there should be for each of us a sphere—however hard it may be to specify its precise boundary—of *fully imputable* acts, and that, within that sphere, there should be no complete determination of any act by the series of past acts and past events; whenever I do an act which is fully imputable to me, it remains undetermined which of the alternatives open to me will be adopted until *I* determine what I will do. My fully imputable actions are not even determined (*ad unum*) by past imputable acts; they are, in the last resort, determined by me, and I am other than the series of my past acts. But this does not mean that I determine them without a *motive*; motiveless willing is the merest fiction, the *motive* is the recognition of the act determined upon as 'best', or as 'obligatory'. The libertarian who knows his business will not attempt to prove that the 'free choice' has no motive, but he will insist on the radical distinction in character between determination by 'motives' and the kind of determination by antecedent events, which is what is meant when we talk about 'causation' in natural science. To say that I now do *A* rather than leave it undone *because* I now judge *A* to be what it is obligatory on me to do presupposes that, however narrowly my choice may be circumscribed as a consequence of the past, there really *is* now an open alternative before me 'to do *A* or to leave *A* undone'; which of the two lines of action shall be followed has *not* been settled by my past or by the past of the whole universe; it is precisely what I have now to settle, and to settle for myself. It is only in the actions of persons that we meet with clear evidence of the reality of such a situation, and, as Kant saw, the only convincing evidence that we meet with it there is just our moral conviction of the *obligatoriness* of morally right action. No philosophy which begins by confusing a personal agent with the series of his acts, or, like Spinoza's, defines his mind as a 'complex idea', can consistently recognise this evidence, and no such philosophy, therefore, can construct a genuine ethics without deserting its own professed principles, any more than Hobbes could succeed, on his professed principles, in establishing the proposition, which is vital to his whole moral doctrine, that men absolutely ought 'to perform their covenants'. For that reason it has long seemed to me that the real imperishable service of Kant to philosophy is to be looked for not in the confused and self-contradictory epistemology of the first *Critique*, but in his triumphant reassertion, against all the superficialities of the eighteenth century, of the significance and implications of the idea of moral obligation and his elucidation of the meaning of a good will.

It is said, of course, that so long as we remain at the level of obligation we are still concerned only with *mere* morality, and that the truly religious man has transcended all such *mere* morality. He has substituted the higher motive of love for that of cold duty. Now I have no quarrel with the view that in a worthy religion morality is transfigured, and, if you like to say so, transcended. But to transfigure morality is one thing, to ignore it quite another, and too much of the modern 'idealism' which draws deeply upon at any rate *Pt.* V. of Spinoza's *Ethics* seems to me to be merely ignoring morality when it supposes itself to have transcended it. It supposes itself to have risen above the ethical sphere by disparaging *Moralität* in favour of something which is called *Sittlichkeit*, but proves on examination to be no more than the apotheosis of the supreme Antichrist, the 'totalitarian State'. 'Free conscience', because not infallible, is vilified in the interests of the conscienceless will of a dictator or group of dictators, and thus we are left with an immoral 'morality' and an 'idolatrous' religion.

Spinoza was himself protected from excess of this kind by his personal sincere adherence to the principles of a free constitution; *he* was no worshipper of Napoleons. But one can see the moral mischief beginning even in him when he tells us, for example, in the *Tractatus Theologico-Politicus*[5] that though forgiveness of injuries would be right in a state of nature, in civil society it becomes a 'pious' act

[5] C. 19, pium est ei qui mecum contendit, et meam tunicam vult capere, pallium etiam dare; at ubi judicatur hoc reipublicae conservationi perniciosum esse, pium contra est eum in judicium vocare, *tametsi mortis damnandus sit.*

to prosecute any one who has 'taken my cloak' even to death, if the
State in which I live has provided 'hanging laws' for the purpose.
The State is here beginning to usurp the place of common humanity, and I could wish that the philosopher could have profited by the
indignant language in which Cromwell, in his own life-time, remon-
strated with his Parliament on the barbarity of the contemporary
laws of England. It is worse still that, as we all know, Spinoza should
have openly proclaimed that any State may at any moment and
without warning of any kind, violate all its most solemn engage-
ments to another purely from consideration of its own convenience
(*Tractatus Politicus, c.* 3). I would commend the whole chapter of
the *Tractatus Politicus* in which this State immoralism is inculcated
to the serious meditations of any one who is tempted to hope much
for mankind from a religion founded on an 'intellectual love of
God' which transcends moral obligation by simply ignoring it.

It is the more important not to lose sight of these deliverances because the stress laid in the *Ethics* on the thought that *homo* (so far
as he is led by the 'dictate of reason') is *homini deus* tends to make
us forget that the *homines* who behave so handsomely to one another are, after all, only those who happen to be connected by common subjection to the same sovereign, they are *concives,* and according to Spinoza's own explanations, any man who is not my *concivis*
is a *hostis* outside the sphere of rights. (*Tractatus Politicus, c.* 3,
*homines enim in statu naturali hostes sunt; qui igitur Jus Naturae
extra civitatem retinent hostes manent.*)[6] As far as the words go, this
is, to be sure, no more than the well-known doctrine of Hobbes. But
there is the very real difference that Hobbes obstinately holds to his
declaration that it is a 'law of nature' that men perform their covenants, and that even in the 'state of nature', this obligation is binding in *foro interno,* that is, it is a matter of conscience to *endeavour*
to fulfil it, though not always binding *in foro externo* (not always to
be acted on without qualification), whereas Spinoza simply ignores
the obligation in *foro interno.* In practice this would work out to a
real difference. Hobbes is only saying that where there is nothing
but my own wit and my own arm to protect me, I must judge for
myself whether the conduct of another justifies me in going back,
for my own self-preservation, on a promise I have made, and this

---

[6] *Cf. Tractatus Theologico-Politicus, c.* 16. Hostis est quicumque extra civitatem
ita vivit ut neque ut confoederatus, neque ut subditus, imperium civitatis
agnoscat.

is no more than any moralist might concede in the case, for example, of a solitary Briton or Frenchman surrounded by a tribe of savages. A man in such a case must do for himself what he would not be entitled to do in a settled society, judge for himself whether the presumption of *mala fides* in the other party cancels the moral obligation originated by his promise. Spinoza is tacitly legitimating unlimited deceit and bad faith towards any one who is "outside the pale". Hence I cannot but agree with Prof. Laird that Spinoza's *theory*—his practice would, no doubt, have been much better—is tainted by a *wickedness* from which Hobbes, as his fellow-countrymen may be glad to recognise, is entirely free. The maxim *nulla fides haeretico praestanda* may conceivably—I do not know—have originally had an innocent meaning; the thought may have been that I should never trust the heretic's word without substantial guarantees, because I can have no assurance that *he* respects the same ultimate "sanctions" as I do. But whatever the original meaning of the maxim, it became one of the most abominable principles of the worst kind of ecclesiastic, and Spinoza has adopted it, in its full extent, and enlarged its scope by making it apply to any man whose political allegiance is other than my own. By an entertaining irony of history the ardent defender of the 'liberty of prophesying', whose *Tractatus Theologico-Politicus* was undertaken as an *apologia* for the broadest toleration, has also supplied the 'totalitarian State' with the standing defence of its fanatical particularism.

I do not make these remarks in the interests of a narrowly 'deontological' conception of ethics. I should myself be the first to admit that our sense of obligation itself is due in the end to the drawing power of good recognised for what it is, that it is the ἀγαθόν which is also the δέον. What I am contending for is not any *independence* of the notion of *right* as against that of *good*, but the impossibility of separating the two. It is, I should say, characteristic of the morally good to be obligatory, and any professed account of it which leaves this feature of it out of account is at once discredited.[7] You cannot even reduce the good to the *desirable*, unless you are careful to explain that by the *desirable* you mean not that which *can* be desired, but that which *cannot but be desired* by sane and properly informed minds; the further reduction of *good* to the *actually desired* at-

---

[7] *Cf.* M. C. D'Arcy, *Thomas Aquinas*, p. 230. "The good for man must appeal to him as his duty, for the reason that he is possessed of a mind and will which of their natures move in the world of the absolute."

tempted by Spinoza, as by so many others, is positively preposterous, unless its meaning is completely transformed by the explanation that no man knows, except in the vaguest way, what it is that he actually desires, while most men suppose themselves to be desiring what in reality they do not desire. If it is a fact that all of us desire the good, as Socrates and Plato held, it is no less a fact that many of the things most of us believe ourselves to desire are actually bad. A moral philosophy of the naturalistic type, professing to found itself upon empirical fact, cannot, of course, treat of *unconscious* desires as ascertained facts; at most it can only allow itself to speculate about them as an unverifiable imaginative hypothesis. The ascertained and certain "facts" from which it starts must be statements about what men suppose themselves to desire and say that they desire, and if many of these supposed objects of desire are, as they certainly are, evil, such a moral philosophy is bound to go wrong from the outset.

And now what is to be said about the concluding section of the *Ethics,* the famous doctrine of the "intellectual love of God" and the deathlessness which that love confers on a certain 'part' of the mind? In the first place, I fully admit the contention of Martineau that the strict logic of Spinozism requires us to hold that this 'love' (though it is said to be 'part of the infinite intellectual love with which God loves himself', and even spoken of as a 'love of God for man') does not exist in God 'as infinite', but only as 'constituting this or that finite mind', and would thus seem to mean no more than that content or delight which the human thinker derives from his passionless insight into truth, and that its 'eternity' similarly should only mean that while we are engaged in the contemplation of scientific truth, we are lifted into a region in which we forget our concern with our own personal destinies. But it seems to me no less clear that, whether his own logic can justify him or not, Spinoza really meant more than this; he did suppose himself to have found in the doctrine a message of personal hope for himself. This comes out plainly enough in the fact that, though for obvious reasons he makes a point of avoiding the word *immortality,* with its suggestions of survival, in favour of the term *eternity,* he does incidentally allow himself to talk of 'deathlessness', and a 'part of the mind which cannot be *destroyed',* and what is this but to give back with one hand what he has taken away with the other?

And there is an obvious difficulty which Martineau and those

who agree with him in accepting a minimising exegesis of the famous propositions never really face. It should be clear that the
eternity ascribed to a 'part' of the thinker's mind cannot be simply
the same thing as the eternity which Spinoza, like Descartes and
Leibniz, attributes to scientific truths as such. In the sense in which
the Pythagorean theorem can be said to be an *aeterna veritas,* the
same thing can be said about any proposition which is really true.
True statements about the mind subject to the domination of the
passions are no less *aeternae veritates* than true propositions about
the mind which has emancipated itself. If all that were meant by
the eternity of that 'part of the mind' which has adequate knowledge, were that 'timelessly true' propositions can be made about it,
there would be no reason why this eternity should be treated as a
prerogative of one particular part of the mind, or why it should be
represented as something only to be won by a life of arduous mental
and moral discipline. In any case, then, something more than this
must be intended. But what? Martineau has, I think, tried to answer
the question, but his solution comes only to this, that the true
thought, once conceived, persists indefinitely as a thought in some
one's mind, though not necessarily in the mind of any particular
person. Thus the mind of Newton may long have ceased to function,
but the Binomial Theorem remains, and will remain, a truth entertained by the minds of all mathematicians, and this is all that Spinoza means by his language about deathlessness. He means only that
my thoughts, so far as they are true, persist in God as 'constituting
the *essentia* of *some* human mind'.[8]

Now I admit at once that, owing to Spinoza's neglect to distinguish the concipient from the *conceptum* and the *conceptio,* there
is a standing equivocation in his use of the expression 'the mind of
X'; he never seems to be clear whether he means the propositions
entertained as true by X, or the X who so entertains them, and this
would make it very easy for him to talk of the survival of Newton's
thought as though it were the same thing as the survival of the
thinker. And yet I feel, and I think reasonably feel, a difficulty in
supposing that this is all that he intends. For it simply is not true,
and I should have thought that even a thinker of the optimistic
'century of genius' must have known it not to be true, that a true
proposition once discovered must persist continuously and indefi-

[8] *Types of Ethical Theory,*[2] I, 381.

nitely in being entertained by all posterity. Can Spinoza not have known that a truth may be discovered only to be lost again?

I may take as an illustration the case of some of the propositions about numbers enunciated by Fermat.[9] Some of these, as I am given to understand by mathematical friends, remain to this day un-demonstrated, though believed to be true. In other words it is be-lieved that they can be proved, though no one knows what the proof is. Let us suppose then, what I take it is at least possible, that one of these propositions is true and that Fermat had a proof of it which he never made known. (In the early years of the nineteenth century, Legendre writes about one such theorem as one which may well be true though no successor of Fermat has ever succeeded in demon-strating it in its complete generality.) [10] If, then, Fermat's theorem is true, his knowledge of that truth did not persist endlessly, though in some other mind than that of Fermat; that 'part of his mind' did not escape the doom of destruction by death.

On the other side, it is not only truths but 'vulgar errors' which enjoy a persistence of this kind. No one has been more emphatic than Spinoza in insisting that *fieri non potest* that men should get rid of 'inadequate ideas'. He certainly regarded the belief in our own freedom, for example, as a mere illusion due to our ignorance, until enlightened by a philosophy like his own, of the causes of our acts. Equally certainly he held that this ignorance with the conse-quent false belief in our freedom, is an inevitable and incurable consequence of our situation in the universe. The truest thinking of Galileo or Newton is, at best, no more 'eternal' than the vulgar error of believing in freedom. Once more, then, with what right, on Mar-

---

[9] For example, take the proposition that if a, b, c be integers the equation $a^n + b^n = c^n$ is always false if $n > 2$. This is, I understand, believed to be true, but no general proof is known, though Fermat said that he had discovered a *demonstratio mirabilis* (Peano, *Formulario*, II § 9.4).

[10] Legendre, *Théorie des nombres*, 204–206. The theorem specially discussed here is Fermat's proposition that any integer can be represented as the sum of not more than three 'triangular' numbers. Legendre says that while he knows of no proof of this, it may be considered as probably true, because one can from it immediately deduce the known and demonstrable consequence that any integer can be represented as the sum of not more than four squares. But Fermat's lan-guage, as quoted by Legendre, shows that *he* believed himself to be able to demonstrate the primary proposition itself. It would be no way out to suggest that the knowledge of such a truth survives in the *infinitus intellectus Dei;* that is, for Spinoza, a 'creature' with no existence apart from that of individual minds.

tineau's interpretation, does Spinoza make *eternity* a prerogative in particular of *true* thinking?

He can only do so, as it seems to me, if he intends to ascribe 'indestructibility by death' not simply to the true thought, but to the mind which thinks it. If that is his meaning, we can understand him. For if it is true that he who has a true idea *knows* that he has it, error and prejudice may be as perennial in the human species as truth, and truth may only be discovered by a solitary thinker to be lost again by his successors, but for the thinker who has found a truth, what he has found is henceforth a genuine possession; if he, in some way, persists, and not otherwise, the possession is really a κτῆμα εἰς ἀεί. Such considerations lead me to think that Spinoza really meant to ascribe an eternity which may not be exhausted by, but yet includes, persistence in despite of death to the individual mind, or rather to that 'part of it' which thinks. (His phraseology, we must remember, comes to him from Maimonides, and Maimonides, in turn, clearly took it from Aristotle's mysterious words in *de Anima III*. about the imperishability of the *intellectus agens*. And whatever Aristotle may have meant by his few broken phrases, there is really nothing in them to suggest that he regarded the *intellectus agens* as detachable from the individual person. He says, indeed, in the *de Generatione Animalium* that it 'comes from outside', but that only means that it is not derived by generation from a man's parents, and is, in fact, just as much a part of the philosophy of Plato as of that of Aristotle.)

But if Spinoza really meant what it seems to me he must have meant, he is breaking away here from the very foundations of his own doctrine. Manifestly he does so when he converts the intellectual love of God into a 'part' of an infinite love of God for Himself. On an interpretation like Martineau's this 'infinite' love can, of course, only 'exist in God' as 'constituting the *essentiae* of particular minds', and will mean simply the summed devotion of countless such minds to truth. But the truth-lover's devotion to truth can hardly be described intelligibly as a devotion to *himself*. The meaning would have to be that I, who am a finite 'mode' of God, love God, not in so far as God is the finite mode which I call myself, but precisely in so far as God is envisaged as the absolute 'substance', as being what I am *not*. And it is of God precisely as *absolute infinitus* that we are told in V. 35 that he *gaudet infinita perfectione,* and that *concomitante idea sui.* That is, this intellectual love belongs to God not as *natura naturata* but as *natura naturans,* for it is only as *natura naturans* that God is "absolutely" infinite. (Even the *infinitus intellectus Dei,* being a mode of one particular attribute, could only be said to be infinite *in suo genere.*) Thus if Spinoza is to be taken at his word the 'infinite intellectual love of Himself' belongs to God, or should belong to God, as the *author* of nature, though this would not really be strictly consistent with the earlier declarations that the *infinitus intellectus* itself belongs to *natura naturata,* and is a mode 'produced' by God, who Himself *has* not *intellectus,* but merely produces *intellectus* in the 'creatures'. But a God who *has intellectus,* and feels a *gaudium* 'with a concomitant idea of Himself as its cause' is a *personal* God. You really cannot have it both ways. If you are going to admire Spinoza for his account of this intellectual love of God for Himself, you must be prepared to believe in a Deity who has both *intellectus* and *voluntas.* If you are to admire him for his superiority to the 'vulgar prejudice' which attributes understanding and will to God, you must deny the very existence of the 'intellectual love' *as* Spinoza describes it. For, as I have said, if the phrase means nothing more than that *I* feel a peculiar "thrill" when I know the truth and know that I know it, that "joy" is not accompanied with an 'idea of *myself* as its cause'. I am, according to the theory, 'God as constituting the idea of a particular body', but it is *not* to God as constituting the idea of that body that 'absolute perfection' belongs. (And Spinoza indicates this plainly enough by appealing to his definition of *ens absolute infinitum* for the proof of his proposition.)

Where there is already so utter a failure in consistency, it becomes by comparison a secondary contradiction that the God who loves Himself with an infinite intellectual love has already been declared (V. 17 and Corr.) incapable of feeling pleasure or pain and therefore incapable of loving or hating anything. If it was to escape from making *this* contradiction too glaring that Spinoza avoided using the word *laetitia* in connection with the love of God for Himself, and preferred to speak of *gaudium,* he cannot well be said to have mended matters, for the *definition* propounded of gaudium in the appendix to *Pt.* III. (§ 16) had made *gaudium* a subspecies of *laetitia,* and a subspecies particularly hard to attribute to God (whether God be understood in the Theist's sense or in that of *Ethics* I.). *Gaudium* had been said to be '*laetitia* accompanied by the idea of a matter in the past which has fallen out beyond one's hopes'. But be the mind which entertains the idea of God as the absolutely infinite substance whose mind it may, the thought of that substance is not the thought of an unexpected stroke of past good fortune. (It is, to be sure, a very minor fault that by the time Spinoza had reached the end of his book he had forgotten his own definition of *gaudium* given in the middle of it. I only remark on the point because the psychological accuracy of the philosopher has been almost as much over-rated as his supposed logical rigour. Spinoza's empirical psychology is full of good things, but it has its full share of internal discrepancies and distortions of fact, if any one cares to take the trouble to look for them.)

The one point of capital importance in connection with the famous concluding section of the *Ethics* on which I want to insist is simply that somehow the conception of God with which the treatise opened, and to which it adhered faithfully enough down to the middle of *Pt.* V. is wholly transformed when we come to V. 35. If it is mainly on the strength of that proposition and those which follow it that a man admires Spinoza—and I believe that it is just these pages of the *Ethics* which have done most to foster the attitude of Spinoza-worship—it is not for his eminence as a rigidly logical thinker that he is admiring him, but rather for his refusal to be logical. He is being revered for a personal religious faith which he entertains to the ruin of his whole metaphysical construction. It is just those critics who, like Martineau, will allow Spinoza no 'extra-belief' going beyond what his metaphysical postulates can justify, who revere him least, and I think they are in the right from their own standpoint. In many respects (not in all, for he has his share of the bitternesses of the fanatic) one cannot admire Spinoza's personality more than it deserves. But I am not sure that Spinozism, as a pretended coherent metaphysical doctrine, does not deserve the hardest things which have ever been said about it. After all, when these unfavourable verdicts are translated into strictly philosophical and passionless language, they amount to no more than this, that Spinozism is a metaphysic built up in blind reliance on a misconceived "mathematical method" which starts from 'high abstractions' as its foundations and consequently can never reach anything else in its conclusions. And this, as Tschirnhaus seems to have perceived at the time, is no more than the truth.

Spinoza and the Idea
of Freedom

Stuart Hampshire

I BELIEVE THAT everyone who has ever written about Spinoza, and who has tried to interpret his thought as a whole, either has been, or ought to have been, uneasily aware of some partiality in his interpretation, when he turns once again from his own words to the original. Certainly this is my own position. When the study of Spinoza is reviewed historically, one sees that each commentator, unconsciously faithful to his own age and to his own philosophical culture, has seized upon some one element in Spinoza's thought; he then proceeds to develop the whole of the philosophy from this single centre. Spinoza as the critic of Cartesianism: Spinoza as the free-thinker and destroyer of Judaeo-Christian theology: Spinoza as the pure deductive metaphysician: Spinoza as the near-mystic, who imagines a level of intuitive understanding beyond discursive reason: lastly, Spinoza as the scientific determinist, who anticipates the more crude materialists, and the more crude secular moralists, of the nineteenth century: as the precursor of George Henry Lewes. All these masks have been fitted on him and each of them does to some extent fit. But they remain masks, and not the living face. They do not show the moving tensions and unresolved conflicts in Spinoza's *Ethics*. They remain interpretations that have been imposed from outside. They smooth over and cover up the opposing strains within the original thought. His writing has a hard, finished, unyielding surface. One can return to it again and again without ever being sure that one has penetrated to the centre of his intentions. He could only state; he could not loosely explain, or betray his intentions in an approximation. Yet I have the persisting feeling—I cannot yet properly call it a belief—that in the philosophy of mind he is nearer to the truth at certain points than any other philosopher ever has been. I do not therefore propose historical accuracy and historical justice as motives for returning

once again to the original *Ethics* at one of its most difficult points
Rather I believe that there is something very relevant to moral and
political philosophy at this time to be learnt from an entirely literal, unprejudiced, and uncondescending attention to Spinoza's
idea of freedom. Perhaps his conception of freedom is after all a
valid one; and perhaps we are now in a better position than our
ancestors to find the true significance of it.

The two most obvious facts about Spinoza are the two most important facts in understanding his intentions: first, that his defin-
itive philosophical work was justly called *Ethics*: second, that the
only evaluative distinction finally recognized in his philosophy,
other than the distinctions between true and false, and between adequate and inadequate, ideas, is the distinction between freedom
and servitude. These are the terms, positive and negative, in which
a man, and a man's life, his actions and passions, are to be finally
judged. These are the terms in which a wise man reviews and
criticizes his own conduct, his own emotions and attitudes, and it
is by reference to this contrast that he will, if he is wise, make his
own decisions. A man is wise in proportion as his thought at all
times proceeds by active reasoning from premisses that are well
known to him as self-evident truths. These self-evident truths are
necessarily available to him, as instruments for his enlightenment,
among the many confused and inadequate ideas that he must also
have. They are necessarily available to every thinking being, as the
reflections in his thought of the universal and unchanging features
of the natural order of extended things. His inadequate ideas reflect
only his particular and temporary standpoint as one extended thing
among others. If once he concentrates his attention on these timeless truths, independent of his own standpoint and perceptions, and
argues carefully from them, he cannot help coming to the conclusion
that human conduct has to be judged, and his own decisions made,
by reference to this single standard, the standard of freedom of
mind as opposed to servitude of mind; and he will unavoidably
agree that the distinction between freedom and its opposite is the
distinction between active reasoning, internally determined, and
the mind's passive reception of ideas impressed upon it from without.

'He cannot help coming to the conclusion', 'He will unavoidably
agree that it *must* be interpreted'—here already there are the signs
of necessity. As soon as we start to argue strictly, these and other

signs of necessity will always enter in. As will be seen later, these
marks of necessity, rightly understood and in the appropriate context, are the marks of freedom and activity of mind. The mind is
active and free when, and only when, the argument is strict, when
the conclusion of a passage of thought is internally determined by
the thinking process itself. A man whose attention has been drawn
to self-evident, primary truths, the terms of which he understands,
will unavoidably follow a continuous train of thought and will unavoidably affirm the necessary conclusions. If he fully understands,
he has no choice. If he has a choice, and if he can doubt and hesitate until he settles the matter by a decision, his conclusion will be
determined, at least in part, by something that is external to the
thinking process itself.

Some of these primary truths are concerned with the notion of
cause or of explanation, in the widest sense of these words. In the
widest sense of the word 'cause', anything that is an appropriate
answer to the question 'Why?' gives a cause, irrespective of the
category to which the thing to be explained belongs. The question
'Why?' may, for example, be asked with reference to a belief, a
human action, a human attitude or sentiment, the existence of a
physical object, or the properties of numbers and geometrical figures.
Anything that counts as an answer to the question 'Why?" is an explanation, whether true or false, of the belief, action, attitude, sentiment, physical object, or mathematical entity. In the vocabulary that
Spinoza inherited, the word 'cause' can be substituted for the word
'explanation', without prejudging any questions about the type of
explanation appropriate to these different cases. The distinguishing
of different types, or categories, of causes, which is the distinguishing
of different types or categories of explanation, has always been the
proper work of philosophy, and of that reflexive knowledge that is
peculiar to philosophy. Spinoza draws these distinctions between
types of explanation in the *Ethics,* adapting an inherited scholastic
vocabulary for his own purpose.

Let us assume the standpoint of an individual thinker, a finite
mode, with his necessarily limited knowledge. Reflecting on the
range of his knowledge, he will find at least one clear distinction:
the distinction between an understanding of causes that is complete
and self-justifying, and an understanding of causes that is not complete and self-justifying. There are ideas in reference to which the
question 'Why is it so?' receives a complete answer, in the sense
that, in looking for the explanation, we arrive at self-evident truths,

and definitions, in a finite number of steps. There are other ideas in reference to which the question 'Why is it so?' leads us back along an infinite series of ideas, with no final and sufficient explanation to be found within the series, however long we continue. So much is common to Leibniz and Spinoza. They diverge when they specify the limits of application of the two orders of explanation, the complete and the incomplete. For Spinoza the fundamental difference between the two orders of causes is the difference between the series of eternal things and the series of things that come into existence and pass away at a certain time. There is no further difference between the two orders of explanation which is not entailed by this primary difference. There is no ultimate contingency in the existence of things in the common order of nature, no contingency imputable to a creator's free choice among logically possible alternatives. The difference is only between that which is eternal and that which is finite in its existence. The existence of things that are not eternal, and that occupy a determinate position in the time-order, can only be incompletely explained. There must always be an infinite regress of causes required to explain why this particular thing exists at this particular time. The existence of this thing was contingent upon the prior existence of some other thing and so on *ad infinitum*. No limit can be set on the universe of individual things that come into existence and pass away. But there are objects conceived as eternal things, about which it does not make sense to ask when they came into existence and when they will perish: numbers, for example, or the whole of extended Nature, which can be referred to as a thing, as *Res extensa*. About such things an explanation can be given of why their properties must be ordered as they are, an explanation that will terminate in self-evident, primary propositions defining the nature of the objects referred to.

This distinction between the two orders of explanation, the two kinds of answer to 'Why is it so?', the temporal and the non-temporal order, corresponds to Leibniz's distinction between truths of reason and truths of fact, and also to familiar post-Kantian distinctions between analytic and synthetic propositions. But it is a different distinction, not the same distinction with a different label. Every philosopher has to draw some similar line between the two types of knowledge. As the chosen ground of distinction differs, the line will fall in a different place and will suggest different groupings and exclusions. Spinoza expresses the distinction, not only as a distinction between different types of object, eternal things and finite things, but also as a distinction between the ways in which any given subject-matter can be studied. Whether we are inquiring into human emotions, including our own emotions, or into the nature and movements of physical objects, we can always, if we choose, look for the eternally valid laws that explain the variety of human emotions and the movements of physical objects. We can always regard the particular case of an emotion or of a physical movement, occurring at exactly this time and soon to disappear, as an instance, or illustration, of a constant, unchanging pattern. Such a pattern has its own ultimate explanation in the permanent structure of things. We can always regard the thing to be explained *sub specie aeternitatis,* without attention to the date on which it occurred, or to the standpoint from which it was observed, and not *sub specie durationis,* which would involve explaining its place in the time order that leads up to this particular occasion. If we are interested only in ourselves and in our own environment, and therefore in the occurrence of the emotion, or of the physical movement, at this particular time, and if we wish to trace the causes in their historical sequence up to this moment, we will of course need to invoke the eternally valid laws in looking for the historical explanation of this particular case. But the interest is then an historical interest, and this is an interest that can never be finally satisfied. Some uncertainty will always attach to any historical explanation that we attempt. Some of the infinitely numerous factors, which should ideally have been mentioned, have always eluded us. We fall into error, and an error that has serious consequences in our practical activities, if we do not always bear in mind the intrinsic difference between the two types of explanation, the two orders of causes, the intellectual order and the common order of nature. We must always be aware of the incompleteness and necessary uncertainty of any historical explanation of things in the common order of nature. Intellectually, the error is to take some cause picked out from the temporal sequence of events and to concentrate our attention upon it as *the* cause, and then to suppose that we can know that, if only this had been different, which it might have been, the effect would never have followed. Then it will seem to us contingent that things happened as they did. But the appearance of contingency is due to the necessary limitation of our knowledge, to our incapacity to follow to its conclusion every path of investi-

gation, where the paths are infinitely many. When we isolate some
one cause as the sole object of interest, and think of it as something
that really might have been different, we are simply failing to
realize the infinite complexity of the connexions between things in
the temporal order. Practically and morally, the corresponding error
will be to love or to hate with blind concentration the particular
thing which, through weakness of mind, has become isolated in our
thought from the infinitely complex network in the common order
of nature. Instead of being detached and sceptical in reflecting on
the infinite complexity of the causes, we shall be uncritically certain
that we have identified the original good or evil within our own
environment. We shall therefore for a time tend to act as if our
welfare depended solely on the destruction or preservation of this
particular thing. Our conduct will for a time correspondingly exhibit the same blind and helpless partiality, the same imaginative
obsession with one thing, suggested to us by our environment, as the
true cause of our present pleasure or suffering.

Most men spend their lives in an alternation between one object and another as the temporary object of desire or aversion,
absorbed in their own partial view of their own environment, and
unable to see this environment, and their own passive reactions to
it, as formed by a concatenation of causes that extends infinitely in
every direction. They have therefore no consistent plan, no stable
and central direction of their interests. This alternation of desires,
this fluctuation of the mind, is the state of fantasy, obsession, and
unenlightenment. The mind is then to a greater or less degree disintegrated, in the sense that the succession of its states is not determined by the subject's own activity of thought. Their states of
mind are only to be explained as more or less unconnected responses of their imagination to the stimulus of the environment,
which evokes desires and aversions that have no adequate foundation in the subject's own directed reasoning. This condition of un-
freedom, of slavery to the passions, is the equivalent in Spinoza of
the heteronomy of the will in Kant. But it is not an enslavement
of the will, but rather of the understanding. The remedy is the
correction of the understanding and an appeal to its natural powers.
The remedy is available to everyone who is able to reflect upon,
and who never forgets, the two levels of explanation, the two orders
of causes, and therefore the two kinds of knowledge which each
man necessarily possesses. As long as a man is reflectively aware,

whenever he thinks, of the nature of his own thought, as either actively directed towards eternal and demonstrable truths, or else as absorbed in uncriticized fantasies traceable to his own sensations and memories, he is not misled either in that which he claims to know with certainty, or in that which he considers desirable or undesirable, as good or bad. He will reflectively examine the reasons for his own desires and aversions, and he will distinguish those that are to be explained as the effects of events on his imagination, from those that are explained by an active consideration, independent of his own situation, of the tendency of an object to serve the purposes common to all thinking beings as such. Because he knows when he truly knows and when he only incompletely knows, he always knows when he has an entirely sufficient reason for his actions and attitudes, and when he has not. As he is by nature an active thinking being, he will prefer the type of explanation of things that is complete and intellectually satisfying when it is presented to him. As a body naturally tends to maintain itself, and restore itself, against the effects of the environment, so correspondingly a mind tends to assert its power of thought, and to prefer rational argument, whenever it is presented, to the passive association of ideas in the common order of nature. But we need to be awakened to the recognition and the use of the powers that our minds possess. This is part of the work of a philosopher, which includes, as in the example of Spinoza's own writing, exhortation, a call to reflection, alongside purely intellectual analysis.

Perhaps this picture of the free man as self-directing, as an integrated mind with a continuous controlling reason, is so far a clear one. But the notion of freedom itself is still unclarified: what is the precise connexion between a man's knowledge of the distinction between different levels of knowledge and his freedom in action? The connexion is to be found in Spinoza's theory of individuals. Like every other identifiable particular thing in the natural order, a man tries in his characteristic activity to preserve himself and his own distinct nature as an individual, and to increase his own power and activity in relation to his environment. This trying, (*conatus*), or inner force of self-preservation, is that which makes any individual an individual. Regarded as a physical organism, his overriding interest is to preserve his own stability as a distinct organism in relation to the physical environment. Regarded as a thinking being, his overriding interest is to preserve the coherence and continuity of his own thought against the flow of unconnected ideas which are his perceptions, sensations, and imaginations. The conatus of the individual, conceived as a physical organism, is the body's tendency to repair itself and to maintain itself in relation to the environment. The conatus of the individual, conceived as a thinking being, is the *vis animi*, which is the essential and natural tendency of the mind to assert active thinking and knowledge against the passive association of ideas in imagination. The more the sequence of a man's own ideas can be explained without reference to causes outside his own thinking, the more active and self-determining he is, regarded as a thinking being. The more active and self-determining he is, to that degree also he can be more properly regarded as a distinct thing, having an individuality that sets him apart from his particular environment. The more self-determining and active he is, and the more free, in this sense of 'free', the more he can be regarded as a real individual, as real as an individual thinking being.

Because a thing's reality as a distinct individual depends on its activity and freedom, Spinoza must take the word 'free', rather than the word 'good', as the fundamental term of evaluation. He is a scholastic and an Aristotelian in taking it for granted that praise and evaluation of a thing are necessarily an assessment of the degree to which it realizes its nature or essence in its activity. The nearer a thing approaches perfection in the activity proper to it, the more praiseworthy it is. He takes the virtue, objectively regarded, of any thing to be the same as the perfect realization of its nature. But, unlike Aristotle, he identifies the essential nature of any individual thing with its individuality, with that which makes it a distinct individual: and this is its power of self-maintenance in relation to other things. Its virtue is its power as an individual. A particular thing's nature or essence is its nature or essence as a distinct individual rather than as a specimen of a kind. Peter or Paul are therefore not to be judged as being more or less good men, that is, as realizing more or less completely the potentialities of their species. They are to be judged as more or less complete individuals, that is, as more or less distinguishable as active agents from the temporary influences of their environment in the common order of nature. A man's natural tendency or conatus is not to make himself a good or perfect specimen of his kind, to realize in his activity some general ideal of humanity, but rather to preserve himself, this individual, as

an active being, who is, as far as possible, independent in his activity. He has achieved virtue, and succeeded in that which he necessarily desires, when, and only when, he is comparatively free and
self-determining in his activity. He would be a perfect being, if he
were perfectly self-determining, active, and free. His happiness, and
enjoyment of action, does not depend on a choice of ends of action
that he, as an individual, has to make and that he is free to make:
the choice of whether to pursue the ideal of excellence that is
proper to his species. In the last analysis, and speaking philosophically, there is no such choice of an ideal or end. Philosophically
speaking, the choice is of the right means to an end that is already
determined for him by his nature and appetites as an individual
thinking and physical thing. The real choice is between the first
step of reflection, preliminary to the use of his intellectual powers,
and an undirected passive response to experience. His desires, as
they emerge into consciousness, are determined by the thought of
the causes of his pleasure and suffering. If the thought is confused,
and is largely fantasy, he will pursue, *sub specie boni*, temporary
ends, which, by the laws of his nature, must lead to frustration,
instability, and suffering. Therefore he needs to be stirred to take
this first step of reflection. His happiness consists in his sense of his
activities as having their originating cause within him, and in his
enjoyment of his own activity as unimpeded activity. He is frus-
trated, and therefore suffers, when his activity is not self-directed,
but is rather the immediate effect of causes external to himself.
The suffering is the loss of his sense of his own power and vitality
as a distinct and active being.

The notion of an individual nature or essence may be found
altogether obscure. We can, I think, still attach a sense to the
notion of the essential characteristics of a species, and to the judgement of individuals as more or less perfect specimens of their kinds.
But can we intelligibly speak of an individual or particular thing
becoming more or less of an individual? Spinoza provides a criterion by which the approach in perfection of an individual *qua*
individual is to be judged: the criterion is the degree to which the
individual is active and self-determining. Any thing that is identifiable as a particular thing can be judged by this single criterion,
irrespective of the kind to which it is allotted within conventional
classifications. One may review the scale of the increasing activity
and self-determination of particular things, and therefore of their

increasing individuality, from physical objects of various orders of complexity, to living organisms, to human beings. Human beings, at the top of the scale, can be completely self-determining when their activity is continuous thought, with each idea following its predecessor in the intellectual sense of 'follow' as well as in the temporal sense. At such moments—and the moments cannot be indefinitely prolonged—men rise above their normal human condition as finite modes.

In the ordinary vocabulary we conventionally classify things into kinds according to their typical human uses. Spinoza demands that, as moralists and philosophers, we should see through these anthropocentric classifications to the true individuality of particular things. When we group them into kinds, we should follow this single principle in differentiating the kinds: their characteristic power and form of self-maintenance as individuals. From the standpoint of the true natural philosopher, the natural order should be seen as a system of individuals within individuals, of increasing power and complexity, each type of individual differentiated by its characteristic activity in self-maintenance. The more fully we study and understand particular things, not as specimens of the conventionally recognized kinds, but as types of structure each acting and maintaining their identity according to the laws of the type, the more we shall understand Nature as a whole. This is the form in which natural knowledge, objectively valid for the whole of Nature, is properly to be expressed. Psychology as a science can be no exception.

There is one case in which each man is well qualified to achieve such a true understanding of an individual: himself. Starting from this secure example, he can work outwards towards a true and objective understanding of Nature as a whole. He will become dissatisfied with the conventional classifications of things by their ordinary human uses, and he will find a more objective and truly scientific principle of classification in their various modes of self-maintenance. Spinoza's objective study of the emotions, the outline of a psychopathology, illustrates these principles. There are systematic connexions, laws of unconscious memory, to be found behind the conventional classifications of the passions. Systematic knowledge of these is the necessary first step to self-knowledge.

It is now possible to state the connexion between a constant awareness of the distinction between adequate and inadequate knowledge and the notion of freedom. We need to apply the doctrine of the individual as essentially active to a thinking being who is a person. For every belief that I have, and for every claim to knowledge that I make, there is an explanation of why I have this belief and why I claim to have this knowledge. Every passion that can be attributed to me is a pleasure or a pain combined with an idea of the cause of this pleasure or pain. There must therefore be an explanation of my having this idea about the cause of my pleasure or suffering. Suppose then that I am at all times asking myself the question: Is the sequence of ideas that has terminated in this idea a self-contained sequence that, by itself, completely explains my idea of the cause? In other words, was the conclusion reached by a rational process? Or must I mention ideas that are associated in my experience, but that are without intrinsic connexion, in explaining my conclusion? Under these conditions of self-conscious reflection, I never affirm a proposition, or commit myself to a belief, without qualifying it as adequately or inadequately founded. If this condition were fulfilled, I could not be a victim of those passions that consist in the association of my pleasure or suffering with the idea of a particular transient thing, or person, in the common order of nature as its adequate cause. And when I say that I *could* not be a victim of the passion, the impossibility here is a logical impossibility. The unexamined links of association, which are necessary to the belief that is part of the passion, depend for their existence on my not being reflectively aware of them. As soon as I am self-consciously aware of them, I must then know that it is only through the fantasies engendered by my particular history that my present pleasure or suffering has become associated in my mind with the idea of these particular things or persons, which I now in consequence hate or love. If I actively inquire into the true causes of my pleasure or suffering, the passive association of ideas is broken, and the attention focused on the particular thing, or person, as the adequate cause is dissolved. An emotion necessarily involves a thought of the cause or occasion of the pleasure or unpleasure, and it is in this sense directed towards an object. Spinoza's theory of the emotions represents them as states of pleasure or unpleasure, and of desire and aversion, combined with a thought of the causes, simple or complex, of the causes of the pleasure or unpleasure. To change the accompanying thought is therefore to change the emotion, and therefore to change the desire or the aversion that determines conduct. Suppose that I am angry with someone and am angry about something that he has done. To be angry is to be displeased and to be disposed to injure someone, together with the thought that he has been the cause of injury to me. When I consider my true interests as an active thinking being, and also examine a train of unconscious associations that leads to the idea of him as the original cause of my displeasure, and recognize their inadequacy, the passion of anger disappears. When I realize the contributing causes of my displeasure in my own unconscious memories and consequent dispositions, the idea of an adequate external cause disappears, and there is nothing left to be angry with. When on reflection I realize that no one external thing can be isolated as the cause of my displeasure, I not only realize my error in imagining a simple external cause of my state: I open the way to the activity of intellectual inquiry, regarding this particular case wholly as an instance of general laws. I thereby substitute the active enjoyment of my own powers of thought for the suffering associated with my imagination of an adequate external cause of my displeasure.

To interpret Spinoza as expecting emancipation solely from an intellectual understanding of causes is not entirely correct. It is equally incorrect to represent him as defining freedom simply as knowledge of the causes that determine my emotions and actions. Reason is the expression of my primary desire of self-assertion as a thinking being, of the urge to extend my own activity and freedom as far as I can. I am to the highest degree free when I am engaged in an intellectual inquiry, and when the subject of this inquiry is the order of my thought, as an instance of something that may be understood *sub specie aeternitatis,* and not as it is affected by particular causes in the common order of nature. My happiness then consists, first, in immunity from hatred of particular things, and from the other negative and depressive passions, as an immunity that an adequate understanding of causes necessarily brings: secondly, it consists in the positive enjoyment of my own freedom *as* freedom, as the active exercise of the power of thought. These two necessary conditions of happiness, which may be distinguished in other philosophies, are inseparable, even if distinguishable, in Spinoza's thought. He is often represented as implausibly asserting that knowledge of the causes of suffering by itself brings liberation from suffering. This is a double over-simplification. First, the liber-

ation consists in the substitution of a free activity and of self-assertion, which is as such enjoyable, for a passive reaction, which is as
such depressing and frustrating. Secondly, in the definition of any
of the passions the pleasure or suffering, and the thought of its
cause, are indissolubly connected. If the confused thought, or imagination, of an external cause is replaced by thought in an intellectual order, an active emotion replaces a passion.

We may now ask whether, and with what qualifications, this
idea of human freedom is still defensible, and whether it suggests
the true grounds of our present interest in the freedom of the individual as the main end of policy, both in private and political
affairs. Let it be remembered that a man is most free, according to Spinoza, and also feels himself to be most free, when he
cannot help drawing a certain conclusion, and cannot help embarking on a certain course of action in view of the evidently compelling reasons in favour of it. He has a compelling reason for
following a certain course of action when he knows with certainty
that it will promote his power and freedom as an active thinking
being, and therefore that it will promote his enjoyment of his own
existence. Then he cannot hesitate. The issue is decided for him
without any need for the exercise of his will in decision, exactly
as the issue is decided for him when the arguments in support
of a theoretical conclusion are conclusive arguments. The only difference between theoretical conclusions and practical decisions is
that the latter are always governed by the agent's desire for his
own good, rationally or irrationally interpreted. When a man
finds himself divided in mind between conflicting and inconclusive
arguments, and between conflicting inclinations, he is, and feels
himself to be, so much less a free man in his affirmations and in
his actions. In such a case that which has determined his final
decision, whatever it is, must be, at least in part, external to his
own thought. In such cases some explanation could always in principle be given, a cause found in the common order of nature, for his
deciding as he did. But it would not be a complete explanation
of the right kind, namely, something that was present to his mind
as a timelessly sufficient ground. He was moved to affirmation or
action by something that was outside the rational sequence of
thought. He was not entirely active and self-determining, but, at
least in part, unknowing and passive in his motivation, since that
which moved him to action was below the level of conscious thought.

He was not altogether free in his decision, and he knows and feels that he was not, because he did not himself recognize its necessity. When some part of the explanation of my believing something, or of my doing something, is to be found in a cause unrecognized by my reason, and in something external to my thought, I had not sufficient grounds for my belief or action. If I have a full awareness of the adequate explanation of my affirming or acting, I necessarily have sufficient grounds for my affirmation or action. The knowledge of the necessity of affirming something, or of doing something, by itself converts an external cause into an inner ground of affirmation or action. If I know clearly why I believe something or why I am doing something, I must have my own sufficient reasons for affirming or doing. If I cannot completely explain why I reach the conclusion, and if I allow that there are other possibilities open to me, my conclusion, whatever it is, will have been motivated by something other than my own reasoning.

It should now be evident that the too simple question 'Was Spinoza a determinist?' admits of no clear answer. The doctrine of the two orders of causes, the intellectual and the temporal orders, by itself makes the question indeterminate—almost meaningless. But there is a question that always lies behind any mention of 'determinism' and that certainly is worth asking: 'Did Spinoza provide clear and acceptable grounds for familiar moral distinctions? Or is his idea of human freedom incompatible with the acceptance of any familiar moral distinctions?' We cannot answer without considering the concept of morality itself: what kind of classifications of men and of their activities are to be counted as moral classifications, as resting on moral distinctions? There is no philosophically neutral answer to this question. Following Kant, one may distinguish between the moral and natural qualities of men on the basis of some doctrine of the will, which is taken to define the domain of the moral. And there is certainly no place for any such distinction as this in Spinoza's thought. Or one may so restrict the notion of morality that nothing counts as a moral judgement, or as a moral choice, unless the free choice of some specific end, or specific standard, of human activity is prescribed, an end or standard that all men, as men, unconditionally ought to aim to achieve or to conform to. If, following Spinoza, the freedom of the individual, as an individual, is taken as the supreme evaluative term, and not the goodness of a man, as a man, one cannot properly speak of a specific end, or specific standard, of human performance which each man ought to achieve or to conform to. Within the terms of his metaphysical theory, there is no sense in saying that men ought to be free, that they ought to be self-determining, integrated in mind and constant in their desires, and actively rational, in an unconditional sense of 'ought'. The unconditional injunction to them to pursue a certain end implies that they have a choice among various possibilities, and that they may make the wrong choice, unless they are enlightened by the moralist. Philosophically speaking and in the last analysis, they have no such choice of the ultimate ends of action. They are all, the virtuous and the vicious, the enlightened and the unenlightened, in any case trying to survive as active individuals and are trying to assert their power and freedom as individuals. The only question that arises, either in their own decisions or in judgement upon them, is: 'How completely are they succeeding in asserting themselves as self-determining individuals? How can they become more successful than they are in maintaining and extending their own freedom and activity?' Of the ideally free man one can say that he will necessarily have certain virtues— for instance, the virtues of liberality and benevolence. In this sense there is indeed a standard or norm of conduct: that we can specify the dispositions that are inseparable from freedom of mind, and therefore we can specify the essential public and private virtues. Spinoza clearly explains in the Preface to Part IV of the *Ethics*: although the words 'good' and 'bad' indicate nothing positive in the things to which they are applied, we do indeed need to retain them in use, because (I quote) 'we want to form for ourselves an idea of man upon which we may look as a model of human nature'. This is part of the technique of self-improvement, a preparation for the life of reason. And he explains again in Part V that reflection upon maxims of virtue and wise conduct is a useful starting-point for the life of reason. But it is, strictly speaking, a misstatement, a philosophical error of the kind that occurs only in speaking to the unenlightened, to represent the virtues of the free, rational man as duties imposed upon us, or as appropriate matter for unconditional moral imperatives. There is no law, and therefore there are no duties, other than the natural law of self-preservation, which states that we try to extend our power and liberty as far as we can. How far we can, and by what methods of intellectual discipline, is the proper subject of any book that

has the title 'Ethics'. Its conclusions are properly called the dictates
of reason. Most of the duties recognized in conventional morality
are in fact irrational foreshadowings of behaviour that would be
the natural and unconstrained behaviour of a free man. He has his
own adequate reasons for being a peaceful, friendly, just, and
co-operative member of society. He may need to appeal to the myth
of the moral law to persuade the mass of his fellow citizens to co-
operate in civil society. Some of the conventional virtues of civil
society, those associated with renunciation, unworldliness, and re-
pression, are not virtues but vices. They are signs of weakness and
of failure in the individual's realization of his own vitality as an
individual. They have been taken for virtues, when myths of a
transcendent God and of another world have been taken seriously
as metaphysical truths. Preoccupation with death, and with human
weakness, and with the passage of time, rather than with the enjoyment of present activity, are the emotional counterparts of these
false philosophies. In a well-known and significant paragraph
(Scholium to Prop. X in Part V), Spinoza says that the attitude of
the severe moralist, which issues in denunciations of the vices and
vanities of man, and of the common conditions of human life, is
always the mark of a diseased mind. Pathos and virtue are opposed
to each other, because, for Spinoza, virtue is energy—in a rather
more precise sense than Blake intended.

There is therefore a sense in which Spinoza is representing the
study of ethics, in the then dominant Christian and Jewish tradition, as one immense error, as the pursuit of a harmful illusion.
The illusion is that various goals or ends of human effort, towards
which our actions might be directed, are open to us for decision
and for appraisal, and that the discussion and comparison of the
various ends of action is the proper subject-matter of ethics. The
ultimate ends of action are not open for decision or discussion.
They are fixed by the laws of our nature as mind-body organisms
struggling to preserve ourselves against our environment. That
which we generally take, in our ignorance of these natural laws, to
be our own free decision between alternative ends is to be explained
as the complicated working of these laws in our own individual
psychology. They are laws governing increases and decreases of
vitality in the mind-body organism, and, derivatively, of unconscious
appetites and conscious desires. I am only self-directing and independent when I am actively studying the laws of nature themselves,

free from any concentration of interest exclusively on myself and on my relation to other particular things. Unless I continually reflect in this detached, philosophical manner, my particular judgement of ends of action, of good and bad, will correspond only to my particular desires and needs, due to the complications of my particular environment, and to the fantasies that have arisen from this history. I am deceived, if I do not discover the element of fantasy, and of unconscious memories in my original judgements of value. Moral argument, that which replaces the traditional free discussion of ends of action, should be an attempt to bring to light, and to recognize, our own motives and their sources, and thereby to make our pursuit of our own safety, and the enjoyment of our own activity, fully self-conscious and therefore fully rational.

I think it is at least possible that Spinoza is right in his opinion that traditional ethics is the pursuit of an illusion, and that gradually, in the course of years, he may be shown to be right. But for him of course this conclusion was not opinion, but knowledge. Nor did he think that it required, or could receive, confirmation from further observation and scientific inquiry. I am assuming a view of his philosophy, and of philosophy itself, which was not his, and which many living British philosophers would certainly not accept: the view that a philosophy such as his, which began with a claim to final truth demonstrable by *a priori* argument, is to be judged now as a speculative anticipation of truths that may gradually be confirmed by scientific inquiry, and by accumulating human experience. The confirmation, if it comes, will not be like the confirmation of an empirical hypothesis. It will not be direct confirmation, which leaves one with no reasonable alternative other than to accept the hypothesis as true. Rather the confirmation would be that some notions closely resembling Spinoza's key notions become widely accepted as peculiarly appropriate in studying and in evaluating human behaviour. New psychological knowledge might fit better into this framework than into any other, and psychologists themselves, and those who must now be directly or indirectly influenced by them, might come to employ concepts closely akin to Spinoza's. Certainly anyone who altogether rejects Spinoza's naturalistic standpoint, and anyone who has some religious and transcendental ground for his moral beliefs, would remain unpersuaded: and, given his premises, justifiably so. But those of us who have no such transcendental grounds may at least pause and consider the possibility that much of our habitual moralizing about the ends of action is altogether mistaken. Certainly we should not deceive ourselves by dismissing Spinoza as the kind of determinist who allows no possibility of deliberate self-improvement, as if this were the dividing line between him and the traditional moralists. It is not. An unprejudiced reading of the introduction to the *De Intellectus Emendatione,* and of Part V of the *Ethics,* will show that it is not. The dividing line is his theory of individuals maintaining themselves as individuals and of the mind and body as the two aspects of a single organism; and this line can be traced back to his nominalistic logic and to his philosophy of nature.

I have elsewhere suggested that there is an illuminating, and more than superficial, resemblance between Spinoza's and Freud's conception of personality. The more closely one considers this resemblance, the more clearly it appears to be traceable to common philosophical beliefs, which lie far below the surface of a shared terminology. That simple, misleading question 'Was Spinoza, was Freud, a determinist?' has to be put on one side, and for the same reason, in both cases: that determinism, as a label, is associated with a particular model of the type of explanation to be aimed at in individual psychology and in the assessment of character: and this is a type which was certainly not theirs and which they had no interest either in accepting or rejecting. A determinist, as this label is commonly understood, has the single idea that any human behaviour is to be explained by well-confirmed natural laws which, taken together with a statement of initial conditions, exhibit the behaviour, whatever it may be, as always in principle predictable. This is not the kind of understanding, and of self-understanding, that is proposed by Spinoza and Freud.

Let me briefly list their points of agreement. First: there is the 'economic' conception of the mind: that any individual is a psychophysical organism with a quantity of undifferentiated energy that appears in consciousness as desire and, below the level of consciousness, as appetite. This is the instinctual energy that must find its outlet, however deformed and deflected it may be by its interactions with the environment. Desires and appetites are projected upon objects, as objects of love or of hate, in accordance, first, with the primary economic needs of the organism, as objects promoting or depressing its vitality, and, secondly, upon objects that are derivatively associated, through the complex mechanisms of memory, with increase or depression of vitality. Following this conception of a person's undifferentiated energy of self-assertion, Spinoza's account of passive emotions, and of the laws of transference that govern them, is very close to Freud's mechanisms of projection, transference, displacement, and identification, in forming the objects of love and aggression. Second: that the way towards freedom and self-direction is through the recognition of the unreality of the causes with which an individual associates pleasures and sufferings. A man's discrimination between good objects and bad objects will be explained to him as imaginative projection upon reality of unconsciously remembered incidents in his personal history. Third: the purpose of such an explanation is to give him an overriding interest in the objective order of things, an interest independent of his own fantasies and of the passive association of ideas. The recall to reason is a recall from fantasy, and from the attachment to past experience through unconscious memories, towards an active and present enjoyment of his energies. He therefore becomes free to direct his mind as he chooses to its proper objects, instead of endlessly and helplessly repeating patterns of pursuit and aversion that originally established themselves below the level of his consciousness. Fourth: in his original state of uncriticized passive emotions, based upon fantasy, and the projection of his conflicts on to external objects, a man necessarily follows contrary and violently conflicting inclinations, and not a stable and consistent policy. Taken as a whole, his behaviour, in realizing his own desires, is therefore self-defeating. He is in this sense a divided and disintegrated personality. Freedom consists in the integration of all his desires and aversions into a coherent policy, the policy of developing his own powers of understanding, and of enjoying his active energies.

The point of philosophical interest here is the conception of mental causation which in turn determines the conception of freedom as the proper subject of ethics. For both Spinoza and Freud, the starting-point was the individual who, although part of the common order of nature, has to assert his individuality, his activity as an individual, against the common order of nature: in later, un-Spinozistic language, to assert the self, as agent, against the not-self, the external reality which resists him. His only means of achieving this distinctness as an individual, this freedom in relation to the common order of nature, is the power of the mind freely to follow in its thought an intellectual order. Then the flow of his reason-

able thought and his reasonable action is predictable with greater
certainty than when his thoughts and actions were determined by
causes external to his own thinking. Spinoza and Freud alike argued that it is the common condition of men that their conduct
and their judgements of value, their desires and aversions, are in
each individual determined by unconscious memories. This is the
nature of the passions—that their objects can be explained only
from knowledge of unconsciously remembered satisfactions and
frustrations in the individual's history, and not from the properties
of the objects themselves. The future activity of a reasonable man
is predictable on the basis of his present activity, while the future
of the man who is a slave to his passions is to be inferred only from
the fantasies that he formed in the remote past. When a man's
thought follows the objective order of things in nature, he is, and
knows that he is, for a time an autonomous individual, asserting
his own power and independence of mind. I repeat 'for a time'.
For neither Spinoza nor Freud were optimists. Freedom is at the
best only intermittent and partial, and the general condition of
men, as parts of nature, is one of fantasy and of passion determined
by unconscious memory and therefore by conflict and frustration.
But Freud's was certainly the deeper pessimism. Attending to the
evidence of fact, he found no reason to believe that the mere force
of intellect and of reflection could by itself open the way to self-
knowledge, and therefore to freedom of mind. And one traditional
form of philosophical writing, which still survives in Spinoza, is
disappearing from our literature: the exhortation addressed to reason, the call to reflection on the right way of life, which used to be
the preface, as in the *De Intellectus Emendatione*, to intellectual
analysis.

Spinoza's philosophy can be construed as a metaphysical justification of individualism in ethics and politics. In so interpreting him,
we only follow his design of his own work, which has never, I think,
been treated with sufficient seriousness, largely because the attention
of political philosophers has been concentrated on the more crude
and inapplicable metaphysics of Hobbes. Whatever may be our
judgement on the metaphysical premises from which it was deduced, Spinoza's theory of the passions is indeed a justification for
taking the freedom of the individual as the supreme goal of political
action. The now prevailing liberal conceptions of freedom, based
on an empiricist philosophy, leave a mystery: why is the individu-

al's act of choice, free from outside interference and threats of force, the supremely valuable activity of a man? Mill himself drew his answer from his utilitarian philosophy. The freedom of the individual was not for him a supreme and absolute end, but rather a means to the general progress of mankind. The individual's freedom of choice is a means to diversity and experiment, and diversity and experiment are means to the discovery of the most desirable forms of life. There is nothing in this philosophy that requires that the freedom of any individual is as such to be respected before all other things. Perhaps a revived doctrine of natural rights could give a sense to the absolute, as opposed to the conditional, value of the freedom of the individual. But no sense is given to the notion of natural rights within the empiricist philosophies of this time. If every man is by the law of his nature as an individual trying to assert his own power and freedom, in Spinoza's sense, in his thought and action, there is indeed a natural basis for the insistence on freedom as the supreme value in politics as in personal morality. The pursuit of any incompatible end will only lead to conflict and violence.

I return to my starting-point. It is, I think, at least possible that Spinoza has presented the outline of a defensible conception of individual freedom as the ultimate value in politics. In the *Tractatus Theologico-Politicus,* particularly in Chapter 20, he undertakes to show both that a civilized social order, based on freedom of thought and toleration, is a necessary condition of the use of reason, and therefore of the individual's fulfilment and enjoyment of his active powers: also, and more important now, to show that violence and social conflict are the projections into the external world of conflicts of passion within the individual. The first demonstration is in its conclusion, though not in its method, a commonplace. The second is not. We continue to speculate without conviction about freedom and social co-operation in the traditional terms of political philosophy, without any serious attention to the psychopathology of the individual, and as if all the discoveries in clinical psychology in the last fifty years had never been made. And this is, I think, why political philosophy is now dying or dead, and lacks all conviction, except as an interpretation of the past. It has lost contact with the revolutionary and relevant moral science of its time. It is contrary to reason, and contrary also to John Stuart Mill's own principles in philosophy, that we should still cling to Mill's definition of freedom, when the philosophy of mind upon which he based it is discredited. We thereby preserve the letter, and lose the spirit, of empiricism, and of the liberal beliefs that were derived from it.

Thought and Action
in Spinoza

S. Paul Kashap

I PROPOSE TO EXAMINE and analyze Spinoza's use of the terms 'appetite,' 'will,' and 'desire' in an attempt to clarify his concept of action as well as to remove certain misunderstandings that have often occurred in the expositions of Spinoza's views on purposive behavior.

Individual things, according to Spinoza, are affections or modes of the attributes of God, expressed in a determinate manner.[1] Their essence is derived from God (*EI* P25). That is to say, as modes, they cannot exist by themselves, but must depend for both their existence and essence on something other than themselves. The essence of an individual thing is considered to be that without which the thing can neither be nor be conceived, and which itself cannot be or be conceived without the thing.[2] The essence being given, the thing must exist unless some other external cause prevents its existence. This does not mean that an individual thing's essence involves existence, since for Spinoza this is true only of God, but that each individual thing, insofar as its essence follows from God, makes an effort to 'persevere' in its being (*EIII* P6). This effort or tendency of an individual thing to persevere or to continue or to persist in its being is that thing's *conatus,* which Spinoza tells us "is nothing but the actual essence of the thing itself" (*EIII* P7).

Now the human mind, according to Spinoza, knows itself through the ideas of the affections of the body, and in knowing in this way, it is conscious of itself (*EII* P19 & P23). A human being, as an individual thing, makes an effort to persist in his being, and the human mind in knowing the affections of its body is conscious of this effort

---

[1] *Ethics*, Pt. I, Prop. 25, Coroll. (or *EI* P25 C), and Pt. II, Prop. 6, Demonstration (or *EII* P6 D).
[2] *Ethics*, Pt. II, Def. 2 (or *EII* D2).

to preserve its existence.[3] This effort has two aspects: one, "related to the mind alone," is called 'will,' the other, "related at the same time both to the mind and the body . . . is called *appetite*" (*EIII* P9 S). This 'appetite' Spinoza regards as the very essence of man. Thirdly, there is 'desire' or *cupiditas* which is "related to men insofar as they are conscious of their appetite." [4]

The human mind, for Spinoza, is a mode of the attribute 'Thought.' The will, which is the mind's effort to preserve the human individual, exists as determined or caused to exist by something other than itself. And since it is a determinate mode, it must have as its cause another finite determinate mode of the same attribute. For Spinoza, therefore, since the will cannot be the cause of its own existence, it is necessarily 'determined' in the sense that its existence must be explained by reference to a cause other than itself.[5] It is not 'self-caused,' and to say this is the same thing, for him, as to say that it is not a free 'cause.' The will, being a mode, is therefore never free in this sense of 'free.'

Faced with Spinoza's denial of the applicability of the term 'free' to the will, one begins to wonder whether he could be dealing with freedom in the specifically moral sense, as the meaning of that term is generally understood. It is important to keep in mind, therefore, that his refusal to accept that the will is free clearly rests in his assertion (at the metaphysical level) that the modes cannot be self-caused. As modes, they must be dependent for their existence on something other than themselves; and to say that a thing is not self-caused is to say, in his sense, that it is not free. But the interesting point is that Spinoza, while maintaining this notion of freedom, also accepts the idea that a human being has the ability to attain 'salvation' or 'freedom' (in some important sense) without seeming to realize that the freedom which he denies to human beings *qua*

---

[3] Ibid. The phrase 'related to mind alone,' in his definition of the will, is a little ambiguous. Does it mean that, taking an 'act' as a combination of subjective and behavioral elements, the purely subjective part is 'will' and the purely behavioral part is physical appetite? It is difficult to say. It seems, however, that the term 'will' as defined here by Spinoza is a purely conceptual notion. That is to say, that although it is not possible for the 'will' to exist without its extensional counterpart, insofar as one can conceptually isolate the element of thought in the 'effort' from the bodily factor, it is called 'will.'

[4] *Ibid.*

[5] Epistolae [hereafter cited as *Ep.*] 2. All references to correspondence are from *The Correspondence of Spinoza*, trans. A. Wolf (London, 1928).

finite determinate modes, and the freedom which he admits that human beings can attain, are not, and cannot be, one and the same freedom. One wonders if Spinoza tends to forget that the freedom which he denies to finite modes can strictly be applied only to God. For no matter how adequate the knowledge in the human mind may be, so long as a human being is not and cannot be identical with God, and must necessarily remain, even at the highest stage of knowledge, a finite mode, it is impossible for him to attain that freedom which God (by definition) possesses. My suspicion, therefore, is that in speaking of freedom as he does above, he is not speaking of (nor defining) freedom in a strictly *moral sense* in which the notion of "could have done otherwise," in one sense of the phrase, is necessarily involved. I am far from saying that Spinoza does not recognize that the notion of "being able to do otherwise than one does" is implied in actions to which moral value is normally attached. But I submit that when he does discuss or imply this latter sense of freedom, he is not speaking in terms of that freedom which can legitimately and properly be applied only to God.[6]

The confusion that has been caused by this conflicting use of the term 'free' by Spinoza in the two instances—namely (1) with regard to God, and (2) with regard to human beings, with the accompanying implication that there is no distinction between the application of 'freedom' in the two contexts—is perhaps one of the main reasons why Spinoza has been regarded as a rigid determinist. But another notable reason consists in the tendency of serious students of Spinoza to emphasize only a part of his thesis, and to ignore those parts which would be consistent with the view that a human being, as a part of a social system, with its "man-made" laws and rules (including moral laws), can be said to be 'free' in the sense in which freedom implies that a man "could have done otherwise than he did" —a sense that would admit the notion of moral responsibility within his system.

We have noted that 'will,' for Spinoza, is the *conatus* of man when related to mind alone. And mind, for him, is a 'thinking thing,' and the conceptions of the mind are 'ideas' (*E*II D3). These 'ideas' or modifications of Thought must be dependent for their existence on some other modifications of Thought, and are thus

---

[6] See, for example, Spinoza's notion of "wrongdoing" in his *Political Treatise,* chap. II, 19.

'determined.' In Spinoza's view there is no such thing as a 'faculty' of willing distinct from the mind (*E*II P48 D). There are indeed, as he admits, individual volitions or desires, but since these are related to the mind as the mental side of an individual's 'effort' to exist, they are not different from 'ideas.' An individual volition, like an 'idea,' is a mode of Thought by which the mind affirms or denies something (*E*II P49 D). The so-called 'faculty of willing,' consequently, is merely an abstraction from individual volitions, and is, as he says, ". . . either altogether fictitious or else . . . nothing but metaphysical or universal entity." [7] "The intellect and the will are related to this or that idea or volition as rockiness is related to this or that rock, or as man is related to Peter or Paul" (*E*II P48 S & *Ep* 2). There is no difference between the mind, the intellect, and the will. Consequently, he declares that "The will and the intellect are one and the same" (*E*II P49 C).

We remarked earlier that to have an idea, for Spinoza, is to affirm or deny something. And similarly, to choose one thing or another is to assent to this or that. Individual acts of thinking and willing are modes of Thought. An 'act of will' or a volition, as a determinate mode of Thought, is determined by causes from which it follows necessarily. As a volition of an individual human being it is the necessary consequent of his nature as expressed through his mental acts. His nature, as manifested physically, is the necessary consequent of purely extensional causes following from the nature of his body as a mode of Extension. Neither the mental side of *conatus* causes the determination of the body nor does the physical side of *conatus* cause the determination of the mind. So that a volition or mode of Thought cannot in any event be the cause of any change in the body, nor do the changes in the body cause the mind to think (*E*III P2 & D & S). Both exist simultaneously without one being the cause of the other. This is Spinoza's theory, generally described as 'parallelism.' It is on account of this view that commentators such as Joachim have been led to remark that Spinoza makes "the last vestiges of the popular conception of free will disappear." [8] Joachim contends that what Spinoza does "is to admit the fact of conscious desire whilst denying the reality of purposive action." [9]

[7] *E*II P48 S. cf. *Treatise on God and Man*, trans. A. Wolf (London, 1910), chap. 16, p. 108: "Will . . . is . . . a thing of Reason, and not a real thing. . . ."
[8] H. H. Joachim, *A Study of the Ethics of Spinoza* (Oxford, 1901), p. 197.
[9] Ibid., p. 228.

It is therefore the conception of *cupiditas* or desire which he holds as responsible for Spinoza's polemic against the freedom of the will.

Now it must be admitted that when one reads in Spinoza such statements as "There is no difference between appetite and desire, unless in this particular, that desire is generally related to men insofar as they are conscious of their appetites" (*EIII* P9 S), and ". . . whether a man be conscious of his appetite or not, it remains one and the same . . . ,"[10] the impression one generally gets is that man, for him, is not different from any other animate or inanimate being insofar as his behavior is conditioned or determined by his appetitive nature, with one exception—that man is sometimes conscious of his drives and impulses and strivings. This consciousness, however, does not make any difference to a man's behavior, since consciousness of the appetite does not make the slightest alteration in the appetites themselves. So that whether he were conscious of his appetites or not, his behavior would be the same. Man is thus a helpless creature in the hands of fate, like "clay in the hands of a potter," and he has no means to consciously control his behavior.

But when one reads Spinoza's letter to Blyenbergh (*Ep.* 21) repudiating the charge that he "reduces man to the level of plants or stones" by saying that whoever thinks of him in this way "has thoroughly misunderstood my meaning . . . ," one pauses to think that one may have done an injustice to him in accepting the usual orthodox interpretation of his views. And one does not have to go far to justify these suspicions; there are a number of statements made by Spinoza in, for instance, his *Treatise on the Improvement of the Understanding* which do not at all seem consistent with his denial of intentional and purposive behavior. Joachim observes in his commentary on *Ethics* that the purposive action that Spinoza discredits and contemptuously rejects is action toward "ideals not yet real, but to be realized," or "action with a view to the attainment of an unpossessed 'better'! "[11] But if Joachim is right, then it becomes practically impossible to understand Spinoza's use of the phrases (which occur in the first few pages of *Treatise on the Improvement of the Understanding*) such as "I finally resolved . . ."; ". . . I seriously devoted myself to the search for something different and new"; ". . . with this end in view I made many efforts";

[10] *EIII*, Explanation of Def. 1 of Affects, after P59.
[11] Joachim, op. cit., p. 232. W. G. DeBurgh in his article in *Philosophy*, VI, no. 43 (1936), expresses essentially the same attitude as Joachim's.

". . . I compelled myself to seek with all my strength . . ."; ". . . love towards a thing eternal . . . is greatly to be desired and sought for with all our strength"; ". . . man conceives a human character much more stable than his own, and sees that there is no reason why he should not himself acquire such a character. . . . This . . . is the end for which I strive, to attain to such a character myself, and to endeavour that many should attain to it with me." (For the context of these statements see the footnote.[12]) If these are not enough, there is at least one passage in his correspondnce which would seem to furnish unmistakable evidence that Spinoza not only recognizes but even recommends intentional and consciously purposeful action. In this letter (*Ep.* 37) a correspondent named Boumeester seems to have questioned Spinoza regarding the method by which one can safely proceed in the search for the highest knowledge. Spinoza, in response, after having outlined the method, observes: "It remains, however, to warn you that for all these there are required incessant thought and a most constant mind and purpose. To gain these, it is first of all necessary to adopt a definite mode and plan of life, and to set before one a definite end." [13]

These statements indicate beyond any reasonable doubt that Spinoza was not denying "action with a view to the attainment of an

---

[12] "I finally resolved to inquire whether . . . in fact there might be anything of which the discovery and attainment would enable me to enjoy continuous, supreme and unending happiness" (*Tractatus de Intellectus Emendatione* [hereafter referred to as *DIE*], p. 1). Page references are to the R. H. M. Elwes translation, *The Chief Works of Spinoza*, 2 vols. (London, 1908). "I could see the benefits which one acquired through fame and riches, and that I should be obliged to abandon the quest of such objects if I seriously devoted myself to the search for something different and new" (*DIE*, p. 1). "I debated whether it would not be possible to arrive at the new principle or at any rate at a certainty concerning its existence, without changing the conduct and usual plan of my life; with this end in view I made many efforts . . ." (*DIE*, p. 1).

"I thus perceived that I was in a state of great peril and I compelled myself to seek with all my strength for a remedy, however uncertain it might be . . ." (*DIE*, pp. 4–5). Spinoza states that fear, hatred, and all other disturbances of the mind "arise from the love of what is perishable. . . . But love towards a thing eternal and infinite feeds the mind wholly with joy . . . wherefore it is greatly to be desired and sought for with all our strength" (*DIE*, p. 5).

". . . man conceives a human character much more stable than his own, and sees that there is no reason why he should not himself acquire such a character. . . . This . . . is the end for which I strive, to attain to such a character myself, and to endeavour that many should attain to it with me" (*DIE*, p. 6).

[13] See another relevant passage in *EV* P10 S.

unpossessed better," nor was he rejecting intentional and purposive action insofar as that involves a man's acting toward acquiring a certain character which he considers as 'ideal.'

Nor do I see that there is any inconsistency involved in his holding the above view and his contention that God does not act purposively or from final causes.[14] For if purpose were attributed to God, it would imply that God is now defective or imperfect or less than complete. But God cannot be said to produce one thing for the sake of another if that other be something not part of His nature, since there can be nothing "outside" that which is complete; this is the same thing as to say that God is His own cause or that He is the free cause of His own being and activity.[15]

It is not likely that Spinoza could have been unaware of the obvious paradox involved in his holding two seemingly incompatible views, namely, that everything finite has a cause and every effect follows from its cause necessarily and a finite mode must be determined by something other than itself to exist and act, and his view that human beings can legitimately be said to direct their efforts toward an end of which they are conscious. It is more probable that he had in mind some argument to show that these two theses are not incompatible with each other—that determination of an individual finite mode by a series of causes does not preclude the application of the concept of intentional action. What he would, doubtless, have insisted is that any action of a human being, regarded at the philosophical level as a determinate mode of God, must in principle be capable of being shown to be completely explainable by reference to a series of causes which follow from the very nature of God or the universe as it is. And since it makes no sense for him to say that God acts teleologically, and since finite

---

[14] Cf. Professor Hallett's review of Wolfson's *Philosophy of Spinoza*, in *Philosophy*, X, no. 39 (July 1935), p. 369: ". . . the two questions of the purposiveness of the parts of nature, and purposiveness of *Deus sive natura,* should be kept . . . distinct. There is room in Spinoza for a genuine doctrine of teleology which Spinoza does not deny."

[15] Cf. *EI* P18 C, and *Treatise on God and Man*, trans. A. Wolf (London, 1910), chap. IV, Pt. I. Also compare *Encyclopaedia Brittanica* (1953 ed.) section on "Spinoza's Moral Theory" by A. Wolf: "Spinoza's contention that the conception of goodness, like that of purpose, is inapplicable to the cosmic system as a whole does not mean that he denied the validity of the distinction between good and evil in the realm of human conduct. The notions of good and evil involve the conception of an ideal that is desired but not yet realized."

individuals are only modifications existing and acting within the universe as a whole from whence they derive their essential nature, there is a sense in which finite beings can not be said to be acting with a purpose that was not part of them by virtue of the nature of God. Thus what we normally call 'purpose' in human beings is itself, quite understandably, *qua* a modification of God, a manifestation of the nature of God and determined by Him insofar as "He is manifested through the nature of the human mind" (*EII* P11 C).

Joachim observes that Spinoza "makes use" of the concept of conscious purpose although he denies its existence.[16] The core of his argument seems to be that Spinoza denies that human beings have conscious purposes because he fails to distinguish between 'appetite' and 'desire.' The way Joachim appears to develop his argument is as follows: Spinoza is known to have held the view that consciousness of appetite does not make any difference to the appetite; it remains unmodified. This implies that since "the end for the sake of which we do anything" is nothing but appetite (*EIV* D7), therefore the end or the purpose of which we are conscious is the end for which we would have acted anyway, whether we were conscious of it or not.

Now even admitting that Spinoza gives some grounds for deriving such a conclusion, it is not possible to ignore the fact that Spinoza not only "makes use" of the notion of conscious purpose but positively recognizes it as a fact in the distinction—which he takes great pains to make—between appetite and desire. Spinoza's definition of desire is very elusive and hence his notion of desire is very difficult to understand. And a great majority of commentators seem disinclined, for some reason, to examine it closely. Perhaps they believe that nothing much would be gained by it. But this I believe to be a mistake. An adequate analysis of his concept of desire seems to be crucial to the understanding of his philosophy of mind and his concept of action.

Let me make one point immediately. When we read Spinoza's statement in the *DIE*, "Man conceives of a human character much more stable than his own and sees no reason why he should not himself acquire such a character," there arises a question with regard to the nature of this conception. That is to say, is this concep-

---

[16] Joachim, op. cit., p. 235. See also R. Demos, "Spinoza's Doctrine of Privation," pp. 276–288, and A. E. Taylor, "Some Incoherencies in Spinozism (II)," pp. 289–309, in this volume.

tion of "a character more stable than his own," formed at the level
of 'imagination,' or of 'reason,' or of 'intuitive knowledge?' If it is
the expression of 'reason' (*Ratio*) or of 'intuitive knowledge' (*Scientia intuitiva*), then it would appear that man would already have
attained to the level of knowledge he is 'aiming' to attain. And this
seems absurd. But if this conception is formed at the level of 'imagination' (and this seems to be the only alternative left), then it would
imply that it makes sense to say *at the level of imagination* that I
can act with a conscious end in view, and purposive activity is unquestionably permissible at this level. Furthermore, it is conceptually necessary that such purposive activity be recognized as essential
in the process of advance to the stage of 'action' which follows from
the knowledge based on *Ratio*. To seek the means to realize an ideal
certainly involves consciously directed effort, and Spinoza does accept that it is possible for a man both to discover an end and to
find the means to attain it. For he admits without ambiguity: "I
wish to direct all sciences to one end and aim, so that we may attain
to the supreme human perfection. . . . All our actions and thoughts
must be directed to this one end" (*DIE*, p. 6). Spinoza even lays
down some provisional rules of behavior (*DIE*, p. 7) while the
search for 'the end' is in progress. These are offered as preliminary
prescriptions and not as mere descriptions of the way to attain 'the
end.'

It does not seem reasonable for anyone to deny that Spinoza does
make value judgments in speaking of what should be done in order
to attain human perfection. True, he does not specifically use the
term 'ought' in any of his judgments, but it would be highly misleading to say that he merely points to what is the case. Even when he
seems to be merely describing eternal truths, one can detect a note
of 'prescription.' For the question that Spinoza seeks to answer, as
has been rightly pointed out by Wernham,[17] is "What shall I do to
inherit eternal life?" But when Wernham goes on to say that Spinoza's answer to this is "not a command; the *Ethics* contains no

---

[17] A. G. Wernham, *Spinoza's Political Works* (Oxford, 1958), pp. 10 and 20. Mr.
Wernham does not seem, however, to have noticed the implications of these
'provisional rules' offered by Spinoza, nor that of the following paragraph in
Ep. 43 (1671), where Spinoza says: "It is false to assert that I maintain that there
is no room left for precepts or commands or . . . that there is no expectation
of reward or punishment since everything is . . . affirmed to proceed from God
by inexorable necessity."

'oughts,' no imperatives, only 'eternal truths,' " he fails to see that
to accept, as he does, that Spinoza tried to give human beings a
'clear and distinct' understanding of themselves and their emotions
so that he who has this has also love of God and salvation—and to
deny that the context in which these statements are made is a context that allows us to make a prescription about what to do in order
to attain the end—is to miss the point of Spinoza's moral theory.
For there is no doubt that Spinoza's aim was ethical, namely, to
guide human action. How can one reasonably argue then that Spinoza's statements do not contain oughts or imperatives—and yet *be
guided by them?* If Spinoza is pointing out eternal truths, then he
is also suggesting that those who try to understand them will at
the same time make an effort to attain the end. It does not seem
plausible that Spinoza merely describes what is 'supreme good,' and
shows us the method by which to attain it, and yet that there is no
suggestion or assumption involved in this to the effect that the
'supreme good' *ought* to be attained.

*   *   *

It will be remembered that 'will,' 'appetite,' and 'desire' are taken
by Spinoza as related notions. They are parts of the 'striving for
self-preservation' or *conatus.* This striving, which Spinoza holds to
be the essence of man, follows from the eternal nature of God. So
that to talk of *its* being free, as if one had the power to either strive
or not strive to preserve onself, is meaningless. In every form of
human behavior, no matter how self-destructive it may be, man
manifests this striving. A human being cannot free himself of this
striving without ceasing to be alive. In this sense he must (logically
must) be a manifestation of his *conatus.* Now as human beings we
naturally strive for certain things (such as pleasures) and avoid
others (such as pain). Those we strive for are generally described
by us as good and those we avoid are called bad or evil. From this
follows the well-known statement of Spinoza: "We neither strive
for, wish, seek nor desire anything because we think it to be good,
but on the contrary, we adjudge a thing to be good because we
strive for, wish, seek or desire it" (*EIII P9 S*). The significance of
this passage is generally somewhat distorted. Spinoza is not saying
that whenever we seek or strive or wish to have a thing, it becomes
good by the mere fact that we desire it. Nor is he saying that any
thing a human being in fact desires at any moment is always good.

There are also things, Spinoza would hold, that are good even though few people actually desire them. Nor is he saying that what we, at any given moment, like or prefer is identical with that which we describe as good, or what we dislike or avoid is identical with our description of it as bad. He is not, so far as I can see, putting forward any implausible or absurd theory in his statement. It is quite plain that our desires which find expression in our inclination and disinclination toward various things play a decisive role in our recognition and description of something as good or bad. It is a necessary truth that a thing could not be *described* as good if there were no individual who was ever disposed toward it or attracted to it in some sense.

It seems fairly plain that the things that are ordinarily considered and described as 'good' (e.g., knowledge, peace of mind) must in fact have been desired by man at some stage of human history, before they came to be looked upon as worthy of being sought; and with successive advancement in conceptual ability together with intellectual, social, and moral sophistication, human beings have learned to seek things that have been recognized generally as good, even thought they are not necessarily desired and sought after by all. Our beliefs about things that are 'good' are constantly changing. And Spinoza was right in recognizing the dependence of the description of things as good or evil, in general, upon the changes in desires resulting from changes in man's perception of the world and of himself. This also explains the difference in value attached to the same sorts of things in different societies at the same time and in the same society at different times.

Now Spinoza is alleged to have maintained that we cannot desire something that we consciously recognize as good. It may be possible to argue from this point of view that conscious desire for something presupposes the unconscious or latent desire in even a more genuine sense of 'unconscious' than is given by propensity or disposition, from which the conscious desire itself arises. Since Spinoza's notion of appetite seems to comprehend all the potential urges of a human being to desire things, it becomes possible to interpret Spinoza as saying that when a man consciously desires anything, what happens is that appetites which form an essential part of him come to the level of consciousness. So that a man does not consciously seek for anything different from that which he had a potential capacity or disposition to desire. And since the desire of which a man is unconscious, namely appetite, is for Spinoza identical with desire of which he is conscious, namely *cupiditas,* he is shown to be stating a trivial tautology.

It must be admitted that if Spinoza is maintaining this tautology in explaining the nature of desire, then there is no way in which the conclusion can be avoided that consciousness of appetite cannot make any difference to what a man does or would do. But the point that needs to be kept in mind is that even if one admits that what one is conscious of, in being conscious of a desire, is appetite, in Spinoza's sense of the term, it does not follow that the behavior that accompanies or follows from the state of a man when he is conscious of desire is logically identical (in the qualitative sense) with the behavior that would follow from appetite of which he is *not* conscious. Spinoza, contrary to the commonly accepted view of his stand, *does in fact* recognize the difference between desire and appetite, and he makes a definite point of clarifying his position in order to avoid being misunderstood.

It is surprising, therefore, that Spinoza scholars have tended to ignore, generally, the distinction that he makes in *Ethics* III, Definition 1, of Affects, and in his statement in the Demonstration to Proposition 56 of Part III. Spinoza seems to apologize in this passage (*E*III, Aff, Def. 1) for appearing to be guilty of tautology when he defined desire earlier in *E*III P9. He warns us significantly by saying, "I have not explained desire by appetite," and adds that if he had explained desire by appetite, then he would have had to say that "desire is the essence itself of man insofar as it is considered as determined to any action." That is, he would have to say that the determination of an action from appetite and from desire are one and the same. But evidently he is not prepared to say this. For then he would be maintaining that it was the appetite that determined a man to action, which is not what he means to do. He explains further that if he held such a definition of desire, then it would not be possible for him to hold Proposition 23, *Ethics* II. When we turn to that proposition, we find Spinoza saying that the mind knows itself through the ideas of the affections of the body. By this he must mean that the idea or consciousness of the affections of the body is a necessary condition for a person's being determined to any action. The consciousness of the affections of the body involves a consciousness of the effects of the outer world upon the body, and this includes a perceptual knowledge of the circumstances in the situation. So that in the absence of consciousness of the modification of his body, a human being will not be self-conscious, nor will it be possible for him to have a desire, and hence no determinate action can ensue. The presence of desires in man logically presupposes that his body is affected by certain objects in the empirical world. This of course does not entail that if a man's body is being affected by certain objects in the empirical world, then certain desires are necessarily being experienced by him. The affections of the body presupposed by desire are entailed by the presence of appetites without which a human being will not be regarded as a person. And in the absence of desire, as Spinoza would put it, a person will not be "determined toward any action." So that what he is saying is that the difference between desire and appetite is that desire implies a self-conscious cognitive state in which the behavior of a human being is governed by the consciousness of an end or a goal. These desires can vary, just as consciousness of an end can vary, according to a man's changing disposition and the kind of objects by which he is affected (EIII P56 D).

In a letter to Blyenburgh (Ep. 23), Spinoza further indicates the difference between desire and appetite by means of one of the few examples to be found in his works. Blyenburgh, in his letter (Ep. 22), asks in part whether Spinoza would hold that stealing was as good as an honest life. Spinoza answers that if the question meant whether a thief and an honest man were equally perfect specimens as human beings, then his answer was "no." "For," he explains, "by an honest man I mean one who always desires that every one should possess that which is his." The implication clearly is that a man may have an appetite or even an impulse to possess something that does not belong to him—he may even steal something while conscious of his impulse to steal—but if it so happens that the consciousness or awareness of this impulse makes him resist and deviate from it rather than to indulge it, then it is fairly obvious that his desire to steal in the instance when he did steal was in an important sense different from his desire in the instance that was not followed by an act of stealing. Now, granted that in one sense all desire presupposes an inclination or an impulse toward something one wants, and perhaps this is the sense in which desire is 'consciousness of appetite,' but merely to say this is not to account for the difference in behavior in the above two instances. Spinoza's example would seem to indicate his acknowledgment of such a distinction, which consists in the degree of presence or absence of the cognitive element in human behavior.

It is quite possible to take the stand taken by Joachim or Broad [18] and contend that, for Spinoza. a righteous man's desires follow from 'clear knowledge.' And to say this is to say that in the righteous person, the desire certainly is the consciousness of appetite, except that in him the appetite itself is different. So that in the case of the righteous no less than in the case of the unrigheous person, 'desire' is nothing but 'consciousness of appetite'; the implication being that if we do not have an appetite for clear knowledge we shall not seek it, and if we do seek clear knowledge we presuppose an appetite for it. This being the case, there seems no possibility of growth in the scale of knowledge or of improvement in oneself, in Spinoza's system. For it amounts to saying that we desire a thing because we have an appetite, and it is only if we have an appetite that we can be said to desire. If we do not have the appetite, there is nothing we or anyone else can do to bring it about; for in order to bring it about we shall have to be conscious of an end, that is to say, conscious of another appetite (*EIV* D7) which must be presumed to be there for us to be conscious of it. In short, it does not make any sense to say that a man can desire anything in the ordinary sense of desire. And the questions about 'self-improvement' and 'seeking' clear knowledge become equally meaningless.

Clearly, the argument as presented above, if it represents Spinoza's thought, involves either an infinite regress or a vicious circularity, and it is difficult to believe that Spinoza failed to notice it.

It is also evident that if Spinoza maintains, for instance, that desire for clear knowledge presupposes appetite for clear knowledge, then failure to have the appetite would lead to failure to attain to clear knowledge.

Under these conditions, since new appetites cannot be generated, they must be regarded as being, in some sense, present or not-present (given or not given, if you prefer). When they are 'present,' in this sense, the desire for clear knowledge is consciousness of the appetite for clear knowledge. In that case it is questionable whether Spinoza can help (as he appears to assume he can) other people to arrive at the possession of the character that he regards as an 'ideal.' It is difficult to see how he could ever have believed that by studying

[18] See C. D. Broad, *Five Types of Ethical Theory* (London, 1930), chapter II on Spinoza.

what he has outlined in the *Ethics* anyone could possibly be affected in such a way that he would begin to desire to attain what Spinoza regards as the supreme good unless he assumed that there was an underlying appetite that was not yet clear about its aim because it did not yet have the requisite cognition of ends and means which the book now can supply; that it was possible to generate some sort of propensity in men to desire something that they never conceived of until someone directed their attention to it. It seems clear that some modification and progress in the appetites themselves will have to be taken as an essential prerequisite to the process of attaining 'clear knowledge,' as well as to the process of attaining desire itself.

The disturbing aspect of the traditional view of Spinoza's theory is that it misrepresents Spinoza as failing to explain the difference between human behavior that follows from appetite alone and that which follows from the consciousness of appetite. That Spinoza does recognize such a difference seems pretty clear from the passages noted above from *DIE*. And I wish to emphasize that the purport of these passages is consistent with the view that Spinoza in fact held, namely, that desire is not *mere* consciousness of appetite but rather appetite as *modified* by consciousness. For if desire were, for him, mere consciousness of appetite, then he would be guilty of 'explaining desire by appetite.' And he specifically denies having done this (*EIII* Expl. I Aff after P59). The question that then arises is, if he refused to be guilty of this 'tautology,' as he calls it, then did he have in mind some factor that distinguished appetite from desire? The answer is "yes," and the distinction, as he points out, lies in this—that while "Appetite is the essence itself of man insofar as it is determined to such acts as contribute to his preservation, . . . desire is the essence itself of man insofar as it is conceived as determined to any action by one of his affections." [19]

It is important to understand what he means by this statement. The only way in which it can be interpreted, without doing injustice to the philosopher, seems to be as follows. An 'affection,' for Spinoza, is a mode of the attribute of Thought or of Extension or it may be related to both. So any change or modification related to a human body or mind or to both can be described as an 'affection.' Desire, which is consciousness of appetite, is an *idea* of the affection of the body and/or mind. It is by means of having such ideas that a

[19] *EIII*, Expl. I, Aff.

human mind becomes conscious of itself. Having a desire necessarily involves, therefore, a self-conscious state. And there is no qualitative identity between the state of man when he is conscious of his appetite and the state of man when he does not have such consciousness. Spinoza is maintaining, as a synthetic a priori truth, that the nature of man is such that man's desires are invariably conditioned by his innate constitution and the way in which his ideas are formed through the effects of the various kinds of objects upon his body and mind. And with this it seems difficult to find grounds for dispute.

There are other difficulties, however, which call for serious attention. The crucial question that must now be raised is whether granting that appetite and desire are qualitatively distinct for Spinoza permits us to conclude that when we desire something and act to fulfill that desire the movement of the body involved in this activity is *caused* by the desire. Spinoza's answer to this appears to be a categorical "no." "The body cannot determine the mind to thought, neither can the mind determine the body to motion nor rest . . ." (EIII P2). This statement, it needs to be noted, is perhaps the first of its kind in the so-called modern philosophy which suggests the distinction to be drawn between causes and reasons for human behavior.

Let me explain how this conclusion can be justified. "Man," Spinoza tells us, "is composed of mind and body" (EII P13 C). A mode of thought or an idea in the human mind must (logically must) have its correlative mode of extension. It is logically impossible for a mode of thought to be attributed to a man's mind without there being some correlative changes occurring in his body. The ideas in the human mind, however, can be explained only by reference to other *ideas* as their causes or reasons,[20] and finite modes

[20] It is interesting and important to note that Spinoza appears to make a distinction between 'cause' and 'reason.' The first indication of it comes in *EI* P11, first of the two proofs. Spinoza says there: "For the existence or non-existence of everything there must be a reason or cause." It seems on first reading as though Spinoza is using 'reason' and 'cause' synonymously. There is certainly some ambiguity involved in his use of these terms. But a careful reading shows that he may have a distinction in mind between the two. This becomes apparent from the illustration he gives of his use of the term 'reason' in the same proof. "For example," he says, "the nature of the thing itself shows the reason why a square circle involves a contradiction." A square circle is a conceptual impossibility, in other words, and in such cases only *reasons* are relevant, and

of Extension are casually explainable only by reference to other
finite modes of Extension (*E*I P28). The order and connection of
ideas being the same, for Spinoza, as the order and connection of
things (*E*II P7), there cannot be an idea in the human mind without
the correlative affection of the body. Now to say that a man 'willed'
something is the same thing, for Spinoza, as to say that there was
an idea in the human mind, or that the human mind assented to
or affirmed something. So that to 'will' something is to be conscious
of an idea. But as consciousness itself is a mode of thought or an
idea, when I 'will' something I have an idea of an idea. Corresponding to this idea, according to Spinoza, there necessarily is a mode of
extension, but in being conscious of an idea, I am not conscious of
the mode of extension. The desire of which I am aware, being an
idea of an idea, does not involve an awareness of the affection of
the body. So that in having a desire we are not, nor need we be,
conscious of the bodily affection, though the affection of the body
is a necessary condition in any given instance of desiring or willing.

If this reading of Spinoza is correct, then it seems that a plausible
explanation can be found for statements like "I desire such and
such," such that my action following the desire can be said to be
the consequence of that desire and legitimately explainable by reference to it.

One obvious objection to this might be that such an explanation
is entirely opposed to Spinoza's statement in *E*III P2, in which he
says that the mind cannot determine the body to motion. It is, however, not clear to me in what way the above interpretation of
Spinoza's theory is incompatible with Spinoza's denial of interaction between the mind and the body. When, for instance, I claim
that my action was caused by my desire for a specific end, surely I
would not be denying the existence of a mode or modes of Extension
correlative to my desire. Any specific desire must ultimately involve
reference to an identifiable person as a mode of Extension, and
within him to certain physical changes occurring as further modes
of Extension. What I *am* claiming in referring to my desire to explain my action is that in being conscious of the desire, I am not
directly conscious of the extensional correlates of this desire which
are causally connected with the changes occurring in my body. So

---

not causes. After all, what would one say is the *cause* for the non-existence of
a square circle? It would be very odd to refer to the self-contradictory nature
of a concept as the *causal* condition of its non-existence!

that when I say "my action was determined by my desire," the actual efficient cause of the movement in and of my body can only be another mode of Extension (i.e., the explanation in terms of *causal* conditions of the movement of my body can be provided only by reference to other modes of extension), but in being conscious of my desire, the ideatum is not an affection of the body but another idea. And since the bodily motion in purposive behavior necessarily accompanies the conscious desire, the desire is perceived (or 'imagined,' in Spinoza's language) as the source of the motion of the body. To say or maintain or believe that my desire is the causal source of motion in my body is only an elliptical way of saying or believing that the extensional correlate of the desire is the causal source of the motion in the body. And the reason for ignoring any reference to the extensional correlate of desire in explaining an action as intentional is simply that in such behavior it is the idea of conscious end that is predominantly significant. When one is asked "Why did you do what you did?" the answer to this "Why" if the action is regarded as voluntary, is not provided by reference to a series of causal connections in the modes of Extension—or to the external and internal changes in the body. It is not this causal chain of the movement of our body, but the conscious reasons for these movements which are relevant in the context of purposive behavior. And Spinoza's view would seem to be that 'reasons' for actions cannot be identified with 'causes' for actions. For he clearly recognized that Extension and Thought are distinct attributes. And modes of Extension are, therefore, not reducible to modes of Thought. The causal explanation of the existence of a mode of Extension can be given (and this is a logical "can") only by reference to modes belonging to the same category. One idea—be it a belief or desire or judgment, or any other finite aspect of the mind—can be explained only by reference to other 'ideas,' beliefs, desires, judgments, etc. And Spinoza does seem to hold that the connecting link between the series of ideas too is causal, but it is clearly not causal in exactly the same sense as the modal series of extension. The connection between modes of thought can only be a logical connection as between ground and consequence.

Where do 'reasons' fit into this scheme? Spinoza's view clearly is that to attempt to explain voluntary behavior by reference to conscious desires is to provide an answer to the question 'Why did you do what you did?" in terms of one's conscious desires which are *reasons* for doing it. The possibility (in principle) of providing reasons that are *adequate* reasons for explaining an action is made by him to be the very condition of rational behavior. And the explanation of behavior by reference to conscious desires, that is, reasons, is analogous to, but not identical with, the explanation of the movement of the body by reference to the antecedent modes of extension in the form of changes occurring in the body. Thus reasons function as sufficient conditions of conscious behavior. In this sense, desires can be said to be the efficient causes of actions, which Spinoza accepts in the preface to *Ethics,* Part IV. He adds, however, that although the desire to attain an end is to be accepted as the 'efficient cause' of the existence of things, it is not to be construed as the 'final cause' of their existence. This need not create difficulties for us. Spinoza wishes to maintain that the 'final cause' is always and invariably the 'appetite' that forms the necessary part of the nature of man, as man. So that in admitting desire as an efficient cause, Spinoza would be saying that the final cause, namely appetite, is to be viewed as the efficient cause of behavior in those circumstances in which a man becomes conscious or aware of the final cause. Since the final causes of behavior are appetites, as distinct from conscious desires, one's conscious desires which are the efficient causes are no other than appetites as modified by consciousness. To say, therefore, that desire is only an efficient cause of the existence of things does not mean, nor does it imply, that desires are being deprived of the relevant kind of causal efficacy which is required to be attributed to conscious desires in order for them to be regarded as the sufficient conditions for the existence of other affections of the mind and body.

I conclude, therefore, that Spinoza not only makes use of the concept of purposive or intentional behavior, but admits that the effort to attain the 'supreme good' cannot be explained adequately by reference to appetitive dispositions alone but must necessarily involve the modification of appetites through men's consciousness of them.

Select Bibliography

There is a fairly comprehensive bibliography of books and papers on Spinoza in Rudolf Oko's *The Spinoza Bibliography* (Boston, 1964). The following is a selection of writings in English.

Works by Spinoza (translations)

Elwes, R. H. M. (translator), *The Chief Works of Spinoza*. London, 1883 and 1906; New York, 1955 and 1956. 2 vols. This is more comprehensive than any other available edition of Spinoza's works, though it includes only an abridged version of the correspondence and excludes the following two works.

Briton, H. H. (translator), *The Principles of Descartes' Philosophy*. Chicago, 1905. Includes *Cogitata Metaphysica*.

Wolf, A. (translator), *Short Treatise on God, Man and His Well-Being*. London, 1910.

Boyle, Andrew (translator), *Ethics*. London, 1910; revised 1959. Introduction by Santayana in 1910 edition.

White, W. H., and A. H. Sterling (translators), *Ethics*. Oxford, 1927. This is the best translation of the work to date.

Wolf, A. (translator), *Correspondence of Spinoza*. London, 1928. Includes detailed annotations.

Wernham, A. G. (translator), *The Political Works*. Oxford, 1958. The best available translation of Spinoza's political writings.

Works on Spinoza

BOOKS

Alexander, Samuel. *Spinoza;* an address in commemoration of the tercentenary of Spinoza's birth. Manchester, 1933.

——. *Spinoza and Time*. London, 1921.

Bidney, David. *The Psychology and Ethics of Spinoza.* New Haven, Conn., 1940.

Bourget, Paul. *Spinoza.* Chicago, 1912.

Browne, Lewis. *Blessed Spinoza.* New York, 1932.

Caird, J. *Spinoza.* Edinburgh, 1910.

Curley, E. M. *Spinoza's Metaphysics.* Cambridge, 1969.

DeDeugd, C. *The Significance of Spinoza's First Kind of Knowledge.* Netherlands, 1966.

Duff, Robert A. *Spinoza's Political and Ethical Philosophy.* Glasgow, 1903.

Feuer, Lewis Samuel. *Spinoza and the Rise of Liberalism.* Boston, 1958.

Friedlander, M. H. *Spinoza, His Life and Philosophy.* London, 1887.

Gunn, J. A. *Benedict Spinoza.* New York, 1925.

Hallett, H. F. *Aeternitas, A Spinozistic Study.* Oxford, 1930.

———. *Benedict de Spinoza: The Elements of His Philosophy.* London, 1957.

Hampshire, Stuart. *Spinoza.* Harmondsworth, 1951.

Hubbeling, H. G. *Spinoza's Methodology.* Netherlands, 1964.

Joachim, H. H. *A Study of the Ethics of Spinoza.* Oxford, 1901.

———. *Spinoza's Tractatus de Intellectus Emendatione.* Oxford, 1940.

Kayser, Rudolf. *Spinoza.* New York, 1968.

Kline, George. *Spinoza in Soviet Philosophy.* London, 1952.

Knight, W. *Spinoza.* London, 1882.

Levin, Dan. *Spinoza.* New York, 1970.

Martineau, J. *A Study of Spinoza.* London, 1882.

McKeon, Richard. *The Philosophy of Spinoza.* New York, 1928.

Melamed, S. M. *Spinoza and Buddha.* Chicago, 1937.

Meyers, H. A. *The Spinoza-Hegel Paradox.* Ithaca, N.Y., 1944.

Oko, Adolph. *The Spinoza Bibliography.* Boston, Mass., 1964.

Parkinson, G. H. R. *Spinoza's Theory of Knowledge.* Oxford, 1954.

Picton, J. A. *Spinoza; A Handbook to the Ethics.* London, 1907.

Pollock, F. *Spinoza, His Life and Philosophy.* London, 1880.

———. *Spinoza.* London, 1935.

Powell, E. E. *Spinoza and Religion.* Chicago, 1906.

Roth, Leon. *Spinoza, Descartes and Maimonides.* Oxford, 1924.

———. *Spinoza.* London, 1929.

Runes, D. D. *Spinoza: Dictionary.* New York, 1951.

Saw, Ruth L. *The Vindication of Metaphysics; A Study in the Philosophy of Spinoza.* London, 1951.

Shanks, Alexander. *An Introduction to Spinoza's Ethics.* London, 1938.

Strauss, Leo. *Spinoza's Critique of Religion.* Berlin, 1930; New York, 1965.

Sullivan, Celestine J., Jr. *Critical and Historical Reflections on Spinoza's "Ethics."* Berkeley, 1958.

Wolf, A., ed. and trans. *The Oldest Biography of Spinoza.* London, 1927.

Wolfson, Abraham. *Spinoza, A Life of Reason.* New York, 1932.

Wolfson, H. A. *The Philosophy of Spinoza.* Cambridge, Mass., 1934.

ARTICLES (OTHER THAN THOSE INCLUDED IN THIS VOLUME) AND REVIEWS IN ENGLISH

The Monist, vol. 55, October 1971 issue on "The Philosophy of Spinoza." This issue was not yet in print at the time the present volume was ready for the press.

Balz, A. G. "Cartesian Refutations of Spinoza," *Philosophical Review* (1937), pp. 461–484.

Bidney, David. "Joachim on Spinoza's *Tractatus de Intellectus Emendatione,*" *Philosophical Review* (1942), pp. 47–65.

———. "Value and Reality in the Metaphysics of Spinoza," *Philosophical Review* (1936), pp. 229–244.

Broad, C. D. "Hallett's *Aeternitas,*" *MIND* (1933), [two articles] I: 150–169; II: 299–318.

Copleston, F. C. "Pantheism in Spinoza and the German Idealists," *Philosophy* (1946), pp. 42–56.

deBurgh, W. G. "Great Thinkers. VIII: Spinoza," *Philosophy* (1936), pp. 271–288.

Eisenberg, Paul D. "How to Understand *De Intellectus Emendatione,*" *J. of History of Philosophy* (1971), pp. 171–191.

Feibleman, James K. "Was Spinoza a Nominalist?" *Philosophical Review* (1951), pp. 386–389.

Hallett, H. F. "Spinoza's Conception of Eternity," *MIND* (1928), pp. 283–303.

———. Review of Bidney's *The Psychology and Ethics of Spinoza,* in *MIND* (1941), pp. 385–393.

―――. "Some Recent Criticisms of Spinoza," *MIND* (1942), [three articles] I: pp. 134–159; II: pp. 223–243; III: pp. 319–342.

―――. "Some Recent Criticisms of Spinoza," *MIND* (1943), pp. 1–23.

―――. "Knowledge, Reality and Objectivity:II," *MIND* (1940), pp. 303–332.

Hicks, G. Dawes. "The 'Modes' of Spinoza and the 'Monads' of Leibniz," *Proceedings of the Aristotelian Society* (1917–18), pp. 329–362.

Jonas, Hans. "Spinoza and the Theory of Organism," *J. of History of Philosophy* (1965), pp. 43–57.

Kaufmann, Fritz. "Spinoza's System as Theory of Expression," *Philosophy and Phenomenological Research* (1940–41), pp. 83–97.

Latta, R. "On the Relations between the Philosophy of Spinoza and that of Leibniz," *MIND* (1899), pp. 333–356.

MacIntyre, A. "Spinoza," in Paul Edwards (ed.), *Encyclopedia of Philosophy* (New York, 1967) vol. 7, pp. 530–541.

Mackinnon, Flora Isabel. "The Treatment of Universals in Spinoza's *Ethics*," *Philosophical Review* (1924), pp. 345–359.

McKeon, Richard. "Causation and the Geometric Method in the Philosophy of Spinoza," *Philosophical Review* (1930), [two articles] I: pp. 178–189; II: pp. 275–296.

McShea, Robert J. "Spinoza on Power," *Inquiry* (1969), pp. 133–143.

Modak, M. S. "Spinozistic Substance and Upanishadic Self," *Philosophy* (1931), pp. 446–458.

Murray, J. Clark. "The Idealism of Spinoza," *Philosophical Review* (1896), pp. 473–488.

Naess, Arne. "Freedom, Emotion and Self-Subsistence: the Structure of a Small, Central Part of Spinoza's *Ethics*," *Inquiry* (1969), pp. 68–104.

Natanson, Harvey B. "Spinoza's God: Some Special Aspects," *Man & World* (1970), pp. 200–223.

Parkinson, G. H. R. "Language and Knowledge in Spinoza," *Inquiry* (1969), pp. 15–40.

Pearson, Carl. "Maimonides and Spinoza," *MIND* (1883), pp. 338–353.

Pollock, Frederick. "Notes on the Philosophy of Spinoza," *MIND* (1878), pp. 195–212.

Radner, Daisie. "Spinoza's Theory of Ideas," *Philosophical Review* (1971), pp. 338–359.

Ratner, Joseph. "Spinoza on God," *Philosophical Review* (1930), [two articles] I:56–72; II:153–177.

Rice, Lee C. "The Continuity of 'Mens' in Spinoza," *The New Scholasticism* (1969), pp. 75–103.

Ritchie, Eliza. "Notes on Spinoza's Conception of God," *Philosophical Review* (1902), pp. 1–15.

———. "The Reality of the Finite in Spinoza's System," *Philosophical Review* (1904), pp. 16–29.

Roth, Leon. "Spinoza in Recent English Thought," *MIND* (1927), pp. 205–210.

Seligman, Paul. "Some Aspects of Spinozism," *Proceedings of the Aristotelian Society* (1959–60), pp. 109–128.

Smith, T. V. "Spinoza's Political and Moral Philosophy," *Monist* (1933), pp. 23–39.

Taylor, A. E. "A Further Word on Spinoza," *MIND* (1946), pp. 97–112.

Tiebout, Harry M. "Deus, Sive Natura . . . ," *Philosophy and Phenomenological Research* (1955–56), pp. 512–521.

Wernham, A. G. Review of S. Hampshire's *Spinoza*, in *Philosophical Quarterly* (1952), pp. 187–189.

———. Review of G. H. R. Parkinson's *Spinoza's Theory of Knowledge*, in *Philosophical Quarterly* (1957), pp. 285–286.

Wetlesen, Jon. "A Reconstruction of Basic Concepts in Spinoza's Social Psychology," *Inquiry* (1969), pp. 105–132.

White, W. H. "Spinoza's Doctrine of the Relationship between Mind and Body," *International Journal of Ethics* (1895–96), pp. 515–518.

Whittaker, T. "Transcendence in Spinoza," *MIND* (1929), pp. 293–311.

Wolf, A. "Spinoza," *Philosophy* (1927), pp. 3–19.

———. "Spinoza's Synoptic Vision," *Philosophy* (1933), pp. 3–13.

———. "An Addition to the Correspondence of Spinoza," *Philosophy* (1935), pp. 200–204.